On the Pragmatics of Communication

Studies in Contemporary German Social Thought (partial listing)
Thomas McCarthy, general editor

On the Pragmatics of Communication

Jürgen Habermas

edited by Maeve Cooke

The MIT Press, Cambridge, Massachusetts

©1998 Massachusetts Institute of Technology

This volume is published by arrangement with Suhrkamp Verlag, Frankfurt am Main, Germany. The sources on which the translations are based are listed in the acknowledgments.

This book was set in Baskerville by Wellington Graphics and was printed and bound in the United States of America

Library of Congress Cataloging-in-Publication Data

Habermas, Jürgen.
  On the pragmatics of communication / Jürgen Habermas : edited by Maeve Cooke.
    p. cm. — (Studies in contemporary German social thought)
  Essays translated from German.
  Includes bibliographical references and index.
  ISBN 0-262-08265-9 (alk. paper)
  1. Pragmatics. I. Cooke, Maeve. II. Title. III. Series
B831.5.H33 1998
193—dc21   98-18171
                                                                          CIP

Contents

Contents

Editor's Acknowledgments

I would like to thank Thomas McCarthy for initiating this undertaking, for fulfilling the role of series editor in an exemplary manner, and for considerable help over and above his editorial duties with regard to translation difficulties. My thanks are also due to Jürgen Habermas for encouraging the project, for replying promptly to my many queries, and for his unfailing cordiality. Ronald Böhme helped with the proofreading, with financial assistance from the Department of German, University College Dublin, and he also compiled the index. Here, too, I am very grateful. Thanks, finally, to Martin Sauter, not just for his painstaking help in checking translations but for his love and support over the many years it took to put this book together.

The translations of many of the chapters have been based on earlier published translations, as follows:

A translation of chapter 1 by Thomas McCarthy was published in Jürgen Habermas, *Communication and the Evolution of Society*, ©1979 by Beacon Press, Boston.

A translation of chapter 2 by Thomas McCarthy was published in Jürgen Habermas, *The Theory of Communicative Action*, vol. 1, ©1984 by Beacon Press, Boston.

A translation of chapter 3 by Jeremy Gaines and Doris L. Jones was first published in *Communicative Action: Essays on Jürgen Habermas's The Theory of Communicative Action*, edited by Axel Honneth and Hans Joas, ©1991 by Polity Press, Cambridge, U.K.

Editor's Acknowledgments

A partial translation of chapter 4 was published in *Philosophical Problems Today*, edited by Guttorm Fløistad, ©1994 by Kluwer Academic Publishers, Dordrecht.

A translation of chapter 5 was published in *John Searle and His Critics*, edited by Ernest Lepore and Robert Van Gulick, ©1991 by Basil Blackwell, Oxford, U.K.

A translation of chapter 6 by William M. Hohengarten was published in Jürgen Habermas, *Postmetaphysical Thinking*, ©1992 by Massachusetts Institute of Technology, Cambridge, Mass.

A translation of chapter 9 by Frederick G. Lawrence was published in Jürgen Habermas, *The Philosophical Discourse of Modernity*, ©1985 by Massachusetts Institute of Technology, Cambridge, Mass.

A translation of chapter 10 by James Bohman was published in *Habermas and Modernity*, edited by Richard Bernstein, ©1985 by Polity Press, Cambridge, U.K.

Chapters 7 and 8 and the final part of chapter 4 have been translated by Maeve Cooke and appear in English for the first time.

Introduction

Maeve Cooke

This anthology brings together for the first time, in revised or new translation, ten essays that present the main concerns of Habermas's program in formal pragmatics. Its aim is to convey a sense of the overall purpose of his linguistic investigations, while introducing the reader to their specific details. Habermas's formal pragmatics fulfills two main functions. First, it serves as the theoretical underpinning for his theory of communicative action, which is a crucial element in his theory of society. Second, it contributes to ongoing philosophical discussion of problems concerning truth, rationality, action, and meaning. Correspondingly, the aim of the present anthology is twofold. First, in providing better access to essays by Habermas that focus explicitly on language, it may help those interested in social theory to assess critically the linguistic basis for his accounts of communicative action and communicative rationality. Second, it may help those interested in more traditional philosophical problems to understand and to appreciate Habermas's treatment of them.

Habermas's original term for his linguistic research program was "universal pragmatics." The adjective "universal" was meant to indicate the difference between his linguistic project and other pragmatic analyses of language. Whereas earlier pragmatic approaches to language had tended to analyze particular contexts of language use, Habermas set out to reconstruct universal features of using language. This explains the title of his programmatic essay, "What

Is Universal Pragmatics?," first published in 1976. However, in a footnote to the 1979 English translation, Habermas expresses dissatisfaction with the label "universal" and a preference for the term "formal pragmatics." One advantage of the latter terminology, in his view, is that it reminds us that formal pragmatics is related to formal semantics. As we shall see, the nature of this relationship is particularly crucial in Habermas's accounts of meaning and truth.

What is meant by universal or, as we should now say, formal pragmatics? Habermas's starting point is that formal analysis of language should not be restricted to semantic analysis, for formal investigation of the pragmatic dimensions of language is equally possible and important. By the "pragmatic" dimensions of language, Habermas means those pertaining specifically to the *employment* of sentences in utterances. He makes clear that "formal" is to be understood in a tolerant sense to refer to the rational reconstruction of general intuitions or competencies. Formal pragmatics, then, aims at a systematic reconstruction of the intuitive linguistic knowledge of competent subjects, the intuitive "rule consciousness" that a competent speaker has of her own language. It aims to explicate pretheoretical knowledge of a general sort, as opposed to the competencies of particular individuals and groups. Formal pragmatics thus calls to mind the unavoidable presuppositions that guide linguistic exchanges between speakers and hearers in everyday processes of communication in any language. It makes us aware that, as speakers and hearers, there are certain things we must—as a matter of necessity—always already have presupposed if communication is to be successful. In focusing on the formal properties of speech situations in general, Habermas's program may thus be distinguished from empirical pragmatics—for example, sociolinguistics—which looks primarily at particular situations of use.

Habermas's formal-pragmatic investigations into everyday linguistic practices in modern societies are attempts to reconstruct the universal competencies that are involved when social actors interact with the aim of achieving mutual understanding (*Verständigung*).[1] Communicative competence is crucial for Habermas's social theory, which is based on the thesis that action oriented toward reaching understanding is the fundamental type of social action. His name for action of this sort is "communicative," and his analysis of it turns on the thesis that everyday language has an in-built connection with validity. More precisely, linguistic utterances as they are used in everyday processes of communication can be construed as *claims* to validity. From his perspective, everyday linguistic interaction is primarily a matter of raising and responding to validity claims. Habermas does allow for other forms of linguistic interaction, such as strategic, figurative, or symbolic interaction, but he contends that these are parasitic on communicative action.

In its simplest terms, communicative action is action whose success depends on the hearer's responding to the validity claim raised by the speaker with a "yes" or a "no." Here, Habermas identifies three basic types of validity claims that are raised by a speaker with her speech act: a claim to the truth of what is said or presupposed, a claim to the normative rightness of the speech act in the given context or of the underlying norm, and a claim to the truthfulness of the speaker. In using a linguistic expression communicatively, the speaker raises all three of these claims simultaneously. In a typical communicative exchange, however, just one of the claims is raised explicitly; the other two remain implicit presuppositions of understanding the utterance. The three validity claims are described as "universal" by Habermas, in the sense of being raised with *every* communicatively used speech act.

The three universal validity claims—to truth, normative rightness, and truthfulness—provide a basis for classifying speech acts. Thus, communicative utterances can be divided into three broad categories according to the explicit claims they raise: constative speech acts are connected in the first instance with truth claims, regulative speech acts with claims to normative rightness, and expressive speech acts with claims to truthfulness.

The thesis of three universal validity claims has implications for both language theory and social theory. On the one hand, it is meant to provide a more convincing basis for classifying speech acts than, for example, the proposals of Austin and his followers or the more theoretically motivated typologies of Searle and his followers. On the other hand, it proposes that language has an in-built connection with validity claims, thereby giving rise to a particular conception of social order as reproduced through communicative action.

In showing that everyday linguistic interaction depends on raising and recognizing validity claims, Habermas presents a picture of social order as a network of relationships of mutual recognition that have two significant characteristics. They are, first, cooperative relationships of commitment and responsibility: participants in communicative interaction *undertake* to behave in certain ways, and the success of the interaction depends on the *cooperation* of both parties involved. Second, the relationships of mutual recognition characteristic for communicative action have an inherent *rational* dimension: the communicative actor undertakes an obligation to provide reasons for the validity of the claims he raises with his utterances, while his counterpart in action may either accept the proffered reasons or challenge them on the basis of better reasons. In this sense, everyday communicative action involves a rudimentary practice of "argumentation." Furthermore, these everyday practices of giving reasons for and against controversial validity claims—sometimes referred to by Habermas as naive communicative action—point toward the possibility of other, more demanding forms of argumentation, which he calls "discourse." Everyday communicative action normally operates on the assumption that the reasons supporting the validity claims raised are good ones. When this background consensus is shaken—as will happen more frequently in posttraditional societies—communicative action cannot continue routinely. Participants then have three options: they can switch to strategic action; they can break off communication altogether; or they can recommence their communicative activity at a different, more reflective level—namely, argumentative speech. In the processes of argumentation known as discourses, certain idealizing suppositions already operative in everyday communicative action are formalized. These presuppositions are unavoidable in the sense that they belong to the very meaning of what it is to take part in argumentation; they are idealizing in the sense that they are typically counterfactual and will not as a rule be satisfied more than approximately. Thus, Habermas claims, participants in argumentation necessarily suppose, among other things, that they share the common aim of reaching agreement with regard to the validity of the disputed validity claim, that no force except that of the better argument is exerted, that no competent parties have been excluded from the discussion, that no relevant argument has knowingly been suppressed, that participants are using the same linguistic expressions in the same way, and so on. These idealizing suppositions refer both to the practice of argumentation and to its outcome. For Habermas, the various idealizing suppositions unavoidably guiding argumentation are what give meaning to the ideas of truth and justice as ideas that transcend all local contexts of validity. To the extent that the validity claims raised in everyday processes of argumentation have a connection in principle with possible vindication in discourse, they have an inherent context-transcendent power. This power is the rational potential built into everyday processes of communication.

Habermas's picture of everyday communicative action thus has important implications for critical social theory. For one thing, in presenting social order as a network of cooperation involving commitment and responsibility, it opposes models of social order that take interactions between strategically acting subjects as fundamental, for example, models grounded in decision or game theory. For another, in the context-transcendent potential of the validity claims raised in everyday communicative processes, it locates a basis for a "postmetaphysical" conception of communicative rationality and, accordingly, a standard for critique. As that conception refers to a potential already built into everyday communicative action, it situates reason in everyday life: the ideas of truth and justice toward which it points are grounded in idealizing suppositions that are part of everyday human activity. Moreover, communicative rationality is not reducible to the standards of validity prevailing in any local context of communicative activity. Rather, the idealizing suppositions on which it rests provide standards for criticizing local practices of justification, both with regard to the outcomes of the agreements reached and with regard to practices of justification themselves. Thus the idea of communicative rationality is meant to provide a postmetaphysical alternative to traditional conceptions of truth and justice that nonetheless avoids value-relativism.

From a more strictly linguistic-philosophical point of view, Habermas's formal pragmatics offers an approach to questions of meaning and truth that radicalizes the linguistic turn within modern philosophy. In his view, traditional formal-semantic approaches to meaning have been guilty of three kinds of abstractive fallacies: a semanticist abstraction, a cognitivist abstraction, and an objectivist one. The semanticist abstraction is the view that the analysis of linguistic meaning can confine itself to the analysis of *sentences,* abstracting from the pragmatic contexts of the use of sentences in utterances. The cognitivist abstraction is the view that all meaning can be traced back to the propositional content of utterances, thus indirectly reducing meaning to the meaning of *assertoric* sentences. The objectivist abstraction is the view that meaning is to be defined in terms of objectively ascertainable truth conditions, as opposed to the *knowledge* of the truth conditions that can be imputed to speakers or hearers. For Habermas, pragmatic theories of meaning have the advantage that they focus not on sentences but on utterances (he is thinking here primarily of the use-oriented theories of meaning suggested by the later work of Wittgenstein, on the one hand, and the work of Austin and Searle, on the other). Furthermore, pragmatic theories of meaning do not emphasize only the assertoric or descriptive modes of language use; they draw attention to the multiplicity of meaningful ways of using language. Finally, such theories stress the connection between the meaning of utterances and social practices; they draw attention to the institutions and conventions of the forms of life in which communicative activity is always embedded.

In Habermas's view, however, existing pragmatic approaches to meaning have weaknesses complementary to those of formal semantics. The great strength of formal semantics has been its attempt to retain a connection between the meaning of linguistic expressions and some notion of context-transcendent validity. In the main pragmatic approaches, however, this connection either slips from view completely or is interpreted too narrowly in a cognitivist way. For example, use theories of meaning derived from the later work of Wittgenstein have in effect renounced a context-transcendent notion of validity by reducing it to the prevailing validity of local language games and particular forms of life. On the other hand, pragmatic approaches that have attempted to avoid such a reduction—Habermas mentions Searle's speech-act theory—typically have succumbed to the cognitivist abstraction, interpreting validity too narrowly as propositional truth. Habermas sees his own pragmatic theory of meaning as an attempt to combine the productive insights of existing formal-semantic and pragmatic approaches to meaning while avoiding their respective weaknesses. He regards speech-act theory as a fruitful starting point, but insufficient as it stands, and attempts to build into it the formal-semantic emphasis on truth or assertibility conditions. In a sense, then, Habermas's pragmatic theory of meaning can be regarded as the proposed happy marriage of Austin and Searle with Frege and Dummett.

From the speech-act theory of Austin and Searle (whom he praises for rendering Austin's theory more precise), Habermas takes over the emphasis on utterances rather than sentences as the central unit of analysis. He also associates himself with their move beyond the traditional narrow focus on assertoric and descriptive modes of language use to include—potentially on an equal footing—other ways of using language, such as acts of promising, requesting, warning, or confessing. In addition, he finds fruitful speech-act theory's emphasis on the illocutionary force of utterances, that is, on the fact that a speaker in saying something also *does* something. However, it may be helpful here to notice Habermas's distinctive conception of illocutionary force, which goes beyond Austin's in a number of significant respects. Austin used the notion of illocution to refer to the *act* of uttering sentences with propositional content. For him, the force of an utterance consists in the illocutionary act—in the attempt to reach an uptake; he contrasted the force of an utterance with its meaning, conceived as a property of the sentence uttered. Habermas's objection to this is threefold: first, Austin's distinction between force and meaning overlooks the fact that utterances have a meaning distinct from the meaning of the sentences they employ; second, it is connected with a problematic classification of speech acts into constatives and performatives, whereby initially, for Austin, only constatives are connected with validity claims; third, it neglects the rational foundation of illocutionary force. By contrast, Habermas proposes an account of utterance meaning that *brings together* the categories of meaning and force; he *extends* the notion of illocutionary force to all utterances that are used communicatively; and he emphasizes the *rational* foundation of illocutionary force. As we shall see, Habermas's pragmatic theory gives an account of the meaning of utterances as inseparable from the act of uttering them, and defines utterances as acts of raising validity claims. His definition of illocutionary force follows from this: illocutionary force consists in a speech act's capacity to motivate a hearer to act on the premise that the commitment signalled by the speaker is seriously meant. On this conception, illocutionary force is bound up with the speaker's assumption of a warranty, if challenged, to provide reasons in support of the validity of the claims she raises. So understood, illocutionary force is a rational force, for in performing a speech act, the speaker undertakes to support what she says with reasons, if necessary. Thus, although Habermas acknowledges speech-act theory as the most fruitful point of departure for his program of formal pragmatics, he engages with it critically, making use of some of its central categories in distinctive ways.

From the point of view of Habermas's program of formal pragmatics, the main weakness of speech-act theory is its failure to connect all communicatively used utterances with validity claims that are in principle context-transcendent. He attempts to make good this deficiency by drawing on Michael Dummett's account of understanding meaning in terms of knowing assertibility conditions. In analogy with Dummett's formulation of what it is to understand the meaning of an assertoric expression, Habermas proposes that we understand an utterance when we know what makes it acceptable. Truth-conditional semantics runs into difficulties when it explains the meaning of sentences in terms of their truth conditions without mediation through the *knowledge* the speaker or hearer may have of such conditions. Thus Habermas adopts Dummett's "epistemic turn" and criticizes Donald Davidson for offering an objectivist reading of Frege's and Wittgenstein's thesis that to understand an utterance is to know what is the case if it is true. He rejects this objectivist reading as tacitly assuming that for every sentence, or at least for every assertoric sentence, procedures are available for effectively deciding when the truth conditions are satisfied. Such an assumption, he argues, implicitly relies on an empiricist theory of knowledge that regards the simple predicative sentences of an observational language as fundamental. Habermas then follows Dummett, who suggests replacing the emphasis on truth conditions with a consideration of what it is for a speaker to *know* when the truth conditions would be satisfied. This is what he refers to as Dummett's epistemic turn; he, however, wants to turn even further. As Habermas reads it, Dummett's theory of meaning has two main shortcomings that prevent his developing fully the inherent potentials of the epistemic turn. The first is a prioritization of truth claims over other kinds of validity claims: Dummett's notion of assertibility conditions accords priority to assertoric utterances. In order to make room on an equal footing for nonassertoric utterances such as promises, imperatives, or avowals, Habermas prefers to speak of *acceptability* conditions. The second is that Dummett's notion of assertibility conditions is insufficiently pragmatic: it remains on the semantic level of analysis inasmuch as it relies on an ideal of validity that is conceptually independent of discursive practices of redeeming validity claims. This last objection takes us to the heart of Habermas's pragmatic theory of meaning.

Before considering it, however, it may be helpful to clarify the status of the theory. Broadly speaking, it seems possible to distinguish between two accounts of its status. According to the first, a pragmatic theory of meaning is merely an extension of truth-conditional semantics in the sense that it broadens its focus. On this view, Habermas's theory leaves the basic assumption of the formal-semantic account of the meaning of sentences intact, while expanding its range, first, to include *nonassertoric* linguistic expressions and, second, to embrace *utterances* as well as sentences. His earlier essay "What Is Universal Pragmatics?" suggests this account of the tasks of a pragmatic theory of meaning. However, in most of his later writings, he seems to offer a more radical account. According to this, a pragmatic theory of meaning *undercuts* the formal-semantic approach to meaning. This view is suggested, for example, in chapters 2 and 3 in the present volume, where Dummett's assertibility-conditional theory of meaning is criticized for failing to carry through completely the move from the semantic to the pragmatic level of analysis. In a recent response to objections raised by Herbert Schnädelbach (see chapter 7), Habermas clarifies the status of his pragmatic theory of meaning in a way that suggests that both of these interpretations are correct. Starting from a distinction between the communicative and noncommunicative use of language, he acknowledges that epistemically used propositional sentences and teleologically used intentional sentences have a meaning content that is in some sense independent of the illocutionary acts in which they can be embedded. In order to understand propositional sentences that serve purely to represent states of affairs or facts, it is sufficient to know their truth conditions. In order to understand intentional sentences that serve to calculate action consequences monologically—without reference to a second person—it is sufficient to know their success conditions. Such sentences, which are used noncommunicatively, can be analyzed exhaustively with the tools of formal semantics. However, they are special cases of language use, due to a feat of abstraction that suspends their pragmatic dimension: the possible communicative situations in which a speaker would *assert* the proposition *"p,"* or declare the intention *"p,"* with the aim of finding agreement with an addressee are abstracted from. As a rule, however, propositional sentences and intentional sentences are embedded in illocutionary acts in the form of assertions and announcements. The meaning of assertions and announcements, which are part of the communicative use of language, can be explicated only pragmatically. From this we can see that Habermas does not reject the formal semantic approach to meaning, for he acknowledges its ability to account for the meaning of noncommunicatively used propositional and intentional sentences. At the same time, he does challenge the claims of formal-semantic theories to explain the meaning of *utterances* such as assertions and announcements, or more generally, of communicatively used linguistic expressions. Moreover, if formal-semantic theories of meaning can account only for the noncommunicative use of language, then their restricted scope suggests that this approach to meaning is itself limited.

We have ascertained that a pragmatic theory is required to explicate the meaning of communicatively used linguistic expressions. It remains unclear, however, in what sense such a theory is pragmatic. As indicated, in his earlier essay on universal pragmatics, Habermas had justified his preference for the category of acceptability conditions, as opposed to truth or assertibility conditions, on the grounds that it avoids the prioritization of the assertoric mode of language use implicit in the latter categories. In these later writings, however, his objection to truth or assertibility conditions seems to go beyond this. They are said to rest on faulty pictures of truth and justification that fail to recognize internal, conceptual links with *pragmatic contexts of justification* and thus remain trapped in abstractive fallacies of a cognitivist and semanticist kind. In Habermas's view, validity and justification—and hence utterance meaning—are inescapably pragmatic notions. They cannot be explicated independently of discursive processes of redeeming different kinds of validity claims. While Dummett's notion of assertibility conditions pushes in the direction of a pragmatic account of justification and validity, it does not quite arrive there; it remains a semantic theory to the extent that it fails to explicate these notions as *conceptually* linked to discursive processes of redeeming disputed—assertoric and nonassertoric—validity claims.

Habermas proposes that we understand the meaning of a speech act when we know what makes it acceptable. We know what makes a speech act acceptable when we know the *kinds* of reasons that a speaker can offer, if challenged, in order to reach understanding with a hearer concerning the validity of the disputed claim. In everyday processes of communication, the kinds of reasons that a hearer must know in order to understand a given utterance are circumscribed contextually. Let us imagine a request to a passenger by an airline steward to stop smoking. In order to understand this request, the passenger has to be able to reconstruct the kinds of reasons that the airline steward could provide in order to justify his request, if necessary. These reasons might include the argument that smoking is unpleasant for other passengers or that it is against the regulations of the airline or against an international code of airline practice. These reasons are of certain kinds. If other kinds of responses were offered as reasons—for instance, that it is raining outside, or that *Finnegans Wake* is James Joyce's best book, or that there are no snakes in Ireland—the context in question would render them irrelevant and, indeed, unintelligible. Thus, although the set of reasons constituting a given *kind* of reasons is always in principle open-ended, in everyday contexts of communication contextual considerations act as a constraint on the kinds of reasons that are relevant to justification.

The hearer not only has to know the kinds of reasons the speaker could adduce in a given instance, he has to know how the speaker might use them in order to engage in argumentation with a hearer concerning the validity of a disputed claim. This focus on knowing how the speaker might *use* reasons to support a disputed validity claim clearly recalls Dummett's epistemic turn. Like Dummett, Habermas also stresses that the validity of these reasons can never in principle be decided once and for all. Rather, their validity must be construed fallibilistically, that is, as always in principle subject to revision in light of new arguments based on new evidence and insights. This is one sense in which the question of validity is tied to pragmatic contexts of justification, and it constitutes a further reason for describing Habermas's theory of meaning (and, indeed, Dummett's) as pragmatic. However, there is a second, possibly more contentious sense, in which Habermas ties validity to pragmatic contexts of justification. In this second sense, validity is not only always subject in principle to discursive reevaluation, it is *in itself* pragmatic. The pragmatic dimension is not something attached to the idea of validity externally, as it were; rather, it is internal to the very concept of validity. A theory of meaning that sees itself as pragmatic in this stronger sense must therefore offer a pragmatic account of validity itself. To this extent, Habermas's pragmatic theories of truth (empirical and theoretical validity) and justice (moral validity)—and, indeed, his accounts of ethical and aesthetic validity—are crucial ingredients of his pragmatic theory of meaning.

Habermas's theory of moral validity has been the subject of extensive commentary and criticism. From the point of view of the theory of meaning, our question is the following: how is the conception of moral validity it proposes internally connected with processes of discursively redeeming validity claims? A norm or principle is morally valid (right or just), for Habermas, if it is the possible object of a discursively achieved consensus to the effect that it is equally in the interest of all affected. Therefore, agreement reached in discourse—idealized rational acceptability—contributes constructively to the validity of moral norms. It is clear from this that Habermas conceives moral validity as internally linked to the idea of discursively achieved consensus and hence to pragmatic contexts of justification.

Habermas also proposes a pragmatic theory of truth. Discussion of this is complicated by the fact that he significantly amended the account he originally presented in the 1973 essay, "Wahrheitstheorien," without subsequently presenting a fully revised version. However, a recent essay on Richard Rorty's neopragmatism (included here as chapter 8) can be seen as an attempt to rectify this deficiency. For our present purposes, what is most interesting about these recent remarks is their continued insistence on the pragmatic nature of truth. Habermas associates himself with Rorty's aim of radicalizing the linguistic turn within modern philosophy by moving to a pragmatic level of analysis. He criticizes him, however, for drawing the wrong conclusions from his critique of the philosophy of language. Rorty reduces truth to practices of justification, thus losing sight of the potential power of validity claims to explode actual contexts of justification. Habermas, by contrast, wants to hold onto the moment of unconditionality that is part of the idea of truth, while retaining an internal relation between truth and justifiability. His aim, in other words, is to work out a theory of truth that is inherently pragmatic yet retains the idea of an unconditional claim that reaches beyond all the evidence available to us at any given time. What would such a theory look like? In the 1980s, Habermas defended a view not unlike Hilary Putnam's conception of truth as idealized rational acceptability: a proposition was said to be true if it could be justified under conditions of an ideal speech situation. Truth, on this account, is a regulative idea, the anticipation of an infinite rational consensus. In the recent essay, however, Habermas acknowledges convincing objections to this earlier conception. One set of objections is directed against some conceptual difficulties with the very notion of an ideal speech situation, in particular, the paradox involved in aiming for "complete" or "conclusive knowledge." The objection has been raised, for instance, that it would be paradoxical for human beings to strive to realize an ideal, the attainment of which would be the end of human history. Another set of objections draws attention to the difficulties involved in conceptualizing the connection between truth and justified acceptability. On the one hand, if there is an unbridgeable gap between de facto and ideal acceptability, the idea of an idealized rational consensus seems so far removed from actual human practices of justification as to undermine the regulative role ascribed to it. On the other hand, such a gap seems to be necessary in order to preserve the intuition that truth has a moment of context-transcendence.

In the face of these and other difficulties, Habermas no longer conceives truth as idealized rational consensus. He now focuses on the idealizing suppositions guiding the *process* of rational argumentation rather than on the idealizing suppositions marking its *outcome*. The former idealizations pertain to the conduct of discourse rather than to the agreement to which participants in discourse aspire. They include the idealizing suppositions that participants are motivated only by the force of the better argument, that all competent parties are entitled to participate on equal terms in discussion, that no relevant argument is suppressed or excluded, and so on. It is from such idealizations, which guide the process of argumentation, that the idea of truth draws its power as a regulative idea. This power is expressed in the idea that a claim, if true, could withstand all attempts to refute it under ideal discursive conditions. The idea of truth has a "decentering" function that serves to remind us that what is currently regarded as rationally acceptable may conceivably be called into question in the future, as the limitations of our current understanding of argumentation become apparent.

It is important here to beware of confusing Habermas's explication of the idea of truth with an explanation of what makes a proposition true. The thesis that a proposition, if true, can stand up to attempts to refute it under the demanding conditions of rational argumentation explicates the pragmatic meaning of truth. It is not, however, an explanation of what makes the proposition true. As to the latter, Habermas's position is the standard one that a proposition is true if and only if its truth conditions are satisfied. Although we can *establish* whether the truth conditions of a given proposition are satisfied only in argumentation, their satisfaction or nonsatisfaction is not itself an epistemic fact. Whereas, as we have seen, idealized rational acceptability *constitutes* the validity of moral norms, it merely *indicates* the truth of propositions. Nonetheless, it is clear from the foregoing that, on Habermas's account, the *concept* of truth must be unpacked pragmatically; we have no access to truth except by way of a concept of validity explicated in terms of how we talk about truth, that is, in terms of an idealized practice of argumentation.

A further concern of Habermas's program of formal pragmatics is to argue that the communicative use of linguistic expressions is the basic mode of language use on which other modes, for example, strategic or fictional ones, are parasitic. Otherwise, in ignoring these other modes, the demonstration that everyday communicative action has an in-built connection with context-transcendent validity claims would be seriously limited. In arguing for the derivative status of the strategic use of language, Habermas initially drew on Austin's distinction between illocutions and perlocutions (see chapter 2). In response to criticisms of his interpretation of this distinction, however, Habermas subsequently modified and clarified his understanding of Austin's categories (see chapters 3, 4, and 7) while continuing to insist that the strategic use of language is parasitic on the use of language with an orientation toward reaching understanding. His argument for the parasitic status of the symbolic, the figurative, and the fictional modes of language use is that the everyday communicative use of language fulfills indispensable problem-solving functions that require idealizing suppositions not demanded by the world-creating and world-disclosing use of language characteristic for the aesthetic realm. The idealizing suppositions of, for example, consistency of meaning or a shared orientation toward mutual understanding are suspended in the fictional use of language, and with these, the illocutionary binding and bonding power of everyday speech acts (see chapters 9 and 10).

Finally, Habermas's pragmatic theory of meaning attempts to do justice to the relations between utterances and the situations and contexts in which they are embedded. For to understand an utterance is always to understand it as an utterance in a given situation, which in turn may be part of multiple, extended contexts. Here,

Habermas draws attention to various kinds of background knowledge: for instance, knowledge of the speaker's personal history or familiarity with the (culturally specific) contexts in which a given topic is normally discussed. These kinds of knowledge, although usually only implicit in acts of understanding, are relatively close to the foreground and can be rendered explicit without difficulty. Thus they can be contrasted with the deep-seated, prereflective, taken-for-granted background knowledge of the lifeworld that, as a horizon of shared, unproblematic convictions, cannot be summoned to consciousness at will or in its entirety. This background knowledge of the lifeworld forms the indispensable context for the communicative use of language; indeed without it, meaning of any kind would be impossible. It also functions to absorb the risk of social disintegration that arises when a social order is reproduced primarily through mechanisms of communicative action. It is thus a necessary complement to Habermas's theories of meaning and communicative action (see, in particular, chapters 2, 4, and 8).

The essays collected in this anthology were selected with the aim of providing general access to Habermas's treatment of formal pragmatics, from his earliest programmatic essay (chapter 1) to his most recent attempts to resolve some perceived problems with his accounts of meaning and truth (chapters 7 and 8). Whereas, in the process of translating, revising existing translations, and retranslating, every effort has been made to ensure terminological consistency, no attempt has been made to impose consistency on the arguments as they are presented in the various essays. We have seen, for instance, that Habermas's earliest proposal for a pragmatic theory of meaning differs in some respects from his subsequent proposals, and that he himself has modified his distinction between illocutions and perlocutions as initially drawn. In later writings (see chapter 7) he introduces a distinction within the category of *Verständigung* between a weak and strong orientation toward consensus, and (see chapter 8) he takes on board objections to the conception of truth hinted at in chapter 3 of the present volume. With the exception of the last two pieces, which are not directly concerned with the question of meaning, the anthology presents the essays in rough chronology in order to show developments and revisions; the reader is encouraged to look out for them.

In chapter 1 we are introduced to formal pragmatics as a research program aimed at reconstructing the universal validity basis of speech. The procedure of rational reconstruction is elucidated through reference both to empirical-analytic approaches and to Kantian transcendental analysis. This is followed by a sketch of a theory of speech acts, which diverges from Austin's and Searle's theories in several important respects, and in which speech acts are characterized in terms of claims to validity.

Chapters 2, 3, 4, and 6, though situating formal pragmatics in relation to Habermas's theory of communicative action, focus on the theory of meaning. The coordinating power of speech acts is explained through account of understanding utterance meaning in terms of knowing acceptability conditions. This pragmatic theory of meaning is presented as an attempt to overcome the limitations of semantic theories through drawing on Karl Bühler's schema of language functions and on speech-act theory. In addition, a typology of speech acts based on their connection with one of three universal validity claims is set up in chapter 2, forming the background for Habermas's discussion in subsequent chapters. The concept of lifeworld as a kind of deep-seated, implicit, background knowledge is also introduced in chapter 2 and developed, in particular, in chapter 4. Habermas stresses the importance of this concept, on the one hand, as a presupposition for understanding utterance meaning and, on the other, as a risk-absorbing counterpoise to the potentially disintegrative effects of action oriented toward reaching understanding. Further, Austin's distinction between illocutions and perlocutions is a thread running through these chapters, and is used by Habermas to support his thesis that the strategic mode of language use is parasitic on the communicative use. This involves him in discussion about the status of simple imperatives (for example, threats), which as a type of utterance not apparently connected with validity claims, seem to undermine his claim that strategic utterances have a derivative status.

Chapter 5 is a critical discussion of Searle's theory of meaning as developed from the late 1970s onwards. Habermas exposes some problems attached to Searle's view, which he reads as a modified intentionalist one, arguing that his own pragmatic theory is better able to account for the meaning of, in particular, imperatives and promises.

Chapter 7 responds to Herbert Schnädelbach's criticisms of Habermas's concept of communicative rationality. Accepting Schnädelbach's criticism that he has hitherto accorded it a privileged position, Habermas now identifies three core structures of rationality; this leads him to make some new distinctions between different modalities of language use. One noteworthy modification here is his introduction of a distinction between action oriented toward reaching understanding in a weaker sense and action oriented toward agreement in the strict sense and, correspondingly, between weak and strong communicative action. Some implications of these distinctions for the theory of meaning are also discussed.

Chapter 8 examines Richard Rorty's neopragmatism, interpreted by Habermas as an attempt to carry the linguistic turn through to its conclusion, and criticizes it for its assimilation of truth claims to justified assertibility.

Chapter 9 focuses on the relation between the fictional or poetic use of language and language as it is used in everyday communicative action; it criticizes Derrideans for faulty accounts of everyday and poetic language, for a consequent problematic leveling of the distinction between literature and communicative action, and for a failure to appreciate the distinctive mediating roles of philosophy and literary criticism.

In chapter 10, Habermas responds to several criticisms of his theory of communicative action. Against Rorty, he defends his view of philosophy as guardian of reason, while acknowledging that this role must be defined in a new way. He then clarifies his position with respect to modern art and the validity claims connected with it, reaffirms his position that interpretive understanding inescapably involves evaluation, clarifies his idea of the unity of reason as an interplay of validity dimensions, and concludes with a discussion of the objection that his theory concentrates on justice at the expense of happiness.

Introduction

Note

1. *Verständigung* (n.): "reaching understanding," "mutual understanding," or "communication." The corresponding verb is *sich verständigen*. As Habermas acknowledges, this term is ambiguous even in German. Although it embraces linguistic comprehension (*Verstehen*), it goes beyond this to refer to the process of reaching understanding, in the sense of reaching an agreement with another person or persons. However, despite having previously used the two terms interchangeably, Habermas now distinguishes between *Verständigung* and *Einverständnis*, agreement or consensus in the strict sense (see chapter 7). Finally, *Verständigung* can also be used as a synonym for "communication"; thus, for example, communicative rationality is occasionally rendered by Habermas as *Verständigungsrationalität*.

1

What Is Universal Pragmatics? (1976)

I

The task of universal pragmatics is to identify and reconstruct universal conditions of possible mutual understanding (*Verständigung*).[1] In other contexts, one also speaks of "general presuppositions of communication," but I prefer to speak of general presuppositions of communicative action because I take the type of action aimed at reaching understanding to be fundamental. Thus I start from the assumption (without undertaking to demonstrate it here) that other forms of social action—for example, conflict, competition, strategic action in general—are derivatives of action oriented toward reaching understanding (*Verständigung*). Furthermore, since language is the specific medium of reaching understanding at the sociocultural stage of evolution, I want to go a step further and single out explicit speech actions from other forms of communicative action. I shall ignore nonverbal actions and bodily expressions.[2]

The Validity Basis of Speech

Karl-Otto Apel proposes the following formulation in regard to the general presuppositions of consensual speech acts: to identify such presuppositions we must, he thinks, leave the perspective of the observer of behavioral facts and call to mind "what we must necessarily always already presuppose in regard to ourselves and others as normative conditions of the possibility of reaching understanding; and in this sense, what we must necessarily always already have accepted."[3] Apel here uses the aprioristic perfect (*immer schon:* always already) and adds the mode of necessity in order to express the transcendental constraint to which we, as speakers, are subject as soon as we perform or understand or respond to a speech act. In or after the performance of this act, we can become aware that we have involuntarily made certain asssumptions, which Apel calls "normative conditions of the possibility of reaching understanding." The adjective "normative" may give rise to misunderstanding. One can say, however, that the general and unavoidable—in this sense transcendental—conditions of possible mutual understanding have a normative content when one thinks not only of the validity dimension of norms of action or evaluation, or even of the validity dimension of rules in general, but also of the validity basis of speech across its entire spectrum. As a preliminary, I want to indicate briefly what I mean by the "validity basis of speech."

I shall develop the thesis that anyone acting communicatively must, in performing any speech act, raise universal validity claims and suppose that they can be vindicated (*einlösen*). Insofar as she wants to participate in a process of reaching understanding, she cannot avoid raising the following—and indeed precisely the following—validity claims. She claims to be

a. uttering something *intelligibly,*

b. giving (the hearer) *something* to understand,

c. making *herself* thereby understandable, and

d. coming to an understanding with *another person.*

The speaker must choose an intelligible (*verständlich*) expression so that speaker and hearer can *comprehend one another.* The speaker must have the intention of communicating a true (*wahr*) proposition (or a propositional content, the existential presuppositions of which are satisfied) so that the hearer can *share the knowledge* of the speaker. The speaker must want to express her intentions *truthfully* (*wahrhaftig*) so that the hearer can find the utterance of the speaker credible (can trust her). Finally, the speaker must choose an utterance that is right (*richtig*) with respect to prevailing norms and values so that the hearer can accept the utterance, and both speaker and hearer can, in the utterance, thereby *agree with one another* with respect to a recognized normative background. Moreover, communicative action can continue undisturbed only as long as all participants suppose that the validity claims they reciprocally raise are raised justifiably.

The aim of reaching understanding (*Verständigung*) is to bring about an agreement (*Einverständnis*) that terminates in the intersubjective mutuality of reciprocal comprehension, shared knowledge, mutual trust, and accord with one another. Agreement is based on recognition of the four corresponding validity claims: comprehensibility, truth, truthfulness, and rightness. We can see that the word "*Verständigung*" is ambiguous. In its narrowest meaning it indicates that two subjects understand a linguistic expression in the same way; in its broadest meaning it indicates that an accord exists between two subjects concerning the rightness of an utterance in relation to a mutually recognized normative background. In addition, the participants in communication can reach understanding about something in the world, and they can make their intentions understandable to one another.

If full agreement, embracing all four of these components, were a normal state of linguistic communication, it would not be necessary to analyze the process of reaching understanding from the dynamic perspective of *bringing about* an agreement. The typical states are in the gray areas between, on the one hand, lack of understanding and misunderstanding, intentional and involuntary untruthfulness, concealed and open discord, and, on the other hand, preexisting or achieved consensus. Reaching understanding is the process of bringing about an agreement on the presupposed basis of validity claims that are mutually recognized. In everyday life, we start from a background consensus pertaining to those interpretations taken for granted among participants. As soon as this consensus is shaken, and as soon as the presupposition that the validity claims are satisfied (or could be vindicated) is suspended in the case of at least one of the four claims, communicative action cannot be continued.

The task of mutual interpretation, then, is to achieve a new definition of the situation that all participants can share. If this attempt fails, one is basically confronted with the alternatives of switching to strategic action, breaking off communication altogether, or recommencing action oriented toward reaching understanding at a different level, the level of argumentative speech (for purposes of discursively examining the problematic validity claims, which are now regarded as hypothetical). In what follows, I shall take into consideration only consensual speech acts, leaving aside both discourse and strategic action.

In communicative action, participants presuppose that they know what mutual recognition of reciprocally raised validity claims means. If in addition they can rely on a shared definition of the situation and thereupon act consensually, the background consensus includes the following:

a. Speaker and hearer know implicitly that each of them has to raise the aforementioned validity claims if there is to be communication at all (in the sense of action oriented toward reaching understanding).

b. Both reciprocally suppose that they actually do satisfy these presuppositions of communication, that is, that they justifiably raise their validity claims.

c. This means that there is a common conviction that any validity claims raised either are already vindicated, as in the case of the comprehensibility of the sentences uttered, or, as in the case of truth, truthfulness, and rightness, could be vindicated because the sentences, propositions, expressed intentions, and utterances satisfy the corresponding adequacy conditions.

Thus I distinguish (i) the *conditions* for the validity of a grammatical sentence, true proposition, truthful intentional expression, or normatively correct utterance appropriate to its context from (ii) the *claims* with which speakers demand intersubjective recognition for the well-formedness of a sentence, truth of a proposition, truthfulness of an intentional expression, and rightness of a speech act, as well as from (iii) the *vindication* of justifiably raised validity claims. Vindication means that the proponent, whether through appeal to intuitions and experiences or through arguments and action consequences, justifies the claim's worthiness to be recognized and brings about a suprasubjective recognition of its validity. In *accepting* a validity claim raised by the speaker, the hearer recognizes the validity of the symbolic structures; that is, he recognizes that a sentence is grammatical, a statement true, an intentional expression truthful, or an utterance correct. The validity of these symbolic structures is *justified* by virtue of the fact that they satisfy certain adequacy conditions; but the meaning of the validity consists in their *worthiness* to be recognized that is, in the guarantee that intersubjective recognition can be brought about under suitable conditions.[4]

I have proposed the name "universal pragmatics"[5] for the research program aimed at reconstructing the universal validity basis of speech.[6] I would now like to delimit the theme of this research program in a preliminary way. Thus before passing on (in part II) to the theory of speech acts, I shall prefix a few guiding remarks dealing with (i) an initial delimitation of the object domain of the proposed program of universal pragmatics; (ii) an elucidation of the procedure of rational reconstruction, as opposed to an empirical-analytic procedure in the narrower sense; (iii) a few methodological difficulties resulting from the fact that linguistics claims the status of a reconstructive science; and finally (iv) the question of whether the proposed universal pragmatics assumes the status of a transcendental theory of reflection or that of an empirically substantive reconstructive science. I shall restrict myself to guiding remarks because, while these questions are fundamental and deserve to be examined independently, they form only the context of the topic I shall treat and must thus remain in the background.

Preliminary Delimitation of the Object Domain

In several of his works, Apel has pointed to the abstractive fallacy that underlies the approach to the logic of science favored by contemporary analytic philosophy.[7] The logical analysis of language that originated with Carnap focuses primarily on syntactic and semantic properties of linguistic formations. Like structuralist linguistics, it delimits its object domain by first abstracting from the pragmatic properties of language, and subsequently introducing the pragmatic dimension in such a way that the constitutive connection between the generative accomplishments of subjects capable of speaking and acting, on the one hand, and the general structures of speech, on the other, cannot come into view. It is certainly legitimate to draw an abstractive distinction between language as structure and speaking as process. A language will then be understood as a system of rules for generating expressions, such that all well-formed expressions (e.g., sentences) may count as elements of this language. On the other hand, subjects capable of speaking can employ such expressions as participants in a process of communication; for instance, they can utter sentences as well as understand them and respond to them. This abstraction of *language* from the use of language in *speech* (*langue* versus *parole*), which is made in both the logical and the structuralist analysis of language, is meaningful. Nonetheless, this methodological step is not sufficient reason for the view that the pragmatic dimension of language from which one abstracts is beyond formal (or linguistic) analysis. An abstractive fallacy arises in that the successful, or at least promising, reconstruction of linguistic rule systems is seen as justification for restricting formal analysis to this object domain. The separation of the two analytic levels, *language* and *speech,* should not be made in such a way that the pragmatic dimension of language is left to exclusively empirical analysis—that is, to empirical sciences such as psycholinguistics and sociolinguistics.

I would like to defend the thesis that not only language but speech too—that is, the employment of sentences in utterances—is accessible to formal analysis. Like the elementary units of language (sentences), the elementary units of speech (utterances) can be analyzed from the methodological stance of a reconstructive science.

Approaches to a general theory of communication have been developed from the semiotics of Charles Morris.[8] In their framework of fundamental concepts they integrate the model of linguistic behaviorism (the symbolically mediated behavioral reaction of the stimulated individual organism) with the model of information transmission (encoding and decoding signals between sender and receiver for a given channel and an at least partially common store of signs). If the speaking process is conceptualized in this way, the fundamental question of universal pragmatics concerning the general conditions of possible mutual understanding (*Verständigung*) cannot be posed in an appropriate way. For example, the intersubjectivity of meanings that are identical for at least two speakers does not even become a problem (i) if the identity of meanings is *reduced* to extensionally equivalent classes of behavioral properties, as is done in linguistic behaviorism,[9] or (ii) if it is preestablished at the analytic level that there exists a common code and store of signs between sender and receiver, as is done in information theory.

In addition to empiricist approaches that issue, in one way or another, from the semiotics of Morris, there are interesting approaches to the logical analysis of general structures of speech and action. The following analyses can be understood as contributions along the way to a universal pragmatics. Bar-Hillel pointed out quite early the necessity for a pragmatic extension of logical semantics.[10] Also of note are the proposals for a *deontic logic* (Hare, H. von Wright, N. Rescher)[11] and corresponding attempts at a formalization of speech acts such as assertions and questions (Apostel);[12] approaches to a logic of nondeductive argumentation (Toulmin, Botha) belong here as well.[13] From the side of linguistics, the investigation of presuppositions (Kiefer, Petöfi),[14] conversational postulates (Grice, Lakoff),[15] speech acts (Ross, McCawley, Wunderlich),[16] and dialogues and texts (Fillmore, Posner)[17] lead to a consideration of the pragmatic dimension of language from a reconstructionist point of view. The difficulties in semantic theory (Lyons, Katz) point in the same direction.[18] From the side of *formal semantics*, in particular the discussion—going back to Frege and Russell—of the structure of propositions, of referential terms and predicates (Strawson)[19] is significant for a universal pragmatics. The same holds for *analytic action theory* (Danto, Hampshire, Schwayder)[20] and for the discussion that has arisen in connection with the logic of the explanation of intentional action (Winch, Taylor, von Wright).[21] The use theory of meaning introduced by Wittgenstein has universal-pragmatic aspects (Alston),[22] as does the attempt by Grice to trace the meaning of sentences back to the intentions of the speakers (Bennett, Schiffer).[23] As the most promising point of departure for a universal pragmatics, I shall draw primarily on the theory of speech acts initiated by Austin (Searle, Wunderlich).[24]

These approaches developed from logic, linguistics, and the analytic philosophy of language have the common goal of clarifying processes of language use from the viewpoint of formal analysis. However, if one evaluates them with regard to the contribution they make to a universal pragmatics, their weaknesses also become apparent. In many cases I see a danger that the analysis of conditions of possible mutual understanding is foreshortened, either

a. because these approaches do not generalize radically enough and do not push through the level of fortuitous contexts to general and unavoidable presuppositions—as is the case, for instance, with most of the linguistic investigations of semantic and pragmatic presuppositions; or

b. because they restrict themselves to the instruments developed in logic and grammar, even when these are inadequate for capturing pragmatic relations—as, for example, in syntactic explanations of the performative character of speech acts;[25] or

c. because they mislead one into a formalization of basic concepts that have not been satisfactorily analyzed—as can, in my view, be shown in the case of the logics of norms which trace norms of action back to commands; or finally

d. because they start from the model of the isolated, purposive-rational actor and thereby fail—as do, for instance, Grice and Lewis[26]—to reconstruct in an appropriate way the specific moment of mutuality in the understanding of identical meanings or in the recognition of intersubjective validity claims.

It is my impression that the theory of speech acts is largely free of these and similar weaknesses.

Some Remarks on the Procedure of Rational Reconstruction

I have been employing the expression "formal analysis" in opposition to empirical-analytic procedures (in the narrower sense) without providing a detailed explanation. This is, at least, misleading. I am not using formal analysis in a sense that refers, say, to the standard predicate logic or to any specific logic. The tolerant sense in which I understand formal analysis can best be characterized through the methodological attitude we adopt in the rational reconstruction of concepts, criteria, rules, and schemata. Thus we speak of the explication of meanings and concepts, of the analysis of presuppositions and rule systems, and so forth. Of course, reconstructive procedures are also important for empirical-analytic research, for example, for explicating frameworks of basic concepts, for formalizing assumptions initially formulated in ordinary language, for clarifying deductive relations among particular hypotheses, for interpreting results of measurement, and so on. Nonetheless, reconstructive procedures are not characteristic of sciences that develop nomological hypotheses about domains of observable objects and events; rather, these procedures are characteristic of those sciences that *systematically reconstruct the intuitive knowledge of competent subjects.*

In clarifying the distinction between empirical-analytic and reconstructive sciences, I would like to begin with the distinction between sensory experience or *observation* and communicative experience or *understanding* (*Verstehen*). Observation is directed toward perceptible things and events (or states); understanding is directed toward the meaning of utterances.[27] In experiencing, the observer is in principle alone, even if the categorial net in which experiences are organized as experiences laying claim to objectivity is always already shared by several (or even all) individuals. In contrast, the interpreter who understands meaning undergoes her experiences fundamentally as a participant in communication, on the basis of an intersubjective relation established through symbols with other individuals, even if she is in fact alone with a book, a document, or a work of art. I shall not here analyze the complex relationship between observation and understanding any further; I would like to direct attention to just one aspect of this: the difference in level between perceptible reality and the understandable meaning of a symbolic formation. Sensory experience is related to segments of reality without mediation, communicative experience only mediately, as illustrated in the diagram below:

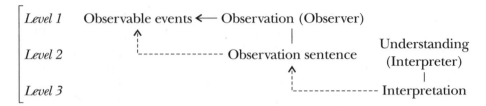

This diagram represents three different relationships:

a. Epistemic relations between experiential acts and their objects. In this sense, the act of understanding relates to the symbolic expression (here of the observation sentence), in a way similar to how the act of observation relates to the objects and events observed.

b. Relations of representing an aspect of reality in a propositional sentence. In this sense, the interpretation represents the semantic content (here of the observation sentence), in a way similar to how the observation sentence represents certain objects and events.

c. Relations of expressing intentional acts. In this sense, the understanding (here of the observation sentence) is expressed in the propositional content of the interpretation, just as the observation is expressed in the propositional content of the observation sentence.

Apart from the fact that all three types of relation simply point to fundamental problems, there is an additional difficulty in specifying the precise differences between the epistemic relations of the observer and the interpreter to their respective objects and between the representational relations of the observation sentence to reality, on the one hand, and that of the interpretation sentence to (symbolically prestructured) reality, on the other. This specification would require a comparison between observation and interpretation, between description and explication. For the time being, the diagram is intended merely to illustrate the two levels of reality to which sensory and communicative experience respectively relate. The difference in level between perceptible and symbolically prestructured reality is reflected in the gap between *direct* access through observation *of* reality and communicatively mediated access through understanding an utterance *concerning* reality.

The two pairs of concepts—"perceptible reality" versus "symbolically prestructured reality" and "observation" versus "understanding"—can be correlated with another pair: "description" versus "explication." With the aid of a sentence that represents an observation, I can *describe* the observed aspect of reality. With the aid of a sentence that represents an interpretation of the meaning of a symbolic formation, I can *explicate* the meaning of such an utterance. Naturally, only when the meaning of the symbolic formation is unclear does the explication need to be set off as an independent analytic step. In regard to sentences that we use to describe objects and events, there can be a lack of clarity at various levels. Depending on the level, we demand explications of different kinds. If the phenomenon described is in need of explanation, we demand an explication that makes clear how reality operates and how the phenomenon in question comes about. If, by contrast, the description itself is incomprehensible, we demand an explication that makes clear what the observer meant by his utterance and how the symbolic expression in need of elucidation comes about. In the first case, a satisfactory explication will have the form of an explanation we undertake with the aid of a causal hypothesis. In the second case, we speak of explication of meaning. (Of course, explications of meaning need not be limited to descriptive sentences; any meaningfully structured formation can be subjected to the operation of meaning explication.)

Descriptions and explications have different ranges; they can begin on the surface and push through to underlying structures. We are familiar with this fact from the explanation of natural phenomena—the more general the theories are with which we explain natural phenomena, the more penetrating the corresponding theoretical descriptions. The same is true of explications of meaning. Of course, in the case of meaning explications, the range of explication does not depend on the level of generality of theoretical knowledge about the structures of an external reality accessible to observation but on knowledge of the deep structures of a reality accessible to understanding—a reality of symbolic formations produced according to rules. The explication of natural phenomena pushes in a different direction from the explication of the meaning of expressions.

Furthermore, I want to distinguish two levels of explication of meaning. If the meaning of a written sentence, action, gesture, work of art, tool, theory, commodity, transmitted document, and so on is unclear, the explication of meaning is directed first to the semantic content of the symbolic formation. In trying to understand its content, we take up the same position as the "author" adopted when he wrote the sentence, performed the gesture, used the tool, applied the theory, and so forth. Often, too, we must go beyond what was meant and intended by the author and take into consideration a context of which he was not conscious.[28] Typically, however, *the understanding of content* pursues connections that link the surface structures of the incomprehensible formation with the surface structures of other, familiar formations. Thus, linguistic expressions can be explicated through paraphrase in the same language or through translation into expressions of another language; in both cases, competent speakers draw on intuitively known meaning relations that obtain within the lexicon of one language or between the lexica of two languages.

If she cannot attain her end in this way, the interpreter may find it necessary to alter her attitude. She then exchanges the attitude of understanding content (directed toward surface structures)—in which she, as it were, looks through symbolic formations to the world about which something is uttered—for an attitude in which she focuses on the generative structures of the expressions themselves. The interpreter then attempts to explicate the meaning of a symbolic formation with the help of the rules according to which the author must have produced it. In normal paraphrase and translation, the interpreter draws on semantic meaning relations (for instance between the different words of a language) in an ad hoc manner, so to speak, in that she simply applies a knowledge shared with competent speakers of that language. In this sense, the role of interpreter can (under suitable conditions) be attributed to the author himself. The attitude changes, however, as soon as the interpreter tries not only to *apply* this intuitive knowledge of speakers but to *reconstruct* it. She then turns away from the surface structure of the symbolic formation; she no longer looks through it *intentione recta* to the world. She attempts instead to peer into the symbolic formation—penetrating through its surface, as it were—in order to discover the rules according to which this symbolic formation was produced (in our example, the rules according to which the lexicon of a language is constructed). The object of understanding is no longer the *content* of a symbolic expression or what specific authors meant by it in specific situations but rather the intuitive *rule consciousness* that a competent speaker has of his own language.

Following a suggestion made by Ryle,[29] we can distinguish between *know-how*, the ability of a competent subject who understands how to produce or accomplish something, and *know-that*, the explicit knowledge of how it is that he is able to do so. In our case, what the author means by an utterance and what an interpreter understands of its content are a first-level know-that. To the extent that his utterance is correctly formed and thus comprehensible, the author produced it in accordance with certain rules or on the basis of certain structures. He knows how to use the system of rules of his language and understands their context-specific application; he has a pretheoretical knowledge of this rule system, which is at least sufficient to enable him to produce the utterance in question. This implicit rule consciousness is a know-how. The interpreter, in turn, who not only shares but wants to understand this implicit knowledge of the competent speaker, must transform this know-how into explicit knowledge, that is, into a second-level know-that. This is the task of reconstructive understanding, that is, of meaning explication in the sense of rational reconstruction of generative structures underlying the production of symbolic formations. Since the rule consciousness to be reconstructed is a categorial knowledge, the reconstruction depends first of all on the operation of conceptual explication.

Carnap put forward four requirements that the explication of a concept must fulfill in order to be adequate:

i. The explicans should be *similar* to the explicandum, that is, from now on the explicans should be able to be used in place of the explicandum in all relevant cases.

ii. Rules should be provided that fix the use of the explicans (in connection with other scientific concepts) in an *exact* manner.

iii. The explicans should prove to be *fruitful* with respect to the formulation of general statements.

iv. (Presupposing that requirements i–iii can be met) the explicans should be as *simple* as possible.[30]

Wunderlich sums up his reflections on the status of concept explication as follows:

Explication always proceeds (in conformity with Carnap's requirements i–iv) *with regard to theories;* either such central concepts (as "meaning") are explicated that entire theories correspond to them as explicans, or different concepts are explicated interconnectedly.

We explicate always *with regard to clear cases,* so as to be able (in connection with these) to replace our intuitions with exact arguments. However, the theory can then also provide answers to borderline cases; or we explicate separately what a clear borderline case is.

The language of explication is *at the same level* as the explicandum language (e.g., ordinary language or a standardized version derived from it). Accordingly, it is not a question here of a descriptive language or a metalanguage relative to the language of the explicandum (the explicans does not describe the explicandum).[31]

In these reflections on the explication of concepts, one point strikes me as insufficiently worked out—the *evaluative accomplishments of rule consciousness.* Reconstructive proposals are directed toward domains of pretheoretical *knowledge,* that is, not to just any implicit opinion, but to a proven intuitive preknowledge. The rule consciousness of competent speakers functions as a court of evaluation, for instance with regard to the grammaticality of sentences. Whereas the understanding of content is directed toward any utterance whatever, reconstructive understanding refers only to symbolic objects characterized as "well formed" by competent subjects themselves. Thus, for example, syntactic theory, propositional logic, the theory of science, and ethics start with syntactically well formed sentences, correctly fashioned propositions, well-corroborated theories, and morally unobjectionable resolutions of norm conflicts, in order to reconstruct the rules according to which these formations can be produced. To the extent that, as in the following examples, universal validity claims (the grammaticality of sentences, the consistency of propositions, the truth of hypotheses, the rightness of norms of action) underlie intuitive evaluations, reconstructions relate to pretheoretical knowledge of a general sort, to *universal capabilities,* and not merely to particular competencies of individual groups (e.g., the ability to utter sentences in a Low-German dialect or to solve problems in quantum physics) or, indeed, to the ability of particular individuals (e.g., to write an exemplary *Entwicklungsroman* even in the middle of the twentieth century). When the pretheoretical knowledge to be reconstructed expresses a universal capability, a general cognitive, linguistic, or interactive competence (or subcompetence), then what begins as an explication of meaning aims at the reconstruction of species competencies. In scope and status, these reconstructions can be compared with general theories.[32]

It is the great merit of Chomsky to have developed this idea in the case of grammatical theory (for the first time in *Syntactic Structures*, 1957). Roughly speaking, it is the task of grammatical theory to reconstruct the intuitive rule consciousness common to all competent speakers in such a way that the proposals for reconstruction represent the system of rules that permits potential speakers, in at least one language *L,* to acquire the competence to produce and to understand any sentences that count as grammatical in *L,* as well as to distinguish these sentences well-formed in *L* from ungrammatical sentences.[33]

Reconstructive versus Empiricist Linguistics

I hope I have sufficiently characterized the reconstructive procedure of sciences that transform a practically mastered pretheoretical knowledge (know-how) of competent subjects into an objective and explicit knowledge (know-that), so that it is clear in what sense I am using the expression "formal analysis." Before mentioning some methodological difficulties with reconstructive linguistics, I would like to contrast, in broad strokes, two versions of linguistics, one empirical-analytic and one reconstructive. (Wunderlich speaks of an empirical-descriptive and an empirical-explicative linguistics.[34]) I will compare both approaches under four headings.

Data
To the extent that the experiential basis is supposed to be secured through observation alone, the data of linguistics consist of meas-

ured variables of linguistic behavior. By contrast, insofar as reconstructive understanding is permitted, the data are provided by the rule consciousness of competent speakers, maieutically ascertained (i.e., through suitable questioning with the aid of systematically ordered examples). Thus the data are distinguished, if you will, according to their ontological level: actual linguistic behavior is part of perceptible reality, and rule consciousness points to the production of symbolic formations in which something is uttered about reality.[35] Furthermore, observations always mean a knowledge of something particular, whereas rule consciousness contains categorical knowledge. Finally, observational data are selected only from the analytic viewpoints of the linguist, whereas, in the other case, competent speakers themselves evaluate and preselect possible data from the point of view of their grammatical well-formedness.

Theory and Object Domain

As long as natural languages count as the object of linguistic description and not as the form of representation of a reconstructible pretheoretical knowledge, linguistic theory relates to its object domain as a causal-analytic theory that explains linguistic descriptions of linguistic reality with the aid of nomological hypotheses. If, on the contrary, linguistic theory is supposed to serve to reconstruct pretheoretical knowledge, theory relates to its object domain as an explication of meaning to its explicandum. Whereas in the empiricist version the relation of linguistic theory to the language to be explained is basically indistinguishable from that between theory and reality in other nomological sciences, in the explicative version the linguistic character of the object necessitates a relation that can hold only between different linguistic expressions: the relation between explication and explicandum, whereby the language of explication (that is, the construct language of linguistics, which is a standardized version of ordinary language) belongs in principle to the same level as the natural language to be explicated. (Neither in the empiricist nor in the explicative case of theory formation can the relation of linguistic theory to its object domain be conceived as that of metalanguage to object language.[36])

Theory and Everyday Knowledge

There is yet another peculiarity arising from these differently oriented conceptualizations. An empirical-analytic theory in the narrow sense can (and as a rule will) refute the everyday knowledge of an object domain that we initially possess prior to science and replace it with a correct theoretical knowledge regarded provisionally as true. A proposal for reconstruction, by contrast, can represent pretheoretical knowledge more or less explicitly and adequately, but it can never falsify it. At most, the representation of a speaker's intuition can prove to be false, but not the intuition itself.[37] The latter belongs to the data, and data can be explained but not criticized. At most, data can be criticized as being unsuitable, that is, either erroneously gathered or wrongly selected for a specific theoretical purpose.

To a certain extent, reconstructions make an *essentialist* claim. One can say, of course, that theoretical descriptions "correspond" (if true) to certain structures of reality in the same sense as reconstructions "bear a likeness" (if correct) to the deep structures explicated. On the other hand, the asserted correspondence between a descriptive theory and its object admits many epistemological interpretations apart from the realistic (e.g., instrumentalist or conventionalist) ones. Rational reconstructions, by contrast, can reproduce the pretheoretical knowledge that they explicate only in an essentialist sense; if they are true, they have to correspond precisely to the rules that are operatively effective in the object domain—that is, to the rules that actually determine the production of surface structures.[38] Thus Chomsky's correlation assumption, according to which linguistic grammar is represented on the part of the speaker by a mental grammar that corresponds exactly to it, is, at least in the first instance, consistent.

Methodological Difficulties

To be sure, serious methodological difficulties have arisen in connection with the Chomskian program for a general science of language as the rational reconstruction of linguistic competence. I would like to consider, from a methodological perspective, two of the problem complexes that have developed. One concerns the status and reliability of the intuitive knowledge of competent speakers; the other, the aformentioned relation between linguistic and mental grammar.

There have been two principal objections against choosing speakers' intuitions as the starting point for reconstructive theory formation.[39] First, the question has been raised whether a reconstructive linguistics can ever arrive at a theory of linguistic competence; whether on the chosen data basis it is not limited to developing, at best, a theory of the intuitive understanding that competent speakers have of their own language. Since the metalinguistic use of one's own ordinary language, to which a science that appeals to speakers' judgments must have recourse, is something other than the direct use of language (and is probably subject to different laws), a grammatical theory of the Chomskian type can at best reconstruct that special part of linguistic competence that regulates the metalinguistic use; it cannot reconstruct the competence that directly underlies speaking and understanding a language.

The empirical question is whether a complete theory of linguistic intuitions is identical with a complete theory of human linguistic competence. . . . Chomsky has no doubt as to this identity. . . . The theory of one kind of linguistic behavior, namely metalinguistic judgment on such things as grammaticality and paraphrase, would then as a whole be built into theories on other forms of linguistic behavior such as speaking and understanding. . . . If we wish to think in terms of primary and derived forms of verbal behavior, the speaking and the understanding of language fall precisely into the category of primary forms, while metalinguistic judgments will be considered highly derived, artificial forms of linguistic behavior, which moreover are acquired late in development. . . . The empirical problem in the psychology of language is in turn divided in two, the investigation of psychological factors in primary language usage, and the psychological investigation of linguistic intuitions.[40]

I think this objection is based on a confusion of the two research paradigms elucidated above, the empirical-analytic and the reconstructive. I wish to make three comments in this regard:

i. Reconstruction relates to a pretheoretical knowledge of competent speakers that is expressed, on the one hand, in the production of sentences in a natural language and, on the other, in the appraisal of the grammaticality of linguistic expressions. The object of reconstruction is the process of production of those sentences held by competent speakers to belong to the set of grammatical sentences. By contrast, the metalinguistic utterances in which competent speakers evaluate the sentences put before them are not the object of reconstruction but part of the data gathering.

ii. Because of the reflexive character of natural languages, speaking about what has been spoken, direct or indirect mention of speech components, belongs to the normal linguistic process of reaching understanding. The expression "metalinguistic judgments" in a natural language about sentences of the same language suggests a difference in level that does not exist. It is one of the most interesting features of natural languages that they can be used as their own languages of explication. (I shall come back to this point below.)

iii. However, it seems to me that the misunderstanding lies, above all, in Levelt's considering the recourse to speakers' intuitions in abstraction from the underlying research paradigm. Only if one presupposes an empirical-analytic approach (in the narrow sense) to the reality of a natural language and the utterances in it can one view speaking and understanding language, on the one hand, and judgments in a language about that language, on the other, as two different object domains. If one chooses a reconstructive approach, then one *thereby* chooses a conceptualization of the object domain according to which the linguistic know-how of a competent speaker is at the root of the sentences she produces with the help of (and only with the help of) this know-how. While this research paradigm may prove to be unfruitful, this cannot be shown at the level of a critique that already presupposes a competing paradigm; it may be shown only in terms of the success or failure of the theories and explanations the competing research paradigms make possible.

The second objection is directed toward the unreliability of intuitively founded speakers' judgments, for which there exists impressive empirical evidence.[41] Nonetheless, it seems to me here that once again an empiricist interpretation of speakers' judgments stimulates false expectations and suggests the wrong remedies. The expression "intuitive knowledge" should not be understood as meaning that a speaker's pretheoretical knowledge about the grammaticality of a sentence (about the rigor of a derivation, about the cogency of a theory, and so forth) is the kind of directly ascertainable intuition that is incapable of being discursively justified. On the contrary, the implicit knowledge has to be brought to consciousness through the choice of suitable examples and counterexamples, through contrast and similarity relations, through translation, paraphrase and so on— that is, through a well-thought-out, maieutic method of interrogation. Ascertaining the so-called intuitions of a speaker is already the first step toward their explication. For this reason, the procedure practiced by Chomsky and many others seems to me to make sense and to be adequate. One starts with clear cases, in which the reactions of the subjects converge, in order to develop structural descriptions on this basis; then, in the light of the hypotheses gained, one attempts to render the less clear cases more precise in such a way that the process of interrogation can lead to an adequate clarification of these cases as well. I do not see anything wrong in this circular procedure; every research process moves in such a circle between theory formation and a more precise rendering of the object domain.[42]

The second methodological question is more difficult. It is one that has been treated as an empirical question in the psycholinguistics of the past decade, and as such has inspired a great amount of research: it asks whether there is a direct correspondence between the linguistic theory of grammar and the mental grammar that is, so to speak, "in the mind" of the speaker.[43] According to the correlation hypothesis, linguistic reconstructions are not simply lucid and economical representations of linguistic data; instead, there is a psychological complexity of the actual production process that corresponds, supposedly, to the transformational complexity that can be read off the structural description of linguistic expressions. I cannot deal with the individual research projects and the various interpretations here. Apparently, in psycholinguistics there is a growing tendency to move away from the original correlation hypothesis; the mental grammar that underlies the psychologically demonstrable production of language and the corresponding processes of understanding cannot, in the opinion of Bever, Watt, and others, be explained in the framework of a competence theory, that is, of a reconstructively oriented linguistics. I am not very certain how to judge this controversy; but I would like to suggest two points of view that have not, so far as I can see, been sufficiently taken into account in the discussion.

i. How strong do the essentialist assertions of a reconstructive linguistics regarding the psychic reality of reconstructed systems of rules have to be? Chomsky's maturationist assumption—that grammatical theory represents exactly the innate dispositions that enable the child to develop the hypotheses that direct language acquisition and that process the linguistic data in the environment—seems to me too strong.[44] Within the reconstructivist conceptual strategy, the more plausible assumption that grammatical theory represents the linguistic competence of the adult speaker is sufficient. This competence in turn is the result of a learning process that may even—in a manner similar to cognitive development or the development of moral consciousness—follow a rationally reconstructible pattern.[45] As Bever suggests, even this thesis can be weakened to allow for restrictions placed on the acquisition and application of grammatical rule-knowledge by nonlinguistic perceptual mechanisms or nonlinguistic epistemic systems in general, without surrendering the categorial framework of a competence theory.

ii. It is not clear to me to what extent the psycholinguistic critique of the admittedly essentialist implications of Chomsky's competence theory can be traced back to a confusion of research paradigms. This could be adequately discussed only if there were clarity about the way in which competence theories can be tested and, as the case may be, falsified. I have the impression that psycholinguistic investigations proceed empirically and analytically, and neglect *a limine* the distinction between competence and performance.[46]

Universal Pragmatics versus Transcendental Hermeneutics

Having presented the idea of a reconstructive science and briefly elucidated it through a consideration of reconstructive linguistics (and two of its methodological difficulties), I would like to touch on one further question: What is the relation of a universal-pragmatic reconstruction of general and unavoidable presuppositions of possible processes of reaching understanding to the type of investigation that has, since Kant, been called transcendental analysis? Kant terms "transcendental" an investigation that identifies and analyzes the a priori conditions of possibility of experience. The underlying idea is clear: in addition to the empirical knowledge that relates to objects of experience, there is, supposedly, a transcendental knowledge of concepts of objects in general that precede experience. The method by which these a priori concepts of objects in general can be shown to be valid conditions of possible experience is less clear. There is already disagreement concerning the meaning of the thesis: "[T]he a priori conditions of possible experience in general are at the same time conditions of the possibility of objects of experience."[47]

The analytic reception of the Kantian program (Strawson's work is a well-known example)[48] leads to a minimalist interpretation of the transcendental. Every coherent experience is organized in a categorial network; to the extent that we discover the same implicit conceptual structure in any coherent experience whatsoever, we may call this basic conceptual system of possible experience "transcendental." This conception renounces the claim that Kant wanted to vindicate with his transcendental deduction; it gives up all claim to a proof of the objective validity of our concepts of objects of possible experience in general.[49] The strong apriorism of Kantian philosophy gives way to a weaker version. From now on, transcendental investigation must rely on the competence of knowing subjects who judge which experiences may be called coherent experiences in order then to analyze this material with a view to finding general and necessary categorial presuppositions. Every reconstruction of a basic conceptual system of possible experience has to be regarded as a hypothetical proposal that can be tested against new experiences. As long as the assertion of its necessity and universality has not been refuted, we term "transcendental" the conceptual structure recurring in all coherent experiences. In this weaker version, the claim that this structure can be demonstrated a priori is dropped.

From this weaker interpretation, consequences ensue that are scarcely compatible with the original program. We can no longer exclude the possibility that our concepts of objects of possible experience can be applied successfully only under contingent boundary conditions that have, for example, heretofore regularly been fulfilled by natural constants.[50] Further, we can no longer exclude the possibility that the basic conceptual structure of possible experience has developed phylogenetically and arises anew in every normal ontogenesis, in a process that can be analyzed empirically.[51] We cannot even exclude the possibility that an a priori of experience that is relativized in this sense is valid only for specific, admittedly anthropologically deep-seated, behavioral systems, each of which makes possible a specific strategy for objectivating reality. The transcendentally oriented pragmatism inaugurated by C. S. Peirce attempts to show that there is such a structural connection between experience and instrumental action;[52] the hermeneutics stemming from Dilthey attempts—over against this a priori of experience—to do justice to an additional a priori of understanding or communicative experience.[53]

From the perspective of a transformed transcendental philosophy (in Apel's sense), two further renunciations called for by the analytic reception of Kant seem precipitate: the renunciation of the concept of the constitution of experience and the renunciation of an explicit treatment of the problem of validity. In my opinion, the reservation regarding a strong apriorism in no way demands limiting oneself to a *logical-semantic* analysis of the conditions of possible experiences. If we surrender the concept of the transcendental subject—the subject that accomplishes the synthesis and that, together with its knowledge-enabling structures, is removed from all experience—this does not mean that we have to renounce the universal-pragmatic analysis of the application of our concepts of objects of possible experience, that is, renounce investigation of the constitution of experience.[54] It is just as little a consequence of giving up the project of a transcendental deduction that one must hand over problems of validity to other domains of investigation, for instance, to the theory of science or of truth. Of course, the relation between the objectivity of possible experience and the truth of propositions looks different than it does under Kantian premises. A priori demonstration is replaced by transcendental investigation of the conditions for argumentatively redeeming the validity claims that lend themselves to possible discursive vindication.[55]

To be sure, in my view the question is more than simply terminologically interesting whether we may still call such investigations of general and unavoidable presuppositions of communication "transcendental" (in this case, presuppositions of argumentative speech). If we want to subject processes of reaching understanding ("speech") to a reconstructive analysis oriented to general and unavoidable presuppositions in the same way as has been done for cognitive processes,[56] then the model of transcendental philosophy undeniably suggests itself—all the more so since the theory of language and action has not (despite Humboldt) found its Kant. Naturally, recourse to this model is understandable only if one has in view one of the weaker versions of transcendental philosophy mentioned above. In this sense, Apel—in order to characterize his approach programmatically—speaks of "transcendental hermeneutics" or "transcendental pragmatics." I would like to mention two reasons for hesitating to adopt this usage.

a. Something like a transcendental investigation of processes of reaching understanding seems plausible to me as long as we view these under the aspect of processes of experience. It is in this sense that I speak of communicative experience; in understanding the utterance of another speaker as a participant in a communication process, the hearer (like the observer who perceives a segment of reality) has an experience. From this comparative perspective, concrete utterances would correspond to empirical objects, and utterances in general to objects in general (in the sense of objects of possible experience). Just as we can analyze our a priori concepts of objects in general—that is, the conceptual structure of any coherent experience whatsoever—we would also be able to analyze our a priori concepts of utterances in general—that is, the basic concepts of situations of possible mutual understanding (*Verständigung*), the conceptual structure that enables us to employ sentences in correct utterances. Concepts such as meaning and intentionality, the ability to speak and act (agency), interpersonal relationships and the like, would belong to this conceptual framework.

The expression "situation of possible mutual understanding" that, from this point of view, would correspond to the expression "object of possible experience," already shows, however, that acquiring the experiences we have in processes of communication is secondary to the goal of reaching understanding that these processes serve. The general structures of speech must therefore first be investigated from the perspective of reaching understanding and not from that of experience. As soon as we admit this, however, the parallels with transcendental philosophy (however conceived) recede into the background. The idea underlying transcendental philosophy is—to oversimplify—that we constitute experiences by objectivating reality from invariant points of view. This objectivation shows itself in the objects in general that necessarily are presupposed in every coherent experience; these objects in turn can be analyzed as a system of basic concepts. However, I do not find any correspondent to this idea under which the analysis of general presuppositions of communication might be carried out. Experiences are, if we follow the basic Kantian idea, constituted; utterances are, at most, generated. A transcendental investigation transposed to processes of reaching understanding would thus have to be guided by *another* model—not the epistemological model of the constitution of experience but perhaps the model of deep and surface structure.

b. Moreover, adopting the expression "transcendental" might conceal the break with apriorism that has been made in the meantime. Kant had to sharply separate empirical and transcendental analysis. If we now understand transcendental investigation in the sense of a reconstruction of general and unavoidable presuppositions of experiences that can lay claim to objectivity, then there certainly remains a difference between reconstructive and empirical-analytic analysis. Against this, the distinction between drawing on a priori knowledge and drawing on a posteriori knowledge becomes blurred. On the one hand, the rule consciousness of competent speakers is for them an a priori knowledge; on the other hand, the reconstruction of this

knowledge calls for inquiries undertaken with empirical speakers—
the linguist procures for herself a knowledge a posteriori. The implicit knowledge of competent speakers is so different from the
explicit form of linguistic description that the individual linguist
cannot rely on reflection on her own speech intuitions. The procedures employed in constructing and testing hypotheses, in apprais-
ing competing reconstructive proposals, in gathering and selecting
data, are in many ways like the procedures customarily used in the
nomological sciences. Methodological differences that can be traced
back to differences in the structure of data (observable events versus
comprehensible signs) and to differences between the structures of
laws and rules do not suffice, for example, to banish linguistics from
the sphere of empirical science.

This is particularly true for ontogenetic theories that, like Piaget's
cognitivist developmental psychology, connect the structural description of competencies (as well as of reconstructed patterns of development of these competencies) with assumptions concerning causal
mechanisms.[57] The paradigms introduced by Chomsky and Piaget
have prompted a type of research determined by a peculiar connection between formal and empirical analysis rather than by their
classical separation. The expression "transcendental," with which we
associate a contrast to empirical science, is thus unsuited to charac-
terizing, without misunderstanding, a line of research such as universal pragmatics. Behind the terminological question can be found
the systematic question concerning the as-yet insufficiently clarified
status of nonnomological empirical sciences of the reconstructive
type. I shall have to leave this question aside here. In any case, the
attempt to play down the interesting methodological differences that
arise here, and to interpret them away in the sense of the unified
science program, seems to have little prospect of success.[58]

II

The discussion of the theory of speech acts has given rise to ideas
on which the fundamental assumptions of universal pragmatics can
be based.[59] The universal-pragmatic point of view from which I shall

select and discuss these ideas leads, however, to an interpretation that diverges in several important respects from Austin's and Searle's understanding of speech-act theory, which remains a semantically determined one.

Three Aspects of Universal Pragmatics

The basic universal-pragmatic intention of speech-act theory is expressed in the fact that it thematizes the elementary units of speech (utterances) from a stance similar to that from which linguistics thematizes the units of language (sentences). The goal of reconstructive language analysis is an explicit description of the rules that a competent speaker must master in order to form grammatical sentences and to utter them in an acceptable way. The theory of speech acts shares this task with linguistics. Whereas the latter starts from the assumption that every adult speaker possesses a reconstructible implicit knowledge in which his linguistic rule competence (to produce sentences) is expressed, speech-act theory postulates a corresponding communicative rule competence, namely the competence to employ sentences in speech acts. It is further assumed that communicative competence has just as universal a core as linguistic competence. A general theory of speech acts would thus describe precisely that fundamental system of rules that adult speakers master to the extent that they can fulfill *the conditions for a happy employment of sentences in utterances,* no matter to which particular language the sentences may belong and in which random contexts the utterances may be embedded.

The proposal to investigate language use in competence-theoretic terms calls for a revision of the concepts of competence and performance. Chomsky initially understands these concepts in such a way that it makes sense to require that the phonetic, syntactic, and semantic properties of sentences be investigated linguistically within the framework of a reconstruction of linguistic competence and that the pragmatic properties of utterances be left to a theory of linguistic performance.[60] This conceptualization gives rise to the question of whether "communicative competence" is not a hybrid concept. I have, to begin with, based the demarcation of linguistics from universal pragmatics on the current distinction between sentences and utterances. The production of sentences according to the rules of grammar is something other than the use of sentences in accordance with pragmatic rules that shape the infrastructure of speech situations in general. But this raises the following two questions. (i) Could not the universal structures of speech—what is common to all utterances independently of their particular contexts—be adequately determined through universal sentential structures? In this case, with his linguistically reconstructible linguistic competence, the speaker would also be equipped for mastering situations of possible mutual understanding (*Verständigung*), for the general task of uttering sentences; and the postulate of a general communicative competence distinguishable from linguistic competence could not be justified. In addition to this there is the question (ii) whether the semantic properties of sentences (or words) may not, in the sense of the use theory of meaning, be explicated in any case only with reference to situations of possible typical employment. Then the distinction between sentences and utterances would be irrelevant, at least to semantic theory (so long as sufficiently typical contexts of utterance were taken into consideration). As soon as the distinction between the linguistic analysis of sentences and the pragmatic analysis of utterances becomes hazy, however, the object domain of universal pragmatics is also in danger of becoming blurred.

With regard to the first question, I would agree, with certain qualifications,[61] that a speaker, in transposing a well-formed sentence into an act oriented toward reaching understanding, merely actualizes what is inherent in the sentence structures. But this is not to deny the difference between the production of a grammatical sentence and the use of that sentence in a situation of possible mutual understanding, or the difference between the universal presuppositions that a competent speaker has to fulfill in each case. In order to utter a sentence, the speaker must fulfill general presuppositions of communication. Even if she fulfills these presuppositions in conformity to the structures that are already given with the sentence employed, she may very well form the sentence itself without at the same time fulfilling the presuppositions specific to speech. This can be made clear by looking at the relations to reality in which every sentence is first embedded through the act of utterance. In being uttered, a sentence is placed in relation to (a) the external reality of that which can be perceived, (b) the internal reality of that which a speaker would like to express as her intentions, and (c) the normative reality of that which is socially and culturally recognized. It is thereby subjected to validity claims that it need not and cannot fulfill as a nonsituated sentence, as a purely grammatical formation. A chain of symbols "counts" as a sentence of a natural language, *L*, if it is well formed according to the system of grammatical rules, *GL*. The grammaticality of a sentence means (from a pragmatic perspective) that the sentence, when uttered by a speaker, is *comprehensible* to all hearers who have mastered *GL*. Comprehensibility is the only universal claim that is to be fulfilled immanently to language that can be raised by participants in communication with regard to a sentence. The validity of a stated proposition, by contrast, depends on whether the proposition represents a fact or experience (or on whether the existential presuppositions of the mentioned propositional content hold); the validity of an expressed intention depends on whether it corresponds to what is actually intended by the speaker; and the validity of the speech act performed depends on whether this action conforms to a recognized normative background. Whereas a grammatical *sentence* fulfills the claim to comprehensibility, a successful *utterance* must satisfy three additional validity claims: it must count as true for the participants insofar as it represents something in the world; it must count as truthful insofar as it expresses something intended by the speaker; and it must count as right insofar as it conforms to socially recognized expectations.

We can, of course, identify features in the surface structures of sentences that have a special significance for the three general pragmatic functions of the utterance: to represent something, to express an intention, to establish an interpersonal relationship. Sentences with propositional content are used to represent an experience or a state of affairs (or to refer to these indirectly); intentional expressions, modal forms, and so on are used to express the speaker's intentions; performative phrases are used to establish interpersonal relations between speaker and hearer. Thus, the general structures of speech are also reflected at the level of sentence structure. But insofar as we consider a sentence as a grammatical formation, that is, independently of speech situations in which it can be uttered, these general pragmatic functions are not yet "occupied." In order to produce a grammatical sentence—as an example, say, for linguists—a competent speaker need satisfy only the claim to comprehensibility. He has to have mastered the corresponding system of grammatical rules; this we call his linguistic ability, and it can be analyzed linguistically. It is a different matter with regard to his ability to communicate; this is susceptible only to pragmatic analysis. By "communicative competence," I understand the ability of a speaker oriented toward reaching understanding to embed a well-formed sentence in relations to reality—that is,

i. to choose the propositional sentence in such a way that either the truth conditions of the proposition stated or the existential presuppositions of the propositional content mentioned are supposedly fulfilled (so that the hearer can share the knowledge of the speaker);

ii. To express his intentions in such a way that the linguistic expression represents what is intended (so that the hearer can trust the speaker); and

iii. To perform the speech act in such a way that it conforms to recognized norms or to accepted self-images (so that the hearer can be in accord with the speaker in shared value orientations).

To the extent that these decisions do not depend on particular epistemic presuppositions and changing contexts but cause sentences in general to assume the universal-pragmatic functions of representation, expression, and the production of interpersonal relationships, what is expressed in them is precisely the communicative competence for which I am proposing a universal-pragmatic investigation.

The part of universal pragmatics that is furthest developed is that related to the representational function of utterances, for example to the use of elementary propositional sentences. This classic

domain of formal semantics has been pursued within analytic philosophy from Frege to Dummett.[62] That this is a matter of universal-
pragmatic investigation can be seen in the fact that the truth value
of propositions is systematically taken into account. The theory of
predication does not investigate sentences in general (as does linguistics) but sentences in their function of representing facts. Analysis is directed above all to the logic of using predicates and those
expressions that enable us to refer to objects. To be sure, this part
of universal pragmatics is not the most important for a theory of
communication. The analysis of intentionality, the discussion of
avowals, and the debate on private speech, in so far as they clear the
way to a universal pragmatics of the expressive function of utterances, are only beginnings.[63] Finally, speech act theory provides a
useful point of departure for the part of universal pragmatics related
to the interpersonal function of utterances.

With regard to the second question raised above, one might see a
further difficulty with my proposal for conceptualizing universal
pragmatics in the fact that formal semantics does not fit well into
the distinction between a linguistic analysis concerned with sentences and a pragmatic analysis concerned with utterances. There is
a broad spectrum of different approaches to semantic theory. *Linguistically oriented theories of meaning*[64] try to grasp systematically the
semantic content of linguistic expressions. In the framework of *transformational grammar,* explanations of the surface structures of sentences either start with semantic deep structures or rely on semantic
projections into syntactic structures. This approach leads as a rule
to a combinatory system, constructed using elementary sentences,
of general semantic markers. *Lexical semantics* proceeds in a similar
manner; it clarifies the meaning structures of a given lexicon by way
of a formal analysis of meaning relations. The weakness of these
linguistic approaches lies in the fact that they accommodate the
pragmatic dimension of the use of sentences only in an ad hoc way.
However, the use theory of meaning developed from the work of
Wittgenstein has provided good reasons for holding that the meaning of linguistic expressions can be identified only with reference to
situations of possible employment.

For their part, *pragmatic theories of meaning*[65] are faced with the difficulty of delimiting a linguistic expression's typical situations of employment from contexts that happen by chance to have additional meaning-generating power but do not affect the semantic core of the linguistic expression. According to which criteria may we extrapolate typical behavior from actual linguistic behavior? *Reference semantics,*[66] whether framed as a theory of extensional or of intensional denotation, determines the meaning of an expression by the class of objects to which it can be applied in true sentences. On this premise, one can explicate the meaning of expressions that appear in sentences with a representational function. I do not see, however, why semantic theory should monopolistically single out the representational function of language and neglect the specific meanings that language develops in its expressive and interpersonal functions.

These preliminary reflections are intended merely to support the conjecture that semantic theory cannot fruitfully be developed as a unified theory. But if it is heterogeneously composed, no objection to the methodological separation of the analysis of sentence structures from that of utterance structures can be inferred from the difficulties of demarcating semantics from pragmatics (difficulties that are equally present in demarcating semantics from syntax). The analysis of general structures of speech can indeed begin with general sentence structures. However, it is directed to formal properties of sentences only from the perspective of the possibility of *using sentences* as elements of speech, that is, for representational, expressive, and interpersonal functions. Universal pragmatics, too, can be understood as semantic analysis. But it is distinguished from other theories of meaning in that the meanings of linguistic expressions are relevant only insofar as these expressions are used in speech acts that satisfy the validity claims of truth, truthfulness, and normative rightness. On the other hand, universal pragmatics is distinguished from empirical pragmatics, for example, sociolinguistics, in that the meaning of linguistic expressions comes under consideration only insofar as it is determined by *formal* properties of speech situations in general, and not by particular situations of use.

I would now like to sum up the different levels of analysis and corresponding object domains of semiotics.

Sentences versus Utterances

If we start with concrete speech acts embedded in specific contexts and then disregard all aspects that these utterances owe to their pragmatic functions, we are left with linguistic expressions. Whereas the elementary unit of speech is the speech act, the elementary unit of language is the sentence. The demarcation is obtained by attending to conditions of validity: a grammatically well-formed sentence satisfies the claim to comprehensibility; a communicatively successful speech act requires, beyond the comprehensibility of the linguistic expression, that the participants in communication be prepared to reach an understanding and that they raise claims to truth, truthfulness, and rightness, and reciprocally impute their satisfaction. Sentences are the object of linguistic analysis, speech acts of pragmatic analysis.

Individual Languages versus Language in General

The first task of linguistics is to develop a grammar for each individual language so that a structural description can be correlated with any sentence of the language. On the other hand, general grammatical theory is concerned with reconstructing the rule system that underlies the ability of a subject to generate well-formed sentences in any language whatsoever. Grammatical theory claims to reconstruct the universal linguistic ability of adult speakers. (In a strong version, this linguistic competence means the ability to develop hypotheses that guide language acquisition on the basis of an innate disposition; in a weaker version, linguistic competence represents the result of learning processes interpreted constructivistically in Piaget's sense.)

Aspects of Linguistic Analysis

Every linguistic expression can be considered from at least three analytic viewpoints. Phonetics examines linguistic expressions as inscriptions in an underlying medium (i.e., as formations of sound).

Syntactic theory investigates linguistic expressions with regard to the formal connections of the smallest meaningful units. Semantic theory examines the meaning content of linguistic expressions. Evidently, only phonetic and syntactic theory are self-sufficient linguistic theories; semantic theory, by contrast, cannot be conducted solely in the attitude of the theoretician of language, that is, in disregard of pragmatic aspects.

Particular versus Universal Aspects of Speech Acts

The task of empirical pragmatics consists, to begin with, in describing speech acts typical of a certain milieu, which can in turn be analyzed from sociological, ethnological, and psychological points of view. General pragmatic theory, on the other hand, is concerned with reconstructing the rule system that underlies the ability of a subject to utter sentences in any relevant situation whatsoever. Universal pragmatics thereby raises the claim to reconstruct the ability of adult speakers to embed sentences in relations to reality in such a way that they can take on the general pragmatic functions of representation, expression, and establishing legitimate interpersonal relations. This communicative competence is expressed inter alia in those accomplishments that hermeneutics stylizes to an art (*Kunstlehre*), namely paraphrasing utterances by means of context-similar utterances of the same language or translating them into context-comparable utterances in a foreign language.

Universal-Pragmatic Aspects

The three general pragmatic functions of an utterance—to represent something in the world using a sentence, to express the speaker's intentions, and to establish legitimate interpersonal relations—are the basis of all the particular functions that an utterance can assume in specific contexts. The fulfillment of those general functions is measured against the validity conditions for truth, truthfulness, and rightness. Thus every speech act can be considered from the corresponding analytic viewpoints. Formal semantics examines the structure of elementary propositions and the acts of reference and predication. A still scarcely developed theory of intentionality examines intentional expressions insofar as they function in first-person sentences. Finally, the theory of speech acts examines illocutionary force from the viewpoint of the establishment of legitimate interpersonal relations. These semiotic distinctions are summarized in the following table:

Theoretical level	Object domain
Linguistics	Sentences
Grammar	Sentences of an individual language
Grammatical theory	Rules for generating sentences in any language whatever
Aspects of linguistic analysis	
Phonetic theory	Inscriptions (language sounds)
Syntactic theory	Syntactical rules
Semantic theory	Lexical units
Pragmatics	Speech acts
Empirical pragmatics	Context-bound speech acts
Universal pragmatics	Rules for using sentences in utterances
Aspects of universal-pragmatic analysis	
Theory of elementary propositions	Acts of reference and predication
Theory of first-person sentences	Linguistic expression of intentions
Theory of illocutionary acts	Establishment of interpersonal relations

For a theory of communicative action, the third aspect of utterances, namely the establishment of legitimate interpersonal relations, is central. I shall therefore take the theory of speech acts as my point of departure.

The Standard Form of the Speech Act—Searle's Principle of
Expressibility

The principal task of speech-act theory is to clarify the performative
status of linguistic utterances. Austin analyzed the sense in which I
can utter sentences in speech acts as the *illocutionary force* of speech
acts. In uttering a promise, an assertion, or a warning, I simultaneously execute an action with the corresponding sentences: I try to
make a promise, to *put forward* an assertion, to *issue* a warning—I do
things by saying something. Although there are other modes of
employing language—Austin mentions, among others, writing po-
ems and telling jokes—the illocutionary use seems to be the foundation on which these other kinds of employment rest. To be
understood in a given situation, every utterance must at least implicitly establish and give expression to a certain *relation* between the
speaker and her counterpart. We can also say that the illocutionary
force of a speech act consists in fixing the communicative function
of the content uttered.

The current distinction between the content and the relational
aspects of an utterance has, to begin with, a trivial meaning.[67] It says
that, in being uttered, the sentence used is embedded in a context,
more precisely, in specific interpersonal relations. In a certain way,
every explicitly performative utterance both establishes and represents an interpersonal relation between at least two subjects capable
of speech and action. This circumstance is trivial so long as under
the relational aspect we merely contrast the utterance character of
speech with its semantic content. If nothing more were meant by the
illocutionary force of a speech act, the concept "illocutionary" could
serve at best to elucidate the fact that linguistic utterances have the
character of actions, that is, are speech *actions.* The point of the
concept cannot lie therein. I find it rather in the peculiarly generative power of speech acts.

It is to this generative power that I trace the fact that a speech act
can succeed (or fail). We can say that a speech act succeeds if a
relation between the speaker and hearer comes to pass—the relation
intended by the speaker—and if the hearer can *understand and accept*
the content uttered by the speaker in the sense indicated (e.g., as a

promise, assertion, suggestion, and so forth). Thus the generative power consists in the fact that the speaker, in performing a speech act, can influence the hearer in such a way that the latter can take up an interpersonal relation with her.[68] It can, of course, be said of every interaction, and not only of speech acts, that they establish interpersonal relations. Whether or not they have an explicitly linguistic form, communicative actions are related to a context of action norms and values. Without the normative background of routines, roles, habitualized forms of life—in short, conventions—the individual action would remain indeterminate. All communicative actions satisfy or violate normative social expectations or conventions. Satisfying a convention in acting means that a subject capable of speaking and acting takes up an interpersonal relation with at least one other such subject. Thus the establishment of an interpersonal relation is a criterion that is not selective enough for our purposes. I emphasized at the start that I am restricting my analysis to paradigmatic cases of linguistically explicit action that is oriented toward reaching understanding. This restriction must now be drawn somewhat more precisely. In doing so, we can begin with the standard examples from which speech-act theory was developed. The following are typical speech-act forms:[69]

"I . . .   you that . . .   ."
     [verb]   [sentence]
e.g., "I (hereby) promise you that I will come tomorrow."

"You are . . .   ."
              [verb] [p. part.]   [sentence]
e.g., "You are requested to stop smoking."

"I . . .   . . .   you that . . .   ."
     [auxiliary verb]   [verb]   [sentence]
e.g., "I can assure you that it wasn't I."

I shall hold to the following terminological rules. An explicit speech act satisfies the *standard form* in its surface structure if it is made up of an *illocutionary* and a *propositional* component. The illocutionary component consists in an *illocutionary* act carried out with the aid of a *performative sentence*. This sentence is formed in the present indicative, affirmative, and has as its logical subject the first person and as its logical (direct) object the second person; the predicate, constructed with the help of a performative expression, permits in general the particle "hereby."[70] This performative component needs to be completed by a propositional component constructed with the help of a sentence with *propositional content.* Whenever it is used in constative speech acts, the sentence with propositional content takes the form of a *propositional sentence (Aussagesatz).* In its elementary form, the propositional sentence contains (i) a name or a referring expression, with the aid of which the speaker denotes an object about which she wants to assert something; and (ii) a predicate expression for the general specification that the speaker wants to grant or deny to the object. In nonconstative speech acts, the propositional content is not stated, but *mentioned,* in this case, propositional content coincides with what is usually called the unasserted proposition. (Thus I distinguish between the nominalized proposition "that *p,*" which expresses a state of affairs, and the proposition "*p,*" which represents a fact and which owes its assertoric force to the circumstance that it is embedded in a speech act of the type "assertion," and is thereby connected with an illocutionary act of asserting. In formal logic, of course, we treat propositions as autonomous units. Only the truth value we assign to "*p*" in contradistinction to "that *p*" is a reminder of the embedding of the proposition in some constative speech act, an embedding that is systematically neglected.)[71]

I shall call speech acts that have this structure *propositionally differentiated.* They are distinguished from symbolically mediated interactions—for instance, a shout of "Fire!" that releases complementary actions, assistance or flight—in that a propositional component of speech is uncoupled from the illocutionary act, so that (i) the propositional content can be held invariant across changes in illocutionary potential, and (ii) the holistic mode of speech, in which representation, expression, and behavioral expectation are still one, can be replaced by differential modes of speech. I shall return to this point in the following section. For the present, it suffices to point out that this level of differentiation of speech is a precondition for an action's ability to take on representational functions, that is, to state something about the world, either directly in the form of an assertion or indirectly, in nonconstative speech acts, through mentioning a propositional content.

Explicit speech acts always have a propositional component in which a state of affairs is expressed. Nonlinguistic actions normally lack this component; thus they cannot fulfill representational functions. Signaling to a taxi so that I can begin work in my office by eight in the morning, reacting to the news of my child's miserable school grades with a desperate look, joining a demonstration march, expressing nonacceptance of an invitation by not showing up, shaking a candidate's hand after he has passed the exam, and so on and so forth, I observe or violate conventions. Naturally, these normative expectations have a propositional content; however, the propositional content must already be known to the participants if the expressed behavior is to be comprehensible as arriving at work, a parent's reacting, taking part in a demonstration—in short as an action. The nonverbal utterance itself cannot bring the propositional content of the presupposed norm to expression because it cannot take on representational functions. It can, of course, be understood as an indicator that calls to mind the propositional content of the presupposed norm.

Owing to their representational function, propositionally differentiated *speech* acts allow the actor a greater degree of freedom in following norms. If work begins at eight in the morning, there is the option only of appearing or not appearing; in the former case, to be on time or to be late; in the latter case, to be excused or not excused, and so on. Nonverbal actions are often the result of such "trees" of "yes" or "no" decisions. But if the actor can express herself verbally, her situation is rich with alternatives. She can express the same speech act, say a command, in a very differentiated way; she will fulfill the same role segment, say that of an English teacher during class dictation, with very different speech acts. In short, propositionally differentiated speech leaves the actor more degrees of freedom in relation to a recognized normative background than does a nonlinguistic interaction.

Of course, propositionally differentiated utterances do not always have a linguistic form, as is shown by the example of a grammaticalized sign language, for instance, the standardized language of the deaf and mute. In this connection, one might also mention pointing gestures, which represent an equivalent for the use of referential terms, thereby supplementing propositional speech. On the other hand, there are also speech acts that are not propositionally differentiated, for example, illocutionarily abbreviated speech acts such as "Hello!" as a greeting formula, or "Check!" and "Checkmate!" as performative expressions for moves in a game of chess and their consequences. The circumstance that a propositional component is lacking places these verbal utterances on a level with normal non-verbal actions; while the latter actions do *refer* to the propositional content of a presupposed convention, they do not *represent* it.

As a first step in delimiting the pragmatic units of analysis, we can specify—out of the set of communicative actions that rest on the consensual foundation of reciprocally raised and recognized validity claims—the subset of *propositionally differentiated speech acts*. But even this specification is not yet selective enough; for among these utterances we find such speech acts as "betting," "christening," "appointing," and so on. Despite their propositionally differentiated content (betting on/for . . . , christening as/with . . . , appointing to . . .), they are bound to a single institution (or to a narrowly circumscribed set of institutions); they can therefore be seen as the equivalent of actions that fulfill presupposed norms, either nonverbally or in an illocutionarily abbreviated way. That these speech acts are *institutionally bound* can be seen in (among other things) the fact that the permissible propositional contents are narrowly limited by the normative meaning of betting, christening, appointing, marrying, and so on. One bets for stakes, christens with names, appoints to official positions, marries a partner, and so on. With institutionally bound speech acts, specific institutions can always be specified. With institutionally unbound speech acts, only general contextual conditions can be specified—conditions that typically must be met for a corresponding act to succeed. Institutionally bound speech acts express a specific institution in the same unmediated way that propositionally nondifferentiated and nonverbal actions express a presupposed norm. To explain what acts of betting or christening mean, I must refer to the institutions of betting or christening. By contrast, commands or advice or questions do not represent institutions but types of speech acts that can fit very different institutions. To be sure, the criterion of being institutionally bound does not always permit an unambiguous classification. Commands can exist wherever relations of authority are institutionalized; appointments presuppose special, bureaucratically developed organizations; and marriages require a single institution (which is, however, to be found universally). But this does not devalue the usefulness of the analytic viewpoint. Institutionally unbound speech acts, insofar as they have any regulative meaning at all, refer to general aspects of action norms; they are not, however, defined by particular institutions.

We can now define the desired analytic units as *propositionally differentiated* and *institutionally unbound speech acts*. To be sure, only those with an explicitly *linguistic* form are suitable for analysis. Frequently, of course, the context in which speech acts are embedded makes standard linguistic forms superfluous; for example, when the performative meaning is determined exclusively by the context of utterance; or when the performative meaning is merely indicated, that is, expressed through inflection, punctuation, word position, or particles such as "isn't it?," "right?," "indeed," "clearly," "surely," and similar expressions.

Finally, we shall exclude those explicit speech acts in standard form that appear in contexts that produce shifts of meaning. This is the case when the pragmatic meaning of a context-dependent speech act diverges from the meaning of the sentences used in it (and from the indicated general contextual conditions that have to be fulfilled for the type of speech act in question). Searle's "principle of expressibility" takes this requirement into account: assuming that the speaker expresses his intention precisely, explicitly, and literally, it is possible in principle for every speech act carried out or capable of being carried out to be specified unequivocally by a complex sentence.

Kanngiesser has given this principle the following form: "For every meaning x, it is the case that, if there is a speaker S in a language community P who means (*meint*) x, then it is possible that there be an expression in the language spoken by P which is an exact expression of x."[72] For our purposes, we can weaken this postulate to require that in a given language, for every interpersonal relation that a speaker wants to take up explicitly with another member of his language community, a suitable performative expression is either available or, if necessary, can be obtained through a specification of available expressions or newly introduced. With this modification, we can take into account reservations that have been expressed concerning Searle's principle.[73] In any case, the heuristic meaning is clear—if the postulate of expressibility is valid, analysis can be limited to institutionally unbound, explicit speech acts in standard form.

The following diagram sums up the viewpoints from which I have delimited the class of speech acts basic for analysis.

Derivation of the Analytic Units of the Theory of Speech Acts

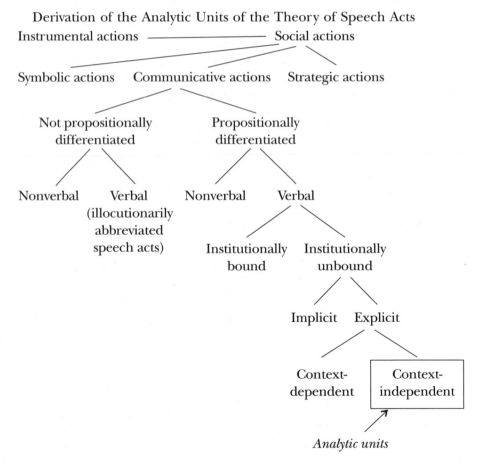

I have not elucidated the embedding of communicative action ("action oriented toward reaching understanding") in other types of action. It seems to me that *strategic action* ("action oriented toward the actor's success" such as competitive behavior or combat games— in general, modes of action that correspond to the utilitarian model of purposive rational action) as well as the still insufficiently analyzed category of *symbolic action* (such as action manifested in a concert or a dance—in general, modes of action that are bound to nonpropositional systems of symbolic expression) differ from communicative action in that individual validity claims are suspended (in strategic action, truthfulness, in symbolic action, truth).[74] My previous analyses of "labor" and "interaction" have not yet adequately captured the most general differentiating characteristics of instrumental and social (or communicative) action. I cannot pursue this here.

On the Double Structure of Speech

I would like to return now to the characteristic *double structure* that can be read off from the standard form of speech acts. Obviously, the two components, the illocutionary and the propositional, can vary independently of one another. We can hold a propositional content invariant vis-à-vis the different types of speech acts in which it occurs. In this abstraction of propositional content from the asserted proposition, a fundamental accomplishment of our language is expressed. Propositionally differentiated speech distinguishes itself therein from the symbolically mediated interaction we can already observe among primates.[75] Any number of examples of the *invariance of propositional content* despite variance in speech act mode can be provided—for instance, for the propositional content "Peter's smoking a pipe," there are the following:

"I assert that Peter smokes a pipe."

"I beg you (Peter) to smoke a pipe."

"I ask you (Peter), do you smoke a pipe?"

"I warn you (Peter) against smoking a pipe."

In a genetic perspective, the speech-act invariance of propositional contents appears as an *uncoupling of the illocutionary and propositional components* in the formation and transformation of speech acts. This uncoupling is a condition for the differentiation of the double structure of speech, that is, for the separation of two communicative levels on which speaker and hearer must *simultaneously* come to an understanding if they want to communicate their intentions to one another. I would distinguish (i) the *level of intersubjectivity* on which speaker and hearer, through illocutionary acts, establish the relations that permit them to come to an understanding with one another, and (ii) the *level of propositional content* about which they wish to reach understanding in the communicative function specified in (i). Corresponding to the relational and the content aspects, from the point of view of which every utterance can be analyzed, there are (in the standard form) the illocutionary and the propositional components of the speech act. The illocutionary act fixes the sense in which the propositional content is employed, and the act-complement determines the content that is understood "as something . . ." in the communicative function specified. (The hermeneutic "as" can be differentiated on both communicative levels. With a proposition "*p*," an identifiable object whose existence is presupposed can be characterized "as something"—e.g., as a "red," "soft," or "ideal," object. In connection with an illocutionary act, that is, through being embedded in a speech act, this propositional content can, in turn, be *uttered* "as something"—e.g., as a command or assertion).

A basic feature of language is connected with this double structure of speech, namely, its inherent reflexivity. The standardized possibilities for directly and indirectly mentioning speech merely make explicit a self-reference that is already contained in every speech act. In filling out the double structure of speech, participants in dialogue communicate on two levels simultaneously. They combine communication of a content with "metacommunication"—communication about the sense in which the communicated content is used. The expression "metacommunication" might be misleading here because it could be associated with *metalanguage* and suggest an idea of language levels such that, at every higher level, metalinguistic statements about the object language of the next lower level can be made. But the concept of a hierarchy of language was introduced for formal languages, in which just that reflexivity of ordinary language is lacking. Moreover, in a metalanguage one always refers to an object language in the objectivating attitude of someone asserting facts or observing events; one forms metalinguistic *statements*. By contrast, on the metacommunicative level of speech, it is precisely statements that are not possible. Instead, at this level, one chooses the illocutionary role in which the propositional content is to be used; and this metacommunication about the sense in which the sentence with propositional content is to be employed requires a performative attitude on the part of those communicating. Thus, the peculiar reflexivity of natural language rests *in the first instance* on the combination of a communication of content—effected in an objectivating attitude—with a metacommunication concerning the relational aspect—effected in a performative attitude—from the point of view of which the content is to be understood.

Of course, participants in dialogue normally have the option of objectifying every illocutionary act performed as the content of a further (constative) speech act. They can adopt an objectivating attitude toward the illocutionary component of an already performed speech act and shift this component to the level of propositional contents. Naturally, they can do so only by peforming a new speech act that contains, in turn, a nonobjectified illocutionary component. The direct and indirect mention of speech standardizes this possibility of rendering explicit the reflexivity of natural language. The metacommunication that takes place on the level of intersubjectivity in a speech act *tn* can be depicted on the level of propositional content in a further (constative) speech act *tn+1*. On the other hand, it is not possible *simultaneously* to perform and to objectify an illocutionary act.[76]

This option is sometimes the occasion for a descriptivist fallacy to which even pragmatic theories fall prey. We can analyze the structures of speech, just like every other object, only in an objectivating attitude. In doing so, the relevant accompanying illocutionary component cannot, as we saw above, become *uno acto* the object. This circumstance misleads many language theorists into the view that communication processes take place at a single level, namely that of transmitting content (i.e., information). From this perspective, the relational aspect loses its independence vis-à-vis the content aspect; the communicative role of an utterance loses its constitutive significance and is counted as part of the information content. The pragmatic operator of the statement, which in formalized presentations (e.g., deontic logics) represents the illocutionary component of an utterance, is then no longer interpreted as a specific mode of reaching understanding about propositional contents but falsely as part of the information transmitted. I do not wish to analyze this fallacy here; I merely point to one of its consequences: that the constitutive meaning of the double structure of speech is neglected in theoretical approaches.

As opposed to this, I consider the task of universal pragmatics to be the rational reconstruction of the double structure of speech. Taking Austin's theory of speech acts as my point of departure (in the next two sections) I would now like to render this task more precise in relation to the problems of meaning and validity.

Universal-Pragmatic Categories of Meaning

Austin's contrasting of locutionary and illocutionary acts set off a broad discussion that has also brought some clarification to the theory of meaning. Austin reserved the concept *meaning* for the meaning of sentences with propositional content, while he used the concept *force* only for the illocutionary act of uttering sentences with propositional content. This leads to the following constellations:

Meaning: sense and reference, locutionary act

Force: attempt to reach an uptake, illocutionary act

Austin could point to the fact that sentences with the same propositional content could be uttered in speech acts of different types, that is, with differing illocutionary force or in different illocutionary modes. Nevertheless, the proposed distinction is unsatisfactory. If one introduces meaning solely in a linguistic sense, as sentence meaning (whereby either sentence meaning is conceived as a function of word meanings or, with Frege, word meanings are conceived as functions of possible sentence meanings), the restriction to the propositional components of speech acts is not plausible. Obviously, their illocutionary components also have a meaning in a linguistic sense. In the case of an explicitly performative utterance, the performative verb employed has a lexical meaning, and the performative sentence constructed with its help has a meaning in a manner *similar* to the sentence with propositional content dependent on it. "What Austin calls the illocutionary force of an utterance is that aspect of its meaning which is either conveyed by its explicitly performative prefix, if it has one, or might have been so conveyed by the use of such an expression."[77]

This plausible argument neglects, however, the fact that force is something that, in a specific sense, belongs only to utterances and not to sentences. Thus, one might first hit upon the idea of reserving "force" for the meaning content that accrues to the sentence through its being uttered, that is, embedded in structures of speech. We can certainly distinguish the phenomenon of meaning that comes about through the employment of a sentence in an utterance from the phenomenon of sentence meaning. We can speak in a pragmatic sense of the meaning of an utterance, as we do in a linguistic sense of the meaning of a sentence. Thus Alston has taken the fact that the same speech act can be performed with very different sentences as a reason for granting pragmatic meaning a certain priority over linguistic meaning. In accordance with a consistent use theory of meaning, he suggests that sentence (and word) meanings are a function of the meaning of the speech acts in which they are "principally" used.[78] The difficulty with this proposal is that it does not adequately take into account the relative independence of sentence meanings in relation to the contingent changes of meaning that a sentence can undergo when used in different contexts. Moreover, the meaning of a sentence is obviously less dependent on the intentions of the speaker than is the meaning of an utterance.

Even if a sentence is very often used with different intentions and in a context that pragmatically shifts meaning, its linguistic meaning does not have to change. Thus, for example, when certain social roles prescribe that commands be uttered in the form of requests, the pragmatic meaning of the utterance (as a command) in no way alters the linguistic meaning of the sentence uttered (as a request). This is an additional reason for singling out the standard conditions under which the pragmatic meaning of an explicit speech act coincides with the linguistic meaning of the sentences employed in it. Precisely in the case of an explicit speech act in standard form, however, the categorial difference between the meaning of the expressions originally used in propositional sentences, on the one hand, and the meaning of illocutionary forces (as well as of expressed intentions), on the other, comes into view. This shows that it does not make sense to explicate the concepts "meaning" versus "force" with reference to the distinction between the linguistic meaning of a sentence and the pragmatic meaning of an utterance.

The linguistic analysis of sentence meaning tends to abstract from certain relations to reality into which a sentence is put as soon as it is uttered and from the validity claims under which it is thereby placed. On the other hand, a consistent analysis of meaning is not possible without some reference to situations of possible use. Every linguistic expression can be used to form statements. Even illocutionary phrases (and originally intentional expressions) can be objectified with the help of a further statement. This suggests that it makes sense to secure a certain uniformity for the linguistic analysis of the meanings of linguistic expressions by relating it in every case to the possibilities for using these expressions in propositions. But this makes sense only for such expressions as can appear *exclusively* in propositional components of speech. By contrast, the meaning of performative expressions should be clarified by referring to the possibilities for using them in illocutionary acts (and the meaning of originally intentional expressions by referring to the possibilities for using them to express intentions directly). The linguistic explication of the meaning of "to promise" should orient itself around the possibilities for using the sentence

(1) "I hereby promise you that . . ."

and not around the possibilities for using the sentence

(2) "He promises her that . . ."

Correspondingly, the explication of the meaning of "to hate" should refer to the sentence

(1′) "I hate you."

instead of to the sentence

(2′) "He hates her."

Only because and so long as the linguistic analysis of meaning is biased in favor of the propositionalized forms (2 or 2′) is it necessary to supplement the meaning of propositional sentences with the meaning of the illocutionary force of an utterance (and the intention of the speaker). No doubt this circumstance motivated Austin to draw his distinction between meaning and force. To my mind, it would be better to start with the linguistic meaning of an expression, as opposed to the pragmatic meaning of an utterance; the linguistic meaning of expressions would then be differentiated according to the universal possibilities for using them in speech acts (and according to the corresponding validity claims), with reference to the original occurrence of such expressions. But what does "original" mean in this context? Let us consider two sentences as examples:

(3) "I'm telling you that father's new car is yellow."

(4) "I'm asking you, is father's new car yellow?"

Understanding the two (different) illocutionary acts is tied to other presuppositions than is understanding their (concordant) propositional content. The difference becomes perceptible as soon as one returns to the conditions that must be fulfilled by situations in which someone who does not know English might learn (i.e., originally understand) the meanings. A hearer can understand the meaning of the sentence with the propositional content "the being yellow of father's car" on condition that he has learned to correctly use the propositional sentence:

(5) "Father's new car is yellow"

in order, for example, to express a corresponding experience, in this case his observation that father's new car is yellow. The ability to make this or a similar observation must be presupposed, for a proper use of the propositional sentence in (5) demands at least the following of the speaker:

a. The existential presupposition: that there is one and only one object to which the designation "father's new car" applies.

b. The presupposition of identifiability: that the (denotatively employed) propositional content contained in the designation "father's new car" is a sufficient indication, in a given context, for a hearer to select the (and only the) object to which the designation applies.

c. The act of predication: that the predicate "yellow" can be attributed to the object that is designated.

Correspondingly, understanding the meaning of the propositional sentence contained in (5) demands of the hearer that he

a'. share the speaker-presupposition,

b'. fulfill the speaker-presupposition, that is, actually identify the object designated, and

c'. undertake for his part the act of predication.

It is a different matter so far as the illocutionary components of utterances (3) and (4) are concerned. A hearer can understand the meaning of notifying or asking on condition that he has learned to take part in successful speech acts of the following type:

(6) "I (hereby) notify you that . . ."

(7) "I (hereby) ask you whether . . ."

The hearer, that is, has learned to assume both the role of the (acting) speaker as well as that of the (cooperating) hearer. The performance of an illocutionary act cannot serve to report an observation as the use of a propositional sentence can; nor must the ability to have perceptions essentially be presupposed here. Rather, conversely, the execution of a speech act is a condition of possibility of an *experience*, namely the communicative experience that the hearer has when he accepts the offer contained in the attempted speech act and enters into an interpersonal relation with the speaker, a relation between one who notifies or informs and one who receives the notification or information—or, alternatively, takes up the relation between a person who questions and a person who answers.

Understanding (5) *presupposes* the possibility of sensory experiences (experiences of the type, observation); by contrast, understanding (6) and (7) itself *represents* a communicative experience (an experience of the type, participatory observation): illocutionary understanding is an experience made possible through communication.

The difference between originally illocutionary and originally propositional meanings ("force" and "meaning" in Austin's sense) can be traced back to differences in possible learning situations. We learn the meaning of illocutionary acts only in the performative attitude of participants in speech acts. By contrast, we learn the meaning of sentences with propositional content in the nonperformative—objectivating—attitude of observers who correctly represent their experiences in propositional sentences.[79] We acquire originally illoctionary meanings in connection with communicative experiences that we have in entering the level of intersubjectivity and establishing an interpersonal relation. We learn originally propositional meanings through reporting experiences with objects and events in the world.

Notwithstanding this difference, meanings learned in a performative attitude can, of course, also occur in sentences with propositional content:

(8) "I assure you that he notified me yesterday that . . ."

(9) "I'm reporting to you that she asked me yesterday whether . . ."

This fact may explain why the indicated difference between the two categories of meaning is often not noticed. In sentences with propositional content, however, we can distinguish the meanings of expressions that may be used in a performative attitude from the word meanings that—like the nominal and predicative expressions in (5)—are permitted *only* as meaning components in sentences with propositional content. In utterances like (8) and (9), "notify" and "ask" bear a shade of meaning derived from the power that they have only in illocutionary roles—as in (6) and (7).

We can retain Austin's distinction between "force" and "meaning" in the sense of these two categories of meaning. "Force" then stands for the meaning of expressions that are originally used in connection with illocutionary acts, and "meaning" for the meaning of expressions originally used in connection with propositions. Thus we distinguish "force" and "meaning" as two categories of meaning that arise with regard to the general pragmatic functions of communication: the establishment of interpersonal relations, on the one hand, and representation (reporting of facts or states of affairs), on the other. (I shall here leave to one side the third category of meaning, which corresponds to the function of *expression*, that is, to the disclosure of subjective experiences (*Erlebnisse*), although reflections similar to those carried out for illocutionary acts apply to intentional sentences as well.)

I would like to hold on to the following results:

a. It is not advisable to reserve the concept *meaning* for the propositional component of a speech act and to characterize the meaning of an illocutionary component only by a pragmatic operator (which designates a specific illocutionary force).

b. On the other hand, it is also unsatisfactory to reconstruct the meaning of a performative sentence in exactly the same way as the meaning of a sentence with propositional content; the illocutionary component of a speech act neither expresses a proposition nor mentions a propositional content.[80]

c. It is equally unsatisfactory to equate illocutionary force with the meaning component that accrues to the meaning of a sentence through the act of uttering it in a given context.

d. Rather, from a universal-pragmatic point of view, the meaning of linguistic expressions can be categorically distinguished according to whether they may appear only in sentences that take on a representational function or whether they can serve specifically to establish interpersonal relations or to express speaker intentions.[81]

Thematization of Validity Claims and Modes of Communication

Austin's contrasting of locutionary and illocutionary acts has become important not only for the theory of meaning; the discussion about basic types of speech acts and basic modes of language use has also taken this pair of concepts as its starting point. At first Austin wanted to draw the boundary in such a way that "the performative should be doing something as opposed to just saying something; and the performative is happy or unhappy as opposed to true and false."[82]

From this the following correlations resulted:

Locutionary acts: constatives, true/untrue

Illocutionary acts: performatives, happy/unhappy

But this demarcation of locutionary and illocutionary acts could not be maintained when it became apparent that all speech acts—the constatives included—contain a locutionary component (in the form of a sentence with propositional content) and an illocutionary component (in the form of a performative sentence).[83] What Austin had initially introduced as the locutionary act was now replaced by (a) the propositional component contained in every explicit speech act, and (b) a special class of illocutionary acts—constative speech acts—that imply the validity claim of truth. Austin himself later regarded constative speech acts as only one among several different classes of speech acts. The two sentences

(1) "I assert that . . ."

(2) "I'm warning you that . . ."

equally express illocutionary acts.[84] But this has the interesting consequence that the validity claim contained in constative speech acts (truth/falsity) represents merely a special case among the validity claims that speakers, in speech acts, raise and offer for vindication vis-à-vis hearers.

In general we may say this: with both statements (and, for example, descriptions) and warnings, etc., the question of whether, granting that you did warn and had the right to warn, did state or did advise, you were *right* to state or to warn or advise, can arise—not in the sense of whether it was opportune or expedient, but whether, on the facts and your knowledge of the facts and the purpose for which you were speaking, and so on, this was the proper thing to say.[85]

In this passage, Austin emphasizes the claim to *be right,* or claim to *validity,* that we raise with any (and not just with constative) speech acts. But he distinguishes these only incidentally from the general contextual conditions—restricted according to speech-act type—that likewise must be fulfilled if a speech act is to succeed (that is, from happiness/unhappiness conditions in general). It is true of assertions, in the same way as it is of warnings, pieces of advice, promises, and so forth, that they can succeed only if *both* conditions are fulfilled: (a) to be in order, and (b) to be right.

> But the real conclusion must surely be that we need . . . to establish with respect to each kind of illocutionary act—warnings, estimates, verdicts, statements, and descriptions—what if any is the specific way in which they are intended, first to be in order or not in order, and second, to be "right" or "wrong;" what terms of appraisal and disappraisal are used for each and what they mean. This is a wide field and certainly will not lead to a simple distinction of true and false; nor will it lead to a distinction of statements from the rest, for stating is only one among very numerous speech acts of the illocutionary class.[86]

Speech acts can be in order with respect to typically restricted contexts (a); but they can be valid (*gültig*) only with respect to the fundamental claim that the speaker raises with his illocutionary act (b). I shall come back to both of these classes of conditions that must be fulfilled in order for speech acts to succeed. At this point I am interested only in the fact that the comparison between constative and nonconstative speech acts throws light on the validity basis that manifestly underlies *all* speech actions.

To be sure, this does initially clarify the special position of constative speech acts. Assertions do not differ from other types of speech acts in their performative/propositional double structure, nor do they differ by virtue of general contextual conditions, for these vary in a typical way for all speech actions; but they do differ from (almost) all other types of speech acts in that they prima facie imply an unmistakable validity claim, a claim to truth. It is undeniable that other types of speech acts also imply *some or other* validity claim; but in determining exactly what validity claim they imply, we seldom encounter such a clearly defined and universally recognized validity claim as "truth" (in the sense of propositional truth). It is easy to see the reason for this; the validity claim of constative speech acts is presupposed in a certain way by speech acts of *every* type. The meaning of the propositional content mentioned in nonconstative speech acts can be made explicit through transforming a sentence of propositional content, "that *p*," into the propositional sentence "*p*;" and the truth claim belongs essentially to the meaning of the proposition thereby expressed. Truth claims are thus a type of validity claim built into the structure of possible speech in general. Truth is a universal validity claim; its universality is reflected in the double structure of speech.

Looking back, Austin assures himself of what he originally had in mind with his contrast of constative and nonconstative speech acts (constatives versus performatives):

With the constative utterances, we abstract from the illocutionary . . . aspects of the speech act, and we concentrate on the locutionary; moreover, we use an oversimplified notion of correspondence with the facts. . . . We aim at the ideal of what would be right to say in all circumstances, for any purposes, to any audience, etc. Perhaps this is sometimes realized. With the performative we attend as much as possible to the illocutionary force of the utterance, and abstract from the dimension of correspondence with facts.[87]

After he recognized that constative speech acts represent only one of several types of speech acts, Austin gave up the aforementioned contrast in favor of a set of unordered families of speech acts. I am of the opinion, however, that what he intended with the contrast "constative" versus "performative" can be adequately reconstructed.

We have seen that communication in language can take place only when the participants, in communicating with one another about something, simultaneously enter two levels of communication—the level of intersubjectivity on which they take up interpersonal relations and the level of propositional contents. However, in speaking, we can make either the interpersonal relation or the propositional content more centrally thematic; in so doing, we make a more interactive or a more cognitive use of our language. In the *interactive use of language,* we thematize the relations into which speaker and hearer enter—as a warning, promise, request—while we merely mention the propositional content of the utterances. In the *cognitive use of language,* by contrast, we thematize the content of the utterance as a statement about something that is happening in the world (or that could be the case), while we express the interpersonal relation only indirectly. This incidental character can be seen, for example, in the fact that in English the explicit form of assertion ("I am asserting (to you) that . . ."), although grammatically correct, is rare in comparison to the short form that disregards the interpersonal relation.

As the content is thematized in the cognitive use of language, only speech acts in which propositional contents can assume the explicit form of propositional sentences are permitted. With these constative speech acts, we raise a truth claim for the proposition asserted. In the interactive use of language, in which the interpersonal relation is thematically stressed, we refer in various ways to the validity of the normative background of the speech act.

For this latter use, the (authorized) command has a paradigmatic significance similar to that of the assertion for the cognitive use of language. Truth is merely the most conspicuous—not the only— validity claim reflected in the formal structures of speech. The illocutionary force of the speech act, which generates a legitimate (or illegitimate) interpersonal relation between the participants, is derived from the binding and bonding force (*bindende Kraft*) of recognized norms of action (or of evaluation); to the extent that a speech act is an action, it actualizes an already established pattern of relations. The validity of a normative background of institutions, roles, socioculturally habitualized forms of life—that is, of conventions—is always already presupposed. This by no means holds true only for institutionally bound speech acts such as betting, greeting, christening, appointing, and the like, each of which satisfies a *specific* norm of action (or a narrowly circumscribed class of norms). In promises, too, in recommendations, prohibitions, prescriptions, and the like, which are not regulated from the outset by institutions, the speaker implies a validity claim that must, if the speech acts are to succeed, be covered by existing norms, and that means by (at least) de facto recognition of *the claim that these norms rightfully exist*. This internal relation between the validity claims implicitly raised in speech acts and the validity of their normative background is emphasized in the interactive use of language, just as is the truth claim in the cognitive use of language.

Just as only constative speech acts are permitted for the cognitive use of language, so for the interactive use of language only those speech acts are permitted that characterize a specific relation that speaker and hearer can adopt to the normative contexts of their action. I call these *regulative* speech acts.[88] With the illocutionary force of speech acts, the normative validity claim—rightness or appropriateness (*Richtigkeit, Angemessenheit*)—is built just as universally into the structures of speech as the truth claim. But the validity claim of a normative background is explicitly invoked only in regulative speech acts (in commands and admonitions, in prohibitions and refusals, in promises and agreements, notifications, excuses, recommendations, admissions, and so forth). The truth reference of the mentioned propositional content remains, by contrast, merely implicit; it pertains only to its existential presuppositions. Conversely, in constative speech acts, which explicitly raise a truth claim, the normative validity claim remains implicit, although these too (e.g., reports, explications, communications, elucidations, narrations, and so forth) must correspond to an established pattern of relations— that is, they must be covered by a recognized normative background—if the interpersonal relations intended with them are to come to pass.

It seems to me that what Austin had in mind with his (later abandoned) classification of speech acts into constative versus performative utterances is captured in the distinction between the cognitive and the interactive uses of language. In the *cognitive use of language,* with the help of constative speech acts, we thematize the propositional content of an utterance; in the *interactive use of language,* with the help of regulative speech acts, we thematize the kind of interpersonal relation established. The difference in thematization results from stressing one of the validity claims universally inherent in speech, that is, from the fact that in the cognitive use of language we raise truth claims for propositions and in the interactive use of language we lay claim to (or contest) the validity of a normative background for interpersonal relations. Austin himself did not draw this consequence because, on the one hand, he took only one universal validity claim into consideration, namely, propositional truth interpreted in terms of the correspondence theory of truth; but he wanted, on the other hand, to make this single validity claim compatible with many types of speech acts (and not just constative speech acts). In his words: "If, then, we loosen up our ideas of truth and falsity we shall see that statements, when assessed in relation to the facts, are not so different after all from pieces of advice, warnings, verdicts and so on."[89] To be sure, this loosening up of the ideas of truth and falsity in favor of a broad dimension of evaluation, in which an assertion can just as well be characterized as exaggerated or precise or inappropriate as true or false, results, on the other hand, in the assimilation of all validity claims to the universal validity claim of propositional truth. "We see that, when we have an order or a warning or a piece of advice, there is a question about how this is related to fact which is not perhaps so different from the kind of question that arises when we discuss how a statement is related to fact."[90] It seems to me that Austin confuses the validity claim of propositional truth, which can be understood in the first instance in terms of a correspondence between statements and facts, with the validity claim of normative rightness, which cannot in any way be interpreted in terms of the correspondence theory of truth.

To the extent that warnings or pieces of advice rest on predictions, they are part of a cognitive use of language. Whether those involved were right to utter certain warnings or pieces of advice in a given situation depends in this case on the truth of the corresponding predictions. As part of an interactive use of language, warnings and pieces of advice can also have a normative meaning. Then the right to issue certain warnings and advice depends on whether the presupposed norms to which they refer are valid (that is, are intersubjectively recognized) or not (and, at a next stage, ought or ought not to be valid, that is, intersubjectively recognized).

Most types of speech acts, however, can be correlated with a single mode of language use. Whether an estimate is good or bad clearly depends on the truth of a corresponding statement; estimates usually appear in the cognitive use of language. Likewise, whether the verdict of a court, the reprimand of a person, or the command of a superior to a subordinate with regard to certain behavior are "justly" pronounced, "deservedly" delivered, or "rightfully" given depends just as clearly on whether a recognized norm has been correctly applied to a given case (or whether the right norm has been applied to the case); legal verdicts, reprimands, and orders can only be part of an interactive use of language. Austin himself once considered the objection that different validity claims are at work in these cases:

Allowing that, in declaring the accused guilty, you have reached your verdict properly and in good faith, it still remains to ask whether the verdict was just, or fair. Allowing that you had the right to reprimand him as you did, and that you have acted without malice, one can still ask whether your reprimand was deserved. . . . There is one thing that people will be particularly tempted to bring up as an objection against any comparison between this second kind of criticism and the kind appropriate to statements, and that is this: aren't these questions about something's being good, or just, or fair, or deserved entirely distinct from questions of truth and falsehood? That, surely, is a very simple black-and-white business; either the utterance corresponds to the facts or it doesn't, and that's that.[91]

In compressing the universal validity claim of truth together with a host of particular evaluative criteria into a single class, Austin blurred the distinction between the clear-cut universal validity claims of propositional truth and normative rightness (and truthfulness). But this proves to be unnecessary if in a given speech act we distinguish among

a. the implicitly presupposed general contextual conditions,

b. the specific meaning of the interpersonal relation to be established, and

c. the implicitly raised general validity claim.

Whereas a. and b. fix the distinct classes (different in different languages) of standardized speech acts, c. determines the universal modes of communication, that is, modes inherent in speech in general.

Before going into a. and b., I would like at least to remark that the Austinian starting point of the distinction between performative and constative utterances provides an overly narrow view; the validity spectrum of speech is not exhausted by the two modes of communication that I developed from this distinction. Naturally, there can be no mode of communication in which the comprehensibility of an utterance is thematically stressed; for every speech act must fulfill the presupposition of *comprehensibility* in the same way. If in some

communication there is a breakdown of intelligibility, the requirement of comprehensibility can be made thematic only through passing over to a hermeneutic discourse, and then in connection with
the relevant linguistic system. The *truthfulness* with which a speaker
expresses her intentions can, however, be emphasized at the level of
communicative action in the same way as the truth of a proposition
and the rightness (or appropriateness) of an interpersonal relation.
Truthfulness guarantees the transparency of a subjectivity representing itself in language. It is especially emphasized in the *expressive
use of language*. The paradigms are first-person sentences in which
the speaker's wishes, feelings, intentions, etc. (which are expressed
incidentally in every speech act) are thematized as such, disclosing
subjective experiences such as

(3)   "I long for you."

(4)   "I wish that . . ."

It is unusual for such sentences to be explicitly embedded in an
illocutionary act:

(3′)   "I hereby express to you that I long for you."

The interpersonal relation, which can take on the function of
self-representation, is not thematic in the expressive use of language
and thus need be mentioned only in situations in which the presupposition of the speaker's truthfulness is not taken for granted; for
this, avowals are the paradigm:

(5)   "I must confess to you that . . ."

(6)   "I don't want to conceal from you that . . ."

For this reason, expressive speech acts such as disclosing, concealing,
revealing, and the like cannot be correlated with the expressive use
of language (which can, in a way, dispense with illocutionary acts)
in the same manner as constative speech acts are correlated with the
cognitive use of language and regulative speech acts with the interactive. Nevertheless, truthfulness, too, is a universal implication of
speech, as long as the presuppositions of communicative action in
general are not suspended. In the cognitive use of language the

speaker must, in a trivial sense, truthfully express his thoughts, opinions, assumptions, and so forth; however, in asserting a proposition, what matters is not the truthfulness of his intentions but the truth of the proposition. Similarly, in the interactive use of language, the speaker expresses the intention of promising, reprimanding, refusing, and so forth; but in bringing about an interpersonal relation with a hearer, the truthfulness of his intention is only a necessary condition, whereas what is important is that the action fit a recognized normative context.

Thus we have the following correlations:

Mode of communication	Type of speech act	Theme	Thematic validity claim
Cognitive	Constatives	Propositional content	Truth
Interactive	Regulatives	Interpersonal relation	Rightness, appropriateness
Expressive	Avowals	Speaker's intention	Truthfulness

N.B.: The modes of language use can be demarcated from one another only paradigmatically. I am not claiming that every sequence of speech acts can be unequivocally classified under these viewpoints. I am claiming only that every competent speaker has in principle the possibility of unequivocally selecting one mode because with every speech act she *must* raise four universal validity claims, so that she *can* single out one of three universal validity claims in order to thematize a component of speech.

The Rational Foundation of Illocutionary Force

Having elucidated the meaning structure and validity basis of basic types of speech acts, I would like to return to the question, in what does the illocutionary force of an utterance consist? At this stage, we know only what it results in if the speech act succeeds—in bringing about an interpersonal relation. Austin and Searle analyzed illocutionary force by looking for conditions of success or failure of speech acts. An uttered content receives a specific communicative function through the fact that the standard conditions for the coming about of a corresponding interpersonal relation are fulfilled. With the illocutionary act, the speaker makes an offer that can be accepted or rejected. The attempt a speaker makes with an illocutionary act may founder for contingent reasons on the refusal of the addressee to enter into the proffered relationship. This case is of no interest in the present context. We shall be concerned with the other case, in which the speaker himself is responsible for the failure of the speech act because the utterance is unacceptable. When the speaker makes an utterance that manifestly contains no serious offer, he cannot count on the relationship intended by him coming about.

I shall speak of the success of a speech act only when the hearer not only understands the meaning of the sentence uttered but also actually enters into the relationship intended by the speaker. And I shall analyze the conditions for the success of speech acts in terms of their "acceptability." Since I have restricted my examination from the outset to communicative action—that is, action oriented toward reaching understanding—a speech act counts as acceptable only if the speaker not merely feigns but sincerely makes a serious offer.[92] A serious offer demands a certain commitment on the part of the speaker. But before going into this, I would like to mention additional reasons for the unacceptability of illocutionary acts.

Austin developed his doctrine of "infelicities" primarily on the basis of institutionally bound speech acts; for this reason, the examples of "misfires" (i.e., misinvocations, misexecutions, misapplications) are typical for all possible cases of rule violation. Thus, the unacceptability of speech acts can stem from transgressions of underlying norms of action. If in a wedding ceremony a priest recites the prescribed marriage formula incorrectly or not at all, the mistake lies at the same level as, let us say, the command of a university lecturer in class to one of her students, who can reply to her (rightly, let us assume): "You can indeed request a favor of me, but you cannot command me." The conditions of acceptability are not fulfilled; but in both cases, these conditions are defined by the *presupposed* norms of action. We are looking, by contrast, for conditions of acceptability that lie within the institutionally unbound speech act itself.

Searle analyzed the conventional presuppositions of different types of speech acts that must be fulfilled if their illocutionary force is to be comprehensible and acceptable. Under the title "preparatory rules," he specifies generalized or restricted *contexts* for possible types of speech acts. A promise, for example, is not acceptable if the following conditions, among others, are not fulfilled: (a) H (the hearer) prefers S's (the speaker's) doing A (a specific action) to his not doing A, and S moreover believes this to be the case; (b) it is not obvious to both S and H that S would do A anyhow in the normal course of events.[93] If conventional presuppositions of this kind are not fulfilled, the act of promising is pointless, that is, the attempt by a speaker to carry out the illocutionary act anyway makes no sense and is condemned to failure from the outset.[94]

The general contextual conditions for institutionally unbound speech acts are to be distinguished from the conditions for applying established norms of action.[95] The two sets of conditions of application, those for types of speech acts and those for established norms of action, must vary (largely) independently of one another if (institutionally unbound) speech acts are to represent a repertory from which the acting subject, with the help of a finite number of types, can put together any number of norm-conformative actions.

To be sure, the peculiar force of the illocutionary—which in the case of institutionally unbound speech acts cannot be derived *directly* from the validity of established norms of action—cannot be explained by means of the speech-act-typical contextual restrictions. It is possible to explain this force only with the help of the specific presuppositions that Searle introduces under the title "essential rules." In doing so, he admittedly appears to achieve no more than a paraphrase of the meaning of the corresponding performative verbs (for example, requests: "count as an attempt to get H to do A;" or questions: "count as an attempt to elicit information from H"). It is interesting, however, that common to these circumscriptions is the specification, "count as an attempt. . . ." The essential presupposition for the success of an illocutionary act consists in the speaker's taking on a specific *commitment* (*Engagement*), so that the hearer can rely on him. An utterance can count as a promise, assertion, request, question, or avowal if and only if the speaker makes an offer that he is ready to make good insofar as it is accepted by the hearer. The speaker must commit himself, that is, indicate that in certain situations he will draw certain consequences for action. The type of obligation determines the *content* of the commitment, from which the sincerity of the commitment is to be distinguished.[96] This condition, introduced by Searle as the "sincerity rule," must *always* be fulfilled in the case of action oriented toward reaching understanding. Thus, in what follows I shall, in speaking of the speaker's commitment, presuppose both that the commitment has a specific content and that the speaker sincerely is willing to take on his commitment. So far as I can see, previous analyses of speech acts have been unsatisfactory, as they have not clarified the commitment of the speaker on which the acceptability of his utterance specifically depends.

The discernible and sincere readiness of the speaker to enter into a specific kind of interpersonal binding and bonding relationship has, compared with the general contextual conditions, a peculiar status. The restricted contexts that specific types of speech acts presuppose must (a) exist and (b) be supposed to exist by those involved. Thus, the following two statements must hold: (a) a statement to the effect that certain contexts obtain, indeed those required by the type of speech act in question; and (b) a statement to the effect that speaker and hearer suppose these contexts to obtain. Interestingly, it does not make sense to analyze the *specific* presupposition of the speaker's commitment in the same way, that is, so that the following two statements would hold: (a) a statement to the effect that there is a certain commitment on the part of the speaker; and (b) a statement to the effect that the hearer supposes this commitment on the part of the speaker to obtain. One *could* choose this strategy of analysis; but I regard it as unsuitable. It would suggest that we speak of the existence of a commitment on the part of a speaker in the same sense as we speak of the existence of restricted contexts. I can ascertain in an appropriate manner through observation or questioning whether certain contexts obtain; on the other hand, I can only *test* whether a speaker commits herself in a specific way and takes on obligations concerning certain consequences for action; I can establish at best whether there are sufficient indicators for the conjecture that the offer would withstand testing.

The binding and bonding relationship into which the speaker is willing to enter with the performance of an illocutionary act signifies a guarantee that, in consequence of her utterance, she will fulfill certain conditions—for example, regard a question as settled when a satisfactory answer is given; drop an assertion when it proves to be false; follow her own advice when she finds herself in the same situation as the hearer; place emphasis on a request when it is not complied with; act in accordance with an intention disclosed by an avowal, and so on. *Thus, the illocutionary force of an acceptable speech act consists in the fact that it can move a hearer to rely on the speech-act-typical obligations of the speaker.* But if illocutionary force has more than a merely suggestive influence, what can motivate the hearer to base his action on the premise that the speaker seriously intends the commitment she indicates? When it is a question of institutionally bound speech acts, he can perhaps rely on the binding and bonding force of an established norm of action. In the case of institutionally unbound speech acts, however, illocutionary force cannot be traced back *directly* to the binding force of the normative background. I would thus like to propose the thesis that the illocutionary force with which the speaker, in carrying out her speech act, influences the hearer can be understood only if, over and above individual speech acts, we take into consideration the "yes" or "no" responses of the hearer to the validity claims raised at least implicitly by the speaker.

With their illocutionary acts, speaker and hearer raise validity claims and demand that they be recognized. But this recognition need not follow irrationally, since the validity claims have a cognitive character and can be tested. I would like, therefore, to defend the following thesis: *In the final analysis, the speaker can illocutionarily influence the hearer, and vice versa, because speech-act-typical obligations are connected with cognitively testable validity claims*—that is, because the reciprocal binding and bonding relationship has a rational basis. The speaker who commits herself normally connects the specific sense in which she would like to take up an interpersonal relationship with a thematically stressed validity claim and thereby chooses a specific mode of communication. Thus, the content of the speaker's commitment is determined by both of the following:

- the specific meaning of the interpersonal relation that is to be established, and
- a thematically stressed universal validity claim.

In this way, assertions, descriptions, classifications, estimates, predictions, objections, and the like have, respectively, specific modal meanings; but the claim put forward in these different interpersonal relations is, or is based on, the truth of corresponding propositions or on the ability of a subject to have cognitions. Correspondingly, requests, orders, admonitions, promises, agreements, excuses, admissions, and the like have a specific modal meaning; but the claim put forward in these different interpersonal relationships is, or refers to, the rightness of norms or to the ability of a subject to assume responsibility. We might say that in different speech acts the content of the speaker's commitment is *determined by a specific way of appealing to the same, thematically stressed, universal validity claim.* And, since as a result of this appeal to universal validity claims, the speech-act-typical obligations take on the character of obligations to provide grounds or to prove trustworthy, the hearer can be rationally motivated by the speaker's signaled commitment to accept the latter's offer. I would like to elucidate this for each of the three modes of communication.

In the cognitive use of language, the speaker proffers a speech-act-immanent *obligation to provide grounds (Begründungsverpflichtung)*. Constative speech acts contain the offer to recur if necessary to the *experiential source* from which the speaker draws the *certainty* that his statement is true. If this immediate grounding does not dispel an ad hoc doubt, the persistently problematic truth claim can become the subject of a theoretical discourse. In the interactive use of language, the speaker proffers a speech-act-immanent *obligation to provide justification (Rechtfertigungsverpflichtung)*. Of course, regulative speech acts contain only the offer on the part of the speaker to indicate, if necessary, the *normative context* that gives him the *conviction* that his utterance is right. Again, if this immediate justification does not dispel an ad hoc doubt, we can pass over to the level of discourse, in this case, practical discourse. In such a discourse, however, the subject of discursive examination is not the rightness claim directly connected with the speech act, but the validity claim of the underlying norm. Finally, in the expressive use of language, the speaker also enters into a speech-act-immanent obligation, namely, the *obligation to prove trustworthy* (*Bewährungsverpflichtung*)—that is, to show in the consequences of his action that he has expressed just that intention that actually guides him. In case the immediate *assurance* expressing what is *evident* to the speaker himself cannot dispel ad hoc doubts, the truthfulness of the utterance can be checked only against the consistency of his subsequent behavior. In the consequences of his action, the obligation taken on with the speech act itself is proven to have been met—and not the validity of a claim that, as in the case of the normative background, is anchored outside of the utterance.

Every speech-act-immanent obligation can be made good at two levels, namely, directly, in the context of utterance—whether through recourse to an experiential certainty, through indicating a corresponding normative background, or through assurance of what is subjectively evident—and indirectly, in discourse or in the sequel of consistent actions. But only in the case of the obligations to ground and to prove trustworthy, into which we enter with constative and with expressive speech acts, do we refer—on both levels—to the *same* truth and truthfulness claim. The obligation to justify, into which we enter with regulative speech acts, refers directly to the claim that the speech act performed fits an existing normative background; whereas with the entrance into practical discourse, the topic of discussion is the validity of the norm itself from which the speaker's rightness claim is merely derived.

Our reflections have led to the following provisional results:

a. A speech act succeeds, that is, it brings about the interpersonal relation that S intends with it, if it is:

- comprehensible and acceptable, and
- accepted by the hearer.

b. The acceptability of a speech act depends on (among other things) the fulfillment of two pragmatic presuppositions:

- the existence of speech-act-typical restricted contexts (preparatory rule); and

- a recognizable commitment on the part of the speaker to enter into certain speech-act-typical obligations (essential rule, sincerity rule).

c. The illocutionary force of a speech act consists in its capacity to move a hearer to act under the premise that the commitment signalled by the speaker is seriously meant:

- in the case of institutionally bound speech acts, the speaker can borrow this force directly from the obligating force of existing norms;

- in the case of institutionally unbound speech acts, the speaker can develop this force by motivating the hearer to the recognition of validity claims.

d. Speaker and hearer can reciprocally motivate one another to recognize validity claims because the content of the speaker's commitment is determined by a specific way of appealing to a thematically stressed validity claim, whereby the speaker, in a testable way, assumes:

- with a truth claim, obligations to provide grounds;

- with a rightness claim, obligations to provide justification; and

- with a truthfulness claim, obligations to prove trustworthy.

A Model of Linguistic Communication

The analysis of what Austin called the illocutionary force of an utterance leads us back to the validity basis of speech. Institutionally unbound speech acts owe their illocutionary force to a cluster of validity claims that must be raised reciprocally by speaker and hearer, and be recognized by them as justified, if grammatical (that is, comprehensible) sentences are to be employed in such a way as to result in successful communication. A participant in communication acts with an orientation toward reaching understanding only under the condition that, in employing comprehensible sentences, he raises with his speech acts three validity claims in an acceptable way.

He claims truth for the stated propositional content or for the existential presuppositions of a mentioned propositional content. He claims rightness (or appropriateness) for norms (or values) that, in a given context, justify an interpersonal relation that is to be established performatively. Finally, he claims truthfulness for the subjective experiences (*Erlebnisse*) expressed. Of course, individual validity claims can be thematically stressed: the truth of the propositional content comes to the fore in the cognitive use of language, the rightness (or appropriateness) of the interpersonal relation in the interactive, and the truthfulness of the speaker in the expressive. But in every instance of communicative action the system of all four validity claims comes into play; they must always be raised *simultaneously* and recognized as justified, although they cannot all be thematic at the same time.

The universality of the validity claims inherent in the structure of speech can perhaps be elucidated with reference to the systematic place of language. Language is the medium through which speakers and hearers realize certain fundamental demarcations. The subject demarcates herself (i) from an environment that she objectifies in the third-person attitude of an observer; (ii) from an environment that she conforms to or deviates from in the performative attitude of a participant; (iii) from her own subjectivity that she expresses or conceals in the first-person attitude; and finally (iv) from the medium of language itself. For these domains of reality I have proposed the somewhat arbitrarily chosen terms *external nature, society, internal nature,* and *language.* The validity claims unavoidably implied in every speech act show that in speech oriented toward reaching understanding these four regions must always simultaneously appear. I shall characterize the way in which these regions appear with a few phenomenological indications.

By *external nature* I mean the objectivated segment of reality that the adult subject (even if only indirectly) is able to perceive and manipulate. The subject can, of course, adopt an objectivating attitude not only toward inanimate nature but toward all objects and states of affairs that are directly or indirectly accessible to sensory experience. *Society* designates that symbolically prestructured segment of reality that the adult subject can understand in a nonobjectivating attitude, that is, as one acting communicatively (as a participant in a system of communication). Legitimate interpersonal relations belong here, as do sentences and actions, institutions, traditions, cultural values, objectivations in general with a semantic content, as well as the speaking and acting subjects themselves. We can replace this performative attitude with an objectivating attitude toward society; conversely, we can switch to a performative attitude in domains in which (today) we normally behave objectivatingly— for example, in relation to animals and plants. I class as *internal nature* all wishes, feelings, intentions, and so forth to which an "I" has privileged access and can express as its own subjective experiences. It is precisely in this expressive attitude that the "I" knows itself not only as subjectivity but also as an authority that has always already transcended the bounds of mere subjectivity in cognition, language, and interaction simultaneously. To be sure, if the subject adopts an objectivating attitude toward herself, this distorts the sense in which intentions can be expressed as *my* intentions.[97]

Finally, I introduced the medium of our utterances as a region of its own; precisely because *language* (including nonpropositional symbol systems) remains in a peculiar half-transcendence in the performance of our communicative actions and expressions, it presents itself to the speaker and actor (preconsciously) as a segment of reality sui generis. Again, this does not preclude our being able to adopt, in regard to linguistic utterances or systems of symbols, either an objectivating attitude directed to the material substratum or a performative attitude directed to the semantic content of illocutionary acts.

The model intuitively introduced here is that of a communication in which grammatical sentences are embedded, by way of universal validity claims, in three relations to reality, thereby assuming the corresponding pragmatic functions of representation, establishing interpersonal relations, and expressing one's own subjectivity.

External nature refers to everything that can be explicitly asserted as the content of statements. Here, "objectivity" might designate the way in which objectified reality appears in speech. And "truth" is the claim with which we assert validity for a corresponding proposition.

The *social reality* of norms of action and values enters speech by way of the illocutionary components of speech acts (penetrating through the performative attitude of the speaker and hearer, as it were) as a slice of nonobjectified reality. In the same manner, the *internal nature* of the subjects involved manifests itself in speech by way of speakers' intentions as a further slice of nonobjectified reality. I would like to propose the terms "normativity" and "subjectivity" for the way in which nonobjectified society or, as the case may be, nonobjectified inner nature appears in speech. "Rightness" is the claim with which we assert validity for the normativity of an utterance; "truthfulness" is the claim with which we assert validity for the intention expressed in that utterance. In this way, the general structures of speech ensure not only a reference to objectified reality, they equally open up space for the normativity of utterances as well as the subjectivity of the intentions expressed therein. Finally, I use the term "intersubjectivity" to refer to the commonality established between subjects capable of speech and action by way of the understanding of identical meanings and the recognition of universal claims. With respect to intersubjectivity, the claim for which validity is asserted is comprehensibility—this is the validity claim specific to speech.

We can examine every utterance to see whether it is true or untrue, justified or unjustified, and truthful or untruthful because in speech, no matter what the emphasis, grammatical sentences are embedded in relations to reality in such a way that in an acceptable speech act segments of external nature, society, and internal nature always appear simultaneously. Language itself also appears in speech, for speech is a medium in which the linguistic means that are employed instrumentally are also reflected. In speech, speech sets itself off from the regions of external nature, society, and internal nature as a reality sui generis, as soon as the sign-substratum, meaning, and denotation of a linguistic utterance can be distinguished.

The following table represents schematically the correlations that obtain for

a. the domains of reality to which every speech act takes up relation,

b. the attitudes of the speaker prevailing in particular modes of communication,

c. the validity claims under which the relations to reality are established, and

d. the general functions that grammatical sentences assume in their relations to reality.

Domains of reality	Modes of communication: Basic attitudes	Validity claims	General functions of speech
"The" world of external nature	Cognitive: Objectivating attitude	Truth	Representation of facts
"Our" world of society	Interactive: Conformative attitude	Rightness	Establishment of legitimate interpersonal relations
"My" world of internal nature	Expressive: Expressive attitude	Truthfulness	Disclosure of speaker's subjectivity
Language	–	Comprehensibility	–

Acknowledgment

I would like to thank E. Tugendhat and G. Grewendorf for their helpful criticisms of a first draft of this essay. They will have their disagreements with this revised version as well. J. H.

Notes

1. [Added to 1979 English translation:] Hitherto the term "pragmatics" has referred to the analysis of particular contexts of language use and not to the reconstruction of universal features of using language (or of employing sentences in utterances). To mark this contrast, I introduced a distinction between "empirical" and "universal" pragmatics. I am no longer happy with this terminology; the term "formal pragmatics"—as an extension of "formal semantics"—would serve better. "*Formalpragmatik*" is the term preferred by F. Schütze, *Sprache Soziologisch Gesehen*, 2 vols. (Munich, 1975); cf. the summary, pp. 911–1024.

2. [Added to 1979 English translation:] I shall focus on an idealized case of communicative action, namely, "consensual interaction," in which participants share a tradition and their orientations are normatively integrated to such an extent that they start from the same definition of the situation and do not disagree about the claims to validity that they reciprocally raise. The following schema locates the extreme case of consensual interaction in a system of different types of social action. Underlying

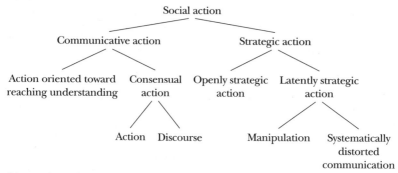

this typology is the question of which categories of validity claims participants are supposed to raise and react to.

These action types can be distinguished by virtue of their relations to the validity basis of speech:

a. *Communicative versus Strategic Action.* In communicative action, a basis of mutually recognized validity claims is presupposed; this is not the case in strategic action. In the communicative attitude, it is possible to reach a direct mutual understanding oriented toward validity claims; in the strategic attitude, by contrast, only an indirect mutual understanding via determinative indicators is possible.

b. *Action Oriented toward Reaching Understanding versus Consensual Action.* In consensual action, agreement about implicitly raised validity claims can be *presupposed* as a background consensus by reason of common definitions of the situations; such agreement is supposed to be *arrived at* in action oriented toward reaching understanding. In the latter case strategic elements may be employed under the proviso that they are meant to lead to a direct mutual understanding.

c. *Action versus Discourse.* In communicative action, it is naively supposed that implicitly raised validity claims can be vindicated (or made immediately plausible by way of question and answer). In discourse, by contrast, the validity claims raised for statements and norms are hypothetically bracketed and thematically examined. As in communicative action, the participants in discourse retain a cooperative attitude.

d. *Manipulative Action versus Systematically Distorted Communication.* Whereas in systematically distorted communication at least one of the participants deceives *himself* about the fact that the basis of consensual action is only apparently being maintained, the manipulator deceives at least one of the *other* participants about her own strategic attitude, in which she *deliberately* behaves in a pseudoconsensual manner.

3. K.-O. Apel, "Sprechakttheorie und transzendentale Sprachpragmatik—zur Frage ethischer Normen," in K.-O. Apel, ed., *Sprachpragmatik und Philosophie* (Frankfurt, 1976), pp. 10–173.

4. In the framework of Southwest German Neo-Kantianism, Emil Lask has earlier reconstructed the concept of "transsubjective validity"—in connection with the meaning of linguistic expressions, the truth of statements, and the beauty of works of art—as worthiness to be recognized. Lask's philosophy of validity combines motifs from Lotze, Bolzano, Husserl, and, naturally, Rickert. "Valid value (*geltender Wert*) is worthiness to be recognized, recognition-value, that which deserves devotion, that to which devotion is due, thus that which demands or requires devotion. To be valid is value, demand, norm. . . . All such terms as 'worthiness,' 'deserve,' 'be due,' 'demand' are correlative concepts; they point to a subjective behavior corresponding to validity: worthy to be treated or regarded in a certain way—this demands a certain behavior." E. Lask, "Zum System der Logik," *Ges. Schriften,* vol. 3 (Tübingen, 1924), p. 92.

5. [Editor's note:] Cf. note 1 above.

6. Y. Bar-Hillel fails to appreciate this in his critique "On Habermas's Hermeneutic Philosophy of Language," *Synthese* 26 (1973): 1–12. His critique is based on a paper I characterized as provisional. "Vorbereitende Bemerkungen zu einer Theorie der kommunikativen Kompetenz," in J. Habermas and N. Luhmann, *Theorie der Gesellschaft oder Sozialtechnologie* (Frankfurt, 1971), pp. 101–141. Bar-Hillel has, I feel, misunderstood me on so many points that it would not be fruitful to reply in detail. I only hope that in the present sketch I can make my (still strongly programmatic) approach clear even to readers who are aggressively inclined and hermeneutically not especially open.

7. E.g., K.-O. Apel, *Transformation der Philosophie,* vol. 2 (Frankfurt, 1971), pp. 406ff., and "Programmatische Bemerkungen zur Idee einer transzendentalen Sprachpragmatik," in *Annales Universitatis Tukuensis Sarja,* Series B, Osa Tom, 126 (Tuku, 1973), pp. 11–35.

8. Charles Morris, "Foundations of the Theory of Signs," in *Encylopedia of Unified Science,* vol. 1, no. 2 (Chicago, 1938), and *Signs, Language, Behavior* (New York, 1955).

9. Cf. my remarks on Morris in *On the Logic of the Social Sciences,* trans. S. W. Nicholsen and G. A. Stark (Cambridge, Mass., 1988), pp. 63ff.

10. Y. Bar-Hillel, "Indexical Expressions," in *Aspects of Language* (Jerusalem, 1970), pp. 69–88, and "Semantics and Communication," in H. Heidrich, *Semantics and Communication* (Amsterdam, 1974), pp. 1–36. Taking Bar-Hillel as his point of departure, A. Kasher has proposed a formal representation embedding linguistic expressions in extralinguistic contexts. "A Step Forward to a Theory of Linguistic Performance," in Y. Bar-Hillel, ed., *Pragmatics of Natural Languages* (Dordrecht, 1971), pp. 84–93; cf. also R. C. Stalnaker, "Pragmatics," in D. Davidson and G. Harman, *Semantics of Natural Language* (Dordrecht, 1972), pp. 380–387.

11. R. M. Hare, *The Language of Morals* (Oxford, 1952); G. H. von Wright, *Norm and Action* (London, 1963); N. Rescher, *Topics in Philosophical Logic* (Dordrecht, 1968).

12. L. Apostel, "A Proposal on the Analysis of Questions," in *Logique et Analyse* 12 (1969): 376–381; W. Kuhlmann, *Reflexion zwischen Theorie und Kritik* (Frankfurt, 1975).

13. S. Toulmin, *The Uses of Argument* (Cambridge, 1974); W. C. Salmon, *The Foundation of Scientific Inference* (Pittsburgh, 1967); cf. the summary chapter on "nondemon-

strative inference" in R. P. Botha, *The Justification of Linguistic Hypotheses* (The Hague, 1973), pp. 25–72.

14. F. Kiefer, "On Presuppositions," in F. Kiefer and N. Ruwet, eds., *Generative Grammar in Europe* (Dordrecht, 1973), pp. 218–242; K. H. Ebert, "Präsuppositionen im Sprechakt," in A. ten-Cate and P. Jordens, eds., *Papers from the Seventh Linguistic Colloquium at Nijmegen* (Tübingen, 1973), pp. 45–60; F. Petöfi, *Präsuppositionen in Linguistik und Philosophie* (Frankfurt, 1974).

15. H. P. Grice, "Logic and Conversation," in P. Cole and J. L. Morgan, eds., *Syntax and Semantics*, vol. 3 (New York, 1974); and D. Gordon and G. Lakoff, "Conversational Postulates" MS (1973).

16. J. R. Ross, "On Declarative Sentences," in J. Rosenbaum, ed., *Readings in English Transformational Grammar* (Waltham, Mass., 1970), pp. 222–277; J. D. MacCawley, "The Role of Semantics in a Grammar," in E. Bach and T. Harms, eds., *Universals in Linguistic Theory* (New York, 1968), pp. 125–170; D. Wunderlich, "Sprechakte," in U. Maas and D. Wunderlich, *Pragmatik und sprachliches Handeln* (Frankfurt, 1972), pp. 69–188, and "Zur Konventionalität von Sprechhandlungen," in D. Wunderlich, ed., *Linguistische Pragmatik* (Frankfurt, 1972), pp. 11–58.

17. C. J. Fillmore, "Pragmatics and the Description of Discourse," in P. Cole, ed., *Radical Pragmatics* (New York, 1981); G. Posner, *Textgrammatik* (Frankfurt, 1973).

18. J. Lyons, *Introduction to Theoretical Linguistics* (New York, 1968); J. J. Katz, *Semantic Theory* (New York, 1972).

19. P. F. Strawson, *Logico-Linguistic Papers* (London, 1971).

20. A. C. Danto, *Analytic Philosophy of Action* (Cambridge, 1973); S. Hampshire, *Thought and Action* (London, 1960); D. S. Schwayder, *The Stratification of Behaviour* (London, 1965); Care and Landesman, eds., *Readings in the Theory of Action* (London, 1968).

21. P. Winch, *The Idea of a Social Science and its Relation to Philosophy* (London, 1958); C. Taylor, "Explaining Action," *Inquiry* 13 (1973): 54–89; H. von Wright, *Explanation and Understanding* (London, 1971), and "On the Logic and Epistemology of the Causal Relation," in P. Suppes, ed., *Logic, Methodology and Philosophy of Science*, vol. 4 (Stanford, 1973), pp. 239–312.

22. W. P. Alston, *Philosophy of Language* (Englewood Cliffs, N.J., 1964).

23. J. Bennett, "The Meaning-Nominalist Strategy," *Foundations of Language* 10 (1973): 141–168; S. R. Schiffer, *Meaning* (Oxford, 1972).

24. Cf. the bibliography by E. von Savigny, in J. L. Austin, *Zur Theorie der Sprechakte* (Stuttgart, 1972), pp. 203ff.

25. G. Grewendorf, "Sprache ohne Kontext," in Wunderlich, ed., *Linguistische Pragmatik*, pp. 144–182.

26. H. P. Grice, "Meaning," *Philosophical Review* 66 (1957): 377–388, and "Utterer's Meaning, Sentence-Meaning, and Word-Meaning," reprinted in Grice, *Studies in the*

Ways of Words (Cambridge, Mass., 1989), pp. 117ff.; D. K. Lewis, *Convention* (Cambridge, 1969).

27. Habermas, *On the Logic of the Social Sciences,* pp. 89ff.

28. H.-G. Gadamer emphasizes this in *Truth and Method* (New York, 1975).

29. G. Ryle, *The Concept of Mind* (London, 1949); cf. the interpretation of E. von Savigny in *Die Philosophie der normalen Sprache* (Frankfurt, 1974), pp. 91ff.

30. R. Carnap and W. Stegmüller, *Induktive Logik und Wahrscheinlichkeit* (Wien, 1959), p. 15.

31. D. Wunderlich, *Grundlagen der Linguistik* (Hamburg, 1974), p. 209.

32. For an analysis of what explication in the sense of rational reconstruction means, cf. H. Schnädelbach, *Reflexion und Diskurs* (Frankfurt, 1977), the chapter on "Explikativer Diskurs," pp. 277–336.

33. N. Chomsky, *Aspects of the Theory of Syntax* (Cambridge, Mass., 1965).

34. Wunderlich, *Grundlagen,* pp. 210–218.

35. Botha, *Justification,* pp. 75ff., speaks in this connection of external versus internal linguistic evidence.

36. Wunderlich, *Grundlagen,* p. 216. If I understand him correctly, H. Schnelle gives an empirical interpretation to the model-theoretic version of linguistics in *Sprachphilosphie und Linguistik* (Hamburg, 1973), pp. 82–114.

37. Botha, *Justification,* p. 224, thinks that a speaker can not only report correct linguistic intuitions falsely but can also have false linguistic intuitions; but the construct of pretheoretical *knowledge* does nor permit this possibility. I think it makes sense to assume that linguistic intuitions can be "false" only if they come from incompetent speakers. Another problem is the interplay of grammatical and nongrammatical (for example, perceptual) epistemic systems in the formation of diffuse judgments about the acceptability of sentences, that is, the question of isolating expressions of grammatical rule consciousness or, as the case may be, of isolating genuinely linguistic intuitions. Cf. T. G. Bever, "The Ascent of the Specious," in D. Cohen, ed., *Explaining Linguistic Phenomena* (New York, 1974), pp. 173–200.

38. In this connection, U. Oevermann points out interesting parallels with Piaget's concept of reflecting abstraction (cf. J. Piaget, *The Principles of Genetic Epistemology* (New York, 1972)): perhaps the procedure of rational reconstruction is merely a stylized and, as it were, controlled form of the reflecting abstraction the child carries out when, for example, she "reads off" her instrumental actions the schema that underlies them.

39. W. J. M. Levelt, *Formal Grammars in Linguistics and Psycholinguistics,* vols. 1–3 (Amsterdam, 1974).

40. Ibid., vol. 3, pp. 5–7.

41. Ibid., pp. 14ff.

42. In responding to the doubts that Botha raises against the "clear case principle" (*Justification*, p. 224), I would like to reproduce an argument that J. J. Katz and T. G. Bever have brought against similar doubts in a paper critical of empiricism, "The Fall and Rise of Empiricism," in T. G. Bever, J. J. Katz, and D. T. Langendoen, eds., *An Integrated Theory of Linguistic Ability* (New York, 1976):

> Such a theory . . . seeks to explicate intuitions about the interconnectedness of phonological properties in terms of a theory of the phonological component, to explicate intuitions about the interconnectedness of syntactic properties in terms of a theory of the syntactic component, and to explicate intuitions about the interconnectedness of semantic properties in terms of a theory of the semantic component. The theory of grammar seeks finally to explicate intuitions of relatedness among properties of different kinds in terms of the systematic connections expressed in the model of a grammar that welds its components in a single integrated theory of the sound-meaning correlation in a language.

These remarks are, of course, by way of describing the theoretical ideal. But as the theory of grammar makes progress toward this ideal, it not only sets limits on the construction of grammars and provides a richer interpretation for grammatical structures but it also defines a wider and wider class of grammatical properties and relations. In so doing, it marks out the realm of the grammatical more clearly, distinctly, and securely than could have been done on the basis of the original intuitions. As Fodor has insightfully observed, such a theory literally defines its own subject matter in the course of its progress:

> There is then an important sense in which a science has to discover what it is about; it does so by discovering that the laws and concepts it produced in order to explain one set of phenomena can be fruitfully applied to phenomena of other sorts as well. It is thus only in retrospect that we can say of all the phenomena embraced by a single theoretical framework that *they* are what we meant, for example, by the presystematic term "physical event," "chemical interaction," or "behavior." To the extent that such terms, or their employments, are neologistic, the neologism is occasioned by the insights that successful theories provide into the deep similarities that underlie superficially heterogeneous events. (J. A. Fodor, *Psychological Explanation* [New York, 1968], pp. 10–11.)

43. H. Leuninger, M. H. Miller, and F. Müller, *Psycholinguistik* (Frankfurt, 1973), and H. Leuninger, M. H. Miller, and F. Müller, eds., *Linguistik und Psychologie* (Frankfurt, 1974); H. Leuninger, "Linguistik und Psychologie," in R. Bartsch and T. Vennemann, eds., *Linguistik und Nachbarwissenschaften* (Kronberg, 1973), pp. 225–241.

44. E. H. Lenneberg, *Biologische Grundlagen der Sprache* (Frankfurt, 1972), and "Ein Wort unter uns," in Leuninger, Miller, and Müller, eds., *Linguistik und Psychologie*, pp. 53–72.

45. L. Kohlberg, "Stage and Sequence," in D. Goslin, ed., *Handbook of Socialization Theory and Research* (Chicago, 1969), and "From Is to Ought," in T. Mischel, ed., *Cognitive Development and Epistemology* (New York, 1971), pp. 151–236.

46. On this point, cf. U. Oevermann, "Kompetenz und Performanz" (Max-Planck-Institut für Bildungsforschung, 1974).

47. I. Kant, *Critique of Pure Reason,* trans. N. Kemp-Smith (New York, 1961), p. 138.

48. B. Stroud, "Transcendental Arguments," *Journal of Philosophy* 9 (1968): 241–254; J. Hintikka, "Transcendental Arguments," *Nous* 6 (1972): 174–281; and M. S. Gram, "Categories and Transcendental Arguments," *Man and World* 6 (1973): 252–269, and "Transcendental Arguments," *Nous* 5 (1971): 15–26.

49. R. Bittner, "Transzendental," in *Handbuch philosophischer Grundbegriffe,* vol. 5 (Munich, 1974), pp. 1524–1539.

50. For example, the reception of Kant by the Erlangen school assumes a transcendental status for the basic concepts of protophysics only in a limited sense; cf. the discussion volume edited by G. Böhme, *Protophysik* (Frankfurt, 1975).

51. Piaget's Kantianism is typical of this approach.

52. Cf. K.-O. Apel's introductions to Volumes 1 and 2 of C. S. Peirce's *Schriften* (Frankfurt, 1967 and 1970).

53. Cf. my "Postscript," in *Knowledge and Human Interests,* trans. J. Shapiro (Boston, 1971); cf. also R. Bubner, "Transzendentale Hermeneutik," in R. Simon-Schäfer and C. W. Zimmerli, eds., *Wissenschaftstheorie der Geisteswissenschaften* (Hamburg, 1975), pp. 57–70.

54. F. Kambartel, *Erfahrung und Struktur* (Frankfurt, 1968).

55. J. Habermas, "Wahrheitstheorien," in *Festschrift für Walter Schulz* (Pfullingen, 1973), pp. 211–265, reprinted in Habermas, *Vorstudien und Ergänzungen zur Theorie des kommunikativen Handelns* (Frankfurt, 1984).

56. W. Sellars, "Presupposing," *Philosophical Review* 63 (1954): 197–215; P. F. Strawson, "A Reply to Mr. Sellars," *Philosophical Review* 63 (1954): 216–231.

57. U. Oevermann, "Theorie der individuellen Bildungsprozesse" (Max-Planck-Institut für Bildungsforschung, 1974).

58. On this point, cf. the controversy between Quine and Chomsky: N. Chomsky, "Quine's Empirical Assumptions," and W. V. O. Quine, "Replies," both in D. Davidson and J. Hintikka, eds., *Words and Objections* (Dordrecht, 1969), pp. 53–68 and 292–352; W. V. O. Quine, "Methodological Reflections on Current Linguistic Theory," in Davidson and Harman, eds., *Semantics of Natural Language.* H. Schnelle, *Sprachphilosophie und Linguistik* (Hamburg, 1973) is also typical of methodological behaviorism in linguistics.

59. J. L. Austin, *How to Do Things with Words* (Oxford, 1962); cf. the bibliography on the theory of speech acts compiled by E. von Savigny for the German edition of this work (see note 24 above), pp. 204–209; J. L. Austin, "Performative Utterances," in his *Philosophical Papers* (Oxford, 1970), pp. 233–252, and "Performative-Constative," in C. E. Caton, ed., *Philosophy and Ordinary Language* (Urbana, Ill., 1963), pp. 22–33. Additional Austin bibliography can be found in von Savigny, *Die Philosophie der normalen Sprache,* pp. 162–166.
See also J. R. Searle, "What Is a Speech Act?," in M. Black, ed., *Philosophy in America* (Ithaca, 1965), pp. 221–239, reprinted in J. Rosenberg and C. Travis, eds., *Readings*

in the Philosophy of Language (Englewood Cliffs, N.J., 1971), pp. 614–628, "Austin on Locutionary and Illocutionary Acts," *Philosophical Review* 77 (1968): 405–424, reprinted in Rosenberg and Travis, eds., *Readings*, pp. 262–275, *Speech Acts* (Cambridge, 1969), and "Linguistik und Sprachphilosophie," in Bartsch and Vennemann, *Linguistik und Nachbarwissenschaften*, pp. 111–126.

Other sources include: W. P. Alston, *Philosophy of Language* (Englewood Cliffs, N.J., 1964), and "Linguistic Acts," *American Philosophical Quarterly* 1 (1964): 138–146; L. J. Cohen, "Do Illocutionary Forces Exist?," *Philosophical Quarterly* 14 (1964): 118–137, reprinted in Rosenberg and Travis, *Readings*, pp. 580–598, and "Speech Acts," *Current Trends in Linguistics* 12 (1970); R. M. Hare, "Meaning and Speech Acts," *Philosophical Review* 79 (1970): 3–24, and "Austin's Distinction between Locutionary and Illocutionary Acts," in R. M. Hare, *Practical Inferences* (London, 1972); D. Holdcroft, "Performatives and Statements," *Mind* 83 (1974): 1–18; P. F. Strawson, "Intention and Convention in Speech Acts," *Philosophical Review* 73 (1964): 439–460, reprinted in Rosenberg and Travis, *Readings*, pp. 599–613; S. Thau, "The Distinction between Rhetic and Illocutionary Acts," *Analysis* 32 (1971/72): 177–183; C. Travis, "A Generative Theory of Speech Acts," in Rosenberg and Travis, *Readings*, pp. 629–644; G. J. Warnock, "Hare on Meaning and Speech Acts," *Philosophical Review* 80 (1971): 80–84; Wunderlich, *Grundlagen*, pp. 309–352.

60. Chomsky, *Aspects of the Theory of Syntax*, pp. 3ff.

61. These qualifications are stated below in the discussion of Searle's principle of expressibility.

62. P. F. Strawson, *Individuals* (London, 1959); M. Dummett, *Frege: Philosophy of Language* (London, 1973); E. Tugendhat, *Traditional and Analytical Philosophy*, trans. P. A. Gorner (Cambridge, 1982).

63. On the analysis of intentionality and the expression of intentions, cf. W. Sellars, "Empiricism and the Philosophy of Mind," in *Metaphysics* (London, 1968); W. Sellars and R. Chisholm, "Intentionality and the Mental," in *Minnesota Studies*, vol. 1 (Minneapolis, 1963), pp. 507–539; W. Sellars, *Science and Metaphysics* (London, 1968); E. Tugendhat, "Phänomenologie und Sprachanalyse," in *Festschrift für Gadamer*, vol. 2 (Tübingen, 1970), pp. 3–24; J. Hintikka, *Knowledge and Belief* (Ithaca, 1962); C. Taylor, "Explaining Action," *Inquiry* 13 (1970): 54–89. On the analysis of expressive speech acts, cf. P. M. S. Hacker, *Insight and Illusion* (Oxford, 1972), chs. 7–9.

64. Cf. D. Steinberg and L. Jakobovits, eds., *Semantics* (Cambridge, 1971), pp. 157–484; H. E. Boekle, *Semantik* (Munich, 1972).

65. The work of P. W. Alston is a good example.

66. F. von Kutschera, *Sprachphilosophie* (Munich, 1971), pp. 117–161; Schnelle, *Sprachphilosophie und Linguistik*, pp. 190–240; Wunderlich, *Grundlagen*, pp. 238–273.

67. P. Watzlawick, J. H. Beavin, and D. D. Jackson, *Pragmatics of Human Communication* (New York, 1967).

68. A communication theory that is supposed to reconstruct conditions of action oriented toward reaching understanding does not necessarily require as its basic unit of analysis pairs of complementary speech acts—that is, reciprocally performed and accepted speech acts; but it does require, at least, a speaker's utterance that can not

only be comprehended but can also be accepted by at least one other subject capable of speech and action.

69. D. Wunderlich, "Zur Konventionalität von Sprechhandlungen," in Wunderlich, ed., *Linguistische Pragmatik*, p. 16; cf. also the linguistic characterization of the standard form given there (which I do not deal with here), and Wunderlich's analysis of advising in *Grundlagen*, pp. 349ff.

70. Exceptions are avowals that, when rendered explicit, can also take on a negative form, for example, "I do not want (hereby) to conceal from you that. . . ."

71. Deviating from a widespread practice, I do not think it advisable to distinguish propositions (*Aussagen*) from assertions (*Behauptungen*) in such a way that, although a proposition is embedded in a specific speech situation through being asserted, it does not receive its assertoric force therefrom. I am of the opinion, rather, that the assertoric force of a proposition cannot be reconstructed except through reference to the validity claim that anyone in the role of a competent speaker raises for it in asserting it. Whether this claim can, if necessary, be discursively vindicated, that is, whether the proposition is "valid" (true), depends on whether it satisfies certain truth conditions. We can, to be sure, view propositions monologically, that is, as symbolic formations with an abstract truth value without reference to a speaker; but then we are abstracting precisely from the speech situation in which a propositional content, owing to the fact that it is asserted as a proposition, receives a relation to reality, that is, fulfills the precondition of being true or false. This abstraction naturally suggests itself (and often remains hidden even from the logician) because the truth claim raised by the speaker is *universalist*—that is, precisely of such a nature that, although it is raised in a particular situation, it could be defended at any time against anyone's doubts.

72. S. Kanngiesser, "Aspekte zur Semantik und Pragmatik," *Linguistische Berichte* 24 (1973): 1–28, here p. 5.

73. Wunderlich, *Grundlagen*, pp. 337ff.

74. Cf. the schema in note 2 above.

75. I. Dornbach, "Primatenkommunikation" MS., (1975). On the relatively early differentiation of different types of speech acts in the linguistic development of the child, see the pioneering dissertation of M. Miller, "Die Logik der frühen Sprachentwicklung" (University of Frankfurt, 1975).

76. In a letter to me, G. Grewendorf cites the following counterexample: signing a contract, petition, and so forth, while simultaneously objectifying the corresponding illocutionary act. But only the following alternative seems possible: either the contract signing is carried out, in such a way that it has legal force, with the help of a performative utterance—in which case there is no objectification—or the nonverbal contract signing is accompanied by a statement: "S signs contract x"—in which case it is a question of two independent illocutionary acts carried out parallel to one another (in such a way that there is, normally, a division of roles: the statesman signs, the reporter reports the signing).

77. Cohen, "Do Illocutionary Forces Exist?," p. 587.

78. W. P. Alston, "Meaning and Use," in Rosenberg and Travis, eds., *Readings*, p. 412: "I can find no cases in which sameness of meaning does not hang on sameness of illocutionary act."

79. For ontogenetic studies, a combination of a Piagetian theory of meaning for the cognitive schemata developed in connection with manipulated objects (cf. H. G. Furth, *Piaget and Knowledge* (Englewood Cliffs, N.J., 1969)) and a Meadian theory of meaning for the concepts developed in connection with interactions (cf. Arbeitsgruppe Bielefelder Soziologen, eds., *Alltagswissen, Interaktion und gesellschaftliche Wirklichkeit,* 2 vols. (Hamburg, 1973)) seems promising to me.

80. B. Richards argues against this in "Searle on Meaning and Speech Acts," *Foundations of Language* 7 (1971): 536: "Austin argued that sentences such as Ra (I promise that I shall pay within one year) never *assert* anything that is either true or false, i.e., never assert propositions. Here we agree; but this in no way upsets the claim that Ra nevertheless *expresses* a proposition . . . viz. the proposition that Ra." Richards does not equate the propositional content of the speech act, Ra, with the propositional content of the dependent sentence: "I shall pay within one year," but with the content of the objectified speech act, Ra, which must, however, then be embedded in a further speech act, Rv; for example, "I tell you, I promised him that I shall pay within one year." I regard the confusion of performative sentences with the assertoric reporting of their content as a category mistake (which, incidentally, diminishes the value of Richards's argument against Searle's principle of expressibility, in particular against his proposal to analyze the meaning of speech acts in standard form in terms of the meaning of the sentences used in the speech acts).

81. It follows from this proposal that each of the universal-pragmatic subtheories, that is, the theory of illocutionary acts as well as the theory of elementary sentences (and that of intentional expressions) can make its specific contribution to the theory of meaning. In Austin's choice of the terms "meaning" and "force," the descriptivist prejudice continues to resonate; it is a prejudice, I might add, that has been out of date since Wittgenstein at the latest, if not since Humboldt, according to which the theory of the elementary sentence, which is to clarify sense and reference, can claim a monopoly on the theory of meaning. (Of course, this prejudice also keeps reference semantics alive.)

82. Austin, *How to Do Things with Words,* p. 132.

83. Ibid., pp. 147–148; Searle, *Speech Acts,* pp. 64ff.

84. Austin, "Performative Utterances," p. 248.

85. Austin, *How to Do Things with Words,* p. 144.

86. Ibid., pp. 145ff. Cf. also Austin, "Performative-Constative," p. 31:

To begin with, it is clear that if we establish that a performative utterance is not unhappy, that is, that its author has performed his act happily and in all sincerity, that still does not suffice to set it beyond the reach of all criticism. It may always be criticized in a different dimension. Let us suppose that I say to you "I advise you to do it;" and let us allow that all the circumstances are appropriate, the conditions for success are fulfilled. In saying that, I actually do advise you to do it—it is not that I *state,* truely or falsely, *that* I advise you. It is, then, a performative utterance. There does still arise, all the same, a little question: was the advice good or bad? Agreed, I spoke in all sincerity, I believed that to do it would be in your interest; but was I right? Was my belief, in these circumstances, justified? Or again—though perhaps this matters less—was it in fact, or as things turned out, in your interest? There is confrontation of my utterance with the situation in, and the situation in respect to which, it was issued. I was fully justified perhaps, but was I right?

87. Austin, *How to do Things with Words,* pp. 144–145.

88. Habermas, "Vorbereitende Bemerkungen," pp. 11ff.

89. Austin, "Performative Utterances," pp. 250–251.

90. Ibid., p. 251.

91. Austin, "Performative-Constative," pp. 31–32.

92. [Added in 1983:] In casually mentioning this restriction, I was unaware of the problems connected with it. What I took at the time to be trivial is in fact in need of careful justification: the thesis that the use of language oriented toward reaching understanding represents the original mode of language use. Cf. chapter 2 in the present volume, pp. 122ff.

93. Searle, *Speech Acts,* p. 63.

94. On Wunderlich's analysis of advising (*Grundlagen,* pp. 349ff.) the general contextual conditions would be as follows:

(A) S makes it understood in a conventional manner that (that is, S should give the advice only if these conditions obtain, and H should accordingly believe that they obtain):

1. S knows, believes, or assumes (depending on preceding communication) that

a. H finds himself in an unpleasant situation Z;

b. H wants or desires to reach some other, more pleasant situation $Z' \neq Z$;

c. H does not know how Z' can be reached;

d. H is in a position to do a.

2. S believes or assumes that

e. H does not already want to do a;

f. H can reach a more pleasant situation Z'' (relative optimum) with a than with any alternative action a'.

3. The following obligations are established for H:
   (7) if one of the subconditions listed under (a) through (f) does not obtain (or, more precisely, if H knows, believes, or assumes that it does not obtain), then H will make this understood to S in a conventional manner.

95. D. Holdcroft ignores this distinction, "Performatives and Statements," *Mind* 83 (1974): 1–18, and thus comes to the false conclusion that only the speech acts that we call institutionally bound are subject to conventional regulations in the sense of the sentence: "A sentence type is a performative if and only if its literal and serious utterance can constitute the performance of an act which is done in accordance with a convention, which convention is not merely a grammatical or semantical one."

96. In Wunderlich's analysis of advising (see *Grundlagen*, p. 350), his conditions B 4–6 make up the content of the obligations.

97. H. Delius, "Zum Wahrheitscharakter egologischer Aussagen," in Brockman and Hofer, eds., *Die Wirklichkeit des Unverständlichen* (The Hague, 1974), pp. 38–77.

2

Social Action, Purposive Activity, and Communication (1981)

If we follow Weber's studies in the sociology of religion, it is an empirical—and thus to begin with an open—question why all three rationality complexes differentiated out after the disintegration of traditional worldviews have not found an institutional embodiment to an equal extent in the orders of life of modern societies, and why they do not determine the communicative practices of everyday life each to the same degree. Through his basic action-theoretic assumptions, however, Weber prejudiced this question in such a way that processes of *societal* rationalization could come into view only from the standpoint of purposive rationality. I would like, therefore, to discuss the conceptual bottlenecks in his theory of action and to use this critique as the starting point for analyzing further the concept of communicative action.

In this sketch I shall not be dealing with the analytic theory of action developed in the Anglo-Saxon world.[1] The studies carried out under this title (the results of which I have drawn upon elsewhere[2]) by no means represent a unified approach. What they do have in common is the method of conceptual analysis and a relatively narrow formulation of the problem. Analytic action theory is fruitful for clarifying the structures of purposive activity. However, it is limited to the atomistic model of action by an isolated actor and neglects the mechanisms for coordinating action through which interpersonal relations come about. It conceptualizes action on the ontological presupposition of exactly one world of existing states of affairs and neglects those actor-world relations that are essential to social interaction. As actions are reduced to purposive interventions in the objective world, the rationality of means-ends relations stands in the foreground. Finally, analytic action theory understands its task to be a metatheoretical clarification of basic concepts; it is not concerned with the empirical usefulness of basic action-theoretic assumptions and thus is scarcely connected with concept formation in the social sciences. It generates a set of philosophical problems that are too unspecific for the purposes of social theory.

On the field of analytic action theory, empiricism is repeating battles long since fought. Once again there are debates concerning the relation of mind and body (idealism versus materialism), concerning reasons and causes (free will versus determinism), concerning behavior and action (objectivistic versus nonobjectivistic descriptions of action), concerning the logical status of explanations of action, concerning causality, intentionality, and so on. To put the matter in a pointed way: analytic action theory treats the venerable problems of the pre-Kantian philosophy of consciousness in a new perspective, without pushing through to the basic questions of a sociological theory of action.

From a sociological point of view, it makes sense to begin with communicative action. "The necessity for coordinated action generates in society a certain need for communication, which must be met if it is to be possible to coordinate actions effectively for the purpose of satisfying needs."[3] Analytic philosophy, with the theory of meaning at its core, does offer a promising point of departure for a theory of communicative action that places linguistic processes of reaching understanding (*sprachliche Verständigung*), as the mechanism for coordinating action, at the focal point of interest. This is less true of the approach to meaning theory that stands closest to action theory in one respect, namely, the intentionalist semantics[4] that goes back to studies by Grice,[5] was further developed by Lewis,[6] and later was worked out by Schiffer[7] and Bennett.[8] This nominalistic theory of meaning is not suitable for clarifying the coordinating mechanism of linguistically mediated interaction because it analyzes the act of reaching understanding according to a model of action oriented toward consequences.

Intentionalist semantics is based on the counterintuitive idea that understanding the meaning of a symbolic expression X can be traced back to understanding the intention of speaker S to give hearer H to understand something by means of a sign. In this way, a derivative mode of reaching understanding, to which speakers can have recourse if the direct road to mutual understanding (*Verständigung*) is obstructed, is stylized into the original mode of reaching understanding. The attempt of intentionalist semantics to base the meaning of the symbolic expression X on what S means (*meint*) by X, or indirectly gives to understand by X, miscarries. For a hearer to understand what S means by X—that is, the meaning (*Bedeutung*) of X—and for him to be aware of the intention that S is pursuing in using X—that is, the purpose that S wants to accomplish with her action—are two different things. S will only then have carried out successfully her intention of inducing in H a meaning-intention (*Bedeutungsintention*) if H recognizes S's intention to communicate with him and understands *what S meant* (*gemeint hat*) in carrying out her communicative intention. H, if he knows only the communicative intention of S, will not understand what S means (*meint*), that is, *that concerning which* she wants to communicate with him.[9]

For a theory of communicative action, only those analytic theories of meaning are instructive that start from the structure of linguistic expressions rather than from speakers' intentions. The theory, however, must keep in view the problem of how the actions of several actors can be linked up with one another with the help of the mechanism of reaching understanding, that is, how they can be interlaced in social spaces and historical times. The organon model of Karl Bühler is representative of this communication-theoretic line of inquiry. Bühler starts from the semiotic model of a linguistic sign used by a speaker (sender) with the aim of coming to an understanding with a hearer (receiver) about objects and states of affairs.[10] He distinguishes three functions of the use of signs: the cognitive function of representing a state of affairs, the expressive function of making known subjective experiences (*Erlebnisse*) of the speaker, and the appellative function of directing requests to addressees. From this perspective, the linguistic sign functions simultaneously as symbol, symptom, and signal. "It is a *symbol* in virtue of being correlated with objects and states of affairs, a *symptom* (indication, index) in virtue of its dependence on the sender, whose inwardness it expresses, and a *signal* in virtue of its appeal to the hearer, whose external or internal behavior it steers like other traffic signs."[11]

There is no need here to go into the reception and critique of this model of language in linguistics and psychology[12] since the decisive developments of it have come, with one exception,[13] from the analytic philosophy of language. At least the three most important analytic theories of meaning can be worked into Bühler's model in such a way that communication theory is further developed from within— through the formal analysis of rules for using linguistic expressions—and not from without—through a cybernetic reformulation of the transmission process. This meaning-theoretic line of development of the organon model leads us away from the objectivistic conception of processes of reaching understanding as information flows between senders and receivers[14] and in the direction of the formal-pragmatic concept of interaction among subjects capable of speaking and acting, interaction that is mediated through acts of reaching understanding.

Linking up with the pragmatist theory of signs introduced by Peirce and developed by Morris, Carnap made the symbolic complex, which Bühler had first considered only functionalistically, accessible to an internally directed analysis of language from syntactic and semantic points of view. The carriers (*Träger*) of meaning are not isolated signs but elements of a language system, that is, sentences whose form is determined by syntactic rules and whose semantic content is determined by the reference to designated objects or states of affairs. With Carnap's logical syntax and the basic assumptions of reference semantics, the way was opened for a formal analysis of the representational function of language. On the other hand, Carnap considered the appellative and expressive functions of language as pragmatic aspects of language use that should be left to empirical analysis. On this view, the pragmatics of language is not determined by a general system of reconstructible rules in such a way that it could be opened up to conceptual analysis like syntax and semantics.

The theory of meaning was finally established as a formal science only with the step from reference semantics to truth-conditional semantics. The semantics founded by Frege and developed through the early Wittgenstein to Davidson and Dummett gives center stage to the relation between sentence and state of affairs, between language and the world.[15] With this ontological turn, semantic theory disengaged itself from the view that the representational function can be clarified on the model of names that designate objects. The meaning of sentences, and the understanding of sentence meanings, cannot be separated from language's inherent relation to the validity of statements. Speakers and hearers understand the meaning of a sentence when they know under what conditions it is true. Correspondingly, they understand the meaning of a word when they know what contribution that word makes to the capacity for truth of a sentence formed with its help. Thus, truth-conditional semantics developed the thesis that the meaning of a sentence is determined by its truth conditions. The internal connection between the *meaning* of a linguistic expression and the validity of a sentence formed with its help was first worked out, then, for the dimension of the linguistic representation of states of affairs.

To be sure, this theory is committed to analyzing all sentences on the model of assertoric sentences. The limits of this approach become visible as soon as the different modes of using sentences are brought under formal consideration. Frege had already distinguished between the assertoric or interrogative force of assertions or questions and the structure of the propositional sentences employed in these utterances. Along the line from the later Wittgenstein through Austin to Searle, the formal semantics of sentences was extended to speech acts. It is no longer limited to the representational function of language but is open to an unbiased analysis of the multiplicity of illocutionary forces. The use theory of meaning makes the pragmatic aspects of the linguistic expression, too, accessible to conceptual analysis. The theory of speech acts then marks the first step toward a formal pragmatics that extends to noncognitive modes of employment. At the same time, as the attempts at a systematization of speech-act classes from Stenius through Kenny to

Searle show, it remains tied to the narrow ontological presuppositions of truth-conditional semantics. The theory of meaning can attain the level of integration of the communication theory that Bühler advanced in a programmatic way only if it is able to provide a systematic grounding for the appellative and expressive functions of language (and perhaps also for the "poetic" function, related to the linguistic means themselves, which is emphasized by Jakobson), in the same way that truth-conditional semantics has done for the representational function. I have taken this path with my reflections on universal pragmatics.[16]

Bühler's theory of language functions could be connected with the methods and insights of the analytic theory of meaning and be made the centerpiece of a theory of communicative action oriented toward reaching understanding if we could generalize the concept of validity beyond the truth of propositions and identify validity conditions no longer only on the semantic level, for sentences, but on the pragmatic level, for utterances. For this purpose, the paradigm change in the philosophy of language that was introduced by Austin (an illuminating historical account of which has been given by Apel)[17] must be radicalized in such a way that the break with the "logos characterization of language," that is, with the privileging of its representational function, also has consequences for the choice of ontological presuppositions in the theory of language. It is not merely a question of admitting other modes of language use on an equal footing with the assertoric; we have to establish validity claims and world relations for these other modes as was done for the assertoric mode.[18] It is with this in mind that I have proposed that we do not oppose the illocutionary role to the propositional component, seeing the former as an irrational force and the latter as that which grounds validity; rather, we should conceive the illocutionary role as the component that specifies *which* validity claim a speaker is raising with her utterance, *how* she is raising it, and for *what*.

With the illocutionary force of an utterance, a speaker can motivate a hearer to accept the offer contained in her speech act and thereby to enter into *a rationally motivated binding and bonding relationship (Bindung)*. This conception presupposes that acting and speaking subjects can relate to more than only one world, and that when they come to an understanding with one another about something in one world, they base their communication on a commonly supposed system of worlds. In this connection I have proposed that we differentiate the external world into an objective world and a social world, and that we introduce the internal world as a complementary concept to the external world. The corresponding validity claims of truth, rightness, and truthfulness (*Wahrhaftigkeit*) can then serve as a guide in the choice of theoretical perspectives for justifying the basic modes of language use, or functions of language, and classifying the speech acts that vary with individual languages. Bühler's appellative function would accordingly have to be split up into regulative and imperative functions. In the regulative use of language, participants raise normative validity claims in various ways and relate to something in their shared social world; in the imperative use of language, they relate to something in the objective world, whereby the speaker raises a claim to power vis-à-vis the addressee in order to get him to act in such a way that the intended state of affairs comes into existence. A theory of communication worked out along these lines in formal-pragmatic terms could be made fruitful for a sociological theory of action if we could show how communicative acts—that is, speech acts or equivalent nonverbal expressions—take on the function of coordinating action and make their contribution to the construction of interactions.

Finally, communicative action is dependent on situational contexts, which in turn represent segments of the lifeworld of the participants in interaction. The connection of action theory to the basic concepts of social theory can be rendered secure only by means of the concept of the lifeworld; this can be introduced as a complementary concept to communicative action via the analyses of background knowledge stimulated by Wittgenstein.[19]

Within the framework of these intermediate reflections, I can at best hope to make this program plausible. Starting from two versions of Weber's action theory, I would like first to make clear the central importance of the problem of coordinating actions. Following this, I shall try to make Austin's distinction between illocutionary and perlocutionary acts fruitful for demarcating action oriented toward reaching understanding from action oriented toward success. On the basis of this, I shall examine the illocutionary binding and bonding (*bindende*) force of the offers contained in speech acts and the role of criticizable validity claims. A discussion of competing proposals for classifying speech acts will serve to confirm my views. Finally, I want to show a few of the transitions from the formal-pragmatic level of analysis to empirical pragmatics, and, on the basis of the relation between the literal and context-dependent meanings of speech acts, to explain why the concept of communicative action has to be supplemented by a concept of the lifeworld.

Two Versions of Weber's Theory of Action

Weber initially introduces "meaning" (*Sinn*) as a basic concept of action theory and, with the help of this category, distinguishes actions from observable behavior: "We shall speak of 'action' insofar as the acting individual attaches a subjective meaning to his behavior—be it overt or covert, omission or acquiescence."[20] Weber does not rely here on a theory of meaning but on an intentional theory of consciousness. He does not elucidate "meaning" in connection with the model of linguistic meanings and does not relate it to the linguistic medium of possible mutual understanding, but to the beliefs and intentions of an acting subject, who is presented in isolation to begin with. At this first switchpoint, Weber parts company with a theory of communicative action. What counts as fundamental is not the interpersonal relation between at least two speaking and acting subjects—a relation that refers back to linguistic processes of reaching understanding—but the purposive activity of a solitary acting subject. As in intentionalist semantics, the process of reaching understanding in language is conceived according to the model of teleologically acting subjects reciprocally influencing one another. "A language community is represented in the ideal-typical, 'purposive-rational' limit case by numerous individual acts . . . which are oriented to the expectation of gaining 'understanding' ('*Verständnis*') from others for an intended meaning."[21] Reaching understanding counts as a derivative phenomenon that is to be construed with the help of a primitive concept of intention. Thus, Weber starts from a teleological model of action and specifies "subjective meaning" as a (precommunicative) action intention. An actor can either pursue his own interests, such as acquiring power or wealth, or he can attempt to live up to values such as piety or human dignity, or he can seek satisfaction in living out affects and desires. These *utilitarian, value-related,* or *affectual* goals, which are broken down into situation-specific purposes, are forms of the subjective meaning that acting subjects can connect with their goal-directed activity.[22]

Since Weber starts from a monologically conceived model of action, he is unable to introduce the concept of "social action" by way of an explication of the concept of meaning. Instead, he has to expand the model of purposive activity with two further specifications so that the conditions of social interaction are satisfied: (a) an orientation toward the behavior of other acting subjects, and (b) a reflexive relation to one another of the action orientations of several interacting subjects. To be sure, Weber vacillates as to whether he should regard condition (a) as sufficient for social interaction or should also require (b). In section 1 of *Economy and Society* he says merely: "Action is 'social' insofar as its subjective meaning takes account of the behavior of others and is thereby oriented in its course."[23] On the other hand, in section 3 Weber stresses that the action orientations of participants have to be *reciprocally* related to one another: "The term 'social relationship' will be used to denote the behavior of a plurality of actors insofar as, in its meaningful content, the action of each takes account of that of the others and is oriented in these terms."[24]

For the construction of a theory of action, another decision is even more important. Should Weber introduce the rationalizable aspects of action on the basis of the teleological action model, or should the concept of social interaction serve as a basis for that purpose? In the first case, Weber has to limit himself to the rationalizable aspects yielded by the model of purposive activity, that is, to the rationality of means and ends. In the second case, the question arises whether there are different kinds of reflexive relations of action orientations and thus also additional aspects under which actions can be rationalized.

The Official Version

Weber distinguishes between purposive-rational, value-rational, affectual, and traditional action. This typology is based on categories
of action goals toward which an actor can orient herself in her
purposive activity: utilitarian, value-related, and affectual goals. Then
"traditional action" follows as a residual category that is, to begin
with, not further determined. This typology is obviously guided by
an interest in distinguishing the degrees to which action is rationalizable. Here, Weber does not start from the social relationship. He
regards as rationalizable only the means-ends relation of teleologically conceived, monological action. If one adopts this perspective,
the only aspects of action open to objective appraisal are the *effectiveness* of a causal intervention into an existing situation and the *truth*
of the empirical statements that underly the maxim or the plan of
action—that is, the subjective belief about a purposive-rational organization of means. Thus Weber chooses purposive-rational (*zweckrational*) action as the reference point for his typology:

Social action, like all action, may be oriented in four ways. It may be: (1)
instrumentally rational (*zweckrational*), that is, determined by expectations as
to the behavior of objects in the environment and of other human beings;
these expectations are used as "conditions" or "means" for the attainment
of the actor's own rationally pursued and calculated ends; (2) *value-rational*
(*wertrational*), that is, determined by a conscious belief in the value for its
own sake of some ethical, aesthetic, religious or other form of behavior,
independently of its prospects of success; (3) *affectual* (especially *emotional*),
that is, determined by the actor's specific affects and feeling states; (4)
traditional, that is, determined by ingrained habituation.[25]

If one follows an interpretation advanced by Wolfgang
Schluchter,[26] this typology can be reconstructed in accordance with
the formal properties of purposive-rational action. An actor behaves
purposive-rationally when she chooses *ends* from a clearly articulated
horizon of *values* and organizes suitable *means* in consideration of
alternative *consequences*. In the series of types of actions proposed by
Weber, the range of what the acting subject takes into consideration
narrows step by step. In value-rational action, the consequences are
screened out of the subjective meaning and thus withdrawn from

Table 2.1
The official typology of action

Types of action in descending order of rationality	Subjective meaning covers these elements:			
	Means	Ends	Values	Consequences
Purposive-rational	+	+	+	+
Value-rational	+	+	+	−
Affectual	+	+	−	−
Traditional	+	−	−	−

rational control; in affectual action, this is true of the consequences and the values; in action that is merely habitualized, of the ends as well (table 2.1).

Of course, Weber can accommodate "value-rational" action in this construction only by attaching to it a restrictive meaning. This type can include only action orientations of an ethics of conviction and not of an ethics of responsibility. Moreover, it does not take into account the principled character on the basis of which the Protestant ethic, for example, qualifies as a framework for a methodical conduct of life. The posttraditional structures of consciousness that Weber finds in ethically rationalized worldviews cannot, on analytic grounds alone, be included in an action typology that rests on a categorization of *nonsocial* actions; for moral consciousness is related to the consensual regulation of *interpersonal* conflicts of action.

The Unofficial Version

When Weber attempts to set up a typology on the conceptual level of social action, he encounters additional aspects of the rationality of action. Social actions can be distinguished according to the mechanisms for coordinating individual actions, for instance, according to whether a social relation is based on *interest positions* alone or also on *normative agreement*. In this way, Weber distinguishes the sheer facticity of an economic order from the social validity of a legal order. In the one case, social relations gain stability through a factual intermeshing of interest positions; in the other, through the recognition of normative validity claims. To be sure, coordination of actions secured, to begin with, merely through a complementarity of interests can be superimposed normatively by the addition of "validity-based agreement," that is, by "deference to convention or legal norms."[27] Weber elucidates this in connection with the development of traditions in the transition from "custom" (*Sitte*) to "convention": "It is by way of conventional rules that merely factual regularities of action, i.e., usages, are frequently transformed into binding norms, guaranteed primarily by psychological coercion."[28]

Interaction based on *complementarity of interests* exists not only in the form of custom—that is, of dull, insensible habituation—but also at the level of rational competitive behavior, for example in modern commerce, in which participants have formed a clear consciousness of the complementarity as well as of the contingency of their interest positions. On the other hand, interaction based on *normative consensus* does not only take the form of tradition-bound, conventional action; thus, the modern legal system is dependent on an enlightened belief in legitimacy, which rational natural law—with the idea of a basic contract among free and equals—traces back to procedures of rational will-formation. If one pursues these considerations, then it makes sense to construe types of social action (a) according to the kind of coordination involved, and (b) according to the degree of rationality of the social relationship (see table 2.2).

There are some indications suggesting such a typology in *Economy and Society*,[29] there is relatively strong evidence for it in the essay "Some Categories of Interpretive Sociology."[30] I shall not pursue this here, however, because Weber does not clearly carry through, at the level of the action orientations themselves, the interesting distinction between social relations mediated by interest positions and those mediated by normative agreement. (I shall remedy this below in the section beginning on page 119.) More serious is the fact that while Weber does distinguish between tradition-bound and rational agreement, he explains this rational agreement inadequately, as we have seen above, using the model of arrangements among subjects of private law. At any rate, he does not trace it back to the moral-practical foundations of discursive will-formation. Otherwise it would have become clear at this point that action in society (*Gesellschaftshandeln*) is distinguished from action in community (*Ge-*

Table 2.2
An alternative typology of action

Coordination	Degree of rationality of action	
	Low	High
Through interest positions	De facto customary action (*Sitte*)	Strategic action (*Interessenhandeln*)
Through normative agreement	Conventional action based on agreement (*Gemeinschaftshandeln*)	Postconventional action based on agreement (*Gesellschaftshandeln*)

meinschaftshandeln) not through the purposive-rational action orientations of the participants, but through the higher, postconventional stage of moral-pratical rationality. Because he does not do this, a *specific* concept of value-rationality cannot gain the significance for action theory that it would have to be accorded if the ethical rationalization that Weber examined at the level of cultural traditions is to be grasped in terms of its consequences for systems of social action.

Weber was not able to make his unofficial typology of action fruitful for the question of societal rationalization. The official version, on the other hand, is so narrowly conceived that within its framework social action can be assessed only under the aspect of purposive rationality. From this conceptual perspective, the rationalization of action systems has to be restricted to the establishment and diffusion of types of purposive-rational action specific to subsystems. If processes of societal rationalization are to be investigated *in their entire breadth*, other action-theoretical foundations are required.

I would like therefore to take up once again the concept of communicative action expounded in the introduction[31] and, by drawing upon speech-act theory, to anchor in its conceptual foundations those rationalizable aspects of action neglected in Weber's official action theory. In this way, I hope to capture in action-theoretic terms the complex concept of rationality that Weber did employ in his cultural analyses. I shall be starting from a classification of action that relies on the unofficial version of Weber's action theory insofar as social actions are distinguished according to two action orientations, corresponding to the coordination of action through interest positions and through normative agreement (see table 2.3).

Table 2.3
Types of action

Action situation	Action orientation	
	Oriented toward success	Oriented toward reaching understanding
Nonsocial	Instrumental action	—
Social	Strategic action	Communicative action

The model of *purposive-rational* action takes as its point of departure the view that the actor is primarily oriented toward attaining an end (which has been rendered sufficiently precise in terms of purposes), that he selects means that seem to him appropriate in the given situation, and that he calculates other forseeable consequences of action as secondary conditions of success. Success is defined as the occurrence in the world of a desired state, which can, in a given situation, be causally effected by goal-oriented action or omission. The effects of action that occur comprise the results of action (to the extent that the set purpose has been achieved), the consequences of action (which the actor foresaw and intended, or made allowance for), and the side-effects (which the actor did not foresee). We call an action oriented toward success *instrumental* when we consider it under the aspect of following technical rules of action and assess the degree of efficiency of an intervention into a complex of circumstances and events. We call an action oriented toward success *strategic* when we consider it under the aspect of following rules of rational choice and assess the degree of efficiency of its influencing the decisions of a rational counterpart in action. Instrumental actions can be connected with social interactions; strategic actions are themselves social actions. By contrast, I shall speak of *communicative* action, whenever the plans of action of the actors involved are coordinated not through egocentric calculations of success but through acts of reaching understanding. In communicative action, participants are not primarily oriented toward their own individual successes; they pursue their individual goals on condition that they can harmonize their plans of action on the basis of common situation definitions. To this extent the negotiation of definitions of the situation is an essential component of the interpretive accomplishments required for communicative action.

Orientation toward Success versus Orientation toward Reaching Understanding

In identifying strategic action and communicative action as types, I am assuming that concrete actions can be classified from these points of view. I use the terms "strategic" and "communicative" not merely to designate two analytic aspects under which one and the same action can be described—on the one hand, as a reciprocal influencing of one another by agents acting in a purposive-rational manner and, on the other hand, as a process of reaching understanding among members of a lifeworld. Rather, social actions can be distinguished according to whether the participants adopt either a success-oriented attitude or one oriented toward reaching understanding. And, under suitable conditions, these attitudes should be identifiable on the basis of the intuitive knowledge of the participants themselves. To begin with, therefore, a conceptual analysis of the two attitudes is required.

Within the framework of action theory, conceptual analysis of the two attitudes cannot be understood as a psychological task. It is not my aim to characterize behavioral dispositions empirically, but to grasp general structures of processes of reaching understanding, from which conditions for participation can be derived that may be characterized formally. To explain what I mean by "an attitude oriented toward reaching understanding," I have to analyze the concept of "reaching understanding" (*Verständigung*). This is not a question of the predicates an observer uses when describing processes of reaching understanding, but of the pretheoretical knowledge of competent speakers, who can themselves distinguish intuitively situations in which they are exerting an influence *upon* others from those in which they are coming to an understanding *with* them, and who further know when their attempts at reaching understanding fail. If we were able to specify explicitly the standards on which the speakers implicitly base these distinctions, we would be in a position to explain the concept of reaching understanding.

Reaching understanding (*Verständigung*) is considered to be a process of achieving unity (*Einigung*) among speaking and acting subjects. However, a group of persons can feel at one in a mood that is so diffuse that it is difficult to specify the propositional content or the intentional object to which it is directed. Such a collective like-mindedness (*Gleichgestimmtheit*) does not satisfy the conditions for the type of agreement (*Einverständnis*) in which attempts at reaching understanding terminate when they are successful. A communicatively achieved agreement, or one that is mutually presupposed in communicative action, is propositionally differentiated. Owing to this linguistic structure, it cannot merely be induced through outside influence; it has to be accepted (or presupposed) as valid by the participants. To this extent it can be distinguished from merely de facto accord (*Übereinstimmung*). Processes of reaching understanding aim at an agreement that meets the conditions of rationally motivated assent (*Zustimmung*) to the content of an utterance. A communicatively achieved agreement has a rational basis; it cannot be imposed by either party, whether instrumentally through intervention in the situation directly, or strategically through exerting influence on the decisions of one party on the basis of a calculation of success. Agreement can indeed objectively be obtained by force; but what comes to pass *manifestly* through outside influence or the use of violence cannot subjectively count as agreement. Agreement rests on common *convictions*. The speech act of one person succeeds only if the other accepts the offer contained in it by taking (however implicitly) a "yes" or "no" position on a validity claim that is in principle criticizable. Both Ego, who raises a validity claim with his utterance, and Alter, who recognizes or rejects it, base their decisions on potential reasons.

If we were not in a position to refer to the model of speech, we could not even begin to analyze what it means for two subjects to come to an understanding with one another. Reaching understanding is the inherent telos of human language (*Sprache*). To be sure, language and reaching understanding are not related to one another as means to end. But we can explain the concept of reaching understanding only if we specify what it means to use sentences with a communicative intent. The concepts of speaking and reaching understanding reciprocally interpret one another. For this reason, we can analyze the formal-pragmatic features of the attitude oriented toward reaching understanding in connection with the model of the attitude of participants in communication, one of whom—in the simplest case—carries out a speech act, to which the other takes a "yes" or "no" position (even though utterances in the communicative practices of everyday life usually do not have a standard linguistic form and often have no verbal form at all).

If we approach the task of distinguishing actions oriented toward success from actions oriented toward reaching understanding by way of an analysis of speech acts, we encounter the following difficulty. On the one hand, we are regarding the communicative acts, with the help of which speakers and hearers come to an understanding about something, as a mechanism for coordinating actions. The concept of communicative action is presented in such a way that the acts of reaching understanding, which link the teleologically structured plans of action of different participants and thereby first combine individual acts into an interaction complex, cannot themselves be reduced to teleological actions. To this extent, the paradigmatic concept of linguistically mediated interaction is incompatible with a theory of meaning that, like intentionalist semantics, tries to conceptualize reaching understanding as the solution to a problem of coordination among subjects acting with an orientation toward success. On the other hand, not every linguistically mediated interaction is an example of action oriented toward reaching understanding. Without doubt, there are countless cases of indirect mutual understanding (*indirekte Verständigung*), whether where one subject, in giving another to understand something through signals, indirectly gets him to form a certain opinion or to adopt certain intentions by way of an inferential processing of perceptions of the situation, or where one subject, on the basis of already habitualized everyday communicative practices, inconspicuously harnesses another for her own purposes, that is, induces him to behave in a desired way by manipulatively employing linguistic means, thereby instrumentalizing him for her own success. Such examples of the use of language with an orientation toward consequences seem to decrease the value of speech acts as the model for action oriented toward reaching understanding.

This will turn out not to be the case only if it can be shown that the use of language oriented toward reaching understanding is the *original mode* of language use upon which indirectly reaching understanding, giving to understand something or letting something be understood—in general, the instrumental use of language—is parasitic. In my view, Austin's distinction between illocutions and perlocutions accomplishes just that.

As is well known, Austin distinguishes between locutionary, illocutionary, and perlocutionary acts.[32] He applies the term "locutionary" to the content of propositional sentences ("*p*") or of nominalized propositional sentences ("that *p*"). Through *locutionary acts*, the speaker expresses states of affairs; she says something. Through *illocutionary acts*, the speaker performs an action by saying something. The illocutionary role establishes the mode of a sentence (Mp) employed as a statement, promise, command, avowal, or the like. Under standard conditions, the mode is expressed by means of a performative verb in the first person present; the action meaning can be seen particularly in the fact that "hereby" can be added to the illocutionary component of the speech act: "I hereby promise you (command you, confess to you) that *p*." Finally, through *perlocutionary acts*, the speaker produces an effect upon the hearer. By carrying out a speech act she brings about something in the world. Thus, the three acts that Austin distinguishes can be characterized with the following phrases: to say *something;* to act *by* saying something; to bring about something *through* acting by saying something.

Austin makes his conceptual incisions in such a way that the speech act (Mp), composed of an illocutionary and a propositional component, is presented as a self-sufficient act that the speaker always performs with a communicative intent, that is, with the aim that a hearer may understand and accept his utterance.[33] The self-sufficiency of the speech act is to be understood in the sense that the communicative intent of the speaker and the illocutionary aim he is pursuing follow from the manifest meaning of what is said. It is a different matter with teleological actions. We identify their meaning only in connection with the intentions their author is pursuing and the ends he wants to realize. Just as *the meaning of what is said* is constitutive for illocutionary acts, *the intention of the actor* is constitutive for teleological actions.

What Austin calls *perlocutionary effects* arise from the fact that illocutionary acts take on a role in a teleological context of action. Speech acts, like actions in general, can produce side effects that the actor did not foresee; these are perlocutionary effects in a trivial sense, which I shall not consider here. Less trivial are the perlocutionary effects that result from the fact that illocutionary acts sometimes take on roles in contexts of strategic interaction. These effects ensue whenever a speaker acts with an orientation toward success and, in doing so, simultaneously connects speech acts with intentions and instrumentalizes them for purposes that are only contingently related to the meaning of what is said.

There yet is a further sense in which to perform a locutionary act, and therein an illocutionary act, may also be to perform an act of another kind. Saying something will often, or even normally, produce certain consequential effects upon the feelings, thoughts, or actions of the audience, or of the speaker, or of other persons: and it may be done with the design, intention, or purpose of producing them; and we may then say, thinking of this, that the speaker has performed an act in the nomenclature of which reference is made either only obliquely . . . or even . . . not at all, to the performance of the locutionary or illocutionary act. We shall call the performance of an act of this kind the performance of a *perlocutionary act* or *perlocution*.[34]

The demarcation between illocutionary and perlocutionary acts has given rise to an extended controversy.[35] From it have emerged four criteria of demarcation.

a. The illocutionary aim a speaker pursues with an utterance follows from the meaning—constitutive for speech acts—of what is said itself; speech acts are, in this sense, self-identifying.[36] With the help of an illocutionary act, a speaker lets it be known that she wants what she says to be understood as a greeting, command, warning, explanation, and so forth. Her communicative intent does not go beyond wanting the hearer to understand the manifest content of the speech act. By contrast, the perlocutionary aim of a speaker, like the ends pursued with goal-directed actions generally, does not follow from the manifest content of the speech act; this aim can be inferred only by way of the actor's intention. For example, a hearer who understands a request directed to him can just as little know thereby what *else* the speaker has in view in uttering it as an observer who sees an acquaintance hurrying along the street can know why he is in a hurry. The addressee could at best infer the speaker's perlocutionary aims from the context.[37] The three remaining criteria have to do with this characteristic self-identification of speech acts.

b. From the description of a speech act, as in (1) and (2) below, we can deduce the conditions for the corresponding illocutionary success of the speaker, but not the conditions for the perlocutionary success that a speaker acting with an orientation toward success might want to achieve, or did achieve, in a given case by carrying out this speech act. In the description of perlocutions, as in (3) and (4) below, kinds of success are included that go beyond the meaning of what is said and thus beyond what an addressee could understand directly.

(1)   *S* asserted to *H* that she gave notice to her firm.

S will have achieved illocutionary success with the utterance represented by (1) if *H* understands her assertion and accepts it as true. The same holds for

(2)   *H* warned *S* not to give notice to her firm.

H will have achieved illocutionary success with the utterance represented by (2) if *S* understands his warning and accepts it as true or right—depending on whether in a given context it has more the sense of a prognosis or of a moral appeal. In any case, accepting the utterance described in (2) provides grounds for obligations to act in a certain way on the part of the addressee and for corresponding expectations on the part of the speaker. Whether or not the expected sequel of action actually comes to pass has no effect on the illocutionary success of the speaker. If, for instance, *S* does not give notice, this is not a perlocutionarily achieved effect but the consequence of a communicatively achieved agreement and thus the fulfillment of an obligation that the addressee took upon himself with his "yes" to a speech act offer. Consider now:

(3)   Through informing H that she had given notice to her firm, S gave H a fright (as she intended to do).

From this description it follows that the illocutionary success of the assertion described in (1) is not a sufficient condition for achieving a perlocutionary effect. In another context, the hearer could just as well react to the same utterance with relief. The same holds for

(4) H made S uneasy with his warning against giving notice to her firm.

In another context the same warning could just as well strengthen S in her resolve, for instance if S harbors a suspicion that H does not wish her well. The description of perlocutionary effects must therefore refer to a context of teleological action that *goes beyond* the speech act.[38]

   c. From considerations of this kind, Austin concluded that illocutionary success stands in a *conventionally* regulated or *internal* connection with the speech act, whereas perlocutionary effects remain external to the meaning of what is said. The possible perlocutionary effects of a speech act depend on fortuitous contexts and, unlike the success of illocutionary acts, are not fixed by conventions.[39] Of course, one might use (4) as a counterexample. Only if the addressee takes the warning seriously is unease a plausible reaction, and only if she does not take it seriously is a feeling of reassurance plausible. In some cases, the meaning conventions of the action predicates with which illocutionary acts are formed exclude certain classes of perlocutionary effects. Nonetheless, these effects are connected with speech acts not merely in a conventional way. When a hearer accepts an assertion by S as true, a command as right, an admission as truthful, he therewith implicitly declares himself ready to bind his further action to certain conventional obligations. By contrast, the feeling of unease which a friend arouses in S with a warning that the latter takes seriously is a state that may or may not ensue.

   d. Similar considerations have motivated Strawson to replace the criterion of conventionality with another criterion of demarcation.[40] A speaker, if she wants to be successful, may not let her perlocutionary aims be known, whereas illocutionary aims can be achieved only through being expressed. Illocutions are expressed openly; perlocutions may not be "admitted" as such. This difference can also be seen in the fact that the predicates with which perlocutionary acts are described (to give a fright to, to cause unease, to plunge into doubt, to put someone in a bad mood, to mislead, to offend, to infuriate, to humiliate, and so forth) cannot appear among those predicates used to carry out the illocutionary acts with the help of which corresponding perlocutionary effects can be achieved. Perlocutionary acts constitute that subclass of teleological actions that can be carried out with the help of speech acts on condition that the agent does not declare or admit to her aims as such.

Whereas the sense of the division into locutionary and illocutionary acts is to separate the propositional content from the mode of speech acts as analytically different aspects, the distinction between these two types of acts, on the one hand, and perlocutionary acts, on the other, is by no means analytical in character. Perlocutionary effects can be achieved with the help of speech acts only if the latter are *incorporated as means* into teleological, success-oriented actions. Perlocutionary acts are an indication of the integration of speech acts into contexts of strategic interaction. They are part of the intended sequel of action or of the results of a teleological action that an actor undertakes with the intention of influencing a hearer in a certain way with the help of successful illocutionary acts. To be sure, speech acts can serve this *nonillocutionary aim of influencing hearers* only if they are suited to achieving illocutionary aims. If the hearer failed to understand what the speaker was saying, a teleologically acting, success-oriented speaker would not be able to bring the hearer, by means of communicative acts, to behave in the desired way. To this extent, what we initially designated as "the use of language with an orientation toward consequences" is not an original use of language but the subsumption of speech acts that serve illocutionary aims under conditions of action oriented toward success.

As speech acts by no means always function in this way, however, it must also be possible to clarify the structures of linguistic communication without reference to structures of purposive activity. The teleological actor orientation toward success is not constitutive for the successful accomplishment of processes of reaching understanding, particularly not when these are incorporated into strategic interactions. What we mean by reaching understanding, and an attitude oriented toward reaching understanding, has to be clarified *solely* in connection with illocutionary acts. An attempt at reaching understanding undertaken with the help of a speech act succeeds when a speaker achieves her illocutionary aim in Austin's sense. From this it also follows that we cannot explain illocutionary success in terms of the conditions for the purposively achieved success of a teleological action. Illocutionary aims are different from those purposes that can be achieved *under the description* of something to be brought about in the world.

Perlocutionary effects, like the successful results of teleological actions generally, may be described as states in the world brought about through intervention in the world. By contrast, illocutionary successes are achieved at the level of interpersonal relations on which participants in communication come to an understanding with one another about something in the world. In this sense, they are not innerworldly, but extramundane. At most, successful illocutionary acts occur within the lifeworld to which the participants in communication belong and that forms the background for their processes of reaching understanding. They cannot be intended under the description of causally produced effects. This model of action oriented toward reaching understanding, which I develop below, is obscured rather than illuminated by Austin's distinction between illocutions and perlocutions.

From the foregoing it appears that we can conceive perlocutions as a special class of strategic interactions in which illocutions are employed as means in teleological contexts of action. As Strawson has shown, this employment is subject to certain provisos. A teleologically acting speaker has to achieve his illocutionary aim— that the hearer understand what is said and enter into the obligations connected with the acceptance of the offer contained in the speech act—without betraying his perlocutionary aim. This proviso lends to perlocutions the peculiarly asymmetrical character of concealed strategic actions. These are interactions in which at least one of the participants is acting strategically, while he deceives other participants regarding the fact that he is *not* satisfying the presuppositions under which illocutionary aims normally can be achieved. For this reason also, this type of interaction is not suitable as the model for an analysis that is supposed to explain the linguistic mechanism of coordinating action with the help of the illocutionary binding and bonding effects of speech acts. For this purpose it would be advisable to select a type of interaction that is not burdened with the asymmetries and provisos of perlocutions. I have called the type of interaction in which *all* participants harmonize their individual plans of action with one another and thus *unreservedly* pursue their illocutionary aims "communicative action."

Austin, too, analyzes speech acts in contexts of interaction. It is precisely the point of his approach to work out the performative character of linguistic utterances on the basis of institutionally bound speech acts such as baptizing, betting, appointing, and the like, in which the obligations issuing from the performance of the speech act are unambiguously regulated by accompanying institutions or norms of action. However, Austin confuses the picture by not treating these interactions, in connection with which he analyzes the illocutionary binding and bonding force of speech acts, as *different in type* from those interactions in which perlocutionary effects occur. Someone who makes a bet, appoints an officer as supreme commander, gives a command, admonishes or warns, makes a prediction, tells a story, makes a confession, reveals something, and so forth is acting communicatively and cannot, *at the same level of interaction,* produce perlocutionary effects at all. A speaker can pursue perlocutionary aims only when he deceives his counterpart concerning the fact that he is acting strategically—when, for example, he gives the command to attack in order to get his troops to rush into a trap, or when he proposes a bet of $3,000 in order to embarrass someone, or when he tells a story late in the evening in order to delay a guest's departure, and so on. It is certainly true that in communicative action unintended consequences may occur at any time; but as soon as there is a danger that these will be attributed to the speaker as intended effects, the latter finds it necessary to offer explanations and denials, and if need be, apologies, in order to dispel the false impression that these side effects are perlocutionary effects. Otherwise, he has to expect that the other participants will feel deceived and adopt in turn a strategic attitude, breaking away from action oriented toward reaching understanding. Of course, in complex action contexts, a speech act that is performed and accepted directly according to the presuppositions of communicative action can at the same time have a strategic status at *other* levels of interaction, that is, can have perlocutionary effects on *third parties*.

Thus, I count as communicative action those linguistically mediated interactions in which all participants pursue illocutionary aims, and *only* illocutionary aims, with their speech acts. On the other hand, I regard as linguistically mediated strategic action those interactions in which at least one of the participants wants to produce perlocutionary effects on his opposite number with his speech acts. Austin did not keep these two cases separate as different types of interaction, because he was inclined to identify speech acts—that is, acts of reaching understanding—with the linguistically mediated interactions themselves. He did not see that speech acts function as a coordinating mechanism for *other* actions. They must be disengaged from such contexts of communicative action before they can be incorporated into strategic interactions. And this is possible in turn only because speech acts have a relative independence in relation to communicative action; however, the meaning of what is said always points to the structures of interaction characteristic of communicative action. The difference between a speech act and the context of interaction that it constitutes through its action-coordinating accomplishments can be recognized more easily if, unlike Austin, one does not remain fixated on the model of institutionally bound speech acts.[41]

Meaning and Validity

On the basis of the controversial relation between illocutionary and perlocutionary acts, I have attempted to show that while speech acts can indeed be employed strategically, they have a constitutive meaning only for communicative action. The latter is distinguished from strategic action by the fact that all participants unreservedly pursue illocutionary aims in order to arrive at an agreement that provides the basis for a consensual coordination of individually pursued plans of action. In what follows I would like to explicate the conditions that have to be satisfied by a communicatively achieved agreement that is to fulfill this function of coordinating action. In doing so, I shall take as my model elementary pairs of utterances, each of which consists of the speech act of a speaker and the affirmative response of a hearer. Consider the following examples:[42]

(1)   I (hereby) promise you that I shall come around tomorrow.

(2)   You are requested to stop smoking.

(3)   I confess to you that I find your actions loathsome.

(4)   I can predict (to you) that the vacation will be spoiled by rain.

We can recognize in each case what an affirmative response would mean and what kind of interaction sequel it would ground.

(1′)   Yes, I shall depend on it.

(2′)   Yes, I shall comply.

(3′)   Yes, I believe you do.

(4′)   Yes, we'll have to take that into account.

With his "yes," the hearer accepts a speech-act offer and grounds an agreement; this agreement concerns the *content of the utterance* on the one hand, and on the other certain *guarantees immanent to speech acts* and certain *obligations relevant for the sequel of interaction*. The action potential typical of a speech act finds expression in the claim that the speaker raises for what she says—in an explicit speech act with the help of a performative verb. In acknowledging her claim, the hearer accepts an offer made with the speech act. This illocutionary success is relevant to the action insofar as an interpersonal relation between speaker and hearer is thereby established that is effective for coordination, that orders the possible scope of action and sequels of interaction, and that opens up to the hearer possible points of connection by way of general alternatives for action.

The question now arises, from where do speech acts draw their power to coordinate actions, when this authority is neither borrowed directly from the social validity of norms (as it is in the case of institutionally bound speech acts) nor owed to a contingently available reservoir of potential sanctions (as it is in the case of imperative expressions of will)? From the perspective of a hearer to whom an utterance is addressed, we can distinguish three levels of reaction to a (correctly perceived) speech act: the hearer *understands* the utterance, that is, he grasps the meaning of what is said; with his "yes" or "no" the hearer *takes a position* on the claim raised with the speech act, that is, he accepts or rejects the speech-act offer; and in consequence of an achieved agreement, the hearer directs his action according to *conventionally fixed obligations to act in a certain way*. The *pragmatic* level of the agreement effective for coordination connects the *semantic* level of understanding meaning with the *empirical* level of further developing—in a manner dependent on the context—the accord relevant to the sequel of interaction. How this connection comes about can be explained by means of the theory of meaning; admittedly, for this purpose, the formal-semantic approach limited to understanding sentences has to be expanded.[43]

The formal-pragmatic approach to meaning theory begins with the question of *what it means to understand an utterance*—that is, a sentence employed communicatively. Formal semantics makes a conceptual distinction between the meaning (*Bedeutung*) of a sentence and the meaning (*Meinung*) of the speaker, who, when she uses the sentence in a speech act, can say something other than what it literally means. But this distinction cannot be developed into a methodological separation between the formal analysis of sentence meanings and the empirical analysis of speakers' meanings expressed in utterances; for the literal meaning of a sentence cannot be explained at all apart from the standard conditions for its communicative employment. To be sure, formal pragmatics must also take precautions to ensure that in the standard case what is meant does not deviate from the literal meaning of what is said. For this reason, our analysis is limited to speech acts carried out *under standard conditions*. This is intended to ensure that the speaker means (*meint*) nothing else than the literal meaning of what she says.

In a distant analogy to the basic assumptions of truth-conditional semantics, I now want to trace back understanding an utterance to knowledge of the conditions under which a hearer may accept it. *We understand a speech act when we know what makes it acceptable.* From the standpoint of the speaker, the conditions of acceptability are identical to the conditions for her illocutionary success. Acceptability is not defined here in an objectivistic sense, from the perspective of an observer, but in the performative attitude of a participant in communication. A speech act may be called "acceptable" if it satisfies the conditions that are necessary in order for the hearer to take a "yes" position on the claim raised by the speaker. These conditions cannot be satisfied one-sidedly, either relative to the speaker or to the hearer. They are rather conditions for the *intersubjective recognition* of a linguistic claim, which, in a way typical of a given class of speech acts, grounds an agreement with a specified content concerning obligations relevant for the sequel of interaction.

From the standpoint of a sociological theory of action, my primary interest must be to make clear the mechanism relevant to the coordinating accomplishments of speech acts. To this end I shall concentrate on those conditions under which a hearer is motivated to accept the offer contained in a speech act, assuming that the linguistic expressions employed are grammatically well formed and that the general contextual conditions typical for a given type of speech act are satisfied.[44] A hearer understands the meaning of an utterance when, in addition to grammatical conditions of well-formedness and general contextual conditions,[45] he knows those *essential conditions* under which he could be motivated by a speaker to an affirmative response.[46] These *acceptability conditions in the narrower sense* relate to the meaning of the illocutionary role that S in the standard case expresses with the help of a performative action predicate.

But let us look first at a grammatically correct imperative sentence, formulated as an imperative under appropriate contextual conditions:

(5) I (hereby) request you to stop smoking.

Imperatives are often understood on the model of perlocutionary acts, as attempts by an actor S to get H to carry out a certain action. On this view, S performs an imperative sentence only when she connects with her utterance the intention that H infer from the utterance that S is attempting to get him to perform an action a.[47] However, this view fails to recognize the illocutionary meaning of such imperatives. In uttering an imperative, a speaker *says what H is to do*. This *direct form* of reaching understanding renders superfluous a speech act by means of which the speaker could indirectly get a hearer to perform a certain action. The illocutionary meaning of imperatives can better be described through the following paraphrases:[48]

(5a) S told H that he should take care to see that "p" comes to pass.

(5b) S signified to H that he should bring about "p."

(5c) The request (demand) uttered by S is to be understood in the sense that H should bring about "p."

Here "p" designates a state in the objective world that, relative to the time of the utterance, lies in the future and that, other conditions remaining constant, can come into existence through an intervention or omission by the addressee—for instance, the state of not smoking that H brings about by putting out his lit cigarette.

A hearer accepts the imperative (5) by responding affirmatively to it with:

(5′) Yes, I shall do what is requested of me.

If we restrict ourselves to conditions of acceptability in the narrower sense, the conditions under which H accepts (5) fall into two components.

a. The hearer should understand the illocutionary meaning of imperatives in such a way that he could paraphrase this meaning with sentences like (5a), (5b), or (5c) and could interpret the propositional content "to stop smoking" as an imperative directed to him. In fact, the hearer understands the imperative (5) if he knows the conditions under which "p" would occur and if he knows what he himself would have to do or not to do in the given circumstances in order that these conditions be satisfied. As one must know the truth conditions of a proposition in order to understand it, one must, in order to understand an imperative, know the conditions under which it would count as satisfied. Within the framework of a pragmatic theory of meaning, these *conditions of satisfaction*—formulated to begin with in semantic terms—are interpreted in terms of obligations relevant for the sequel of interaction. The hearer understands an imperative if he knows what he must do or not do in order to bring about a state "p" desired by S; he thereby also knows how he could link up his actions with those of S.

b. As soon as we conceptualize the understanding of imperatives from this perspective, broadened to include the context of interaction, it becomes clear that knowledge of "satisfaction conditions" is not sufficient for knowing when an imperative is acceptable. A second component is lacking, namely, knowledge of *the conditions of the agreement* that first *grounds adherence* to the obligations relevant for the sequel of interaction. The hearer fully understands the illocutionary meaning of the imperative only if he knows why the speaker expects that she can impose her will on him. With her imperative, the speaker raises a *claim* to power, to which the hearer, if he accepts it, yields. It belongs to the meaning of an imperative that the speaker harbors a *justified* expectation that she will be able to carry through her claim to power; and this holds only under the condition that S knows that her addressee has reasons to yield to her power claim. Since, to begin with, we have understood imperatives as sheer expressions of will, these reasons cannot lie in the illocutionary meaning of the speech act itself; they can reside only in a reservoir of potential sanctions that is externally connected with the speech act. Thus *the conditions of satisfaction have to be supplemented with conditions of sanction* in order to complete the conditions of acceptability.

A hearer understands an imperative (5) if he knows (a) the conditions under which an addressee can bring about the desired state (not smoking) and (b) the conditions under which S has good reasons to expect that H will feel constrained to yield to the will of S (for example, the threat of penalties for violating safety regulations). Only by knowing both components (a) and (b) does the hearer know what conditions have to be met if a hearer is to be able to respond affirmatively, as in (5′), to the imperative (5). In knowing these conditions, he knows what makes the utterance acceptable.

This picture is complicated in an instructive way when we pass from genuine or *simple* imperatives to *normatively authorized* imperatives or commands. Let us compare (5) with the following—a variant of (2):

(6) I (hereby) direct you to stop smoking.

This utterance presupposes recognized norms (for example, the safety regulations for international air travel) and an institutional framework authorizing those holding certain positions (e.g., flight attendants) under certain conditions (e.g., preparing to land) to direct a certain class of persons (here, the passengers) to stop smoking by appealing to certain regulations.

Once again, the illocutionary meaning can be specified initially through the conditions mentioned under (a), but in the case of directives (*Anweisungen*), the illocutionary meaning does not only *point* to conditions (b), which have to be completed on the basis of the context of the speech act; rather, these conditions for accepting the linguistic claim, and thus for agreement between S and H, *result from* the illocutionary act itself. In the case of imperative expressions of will, S has good reasons to expect that H will yield to her will only if she has at her disposal sanctions with which she can, in a recognizable manner, threaten or entice H. So long as S does not appeal to the validity of norms, it makes no difference whether the reservoir of potential sanctions is de jure or de facto. For so long as S utters a genuine (simple) imperative, that is, expresses nothing other than her own will, she influences H's motives in a merely empirical way by threatening him with harm or by offering him rewards. The grounds for accepting expressions of will are related to motives of the hearer that the speaker can influence only empirically, in the final instance by means of violence or goods. It is a different matter with normatively authorized imperatives such as commands and directives. In contrast to (5), with (6) the speaker appeals to the validity of safety regulations and, in issuing directives, raises a claim to validity.

Registering a *validity claim* is not the expression of a contingent will; and responding affirmatively to a validity claim is no merely empirically motivated decision. Both acts, putting forward and recognizing a validity claim, are subject to conventional restrictions, because such a claim can be rejected only in the form of criticism and can be defended against a criticism only in the form of a refutation. Someone who resists a directive is referred to prevailing regulations and not to the penalties that can be expected if they are not followed. And one who doubts the validity of the underlying norms has to give *reasons*—whether challenging the legality of the regulation, that is, challenging the lawfulness of its social validity, or challenging the legitimacy of the regulation, that is, its claim to be right or justified in a moral-practical sense. Validity claims are *internally* connected with reasons. To this extent, the conditions for the acceptability of directives can be taken from the illocutionary meaning of a speech act *itself;* they do not need to be completed by *additional* conditions of sanction.

Thus a hearer understands the directive (6) if he knows (a) the conditions under which an addressee could bring about the desired state (not smoking), and (b) the conditions under which S could have convincing reasons to regard an imperative with the content (a) as valid—that is, as normatively justified. The conditions (a) pertain to obligations to act in a certain way that arise out of an agreement based on the intersubjective recognition of the normative validity claim raised for a corresponding imperative.[49] The conditions (b) pertain to the acceptance of the validity claim itself. We have to distinguish here between the *validity* of an action or of the norm underlying it, the *claim* that the conditions for its validity are satisfied, and the *redemption* of the validity claim raised, that is, the justification (of the claim) that the conditions for the validity of an action or of the underlying norm are satisfied. We are now in a position to say that a speaker can *rationally motivate* a hearer to accept her speech act offer because—on the basis of an internal connection between validity, validity claim, and the redemption of a validity claim—she can assume the warranty (*Gewähr*) for providing, if necessary, convincing reasons that would stand up to a hearer's criticism of the validity claim. Thus a speaker owes the binding and bonding force of her illocutionary success not to the validity of what is said but to *the coordinating effect of the warranty* that she offers—a warranty to redeem, if necessary, the validity claim raised with her speech act.

In all cases in which the illocutionary role expresses not a power claim but a validity claim, the place of the empirically motivating force of a reservoir of potential sanctions (contingently linked with speech acts) is taken by the rationally motivating force of the speaker's assuming a warranty for validity claims.

This holds not only for regulative speech acts like (1) and (2), but also for expressive and constative speech acts like (3) and (4). Just as with (1) a speaker *produces* a normative validity claim for her intention to bring about a desired state, and just as with (2) she *raises* a normative validity claim for her imperative that *H* bring about a state desired by *S*, so with (3) the speaker makes a claim to truthfulness for a disclosed intentional subjective experience (*Erlebnis*), and with (4) a truth claim for a proposition. In (3) it is the disclosure of a previously concealed emotional attitude, in (4) the putting forward of a proposition, for the validity of which the speaker assumes a warranty in making a confession (3) or a prediction (4). Thus a hearer understands the avowal (3) if he knows (a) the conditions under which a person could experience loathing for "*p*," and (b) the conditions under which *S* says what she means and thereby takes on a warranty for the consistency of her further behavior with this avowal. A hearer understands (4) if he knows (a) the conditions that would make the prediction true, and (b) the conditions under which *S* could have convincing reasons for holding a statement with the content (a) to be true.

Of course, there are also important asymmetries. Thus the conditions mentioned under (a) do *not*, in the cases of expressive and constative speech acts like (3) and (4), have to do with obligations to act in a certain way resulting from the intersubjective recognition of the validity claims in question; they relate only to understanding the propositional content of a first-person sentence or an assertoric sentence for which the speaker claims validity. In the case of regulative speech acts like (1) and (2), the conditions (a) likewise relate to understanding the propositional content of an intention or imperative sentence for which the speaker produces or claims normative validity; but here the content *simultaneously* circumscribes the obligations relevant for the sequel of interaction that arise for the hearer from acceptance of the validity claim.

In general, obligations to act in a certain way result from the meaning of expressive speech acts only in the sense that the speaker specifies actions with which her behavior may not be inconsistent. That a speaker means what she says can be made credible only in the consistency of what she does and not through providing reasons. Thus, addressees who have accepted a claim to truthfulness can expect a consistency of behavior in certain respects; however, this expectation follows from the conditions given under (b). Of course, consequences also arise from the warranties offered with the validity claims in regulative and constative speech acts, but these *validity-related* obligations to provide, if necessary, justification for norms or grounding for propositions have relevance for action only on a metacommunicative level. Only those obligations to prove trustworthy (*Bewährungsverpflichtungen*) that the speaker takes on with expressive speech acts have direct relevance for the continuation of interaction. They contain an offer to the hearer to check against the consistency of the speaker's sequences of action whether she means what she says.[50]

In general, no *special* obligations to act in a certain way follow from the meaning of constative speech acts. Obligations relevant for the sequel of interaction arise from the satisfaction of the acceptability conditions stated under (a) and (b) only insofar as speaker and hearer obligate themselves to base their action on interpretations of situations that do not contradict the statements accepted as true.

We have distinguished genuine (or simple) imperatives, with which the speaker connects a claim to power, from speech acts with which the speaker raises a criticizable validity claim. Whereas validity claims are internally connected with reasons and accord a rationally motivating force to the illocutionary role, power claims have to be covered by a reservoir of potential sanctions if they are to be capable of being carried through. However, imperatives admit of a *secondary normativization*. This can be illustrated by the relation that holds between intentional sentences and declarations of intention. Intentional sentences belong in the same category as the imperative sentences with which imperatives are formed. We can interpret intentional sentences as internalized imperatives addressed by the speaker to herself.[51] Of course, imperatives are illocutionary acts, whereas intentional sentences acquire an illocutionary role only through being transformed into declarations of intention or *announcements.* Whereas imperatives have in themselves an illocutionary force—albeit one that calls for supplementation by sanctions—intentional sentences, which have, so to speak, lost their imperative force *in foro interno,* can regain an illocutionary force through being connected with validity claims, whether in the form of expressive speech acts like

(7) I confess to you that it is my intention to . . .

or in the form of normative speech acts like

(8) I (hereby) declare to you my intention to . . .

With announcements like (8) the speaker enters into a weak normative binding and bonding relationship to which the addressee can appeal in a similar way as to a promise.

The normativization of intentional sentences can serve as a model for grasping the transformation of simple imperatives into normatively authorized imperatives, or of sheer imperatives into commands. The imperative (5), by being boosted with a normative validity claim, can be transformed into the directive (6). With this, the component of the acceptability conditions given under (b) changes; the conditions of sanction supplementing the imperative power claim are replaced by the rationally motivating conditions for accepting a criticizable validity claim. Because these conditions can be derived from the illocutionary role itself, normatively authorized imperatives gain an autonomy that is missing from simple imperatives.

This makes it clear once again that only those speech acts with which a speaker connects a criticizable validity claim can, by virtue of their own power and owing to the validity basis of linguistic communication oriented toward reaching understanding, motivate a hearer to accept a speech-act offer, and thereby become effective as a mechanism for coordinating action.[52]

Following these reflections, the concept of communicative action, which we have introduced in a provisional way, now needs to be rendered more precise. We began by including in communicative action all interactions in which those involved coordinate their individual plans unreservedly on the basis of communicatively achieved agreement. With the specification "unreservedly pursuing illocutionary aims," we meant to exclude cases of latently strategic action, in which the speaker *inconspicuously* employs successful illocutionary acts for perlocutionary purposes. However, imperative expressions of will are illocutionary acts with which the speaker *openly* declares her aim of influencing the decisions of her opposite number, whereby she has to rely for the success of her power claim on supplementary sanctions. For this reason, with genuine imperatives or nonnormatively authorized imperatives, speakers can unreservedly pursue illocutionary aims and nonetheless act strategically.

Not all speech acts are constitutive for communicative action, but only those with which the speaker connects criticizable validity claims. In the other cases, when a speaker is pursuing undeclared aims with perlocutionary acts, aims with regard to which the hearer can take no position at all, or when a speaker is pursuing illocutionary aims regarding which the hearer cannot take a *grounded* position, as in relation to imperatives, the potential for a binding and bonding relationship motivated by insight into reasons—a potential that is always contained in linguistic communication—remains unexploited.

Validity Claims

Having distinguished communicative actions from all other social actions through their illocutionary binding and bonding effect, it makes sense to order the multiplicity of communicative acts according to types of speech acts. And to guide our classifying of speech acts we may use the options open to a hearer of taking a rationally motivated "yes" or "no" position on the utterance of a speaker. In our previous examples, we have assumed that the speaker raises precisely one validity claim with her utterance. With the promise (1), she connects a validity claim for a declared intention; with the directive (2), a validity claim for an imperative; with the avowal (3), a validity claim for the expression of a feeling; and with the prediction (4), a validity claim for a statement. Correspondingly, with a "no" response, the addressee contests the rightness of (1) and (2), the truthfulness of (3), and the truth of (4). This picture is incomplete, however, inasmuch as every speech act can be contested (that is, rejected as invalid) under more than one aspect.

Let us assume that a seminar participant understands the following imperative addressed to him by the professor

(9)   Please bring me a glass of water.

not as a naked imperative expression of will but as a speech act carried out in an attitude oriented toward reaching understanding. Then he can in principle reject this request under three validity aspects. He can either contest the normative rightness of the utterance:

(9′)   No. You can't treat me like one of your employees.

or he can contest the subjective truthfulness of the utterance:

(9″)   No. You really only want to put me in a bad light in front of the other seminar participants.

or he can deny that certain existential presuppositions obtain:

(9‴)   No. The nearest water tap is so far away that I couldn't get back before the end of the session.

In the first case, what is contested is that the action of the professor is right in the given normative context; in the second, that the professor means what she says because she wants to achieve a certain perlocutionary effect; in the third, propositions are contested whose truth the professor has to presuppose in the given circumstances.

What we have shown in connection with this example holds true for *all* speech acts oriented toward reaching understanding. In contexts of communicative action, speech acts can always be rejected under *each* of three aspects: the aspect of the rightness that the speaker claims for her action in relation to a normative context (or, indirectly, for these norms themselves); the aspect of the truthfulness that the speaker claims for the expression of subjective experiences to which she has privileged access; and finally, the aspect of the truth that the speaker, with her utterance, claims for a statement (or for the existential presuppositions of the context of a nominalized proposition). This strong thesis can be tested against numerous cases and made plausible by reflections that take us back to Bühler's model of the functions of language.

The term "reaching understanding" ("*Verständigung*") means, at the minimum, that at least two subjects capable of speech and action understand a linguistic expression in an identical way. The meaning of an elementary expression consists in the contribution that it makes to the meaning of an acceptable speech act. And to understand what a speaker wants to say with such an act, the hearer has to know the conditions under which it can be accepted. To this extent, understanding (*Verständnis*) an elementary expression already points beyond the minimal meaning of the term *Verständigung*. When a hearer accepts a speech-act offer, an agreement (*Einverständnis*) comes about between (at least) two subjects capable of speech and action. However, this does not rest only on the intersubjective recognition of a single, thematically emphasized validity claim. Rather, an agreement of this sort is achieved simultaneously at three levels. These may easily be identified intuitively if we bear in mind that in communicative action a speaker selects a comprehensible linguistic expression only in order to reach an understanding *with* a hearer *about* something and thereby to make *herself* understood. It belongs to the communicative intent of the speaker (a) that she perform a speech act that is *right* in respect to the given normative context, so that an intersubjective relation that is recognized as legitimate may come about between her and the hearer; (b) that she express *truthfully* her beliefs, intentions, feelings, wishes, and the like, so that the hearer will give credence to what is said; and (c) that she make a *true* statement (or *correct* existential presuppositions), so that the hearer may accept and share the knowledge of the speaker. The fact that the intersubjective commonality of a communicatively achieved agreement exists at the levels of normative accord, mutual trust in subjective sincerity, and shared propositional knowledge can be explained in turn through the functions of reaching understanding in language.

As the medium for reaching understanding, speech acts serve (a) to establish and renew interpersonal relations, whereby the speaker takes up a relation to something in the world of legitimate orders; (b) to make manifest subjective experiences—that is, to represent oneself—whereby the speaker takes up a relation to something in the subjective world to which she has privileged access; and (c) to represent (or presuppose) states and events, whereby the speaker takes up a relation to something in the world of existing states of affairs. Communicatively achieved agreement is measured against precisely three criticizable validity claims, because actors, in coming to an understanding about something with one another and thereby making themselves understood, cannot avoid embedding each speech act in precisely three world-relations and claiming validity for it under each of these aspects. Someone who rejects a comprehensible speech act contests at least one of these validity claims. In rejecting a speech act as (normatively) wrong or untrue or untruthful, the hearer with his "no" gives expression to the fact that the utterance does not fulfill its functions of securing an interpersonal relationship, of manifesting subjective experiences, or of representing states of affairs—to the fact that it is not in agreement with *our* world of legitimately ordered interpersonal relations, or with the *speaker's* world of subjective experiences or with *the* world of existing states of affairs.

Although speech acts oriented toward reaching understanding are always involved in this way in a complex net of world-relations, the illocutionary role—under standard conditions, the meaning of the illocutionary component—determines the aspect of validity under which the speaker wants her utterance to be understood *first and foremost*. When she makes a statement, asserts, narrates, explains, represents, predicts, discusses something, and the like, she is seeking agreement with the hearer based on the recognition of a truth claim. When the speaker utters a first-person experiential sentence, discloses, reveals, confesses, manifests something, and the like, agreement can come about only on the basis of the recognition of a claim to truthfulness. When the speaker gives an order or makes a promise, appoints or warns somebody, baptizes or weds somebody, buys something, and the like, agreement depends on whether those involved accept the action as right. These basic modes appear in greater purity the more clearly reaching understanding is oriented toward only one dominant validity claim. Considerations of expediency suggest beginning analysis with idealized or *pure cases of speech acts*. I am thinking here of

- constative speech acts in which *elementary propositional (assertoric) sentences* are used;

- expressive speech acts in which *elementary experiential sentences* (in the first person present) appear; and of

- regulative speech acts in which either *elementary imperative sentences* (as in commands) or *elementary intentional sentences* (as in promises) appear.

In analytic philosophy there is an extensive literature on each of these complexes. Here, instruments have been developed and analyses carried out that make it possible to explain the universal validity claims toward which the speaker is oriented and to characterize more precisely the basic attitudes that the speaker thereby adopts. I am referring here to the *objectivating attitude* in which a neutral observer behaves toward something that happens in the world; to the *expressive attitude* in which a subject in representing himself reveals to a public something within him to which he has privileged access; and finally, to the *norm-conformative attitude* in which a member of social groups satisfies legitimate behavioral expectations. To each of these fundamental attitudes there corresponds a concept of "world."

Let Mp represent any explicit speech act, where "M" stands for the illocutionary component and "p" for the propositional component;[53] and let M_c designate the cognitive use of language, M_e the expressive, and M_r the regulative. We can then, on the basis of the aforementioned basic attitudes, distinguish intuitively the senses in which the speaker wants the propositional component of her speech act to be interpreted. In a valid utterance of the type $M_c p$, "p" signifies a state of affairs that *exists* in the objective world; in a valid utterance of the type $M_e p$, "p" signifies a subjective experience that is manifested and ascribed to the *internal world* of the speaker; and in a valid utterance of the type $M_r p$, "p" signifies an action that is recognized as legitimate in the social world.

This distinction among exactly three basic modes of using language with an orientation toward reaching understanding could be grounded only in the form of an elaborated theory of speech acts. I cannot carry out the necessary analyses here, but I would like to take up a few prima facie objections to the proposed program.

Leist has formulated my basic thesis as follows: "For all *S* and all *H*, in all speech acts that belong to action oriented toward reaching understanding and which are illocutionarily and propositionally differentiated and institutionally unbound, it is mutual knowledge that the speaker is required to speak intelligibly, to be truthful, to take his utterance as true, and a norm relevant to his act as right."[54] To begin with, this formulation requires the explanatory comment that, from the standpoint of the theory of interaction, I delimit speech acts "oriented toward reaching understanding" from speech acts that are incorporated into strategic action contexts, either because the latter, like genuine imperatives, are connected only with power claims and thus produce no illocutionary binding and bonding effect on their own, or because the speaker is pursuing perlocutionary aims with such utterances. Next, I would not use the expression "mutual knowledge," which comes from intentionalist semantics, but speak rather of "common suppositions." Furthermore, the term "required" suggests a normative sense; I would rather—despite the weak transcendental connotations—speak of "general conditions" that have to be satisfied if a communicative agreement is to be achieved. Finally, I find lacking here a hierarchical order between the well-formedness or comprehensibility of the linguistic expression as a presupposition of communication, on the one hand, and the claims to truthfulness, propositional truth, and normative rightness, on the other hand. The acceptance of these claims brings about an agreement between *S* and *H* that grounds obligations that are relevant for the sequel of interaction. I distinguish from these the warranty assumed by the speaker to redeem the validity claim he raises, as well as the reciprocal obligation that the hearer undertakes with the negation of a validity claim.

Reservations have been expressed mainly in regard to the assumptions (a) that with *every* speech act oriented toward reaching understanding *exactly three* validity claims are raised; (b) that the validity claims can be *adequately distinguished* from one another; and (c) that validity claims have to be analyzed in *formal-pragmatic terms,* that is, on the level of the communicative employment of sentences.

a. Can we maintain the universality of the claim to truth, even though we obviously cannot raise a truth claim with nonconstative speech acts?[55] It is certainly the case that we can raise the claim that an asserted proposition "*p*" is true only with constative speech acts. But all other speech acts also contain a propositional component, normally in the form of a nominalized propositional sentence "that *p.*" This means that the speaker also relates to states of affairs with nonconstative speech acts, not directly to be sure—that is, not in the propositional attitude of one who thinks or is of the opinion, knows, or believes that "*p*" is the case. The propositional attitudes of speakers who employ first-person experiential sentences in expressive speech acts and imperative or intentional sentences in regulative speech acts are of another kind. They are in no way directed to the existence of the state of affairs mentioned in the propositional component. However, in saying with a nonconstative speech act that she desires or detests something, that she wants to bring about something or see it brought about, the speaker *presupposes* the existence of *other,* not mentioned, states of affairs. It belongs to the concept of an objective world that states of affairs are located in a nexus and do not hang isolated in the air. Therefore, the speaker connects *existential presuppositions* with the propositional component of her speech act; if need be, these presuppositions can be rendered explicit in the form of assertoric sentences. To this extent, nonconstative speech acts, too, have a relation to truth.

Moreover, this holds not only for propositionally differentiated speech acts; illocutionarily abbreviated speech acts—for example, a "hello" uttered as a greeting—are understood as satisfying norms from which the propositional content of the speech act can be supplemented—for example, in the case of a greeting, the well-being of the addressee or the confirmation of his social status. The existential presuppositions of a greeting include, among other things, the presence of a person for whom things can go well or badly, his membership in a social group, and so forth.

The situation is somewhat different with regard to the universality of the claim to rightness. It may be objected that no relation to normative contexts can be inferred from the meaning of nonregulative speech acts.[56] However, communications are sometimes "inappropriate," reports "out of place," confessions "embarrassing," disclosures "hurtful." The fact that they can go wrong under this aspect is by no means extrinsic to nonregulative speech acts; rather it necessarily results from their character *as* speech acts. From their illocutionary component we can see that the speaker also enters into interpersonal relations with constative and expressive speech acts; and whether or not these relations fit the existing normative context in question, they belong to the world of legitimate (social) orders.

There have also been objections with respect to the completeness of the table of validity claims. If one compares this with the conversational postulates proposed by Grice,[57] for example, one finds not only certain parallels but also certain asymmetries. Thus, there is no counterpart to the postulate that the speaker should always make a contribution to the topic that is relevant in the context of the given conversation. Apart from the fact that such a claim to the relevance of a contribution to conversation is raised by the hearer and related to a text (rather than to an individual speech act)—that is, cannot be subjected to a "yes" or "no" test—the universality of such a requirement would be difficult to establish. There are obviously situations—informal social gatherings, for example, or even entire cultural milieus—in which a certain redundancy of contributions is nearly mandatory.[58]

b. Reservations have also been expressed with regard to the possibility of sharply discriminating between claims to truth and claims to truthfulness. Is it not the case that a speaker who truthfully utters the opinion "*p*" must simultaneously raise a truth claim for "*p*"? It appears to be impossible "to expect of *S* that he is speaking the truth in any other sense than that *S* wants to speak the truth—and this means nothing else than to be truthful."[59] This objection is not relevant to the class of expressive speech acts in its entirety but only to those utterances in whose propositional component a cognition verb in the first person present (such as I think, know, believe, suspect, am of the opinion "that p") occurs. At the same time, there is also an internal relation between these propositional attitudes, which can be expressed by means of cognition verbs, and constative speech acts. When someone asserts or ascertains or describes "p," she simultaneously is of the opinion that, knows, or believes "that p." Moore already pointed out the paradoxical character of utterances like

(10+) It is raining now, but I don't believe that it is raining now.[60]

Despite these internal connections, however, a hearer can be rejecting two *different* validity claims with his rejection of

(10) It is raining now.

In taking a negative position, he can mean both

(10′) No, that isn't true.

and

(10″) No, you don't mean what you are saying.

In the first case, the hearer understands (10) as a constative utterance, in the second, as an expressive utterance. Obviously, the negation of the proposition "p" just as little implies the negation of the belief "that p" as, conversely, (10″) implies the negation of the position taken in (10′). To be sure, the hearer may suppose that *whenever* S asserts "p" she also believes "that p." But this does not affect the fact that the truth claim relates to the existence of the state of affairs "p," whereas the truthfulness claim has to do only with the manifestation of the opinion or the belief "that p." A murderer who makes a confession can mean what he says and yet, without intending to do so, be saying what is untrue. He can also, without intending to do so, speak the truth although, in concealing his knowledge of the facts of the case, he is lying. A judge who had sufficient evidence at her disposal could criticize the truthful utterance as untrue in the one case, and the true utterance as untruthful in the other.

As against this, Ernst Tugendhat tries to make do with a single validity claim.[61] He takes up the extended discussion connected with

Social Action, Purposive Activity, and Communication

Wittgenstein's private language argument in order to show that the same assertoric validity claim is connected with such first-person experiential sentences as

(11)   I am in pain.

(12)   I am afraid of being raped.

as with assertoric sentences with the same propositional content:

(13)   He is in pain.

(14)   She is afraid of being raped.

whereby the corresponding personal pronouns in the first and third person are supposed to have the same reference. If Tugendhat's assimiliation thesis is correct, the negation of (11) or (12) has the same sense as the negation of (13) or (14). It would be redundant to postulate a truthfulness claim alongside the claim to truth.

Following Wittgenstein, Tugendhat takes as his starting point an expressive gesture, the cry "ouch," and imagines that this linguistically rudimentary cry of pain is replaced by an expressive utterance represented at the semantic level by the experiential sentence (11). Wittgenstein denies to such experiential sentences the character of statements.[62] He assumes that a continuum exists between both non-cognitive forms of expressing pain, the gesture and the sentence. For Tugendhat, by contrast, the categorial difference consists in the fact that the experiential sentence can be false, but not the gesture. His analysis leads to the result that with the transformation of the cry into an experiential sentence with the same meaning, "an expression is produced that, although it is used according to the same rule as the cry, is true when it is used correctly; and thus there arises the singular case of assertoric sentences which can be true or false but which are nonetheless not cognitive."[63] For this reason, experiential sentences like (11) are *not* supposed to be distinguishable from assertoric sentences with the same propositional content like (13) on the basis of the criterion of whether or not they admit of truth. Both can be true or false. Of course, experiential sentences exhibit the peculiarity that they express an "incorrigible knowledge;" thus, whenever they are used according to the rules they *must* be true. Between the sentences (11) and (13) there exists a "verificatory symmetry," in the sense that (13) is true whenever (11) is used in conformity with the rules.

Tugendhat explains this connection through the special properties of the singular term "I," with which the speaker designates herself without at the same time thereby identifying herself. Even if his thesis is correct, however, this does not solve the problem of explaining how a sentence can have an assertoric character and thus admit of truth and yet not admit of being employed cognitively, that is, for representing existing states of affairs.

In general, the rules for employing assertoric sentences *indicate* a cognition; only in the case of expressive sentences is the correct employment of the linguistic expression also supposed to *guarantee* its truth. But a hearer who wants to ascertain whether a speaker is deceiving him with the sentence (11) has to *test* whether or not the sentence (13) is true. This shows that expressive sentences in the first person do not primarily serve the purpose of expressing cognitions, that at most they *derive* the truth claim ascribed to them from the corresponding assertoric sentences in the third person; for only the latter can *represent* the state of affairs to whose existence the truth claim refers. Thus Tugendhat falls into the dilemma of having to characterize in a contradictory way what a speaker means with experiential sentences. On the one hand, this is supposed to be a matter of knowledge for which the speaker claims validity in the sense of propositional truth; on the other hand, this knowledge cannot have the status of a cognition, for cognitions can be represented only in assertoric sentences that can in principle be contested as untrue. But this dilemma arises only if the validity claim to truthfulness—which is *analagous* to truth—is *identified with* the claim to truth. The dilemma dissolves as soon as one shifts from the semantic to the pragmatic level and compares speech acts rather than sentences. Consider

(15) I have to confess (to you) that I've been in pain for days.

(16) I can report (to you) that he's been in pain for days.

whereby the personal pronoun in the first person in (15) and the personal pronoun in the third person in (16) are to have the same reference. It becomes clear at a glance that if (15) is invalid, the speaker is deceiving the hearer, whereas if (16) is invalid, the speaker is telling the hearer something that is not true, although she need not intend to deceive him. Thus it is legitimate to postulate for expressive speech acts a *different* validity claim than for constative speech acts with the same meaning. Wittgenstein comes very close to this insight at one point in his *Philosophical Investigations,* where he is showing, in connection with the paradigm case of a confession, that expressive utterances do not have a descriptive sense—that is, do not admit of truth—and yet can *be valid or invalid.*

> The criteria for the truth of the *confession* that I thought such-and-such are not the criteria for a true *description* of a process. And the importance of the true confession does not reside in the fact that it is a reliable report of a certain process. It resides rather in the special consequences which can be drawn from a confession whose truth is guaranteed by the special criteria of *truthfulness.*[64]

c. With these arguments we have already touched upon the third group of objections, which is directed against a formal-pragmatic approach to the analysis of validity claims. These validity claims, following the model of legal claims, have to do with relations between persons and are oriented toward intersubjective recognition. They are raised for the validity of symbolic expressions, in the standard case for the validity of the sentence with propositional content that is dependent on an illocutionary component. It thus makes sense to regard a validity claim as a complex and derivative phenomenon that can be traced back to the underlying phenomenon of the satisfaction of conditions for the validity of sentences. But then should we not look for these conditions on the semantic level of analyzing assertoric, experiential, imperative, and intentional sentences, rather than on the pragmatic level of the employment of such sentences in constative, expressive, and regulative speech acts? Is not precisely a theory of speech acts, which hopes to explain the illocutionary binding and bonding effect through a warranty offered by the speaker for the validity of what she says, and through a corresponding rational motivation on the part of the hearer, dependent on a theory of meaning that explains for its part under what conditions the sentences employed are valid?

At issue in this debate are not questions of territorial boundaries or of nominal definitions but whether the *concept of the validity* of a sentence can be clarified independently of the *concept of redeeming the validity claim* raised through the utterance of the sentence. I am defending the thesis that this is not possible. Semantic investigations of descriptive, expressive, and normative sentences, if only they are carried through consistently enough, force us to change the level of analysis. The very analysis of the conditions for the validity of sentences *itself* compels us to analyze the conditions for the intersubjective recognition of corresponding validity claims. An example of this can be found in Dummett's development of truth-conditional semantics.[65]

Dummett starts from the distinction between the conditions that an assertoric sentence has to satisfy to be true and the knowledge that a speaker who asserts the sentence as true has of these truth conditions—conditions that at the same time determine the meaning of the sentence. Knowing the truth conditions consists in *knowing how one ascertains* whether or not they are satisfied in a given case. The orthodox version of truth-conditional semantics, which tries to explain understanding the meaning of a sentence in terms of knowing its truth conditions, is based on the unrealistic assumption that for every sentence, or at least for every assertoric sentence, procedures are available for effectively deciding whether or not its truth conditions are satisfied. This assumption rests tacitly on an empiricist theory of knowledge that ascribes a fundamental status to the simple predicative sentences of an observation language. But not even the argumentation game that Tugendhat postulates for verifying such seemingly elementary sentences consists in a decision procedure that could be applied like an algorithm, that is, in such a way that further demands for grounding are excluded in principle.[66] It is especially clear in the case of counterfactuals, universal existential sentences, and sentences with a temporal index—in general, any sentences referring to places and times that are actually inaccessible—that effective decision procedures are lacking. "The difficulty arises because natural language is full of sentences which are not effectively decidable, ones for which there exists no effective procedure for determining whether or not their truth conditions are fulfilled."[67]

Because knowing the truth conditions of assertoric sentences is problematic in many, if not in most cases, Dummett stresses the difference between knowing the conditions that make a sentence true and knowing the grounds that entitle a speaker to assert a sentence as true. Relying on basic assumptions of intuitionism, he goes on to reformulate the theory of meaning as follows: "[A]n understanding of a statement consists in a capacity to recognize whatever is counted as verifying it, i.e., as conclusively establishing it as true. It is not necessary that we should have any means of deciding the truth or falsity of the statement, only that we be capable of recognizing when its truth has been established."[68]

It is part of understanding a sentence that we are capable of recognizing *grounds* through which the *claim* that its truth conditions are satisfied *could be redeemed*. Thus, this theory explains the meaning of a sentence only indirectly through knowing the conditions of its validity, but directly through knowing grounds that are objectively available to a speaker for redeeming a truth claim.

Now a speaker might still produce such grounds according to a procedure that can be applied monologically; then even an explanation of truth conditions in terms of grounding a truth claim would not make it necessary to move from the semantic level of sentences to the pragmatic level of using sentences communicatively. Dummett stresses, however, that the speaker is by no means able to undertake the required verifications in a deductively compelling manner on the basis of rules of inference. The set of grounds available in any given instance is circumscribed by internal relations of a universe of linguistic structures that can be surveyed only argumentatively. Dummett pursues this idea so far that in the end he gives up entirely the basic idea of verificationism.

A verificationist theory comes as close as any plausible theory of meaning can do to explaining the meaning of a sentence in terms of the grounds on which it may be asserted; it must of course distinguish a speaker's actual grounds, which may not be conclusive, or may be indirect, from the kind of direct, conclusive grounds in terms of which the meaning is given, particularly for sentences, like those in the future tense, for which the speaker cannot have grounds of the latter kind at the time of utterance. But a falsificationist theory . . . links the content of an assertion with the commitment that a speaker undertakes in making that assertion; an assertion is a kind of gamble that the speaker will not be proved wrong.[69]

I see this as an indication of the fallibilistic character of the discursive vindication of validity claims. I cannot go into the details of Dummett's theory of meaning here. What is important is only that the illocutionary claim the speaker raises for the validity of a sentence be criticizable in principle. In any case, truth-conditional semantics in its revised form takes into consideration the fact that truth conditions cannot be explicated independently from knowing how to redeem a corresponding truth claim. To understand an assertion is to know when a speaker has good reasons to assume a warranty that the conditions for the truth of the asserted sentence are satisfied.

As in the case of the meaning of assertoric sentences, it can also be shown for expressive and normative sentences that semantic analysis pushes beyond itself. The discussion that has arisen from Wittgenstein's analysis of experiential sentences makes clear that the claim connected with expressions is genuinely addressed to *others*. The meaning of the expressive and declarative function already suggests a primarily communicative employment of such expressions.[70] The intersubjective character of the validity of norms is even clearer. Here, too, an analysis that starts with simple predicates for seemingly subjective emotional reactions to violations or impairments of personal integrity leads step-by-step to the intersubjective, indeed transsubjective, meaning of basic moral concepts.[71]

On the Classification of Speech Acts

If our thesis holds that the validity of speech acts oriented toward reaching understanding can be contested under precisely three universal aspects, we might conjecture that a system of validity claims also underlies the differentiation of types of speech acts. If so, the universality thesis would also have implications for attempts to classify speech acts from theoretical points of view. Thus far I have tacitly been dividing speech acts into three classes: regulative, expressive, and constative. I would now like to justify this classification by way of a critical examination of other classificatory schemes.

As is well known, at the end of his series of lectures on "How to Do Things with Words," Austin tried his hand at a typology of speech acts. He ordered illocutionary acts on the basis of performative verbs and distinguished five types (verdictives, exercitives, commissives, behabitives, and expositives), without denying the provisional character of this classification.[72] In fact, it is only for the class of commissives that Austin gives us a clear criterion of demarcation: with promises, threats, announcements, vows, contracts, and the like, the speaker commits himself to carrying out certain actions in the future. The speaker enters into a normative binding relationship that obliges him to act in a certain way. The remaining classes are not satisfactorily defined, even if one takes into account the descriptive character of the classification. They do not meet the requirements of distinctness and disjunctiveness;[73] Austin's classificatory scheme does not require us always to assign different phenomena to different categories nor to assign each phenomenon to at most one category.

The class of verdictives comprises utterances with which "judgments" or "verdicts"—in the sense of appraisals and assessments—are made. Austin does not distinguish here between judgments with descriptive content and those with normative content. Thus there is some overlap with both the expositives and the exercitives. The class of exercitives comprises, to begin with, all declaratives, that is expressions for institutionally—for the most part, legally—authorized decisions (such as sentencing, adopting, appointing, nominating, resigning, and so forth). There is overlap not only with verdictives (such as naming and awarding) but also with behabitives (such as protesting). These behabitives in turn form a class that is pretty heterogeneous in composition. In addition to verbs for standardized expressions of feeling (such as complaints and commiserations), it contains expressions for institutionally bound utterances (congratulations, curses, toasts, expressions of welcome) as well as expressions for satisfactions (apologies, thanks, all sorts of making good). Finally, the class of expositives does not discriminate between constatives, which serve to represent states of affairs, and communicatives, which (like asking, replying, addressing, citing, and so forth) refer to speech itself. Also to be distinguished from these are the expressions with which we designate the execution of operations (such as deducing, identifying, calculating, classifying, and the like).

Searle has attempted to sharpen Austin's classification.[74] He no longer orients himself toward a list of performative verbs differentiated within a specific language, but toward the illocutionary intentions or aims that speakers pursue with various types of speech acts, independently of the forms in which they are realized in individual languages. He arrives at a clear and intuitively convincing classification of speech acts: assertive (or constative), commissive, directive, declarative, and expressive. To start with, Searle introduces assertive (constative, representative) speech acts as a well defined class. From Austin he further takes over the class of commissives and contrasts these with the directives. Whereas with the former the speaker commits herself to an action, with the latter she tries to motivate the hearer to carry out a certain action. Among the directives, Searle counts ordinances, requests, instructions, imperatives, invitations, as well as questions and entreaties. Here, he does not discriminate between normatively authorized imperatives—such as petitions, reprimands, commands, and the like—and simple imperatives, that is, nonauthorized expressions of will. For this reason, the delimitation of directives from declaratives is also not very sharp. It is true that for declarative utterances particular institutions are required to secure the normative obligatory character of, for instance, appointing, abdicating, declaring war, and giving notice; but their normative meaning is similar to that of commands and directives. The last class comprises expressive speech acts. These are defined by their aim— namely, that with them, the speaker sincerely brings to expression her psychological attitudes. But Searle is uncertain in his application of this criterion; thus, the exemplary cases of avowals, disclosures, and revelations are missing. Apologies and expressions of joy and sympathy are mentioned. Evidently, Searle has allowed himself to be led astray by Austin's characterization of behabitives and has tacked onto this class institutionally bound speech acts like congratulations and greetings as well.

Social Action, Purposive Activity, and Communication

Searle's sharpened version of Austin's speech-act typology marks the starting point of a discussion that has developed in two different directions. The first is characterized by Searle's own efforts to provide an ontological grounding for the five types of speech acts; the other is determined by the attempt to develop the classification of speech acts from the standpoint of empirical pragmatics so as to make it fruitful for the analysis of speech-act sequences in everyday communication.

It is along this latter path that we find the work of linguists and sociolinguists such as Wunderlich, Campbell, and Kreckel.[75] For empirical pragmatics, social life-contexts present themselves as communicative actions that intermesh in social spaces and historical times. The patterns of illocutionary forces realized in particular languages reflect the structure of these networks of actions. The linguistic possibilities for performing illocutionary acts—whether in the fixed form of grammatical modes or in the more flexible forms of performative verbs, sentence particles, sentence intonations, and the like—provide schemata for establishing interpersonal relations. The illocutionary forces constitute the knots in the network of communicative socialization (*Vergesellschaftung*); the illocutionary lexicon is, as it were, the sectional plane on which the language and the institutional order of a society interpenetrate. This societal infrastructure of language is itself in flux; it varies in dependence on institutions and forms of life. But these variations *also* embody a linguistic creativity that gives new forms of expression to the innovative mastery of unforeseen situations.[76]

Indicators that relate to general dimensions of the speech situation are important for a pragmatic classification of speech acts. With regard to the *temporal dimension* there is the question of whether participants are oriented more toward the future, the past, or the present, or whether the speech acts are temporally neutral. With regard to the *social dimension* there is the question of whether obligations relevant for the sequel of interaction arise for the speaker, the hearer, or for both parties. And with regard to the *dimension of objectivity (die sachliche Dimension)* there is the question of whether the thematic emphasis lies more on the objects, the actions, or the actors themselves. Kreckel uses these indicators to propose a classification on which she bases her analyses of everyday communication (see table 2.4).

Certainly, the advantage of this and similar classifications consists in the fact that they provide us with a guideline for ethnolinguistic and sociolinguistic descriptive systems; they are better able to cope with the complexities of natural settings than are typologies that start from illocutionary intentions and aims rather than from features of situations. But they pay for this advantage by relinquishing the intuitively evident character of classifications that link up with semantic analyses and take account of the elementary functions of language (such as the representation of states of affairs, the expression of experiences, and the establishment of interpersonal relations). The classes of speech acts that are arrived at inductively and constructed in accordance with pragmatic indicators do not consolidate into intuitively evident types; they lack the theoretical power to illuminate our intuitions.

Searle makes the move toward a *theoretically motivated typology of speech acts* by giving an ontological characterization of the illocutionary intentions and the propositional attitudes that a speaker pursues or adopts when she performs assertive (constative), directive, commissive, declarative, and expressive speech acts. In doing so, he draws upon the familiar model that defines the world as the totality of existing states of affairs, sets up the speaker/actor as an authority outside of this world, and allows for precisely two linguistically mediated relations between actor and world: the cognitive relation of ascertaining facts, and the interventionist relation of realizing a goal of action. The illocutionary intentions may then be characterized in terms of the direction in which sentences and facts are supposed to be brought into accord. The arrow pointing downwards ($\downarrow$) says that the sentences are supposed to fit the facts; the arrow pointing upwards ($\uparrow$) says that the facts are to be fitted to the sentences. Thus, the assertoric force of constative speech acts and the imperative force of directive speech acts appear as follows:

Constative $\vdash$ $\downarrow C(p)$

Directive ! $\uparrow I(H$ brings about $p)$

Social Action, Purposive Activity, and Communication

Table 2.4
Classification according to three paradigmatic indicators

	Speaker (S)	Hearer (H)
Present	*Cognition oriented (C)* Does the speaker indicate that he has taken up the hearer's message? Examples: agreeing acknowledging, rejecting	*Cognition oriented (C)* Does the speaker try to influence the hearer's view of the world? Examples: asserting, arguing, declaring
Past	*Person oriented (P)* Does the speaker refer to himself and/or his past action? Examples: justifying, defending, lamenting	*Person oriented (P)* Does the speaker refer to the person of the hearer and/or his past action? Examples: accusing, criticizing, teasing
Future	*Action oriented (A)* Does the speaker commit himself to future action? Examples: promising, refusing, giving in	*Action oriented (A)* Does the speaker try to make the hearer do something? Examples: advising, challenging, ordering

Source: M. Kreckel, *Communicative Acts and Shared Knowledge in Natural Discourse* (London, 1981), p. 188.

whereby C stands for cognitions or the propositional attitudes of thinking, being of the opinion, believing, and the like, and I stands for intentions or the propositional attitudes of wanting, wishing, intending, and the like. The assertoric force signifies that S raises a truth claim for "p" vis-à-vis H; that is, she assumes a warranty for the agreement of the assertoric sentence with the facts ($\downarrow$); the imperative force signifies that S raises a power claim vis-à-vis H for seeing to it that "H brings about 'p,'" that is, she assumes a warranty for having the facts brought into agreement with the imperative sentence ($\uparrow$). In describing illocutionary forces by means of the relation between language and the world, Searle has recourse to conditions for the validity of assertoric and imperative sentences. He finds his theoretical standpoint for classifying speech acts in the *dimension of validity.*

But he restricts himself to the perspective of the speaker and disregards the dynamics of the negotiation and intersubjective recognition of validity claims—that is, *consensus-formation*. The model of two linguistically mediated relations between a solitary actor and the one objective world has no place for the intersubjective relation between participants in communication who come to an understanding with one another about something in the world. When worked out, Searle's ontological conception proves to be too narrow.

The commissive speech acts seem at first to fit easily into the model. With a speech act of this type, S assumes a warranty vis-à-vis H for bringing the facts into agreement with the intentional sentence uttered ($\uparrow$):

Commissive C′ $\uparrow$I(S brings about p)

However, in analyzing the use of intentional sentences in announcements, we saw that the illocutionary force of commissive speech acts cannot be explained through the conditions of satisfaction for the announced intention to act in a certain way. It is only the latter that is meant by ($\uparrow$). Rather, with commissive speech acts, the speaker *binds* her will in the sense of a *normative obligation;* and the conditions for the *reliability of a declaration* of intention are of quite a different sort than the conditions that the speaker satisfies when she, as an actor, realizes her intention. Searle would have to distinguish conditions of validity from conditions of success.

In a similar way, we distinguished normatively authorized imperatives such as directives, commands, ordinances, and the like from sheer imperatives; with the former the speaker raises a normative validity claim, with the latter an externally sanctioned claim to power. For this reason, not even the imperative sense of simple imperatives can be explained through the conditions for satisfying the imperative sentences employed therein. Even if that were sufficient, Searle would have difficulty restricting the class of directives to the class of genuine imperatives and demarcating the former from directives and commands, since his model does not allow for conditions for the validity (or for the satisfaction) of norms. This lack is especially noticeable when Searle tries to accommodate declarative speech acts in his system.

It is evident that the illocutionary force of a declaration of war, a resignation, the opening of a session, the reading of a bill, or the like cannot be interpreted according to the scheme of two directions of fit. In producing institutional facts, a speaker does not at all refer to something in the objective world; rather he acts in accordance with the legitimate orders of the social world and at the same time initiates new interpersonal relations. It is purely out of embarrassment that Searle symbolizes this meaning, which belongs to *another* world, by a double arrow coined in respect to the objective world:

declarative $\quad$ D$\updownarrow$(p)

whereby no special propositional attitudes are supposed to be required. This embarrassment recurs once again in the case of expressive speech acts, whose illocutionary force can just as little be characterized in terms of an actor's relations to the world of existing states of affairs. Searle is consistent enough to give expression to the inapplicability of his scheme through a neither/nor sign:

expressive speech acts $\quad$ E $\varnothing$ (p)

whereby any propositional attitude at all is possible.

We can avoid the difficulties of Searle's attempt at classification, while retaining his fruitful theoretical approach, if we start from the fact that the illocutionary aims of speech acts are achieved through the intersubjective recognition of claims to power and validity, and if we further introduce normative rightness and subjective truthfulness as validity claims analogous to truth and interpret them too in terms of actor/world relations.

This revision yields the following classification:

• With *imperatives* the speaker refers to a desired state in the objective world, and in such a way that he would like to get *H* to bring about this state. Imperatives can be criticized only from the standpoint of whether the action demanded can be carried out, that is, on the basis of conditions of success. However, rejecting imperatives normally means rejecting a claim to power; such rejection is not based on criticism but itself *expresses a will.*

• With *constative speech acts* the speaker refers to something in the objective world, and in such a way that he would like to represent a state of affairs. The negation of such an utterance means that *H* *contests* the claim to truth raised by *S* for the proposition asserted.

• With *regulative speech acts* the speaker refers to something in a common social world, and in such a way that he would like to establish an interpersonal relation recognized as legitimate. The negation of such an utterance means that *H* *contests* the normative rightness claimed by *S* for his action.

• With *expressive speech acts* the speaker refers to something in his subjective world, and in such a way that he would like to reveal to a public an experience to which he has privileged access. The negation of such an utterance means that *H* *doubts* the claim raised by *S* to the truthfulness of his self-representation.

Communicatives constitute a further class of speech acts. They can also be understood as that subclass of regulative speech acts—questioning and answering, addressing, objecting, admitting, and the like—that serve the *organization of speech,* its arrangement into topics and contributions, the distribution of conversational roles, the regulation of turn-taking in conversation, and the like.[77] But it makes more sense to regard the communicatives rather as an independent class and to define them through their *reflexive relation to the process of communication;* for then we can also include those speech acts that either refer directly to validity claims (affirming, denying, assuring, confirming, and the like) or that refer to how validity claims are dealt with argumentatively (grounding, justifying, refuting, supposing, proving, and the like).

Finally, there is the class of *operatives,* that is, speech acts—such as inferring, identifying, calculating, classifying, counting, predicating, and the like—that designate the application of constructive rules (of logic, grammar, mathematics, and the like). Operative speech acts have a performative sense but *no genuine communicative sense;* they serve simultaneously to *describe* what one does in constructing symbolic expressions in conformity with rules.[78]

If one takes this classification as basic, commissives and declaratives, as well as institutionally bound speech acts (betting, marrying, oath-taking) and satisfactives (which relate to excuses and apologies for violating norms, as well as to reparations), must all be subsumed under the same class of regulative speech acts. One can see from this that the basic modes are in need of further differentiation. They cannot be used for the analysis of everyday communication until we succeed in developing taxonomies for the *whole spectrum of illocutionary forces* differentiated in a particular language within the boundaries of a specific basic mode. Only very few illocutionary acts—like asserting and ascertaining, promising and commanding, confessing and disclosing—are so general that they can characterize a basic mode as such. Normally, the possibilities of expression standardized in particular languages characterize not only the relation in general to validity claims, but the *way* in which a speaker lays claim to truth, rightness, or truthfulness for a symbolic expression. Pragmatic indicators—such as the degree of institutional dependence of speech acts, the orientation toward past and future, the speaker/hearer orientation, the thematic focus, and so forth—can henceforth help us to grasp systematically the *illocutionary modifications of validity claims*. Only an empirical pragmatics that is theoretically guided will be able to develop speech-act taxonomies that are informative, that is, neither blind nor empty.

However, the pure types of language use oriented toward reaching understanding are suitable as guidelines for constructing typologies of linguistically mediated interaction. In communicative action, the plans of action of individual participants are coordinated by means of the illocutionary binding and bonding effects of speech acts. For this reason, we might conjecture that constative, regulative, and expressive speech acts also constitute corresponding types of linguistically mediated interaction. This is obviously true of regulative and expressive speech acts, which are constitutive for normatively regulated and dramaturgical action, respectively. At first glance there seems to be no type of interaction that would correspond in a similar way to constative speech acts. However, there are contexts of action that do not primarily serve the purpose of carrying out communicatively harmonized plans of action (that is, purposive activities) but themselves make communication possible and stabilize it—for instance, chatting, conversing, and arguing—in general, conversation that in a certain context becomes an end in itself. In such cases, the process of reaching understanding is detached from the instrumental role of serving as a mechanism for coordinating action, and the communicative negotiation of topics gains independence and becomes the purpose of the conversation. I shall speak of "conversation" whenever the weight is shifted in this way from purposive activity to communication; argumentation is perhaps the most important special case of conversation. As interest in the topics negotiated is predominant here, we could perhaps say that constative speech acts have constitutive significance for conversations.

Thus our classification of speech acts can serve to introduce three pure types—or better, *limit cases*—of communicative action: conversation, normatively regulated action, and dramaturgical action. If we further take into account the internal relations between strategic action and perlocutionary acts or imperatives, we arrive at the classification of linguistically mediated interactions in table 2.5.

Formal and Empirical Pragmatics

Even if the program for a theory of speech acts that I have here merely outlined were carried out in detail, one might ask what would be gained for a useful sociological theory of action by such a formal-pragmatic approach. The question arises, at least, why would not an empirical-pragmatic approach be better for this, an approach that did not dwell on the rational reconstruction of isolated, highly idealized speech acts but started at once with everyday communicative practices. From the side of linguistics there are interesting contributions to the analysis of stories and texts,[79] from sociology contributions to conversational analysis,[80] from anthropology contributions to the ethnography of speaking,[81] and from psychology investigations into the pragmatic variables of linguistic interaction.[82] By comparison, formal pragmatics—which, in its reconstructive intention (that is, in the sense of a theory of competence) is directed to the conditions under which reaching understanding is possible[83]—seems to be hopelessly removed from actual language use.[84] Under these circumstances, does it make any sense to insist on a formal-pragmatic grounding for a theory of communicative action?

I would like to respond to this question by first (a) enumerating the methodological steps through which formal pragmatics can be

Social Action, Purposive Activity, and Communication

Table 2.5
Pure Types of Linguistically Mediated Interaction

| Type of action | Formal-pragmatic features | | | | | |
	Characteristic speech acts	Functions of speech	Action orientations	Basic attitudes	Validity claims	World relations
Strategic action	Perlocutions, imperatives	Influencing one's opposite number	Oriented toward success	Objectivating	(Effectiveness)	Objective world
Conversation	Constatives	Representation of states of affairs	Oriented toward reaching understanding	Objectivating	Truth	Objective world
Normatively regulated action	Regulatives	Establishment of interpersonal relations	Oriented toward reaching understanding	Norm-conformative	Rightness	Social world
Dramaturgical action	Expressives	Self-representation	Oriented toward reaching understanding	Expressive	Truthfulness	Subjective world

connected up with empirical pragmatics; then I shall (b) identify the problems that make it necessary to clarify the rational foundations of processes of reaching understanding; finally, I would like (c) to take up a strategically important argument, concerning which formal pragmatics has to learn from empirical pragmatics if it is to avoid locating the problem of rationality in the wrong place—that is, not in action-orientations, as is suggested by Weber's theory of action, but rather in the general structures of the lifeworlds to which acting subjects belong.

a. The pure types of linguistically mediated interaction can step by step be brought closer to the complexity of natural situations without sacrificing theoretical perspectives for analyzing the coordination of action. This task consists in reversing in a controlled manner the strong idealizations to which we owe the concept of communicative action:

• In addition to the basic modes, we admit the multiplicity of the concretely shaped illocutionary forces that form the culture-specific network of possible interpersonal relations standardized in each individual language.

• In addition to the standard form of speech acts, we admit other forms of the linguistic realization of speech acts.

• In addition to explicit speech acts, we admit elliptically foreshortened, extraverbally supplemented, implicit utterances, the understanding of which is dependent upon the hearer's knowledge of nonstandardized, contingent contextual conditions.

• In addition to direct speech acts, we admit indirect, nonliteral, and ambiguous utterances, the meaning of which has to be inferred from the context.

• The focus is enlarged from isolated speech acts (and "yes" or "no" responses) to sequences of speech acts, to texts, or to conversations, so that conversational implications can come into view.

• In addition to the objectivating, norm-conformative, and expressive basic attitudes, we admit an overarching performative attitude to take account of the fact that with every speech act participants in communication relate simultaneously to something in the objective, social, and subjective worlds.[85]

• In addition to the level of processes of reaching understanding (that is, speech), we bring in the level of communicative action (that is, the coordination through agreement of the plans of action of individual participants).

• Finally, in addition to communicative action, we include in our analysis the resources of the background knowledge (that is, life-worlds) from which participants nourish their interpretations.

These extensions amount to dropping the methodological provisions that we intended initially with the introduction of standard speech acts. In the standard case, the literal meaning of the sentences uttered coincides with what the speaker means (*meint*) with her speech act.[86] However, the more that which the speaker means with her utterance is made to depend on a background knowledge that remains implicit, the more the context-specific meaning of the utterance can diverge from the literal meaning of what is said.

When one drops the idealization of a complete and literal representation of the meaning of utterances, the resolution of another problem is also made easier—namely, distinguishing and identifying in natural situations between actions oriented toward reaching understanding and actions oriented toward success. Here we must take into consideration that not only do illocutions occur in contexts of strategic action but perlocutions appear in contexts of communicative action as well. Cooperative interpretive processes run through different phases. As a rule, their initial phase is defined by the fact that the participants' interpretations of the situation do not overlap sufficiently for the purpose of coordinating actions. In this phase, participants have either to shift to the level of metacommunication or to employ means of indirectly coming to an understanding. Reaching understanding indirectly proceeds according to the model of intentionalist semantics: through perlocutionary effects the speaker gives the hearer to understand something that she cannot (yet) communicate directly. In this phase, then, perlocutionary acts have to be embedded in contexts of communicative action. These *strategic elements within a use of language oriented toward reaching understanding* can nonetheless be distinguished from *strategic actions* through the fact that the entire sequence of a segment of speech stands—on the part of all participants—under the presuppositions of the use of language oriented toward reaching understanding.

b. An empirical pragmatics that did not ensure for itself a formal-pragmatic point of departure would not have at its disposal the conceptual instruments needed to recognize the rational bases of linguistic communication in the confusing complexity of the every-day scenes observed. It is only in formal-pragmatic investigations that we can secure for ourselves an idea of reaching understanding that can guide empirical analysis into challenging problems—such as the linguistic representation of different levels of society, the manifestations of communication pathologies, or the development of a decentered understanding of the world.

The linguistic *demarcation of the levels of reality* of "play" and "seriousness," the linguistic construction of a fictitious reality, wit and irony, nonliteral and paradoxical uses of language, puns and allusions, and the contradictory withdrawal of validity claims at a metacommunicative level—all these accomplishments rest on intentionally confusing modalities of existence. For the clarification of the mechanisms of deception that a speaker has to master in order to do this, formal pragmatics can contribute more than even the most precise empirical description of the phenomena to be explained. With training in the basic modes of language use, the growing child gains the ability to demarcate by himself the subjectivity of his own experiences from the objectivity of objectified reality, from the normativity of society, and from the intersubjectivity of the medium of language. In learning to deal hypothetically with the corresponding validity claims, he practices drawing the categorial distinctions between essence and appearance, existence and illusion, "is" and "ought," sign and meaning. With these modalities of being, he himself gets a grip on the deceptive phenomena that initially spring from the involuntary confusion between his own subjectivity, on the one hand, and the domains of the objective, the normative, and the intersubjective, on the other. He now knows how one can master the confusions, produce de-differentiations intentionally, and employ them in fiction, wit, irony, and the like.[87]

The situation is similar with manifestations of *systematically distorted communication.* Here, too, formal pragmatics can contribute to the explanation of phenomena that are identified initially only on the basis of an intuitive understanding matured by clinical experience. Such communication pathologies can be conceived of as the result of a confusion between actions oriented toward reaching understanding and actions oriented toward success. In situations of latent strategic action, at least one of the parties behaves with an orientation toward success, but leaves others to believe that all the presuppositions of communicative action are satisfied. This is the case of manipulation that we mentioned in connection with perlocutionary acts. By contrast, the kind of unconscious dealing with conflicts that psychoanalysis explains in terms of defense mechanisms leads to disturbances of communication on both the intrapsychic and interpersonal levels simultaneously.[88] In such cases, at least one of the parties is deceiving herself about the fact that she is acting with an attitude oriented toward success and is merely keeping up the appearance of communicative action. The place of such systematically distorted communication within the framework of a theory of action can be seen below.

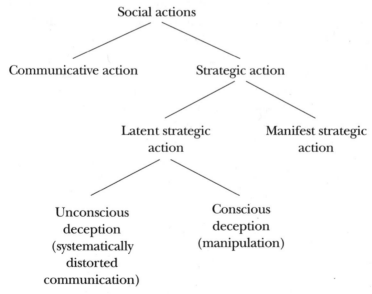

In the present context, the main advantage of a formal pragmatics is that it highlights, by means of the pure types of linguistically mediated interaction, precisely those aspects under which social actions embody different sorts of knowledge. The theory of communicative action can make good the weaknesses we found in Weber's action theory, to the extent that it does not remain fixated on purposive rationality as the only aspect under which action can be criticized and improved. Drawing on the types of action introduced above, I would now like to comment briefly on different aspects of the rationality of action.

Teleological actions can be judged under the aspect of effectiveness. The rules of action embody technically and strategically usable knowledge, which can be criticized through reference to truth claims and can be improved through a feedback relation to the growth of empirical-theoretical knowledge. This knowledge is stored in the form of technologies and strategies.

Constative speech acts, which not only embody knowledge but explicitly represent it and make conversations possible, can be criticized under the aspect of truth. In cases of more obstinate controversy concerning the truth of statements, theoretical discourse offers its services as a continuation, with different means, of action oriented toward reaching understanding. When discursive examination loses its ad hoc character and empirical knowledge is systematically called into question, when quasi-natural learning processes are guided through the sluice gates of argumentation, cumulative effects result. This knowledge is stored in the form of theories.

Normatively regulated actions embody moral-practical knowledge and can be contested under the aspect of rightness. Like claims to truth, controversial claims to rightness can be made thematic and examined discursively. In case of disturbance in the regulative use of language, practical discourse offers its services as a continuation, with other means, of consensual action. In moral-practical argumentation, participants can test both the rightness of a given action in relation to a given norm and, at the next level, the rightness of such a norm itself. This knowledge is handed down in the form of legal and moral ideas.

Dramaturgical actions embody a knowledge of the actor's own subjectivity. These expressions can be criticized as untruthful, that is, rejected as deceptions or self-deceptions. Self-deceptions can be dissolved in therapeutic dialogue by argumentative means. Expressive knowledge can be explicated in terms of those values that underlie interpretations of needs, and of desires and emotional attitudes. Value standards are dependent in turn on innovations in the domain of evaluative expressions. These are reflected in an exemplary manner in works of art. The aspects of the rationality of action are summarized in table 2.6.

c. This complex of action orientations, types of knowledge, and forms of argumentation is, of couse, inspired by Weber's idea that in European modernity, with the development of science, morality, and art, stores of explicit knowledge have been differentiated from one another. These flow into various domains of institutionalized everyday action and, so to speak, subject to the pressure of rationalization certain action orientations that had previously been determined in a traditionalist manner. The aspects of the rationality of action that can be read off from communicative action should now permit us to grasp processes of societal rationalization across their whole breadth, and no longer solely from the selective viewpoint of the institutionalization of purposive-rational action.

In posing the problem in this way, however, the *role of implicit knowledge* is not given its due. It remains unclear what the horizon of everyday action, into which the explicit knowledge of cultural ex-

Table 2.6
Aspects of the rationality of action

Type of action	Type of knowledge embodied	Form of argumentation	Model of transmitted knowledge
Teleological action: (instrumental, strategic)	Technically and strategically useful knowledge	Theoretical discourse	Technologies, strategies
Constative speech acts (conversation)	Empirical-theoretical knowledge	Theoretical discourse	Theories
Normatively regulated action	Moral-practical knowledge	Practical discourse	Legal and moral representations
Dramaturgical action	Aesthetic-practical knowledge	Therapeutic and aesthetic critique	Works of art

perts is injected, looks like, and how everyday communicative practices actually change with this influx. The concept of action oriented toward reaching understanding has the additional—and quite different—advantage of throwing light on this background of implicit knowledge that enters *a tergo* into cooperative processes of interpretation. Communicative action takes place within a lifeworld that remains at the backs of participants in communication. It is present to them only in the prereflective form of taken-for-granted background assumptions and naively mastered skills.

If the investigations of the last decade in socio-, ethno-, and psycholinguistics converge in any one respect, it is on the recognition—demonstrated in various ways—that the collective background knowledge and contextual knowledge of speakers and hearers determines the interpretation of their explicit utterances to an extraordinarily high degree. Searle has taken up this doctrine of empirical pragmatics. He criticizes the long-dominant view that sentences acquire *literal meaning* solely by virtue of the rules for using the expressions contained in them.[89] So far, I too have construed the meaning of speech acts as literal meaning in this sense. Certainly, literal meaning could not be conceived at all independently of contextual conditions; for each type of speech act there are *general* contextual conditions that must be met if the speaker is to be able to achieve illocutionary success. But these general contextual conditions are in turn supposed to be derivable from the literal meaning of the linguistic expressions employed in the standard speech acts. As a matter of fact, if formal pragmatics is not to lose its object, knowledge of the conditions under which a speech act may be accepted as valid cannot depend *completely* on contingent background knowledge.

However, Searle has shown—on the basis of simple assertions such as "The cat is on the mat" and imperatives such as "Give me a hamburger"—that the truth conditions and satisfaction conditions of the assertoric and imperative sentences employed therein cannot be specified independently of the context. Once we begin to vary relatively deep-seated and trivial background assumptions, we notice that the seemingly context-invariant validity conditions change their meaning and are thus by no means absolute. Searle does not go so far as to deny to sentences and utterances any literal meaning at all;

but he does defend the thesis that the literal meaning of an expression is relative to a background of variable implicit knowledge that participants normally regard as trivial and obvious.

The sense of this relativity thesis is not to reduce the meaning of a speech act to what a speaker means by it in a contingent context. Searle is not maintaining a simple relativism of the meaning of linguistic expressions; for their meaning in no way changes as we pass from one contingent context to the next. Rather, we discover the relativity of the literal meaning of an expression only through a sort of problematization that is not straightforwardly under our control. It emerges as a result of problems that occur objectively and have an unsettling effect on our natural worldview. This fundamental background knowledge, which must tacitly supplement our knowledge of the acceptability conditions of linguistically standardized utterances if hearers are to be able to understand their literal meanings, has remarkable features: It is an *implicit* knowledge that cannot be represented in a finite number of propositions; it is a *holistically structured* knowledge, the basic elements of which define one another; and it is a knowledge that *does not stand at our disposal,* to the extent that we cannot make it conscious and place it in doubt as we please. When philosophers nevertheless seek to do so, then that knowledge appears in the shape of commonsense certainties in which Moore, for instance, took an interest,[90] and to which Wittgenstein refers in his reflections *On Certainty.*

Wittgenstein calls these certainties elements of a worldview that are "anchored in all my *questions and answers,* so anchored that I cannot touch [them]."[91] Only those beliefs that do not fit such convictions—convictions that are as beyond question as they are fundamental—appear to be absurd. "Not that I could describe the system of these convictions. Yet my convictions do form a system, an edifice."[92] Wittgenstein characterizes the dogmatism of everyday background assumptions and skills in a way similar to that in which Schütz describes the mode of taken-for-grantedness in which the lifeworld is present as a prereflexive background: "The child learns to believe a host of things. I.e., it learns to act according to these beliefs. Bit by bit there forms a system of what is believed, and in that system some things stand unshakably fast and some or more are less liable to shift. What stands fast does so, not because it is intrinsically obvious or convincing; it is rather held fast by what lies around it."[93]

Literal meanings, then, are relative to a deep-seated, implicit knowledge, *about which* we normally know nothing because it is simply unproblematic and does not reach into the domain of communicative utterances that can be valid or invalid. "If the true is what is grounded, then the ground is not true, nor yet false."[94]

Searle uncovers this layer of worldview knowledge functioning in everyday life as the background with which a hearer has to be familiar if he is to understand the literal meaning of speech acts and to act communicatively. He thereby directs our gaze to a continent that remains hidden so long as the theoretician analyzes speech acts from the perspective of the speaker who relates with her utterances to something in the objective, social, and subjective worlds. It is only in turning back to the context-forming horizon of the lifeworld, from within which participants in communication come to an understanding with one another about something, that our field of vision changes in such a way that we can see the points of connection between the theory of action and social theory; the concept of society has to be linked up to a concept of the lifeworld that is complementary to the concept of communicative action. Then communicative action becomes interesting primarily as a principle of socialization (*Vergesellschaftung*); and at the same time, processes of societal rationalization acquire a different status. They take place primarily more within the implicitly known structures of the lifeworld than in explicitly known action orientations, as Weber suggested.

Notes

1. M. Brand and D. Walton, eds., *Action Theory* (Dordrecht, 1976); A. Beckermann, ed., *Analytische Handlungstheorie. Handlungserklärungen* (Frankfurt, 1977); G. Meggle, ed., *Analytische Handlungsbeschreibungen* (Frankfurt, 1977).

2. See J. Habermas, *The Theory of Communicative Action*, vol. 1, trans. T. McCarthy (Boston, 1984), pp. 96ff.

3. S. Kanngiesser, "Sprachliche Universalien und diachrone Prozesse," in K.-O. Apel, ed., *Sprachpragmatik und Philosophie* (Frankfurt, 1976), p. 278. See also T. Frentz and

Social Action, Purposive Activity, and Communication

T. Farrell, "Language Action. A Paradigm for Communication," *Quarterly Journal of Communication* 62 (1976): 333–334.

4. J. Heal, "Common Knowledge," *Philosophical Quarterly* 28 (1978): 116ff.; G. Meggle, ed., *Grundbegriffe der Kommunikation* (Berlin, 1981).

5. H. P. Grice, "Meaning," *Philosophical Review* 66 (1957): 377–388. See also "Utterer's Meaning, Sentence-Meaning and Word-Meaning," and "Utterer's Meaning and Intentions," both reprinted in H. P. Grice, *Studies in the Ways of Words* (Cambridge, Mass., 1989).

6. D. Lewis, *Conventions* (Cambridge, Mass., 1969).

7. S. R. Schiffer, *Meaning* (Oxford, 1972).

8. J. Bennett, *Linguistic Behaviour* (Cambridge, 1976).

9. Cf. J. Habermas, "Intentionalistische Semantik," in *Vorstudien und Ergänzungen zur Theorie des kommunikativen Handelns* (Frankfurt, 1984), pp. 307ff.; A. Leist, "Über einige Irrtümer der intentionalen Semantik," Linguistic Agency, University of Trier, Series A, Paper No. 51 (1978). On the critique of linguistic nominalism, see also K.-O. Apel, "Intentions, Conventions, and Reference to Things," in H. Parret and J. Bouveresse, eds., *Meaning and Understanding* (Berlin, 1981), and "Three Dimensions of Understanding and Meaning in Analytic Philosophy," *Philosophy and Social Criticism* 7 (1980): 115–142.

10. K. Bühler, *Sprachtheorie* (Jena, 1934).

11. Ibid., p. 28.

12. W. Busse, "Funktionen und Funktion der Sprache," in B. Schlieben-Lange, ed., *Sprachtheorie* (Hamburg, 1975), p. 207; G. Beck, *Sprechakte und Sprachfunktionen* (Tübingen, 1980).

13. R. Jakobson, "Linguistics and Poetics," in T. A. Sebeok, ed., *Style in Language* (New York, 1960), pp. 350–377.

14. P. Watzlawick, J. H. Beavin, and D. D. Jackson, *Pragmatics of Human Communication* (New York, 1962); H. Hörmann, *Psychologie der Sprache* (Heidelberg, 1967), and *Meinen und Verstehen* (Frankfurt, 1976).

15. K.-O. Apel, *Analytic Philosophy of Language and the Geisteswissenschaften* (Dordrecht, 1967); see also S. Davis, "Speech Acts, Performance and Competence," *Journal of Pragmatics* 3 (1979): 497ff.

16. J. Habermas, "What Is Universal Pragmatics?," chapter 1 in the present volume.

17. K.-O. Apel, "Zwei paradigmatische Antworten auf die Frage nach der Logosauszeichnung der Sprache," in *Festschrift für W. Perpeet* (Bonn, 1980).

18. See Habermas, *Theory of Communicative Action,* vol. 1, pp. 98ff.

19. L. Wittgenstein, *On Certainty,* trans. D. Paul and G. E. M. Anscombe (Oxford, 1969).

20. M. Weber, *Economy and Society,* G. Roth and C. Wittich, eds., 2 vols. (Berkeley, 1978), p. 4. Hereafter cited as *ES.*

21. M. Weber, "Some Categories of Interpretive Sociology," *Sociological Quarterly* 22 (1981): 151–180.

22. H. Girndt, *Das soziale Handeln als Grundkategorie der erfahrungswissenschaftlichen Soziologie* (Tübingen, 1967).

23. *ES,* p. 4.

24. *ES,* p. 26.

25. *ES,* pp. 24–25.

26. W. Schluchter, *Die Entwicklung des okzidentalen Rationalismus* (Tübingen, 1979), p. 192.

27. *ES,* p. 327.

28. *ES,* p. 326.

29. *ES,* pp. 26–36; pp. 319–333.

30. See note 21.

31. [Editor's note:] Habermas's introduction to his *Theory of Communicative Action,* vol. 1.

32. J. L. Austin, *How to Do Things with Words* (Oxford, 1962).

33. I shall leave aside the development that speech-act theory underwent in the hands of Austin himself [see "What Is Universal Pragmatics?," chapter 1 in the present volume] and take as my point of departure the interpretation that Searle has given to this theory. John Searle, *Speech Acts* (Cambridge, 1969); D. Wunderlich, *Studien zur Sprechakttheorie* (Frankfurt, 1976).

34. Austin, *How to Do Things with Words,* p. 101.

35. B. Schieben-Lange, *Linguistische Pragmatik* (Stuttgart, 1975), pp. 86ff.

36. D. S. Shwayder, *The Stratification of Behavior* (London, 1965), pp. 287ff.

37. M. Meyer, *Formale und handlungstheoretische Sprachbetrachtungen* (Stuttgart, 1976).

38. M. Schwab, *Redehandeln* (Königstein, 1980), pp. 28ff.

39. Austin, *How to Do Things with Words,* p. 118.

40. P. Strawson, "Intention and Convention in Speech Acts," *Philosophical Review* 73 (1964): 439ff.

Social Action, Purposive Activity, and Communication

41. Cf. Habermas, "What Is Universal Pragmatics?," chapter 1 in the present volume:

> With institutionally bound speech acts, specific institutions can always be specified. With institutionally unbound speech acts, only general contextual conditions . . . typically must be met for a corresponding act to succeed. . . . To explain what acts of betting or christening mean, I must refer to the institutions of betting or christening. By contrast, commands or advice or questions do not represent institutions but types of speech acts that can fit very different institutions. To be sure, the criterion of being institutionally bound does not always permit an unambiguous classification. Commands can exist wherever relations of authority are institutionalized; appointments presuppose special, bureaucratically developed organizations; and marriages require a single institution (which is, however, to be found universally). But this does not devalue the usefulness of the analytic viewpoint. Institutionally unbound speech acts, insofar as they have any regulative meaning at all, refer to general aspects of action norms; they are not, however, defined by particular institutions (pp. 60–61).

42. Cf. D. Wunderlich, "Zur Konventionalität von Sprechhandlungen," in D. Wunderlich, ed., *Linguistische Pragmatik* (Frankfurt, 1972), pp. 16–17; Here, Wunderlich also provides a linguistic characterization of speech acts in standard form.

43. Even the use theory of meaning stemming from the later work of Wittgenstein— see W. P. Alston, *The Philosophy of Language* (Englewood Cliffs, N.J., 1964); Ernst Tugendhat, *Traditional and Analytical Philosophy*, trans. P. A. Gorner (Cambridge, 1982)—remains fixated on the solitary employment of sentences. Like Frege's theory of meaning, it takes its orientation from the noncommunicative use of assertoric sentences *in foro interno;* it abstracts from the interpersonal relations between speakers and hearers who reach understanding with one another about something in the world with the aid of communicative acts. Tugendhat justifies this self-limitation of semantics with the argument that the communicative use of language is constitutive only for special linguistic expressions, in particular for the performative verbs and for the speech acts formed with them; in the areas essential to semantics, however, language can be employed in a monological train of thought. There is in fact an intuitively easily accessible distinction between thinking in propositions in abstraction from speaker–hearer relations and making interpersonal relations present in the imagination. In imagining stories in which the "I"—as imagining subject—accords itself a place in a context of interaction, the roles of participants in communication in the first, second, and third person—however internalized—remain constitutive for the sense of what is thought or represented. But solitary thinking in propositions is also discursive in more than a figurative sense. This becomes evident as soon as the validity, and thereby the assertoric force, of a proposition becomes problematic and the solitary thinker has to move from inferring to devising and weighing up hypotheses. He then finds it necessary to assume the argumentative roles of proponent and opponent as a communicative relation in his thought—as the daydreamer takes up the narrative structure of speaker–hearer relations when she recalls scenes from everyday life.

44. If, for example, a promise were to take the form

(1+) I promise you that I was in Hamburg yesterday.

one of the conditions of grammatical well-formedness would be violated. By contrast, if *S* uttered the correct sentence (1) in a situation in which it was presupposed that *H* could count on a visit from *S* in any case, one of the contextual conditions typically presupposed for promises would be violated.

45. Contributions to speech-act theory from philosophy and linguistics are chiefly concerned with analyzing these conditions. D. Wunderlich analyzes speech acts of the type "advising," from the theoretical perspective developed by Searle, in *Grundlagen der Linguistik* (Hamburg, 1974), pp. 349ff.

46. R. Bartsch, too, speaks in this sense of "acceptability conditions" in contrast to conditions of correctness or validity, in "Die Rolle von pragmatischen Korrektheitsbedingungen bei der Interpretation von Äußerungen," in G. Grewendorf, ed., *Sprechakttheorie und Semantik* (Frankfurt, 1979), pp. 217ff.

47. Surprisingly, Searle also comes close to this view of intentionalist semantics in *Speech Acts*, p. 66. Cf. Schiffer, *Meaning*.

48. Schwab, *Redehandeln*, p. 65.

49. In the case of commands or directives, principally for the addressee; in the case of promises or announcements, principally for the speaker; in the case of agreements or contracts, symmetrically for both parties; in the case of advice (with a normative content) or warnings, for both sides, but asymmetrically.

50. On these speech-act immanent obligations, see "What Is Universal Pragmatics?," chapter 1 in the present volume, pp. 85ff.

51. See J. Habermas, *The Theory of Communicative Action*, vol. 2, trans. T. McCarthy (Boston, 1987), pp. 31ff.

52. Because Schwab distinguishes neither between simple and normatively authorized imperatives—that is, between imperative and command—nor between monologically and communicatively employed intentional sentences—that is, between intentions and declarations of intention—he draws a mistaken parallel between imperatives and declarations of intention and distinguishes both from constative speech acts by virtue of the separation, and hierarchical ordering, of two types of success: success in the sense of validity and success in the sense of satisfaction. *Redehandeln*, pp. 72–73, 74ff., 95ff.

53. E. Stenius, "Mood and Language Game," *Synthese* 17 (1967): 254ff.; cf. D. Follesdal, "Comments on Stenius's 'Mood and Language Game,'" *Synthese* 17 (1967): 275ff.

54. A. Leist, "Was heißt Universalpragmatik?," *Germanistische Linguistik* 5/6 (1977): 93.

55. Ibid., pp. 97–98.

56. Ibid., p. 109.

57. H. P. Grice, "Logic and Conversation," in P. Cole and J. L. Morgan, eds., *Syntax and Semantics*, vol. 3 (New York, 1974), pp. 41ff.; A. P. Martinich, "Conversational Maxims and Some Philosophical Problems," *Philosophical Quarterly* 30 (1980): 215ff.

58. For other objections of this kind, see J. Thompson, "Universal Pragmatics," in J. Thompson and D. Held, eds., *Habermas: Critical Debates* (London, 1982), pp. 116–133.

59. Leist, "Was heißt Universalpragmatik?," p. 102; K. Graham, "Belief and the Limits of Irrationality," *Inquiry* 17 (1974): 315ff.

60. Searle refers to this argument in *Intentionality* (Cambridge, 1983), p. 9.

61. E. Tugendhat, *Self-Consciousness and Self-Determination*, trans. P. Stern (Cambridge, Mass., 1986), lectures 5 and 6.

62. L. Wittgenstein, *Zettel*, G. E. M. Anscombe and G. H. von Wright, eds. (Berkeley, 1970), §§404, 549.

63. Tugendhat, *Self-Consciousness and Self-Determination*, p. 114.

64. L. Wittgenstein, *Philosophical Investigations*, trans. G. E. M. Anscombe (London, 1958), p. 222. Cf. S. Hampshire, *Feeling and Expression* (London, 1961); B. Aune, "On the Complexity of Avowals," in M. Black, ed., *Philosophy in America* (London, 1965), pp. 35ff.; D. Gustafson, "The Natural Expression of Intention," *Philosophical Forum* 2 (1971): 299ff., and, "Expressions of Intentions," *Mind* 83 (1974): 321ff.; N. R. Norrick, "Expressive Illocutionary Acts," *Journal of Pragmatics* 2 (1978): 277ff.

65. M. Dummett, "What Is a Theory of Meaning?," in G. Evans and J. McDowell, eds., *Truth and Meaning* (Oxford, 1976), pp. 67ff.

66. Tugendhat, *Traditional and Analytical Philosophy*.

67. Dummett, "What Is a Theory of Meaning?," p. 81.

68. Ibid., pp. 110–111.

69. Ibid., p. 126.

70. P. M. S. Hacker, *Insight and Illusion (Oxford, 1972), chaps. 8 and 9.*

71. A convincing example of this is P. F. Strawson's analysis of the resentment called forth by moral violations, in *Freedom and Resentment* (London, 1974).

72. Austin, *How to Do Things with Words*, pp. 150ff.

73. One should not, however, make the requirements as strong as T. Ballmer does in "Probleme der Klassifikation von Sprechakten," in Grewendorf, ed., *Sprechakttheorie und Semantik*, pp. 247ff.

74. J. Searle, "A Taxonomy of Illocutionary Acts," in *Expression and Meaning*, pp. 1ff.

75. D. Wunderlich, "Skizze zu einer integrierten Theorie der grammatischen und pragmatischen Bedeutung," in *Studien zur Sprechakttheorie* (Frankfurt, 1976), pp. 51ff., "Was ist das für ein Sprechakt?," in Grewendorf, ed., *Sprechakttheorie und Semantik*, pp. 275ff., "Aspekte einer Theorie der Sprechhandlungen," in H. Lenk, ed., *Handlungstheorien*, vol. 3 (Munich, 1980), pp. 381ff.; B. G. Campbell, "Toward a Workable

Taxonomy of Illocutionary Forces and Its Implication to Works of Imaginative Literature," *Language and Style* 8 (1975): 3ff.; M. Kreckel, *Communicative Acts and Shared Knowledge in Natural Discourse* (London, 1981).

76. One measure of the flexibility of a society is the share of the totality of available illocutionary possibilities for linking up action that is made up by institutionally more-or-less bound, idiomatically fixed, ritualized speech acts. Thus Wunderlich distinguishes speech acts according to whether they depend more on action norms or on action situations (Wunderlich, "Skizze," pp. 86ff.). For this Campbell uses the dimensions "institutional vs. vernacular" and "positional vs. interactional" (Campbell, "Workable Taxonomy"). In this regard, the dimension "initiative vs. reactive" is also relevant (Wunderlich, "Skizze," pp. 59ff.).

77. On the speech acts that serve to organize speech, see E. Schegloff, G. Jefferson, and H. Sacks, "A Simplest Systematics for the Organization of Turn-Taking for Conversation," *Language* 50 (1974): 696ff., which draws on the work of Harvey Sacks; see also Wunderlich, *Studien zur Sprechakttheorie*, pp. 330ff.

78. The thesis that *S*, with an illocutionary act, informs the hearer of the execution of this act, or tells him that the act is being executed, could be applied most easily to this class of speech acts. For a critique of this thesis (which has been advanced by Lemmon, Hedenius, Wiggins, D. Lewis, Schiffer, Warnock, Cresswell, and others), see G. Grewendorf, "Haben explizit performative Äußerungen einen Wahrheitswert?," in Grewendorf, ed., *Sprechakttheorie*, pp. 175ff. It is, of course, wrong to assimilate operatives, which express the bringing about of constructive accomplishments, to constative speech acts. With the former, the speaker connects a claim not to propositional truth but to constructive well-formedness or intelligibility.

79. W. Kummer, *Grundlagen der Texttheorie* (Hamburg, 1975); M. A. K. Halliday, *System and Function in Language: Selected Papers* (Oxford, 1976); K. Bach and R. M. Hanisch, *Linguistic Communication and Speech Acts* (Cambridge, Mass., 1979).

80. M. Coulthard, *An Introduction into Discourse Analysis* (London, 1977); L. Churchill, *Questioning Strategies in Sociolinguistics* (Rowley, Mass., 1978); J. Schenken, ed., *Studies in the Organization of Conversational Interaction* (New York, 1978); S. Jacobs, "Recent Advances in Discourse Analysis," *Quarterly Journal of Speech* 66 (1980): 450ff.

81. D. Hymes, ed., *Language in Culture and Society* (New York, 1964) and "Models of the Interactions of Language and Social Life," in J. J. Gumperz and D. Hymes, eds., *Directions in Sociolinguistics* (New York, 1972), pp. 35ff.

82. R. Rommetveit, *On Message-Structure* (New York, 1974).

83. K.-O. Apel, "Sprechakttheorie und tranzendentale Sprachpragmatik," in Apel, ed., *Sprachpragmatik und Philosophie,* pp. 10ff.; Habermas, "What Is Universal Pragmatics?"

84. See the critical appraisal of the formal-pragmatic approaches of Allwood, Grice, and myself in Kreckel, *Communicative Acts,* pp. 14ff.

85. Classification into constative, regulative, and expressive speech acts means that in each case we attribute one dominant basic attitude to the speaker. In allowing for a performative attitude, we take account of the fact that complex processes of

Social Action, Purposive Activity, and Communication

reaching understanding can succeed only if each speaker undertakes a regulated—that is, rationally controlled—transition from one attitude (be it objectivating, norm-conformative, or expressive) to the others. Such transformations rely on intermodal invariances of validity. This area of the logic of speech acts has scarcely been studied. Why, for example, may we infer from the validity of an expressive speech act $M_e p$, the validity of a corresponding speech act of the form $M_c p$? If Peter truthfully confesses to loving Frances, we feel entitled to accept as true the assertion that Peter loves Frances. And if, conversely, the assertion that Peter loves Frances is true, we feel entitled to accept as truthful Peter's confession that he loves Frances. This transition could be justified according to the rules of propositional logic only if we could assimilate expressive to constative speech acts or (first person) experiential sentences to assertoric sentences. Since we cannot, we have to look for formal-pragmatic rules for the connections between such speech acts, which appear with the same propositional content in different modes. Table 2.7 is meant merely to illustrate which transitions we intuitively regard as permissable (+) and which not (–). These phenomena cannot be explained satisfactorily by the familiar modal logics. However, on the constructivist approach to a pragmatic logic, see C. F. Gethmann, ed., *Theorie des wissenschaftlichen Argumentierens* (Frankfurt, 1980), part 3, pp. 165–240; C. F. Gethmann, *Protologik* (Frankfurt, 1979).

86. This is the methodological meaning of Searle's "principle of expressibility"; cf. *Speech Acts*, pp. 87–88. Compare T. Binkley, "The Principle of Expressibility," *Philosophy and Phenomenological Research* 39 (1979): 307ff.

87. J. Habermas, "Universalpragmatische Hinweise auf das System der Ich-Abgrenzungen," in M. Auwärter, E. Kirsch, M. Schröter, eds., *Kommunikation, Interaktion, Identität* (Frankfurt, 1976), pp. 332ff., "Some Distinctions in Universal Pragmatics," *Theory and Society* 3 (1976): 155–167. See also the empirical study by M. Auwärter and E. Kirsch, "Die konversationelle Generierung von Situationsdefinitionen im Spiel 4-bis 6-jähriger Kinder," in W. Schulte, ed., *Soziologie in der Gesellschaft* (Bremen, 1981), pp. 584ff.

88. J. M. Ruskin, "An Evaluative Review of Family Interaction Research," *Family Process* 11 (1972): 365ff. J. H. Weakland, "The Double Bind Theory: A Reflexive Hindsight," *Family Process* 13 (1974): 269ff.; S. S. Kety, "From Rationalization to Reason," *American Journal of Psychiatry* 131 (1974): 957ff.; D. Reiss, "The Family and Schizophrenia," *American Journal of Psychiatry* 133 (1976): 181ff.

Table 2.7
Intermodal transfer of validity between speech acts with the same propositional content

From	To		
	Constative speech acts (truth)	Expressive speech acts (truthfulness)	Regulative speech acts (rightness)
Constative speech acts (truth)	x	+	–
Expressive speech acts (truthfulness)	+	x	–
Regulative speech acts (rightness)	–	+	x

89. J. Searle, "Literal meaning," in *Expression and Meaning,* pp. 117ff. See also R. D. Van Valin, "Meaning and Interpretation," *Journal of Pragmatics* 4 (1980): 213ff.

90. G. E. Moore, "Proof of an External World," *Proceedings of the British Academy* (London, 1939).

91. Wittgenstein, *On Certainty,* §103, p. 16.

92. Ibid., §102, p. 16 [amended translation].

93. Ibid., §144, p. 21.

94. Ibid., §205, p. 28.

3

Communicative Rationality and the Theories of Meaning and Action (1986)

On the Concept of Communicative Rationality

Charles Taylor's objections to my theory should be seen in the context of his own theory of language, which follows in the tradition of Wilhelm von Humboldt's work in the same area.[1] . . . [Taylor] reconstructs my conception of language accurately from the perspective of Humboldt's philosophy of language. The distinction between the structure of language (the linguistic structure or organism of language) and practices of language usage (the living process of speech)—in other words, Humboldt's distinction between language as *ergon* and as *energeia*—has, of course, been taken up by more recent theories of language (*langue* versus *parole*, linguistic competence vs. linguistic performance). In the process, however, language has been deprived of a decisive dimension: the intersubjectivity of possible mutual understanding (*Verständigung*). Unlike Humboldt,[2] neither Saussure nor Chomsky conceives of dialogue (*Gespräch*[3]) as the central point of language. Taylor correctly perceives that the theory of communicative action can be understood as an attempt to develop a theory of society from precisely this approach to the theory of language. Yet there is a tension in Humboldt's writings between the basic presuppositions with which he works, which are grounded in a theory of intersubjectivity, and the figures of thought in which these are couched, which are taken from the philosophy of the subject. My theory is drawn more toward the one pole, Taylor's more toward the other. This is the source of the controversy between us. Before proceeding further, therefore, a brief review of the issues involved is advisable.

Humboldt characterizes the status of the linguistic medium of reaching understanding (*Verständigung*) in a manner similar to Hegel's characterization of objective spirit. Language acts upon the speaking subject as an incisively molding and suprasubjective force without confronting her as something purely external—as is the case, for instance, with the contingent influence of nature. The structure of language maintains and renews itself solely through the linguistic community's practices of reaching understanding. The language system makes speech acts possible that, in turn, reproduce the language and, in so doing, make innovative changes in it, however imperceptible these may be.[4] Everything else depends on which model Humboldt adopts when conceiving of the mediating unity of the structure of language and speech practices. Is language as a whole a self-referential subject that holds together the living process of language by means of its synthesizing achievements, or is this synthesis accomplished solely in the forms taken by the fractured intersubjectivity of dialogue (*Gespräch*)? Humboldt did not completely relinquish the model of the self-referentiality of the active, knowing subject. His notion of language as an organism clearly still bears the Romantic traits of language as an expressive whole that externalizes its essential powers and assures itself of its creative subjectivity by contemplating these objectivations. Humboldt's conception of language appears simply to be a variation on Hegel's concept of the concrete universal: language as such relates to the multiplicity of national languages, and these in turn relate to concrete speech acts as the moments of the universal, the particular, and the individual in the processual web of relations of an individual totality.

On the other hand, Humboldt is *not* able to articulate in these basic concepts of the philosophy of consciousness the insight that was of paramount importance to him, both as the liberal philosopher of a bourgeois individualism and in his philosophy of language. For he is convinced

that the individuality of a language is only such by comparison, but that its true individuality resides only in the given speaker at a given time. Only in the individual does language attain its final determination. No one person thinks with a given word exactly what another person thinks, and this variation, no matter how slight it is, skitters through the entire language like concentric ripples over water. All understanding is thus simultaneously a nonunderstanding, all agreement in ideas and feelings is simultaneously a divergence. In the manner in which language is modified in each individual, there is revealed, in contrast to its previously expounded potency, the power of man over it.[5]

Of course, Humboldt is not an empiricist who robbed the process of reaching understanding of the rails on which it runs and allowed the identity of linguistic meanings to emanate from the intentions—arbitrarily iterated and reciprocally superseding one another—of isolated individual speakers. For him, the intersubjectivity of a common perspective does not dissolve, for example, into a series of isolated I-perspectives that are reflected merely in one another; rather it arises equiprimordially (*gleichursprünglich*) with the intersubjective validity of linguistic expressions that are identical in meaning. But Humboldt is no less adverse to understanding language as a totality that would have to prejudge the initiatives and "yes" or "no" positions of autonomous and unique subjects through a predetermined—fateful, as it were—preunderstanding. Humboldt wants to do justice to both aspects: first, to the at once unavoidable and counterfactual supposition that, in a given instance, all participants use the same expressions in a semantically identical way, for without this idealizing supposition they would not even be able to enter into a dialogue; and second, to the fact that the intentions of the speakers invariably deviate from the standard meanings of the expressions used and that this difference casts its shadow over every linguistically achieved agreement.

It is my impression that Taylor does not pay sufficient attention to this difference. Certainly, "I" and "We" perspectives are supposed to complement one another; but in Taylor's work the latter ends up taking precedence over the former. Taylor speaks of temporary breaches in a processually secured consensus, so that the breaks that have occurred would have to be sealed over by processes of reaching understanding. We can detect signs of the Romantic conception of language in this view, for which the synthesizing achievements and the unifying productive activities of a self-referentially operating

Spirit of Language are a first principle. The organic life of the linguistic totality branches out by way of the structural differences of national languages into the multiplicity of speech acts, yet asserts itself within these differentiations as the *superordinated* universal. Against this totalizing conception of language, Humboldt rightly brings into play the fractured intersubjectivity of a mutual understanding (*Verständigung*) that permits the *divergence,* within the successfully achieved agreement itself, of individually nuanced thoughts and feelings.

Objective agreement about something in the world—that is, agreement, the validity of which is open to question—is dependent on bringing about an *intersubjective* relationship between the speaker and at least one hearer capable of adopting a critical position.[6] The model of dialogue (*Gespräch*), taken from the ideal of Platonic dialogue,[7] suggests a notion of dialogic synthesis that no longer ensures—in the manner of the reflexive force of an "I think"—a monologic unity within the multiplicity of ideas. Rather, the communicatively achieved consensus relies both on the idealizing supposition of the identity of linguistic meanings and on the power of negation and autonomy of unique, irreplaceable (*unvertretbar*[8]) subjects from whom intersubjective agreement to criticizable validity claims has to be obtained—to be *won*—in every case. Every discursively achieved consensus rests on the power of negation of independent subjects who, in entering into an interpersonal relationship, recognize one another reciprocally as accountable subjects—whereby accountability (*Zurechnungsfähigkeit*) means that they orient their action toward validity claims.

Even when applied to linguistic phenomena, self-consciousness—the basic figure of thought of the philosophy of the subject—does not offer a sound basis for a theory of society. If the subject, in knowing its objects, relates at the same time to itself, it encounters itself in a double position: both as a single empirical entity in the world and as the transcendental subject facing the world as a whole. It encounters itself as one among many and as one against all (Henrich). Between these two positions of the subject there is no space left for the symbolically prestructured, linguistically constituted domains of culture, society, and socialized individuals.

Things are quite different with respect to the basic configuration in the theory of communication, which is one of subjects capable of speech and action reaching understanding about something in the world. What is constitutive for this configuration is the relation of an "I" to an *equiprimordial* Alter Ego. Space opens up between the two for an intersubjectively shared lifeworld; participants in communication are situated within the horizon of this lifeworld when they refer to objects or states of affairs in the world: "In order to designate this, a sensuous concept that nonetheless abstracts from all qualitative differences must be used; a concept that embraces the "I" and the "You" in one sphere and yet allows for a mutually determining division within this sphere. The notion of space (referring to personal pronouns) is such a concept."[9] The social space of a lifeworld inhabited in common that opens up in the course of dialogue provides the key to the conception of society proposed by the theory of communication. Humboldt already understood speech acts as connecting up for interaction; he conceives of reaching understanding as the generative mechanism of socialization (*Vergesellschaftung*)— first as the mechanism of action coordination and social integration, but then also as the medium both of socialization and for the continuation of cultural traditions. Language, worldview, and form of life are entwined.

I have recalled these interrelationships because of my interest in a point made by Humboldt who thereby preempted George Herbert Mead in certain respects by a hundred years. For Humboldt already conceives of reaching understanding as a mechanism that *socializes* and *individuates* in one act. In the structures of fractured intersubjectivity—which demand of competent speakers that they master the system of personal pronouns[10]—singularization is just as impossible without the inexorable compulsion to universalization as is socialization without concomitant individuation. Language contains "the possibility of universal understanding (*Verständnis*[11]) within the shell of the most individual expression;" "in singling out, it connects." On the other hand, the person who communicates with others will, in order to step beyond the dividing boundaries of his individuality, at the same time also "increase his individuality in this more elevated struggle."[12] And what holds true for individuals holds to an even greater degree for nations: "In its capacity for dividing peoples, language unifies the difference between individualities without detracting from them in any way, by means of the mutual understanding of foreign speech."[13] Language compels the individuation of peoples and individual persons, "but in such a wonderful way that, precisely in dividing, it awakens a feeling of unity; it appears indeed as a means of creating unity, at least as an idea."[14]

The idea to which Humboldt is alluding here gives expression to the rational potential of speech, that is, to the telos inherent in the very process of reaching understanding through language. This goal of reaching universal understanding has to be conveyed as a tendency of society as a whole because, and in so far as, society makes use of the mechanism of reaching understanding for its own coordinating purposes.

Taylor objects at this point that my explanation of communicative rationality is false because I explain it in terms of a formalist and cognitivist ethics, although he in no way denies that it is a potential contained in rational speech. Here, Taylor is too quick to introduce philosophical ethics into the debate. In my opinion, communicative rationality is not exhausted by its moral-practical component. Everyday communicative practices extend across a wider spectrum of validity; claims to normative rightness constitute only one among several aspects of validity. Moral issues arise only when conflicts of action are to be resolved with the consensus of the participants from the point of view of this one aspect alone. Philosophy may take moral questions as its point of departure in order to explain the moral point of view, from which such questions can be answered rationally—that is, by providing good reasons. Such an ethics cannot, however, exhaust the rational content of everyday communicative practices but can only grasp it in terms of one of its aspects; moreover, it can only do this within the framework of a normative theory. Taylor could agree to these reservations and insist nonetheless that his objections can be raised not only against a procedural ethics but against procedural rationality as a whole. The case Taylor makes against a procedural ethics is also directed against the unity of communicative rationality as whole, when this unity is understood merely procedurally. Does not *every* concept of rationality have to remain enmeshed with the substantive contents of a particular form of life, with a particular vision of the good life?

This question leads us back to the paradigm shift, signs of which are already apparent in Humboldt's philosophy of language, at least on a reading that strictly takes the viewpoint of a theory of intersubjectivity. According to such a reading, the moments of the universal, the particular, and the individual are no longer bound up with the ongoing process of self-relation of a higher-level subjectivity. Rather, they are released from their relation to a totality and are conceived of as equiprimordial reference points of a process of differentiation that moves outward radially in three directions. As a mechanism of socialization, the first act of reaching understanding itself sets in motion a dialectic of universalization, particularization, and individualization, a dialectic that leaves *only* the differentiated *particular* in the position of an individual totality. Within the structures of the fractured intersubjectivity of possible mutual understanding, general structures of the lifeworld, collective forms of life, and individual life histories arise and are simultaneously differentiated. The "I" is thereby formed equiprimordially as a subject in general, as a typical member of social collectives, and as a unique individual. The universal, particular, and individual constitute themselves radially, as it were, and no longer as interlocking moments within a totality. This became clear to Humboldt as a result of his studies of the cultural development of civilized peoples.[15]

Here, individual language, the development of ideas, and national character are entwined in such a way that internal correspondences obtain between the linguistic worldviews and the sociocultural forms of life of the linguistic community. However, the same national languages not only constitute the boundaries of a form of life, they serve simultaneously as a medium that traverses these boundaries; a medium in which different totalities—each one of which is the Spirit of a People—meet and where they, from their own respective standpoints, come to an agreement with each other about the world of all that is knowable "which lies in the middle."[16] Thus, national languages, as form-giving principles guiding the shape taken by the individual totality of each particular worldview and of each particular way of life, come into their own only to the extent that, by virtue of their universalist core, they both enable translations to be made from each language into every other language and determine the point of convergence toward which all cultural developments move. In this respect, Humboldt speaks of the "constant and uniform work" of the Spirit: "The purpose of this work is understanding (*Verständnis*). Thus, nobody may speak to another person in a manner different from that in which the latter, under identical conditions, would have spoken to him."[17]

By putting it this way, Humboldt has already given a normative twist to what, in formal-pragmatic terms, is discernible—on the basis of the necessarily idealizing suppositions of communicative action—as the rational potential of speech. Of course, the grammatically regulated worldviews and forms of life appear only in the plural; however, they constitute totalities over which there is not some further, overarching supertotality but that rather correspond to one another in their formal and most general structures. Because all lifeworlds have to reproduce themselves through the medium of action oriented toward reaching understanding, the general character of communicative rationality asserts itself in the multiplicity of concrete forms of life.

If moral philosophy appeals to this universalist potential of speech—and Humboldt did in fact use it as a basis for deriving something like a cosmopolitan ethics of reaching understanding[18]— then it can develop no more than a formal or procedural ethics from it. In so doing, moral philosophy has to accept the fact that, with the concept of morality, only one of several general aspects of rationality inherent in linguistically structured forms of life can be reconstructed—and this only from the reflexive attitude of a participant in argumentation who considers normative validity claims hypothetically. Such an ethics must also concede that it can explain only the formal conditions of valid moral judgments, but not the empirical conditions under which moral insights can be put into practice. Every universalist morality is dependent on structurally analogous forms of life to complement and supplement it. The circumstances under which it can count on this is less a matter for moral philosophy than for social theory.[19] One cannot, however, as Taylor proposes, develop an ethics of language on a Humboldtian plane and at the same time attempt to reconnect the universal core of morality to the ethical life (*Sittlichkeit*) of concrete forms of life.[20]

Of course, the reproduction of the lifeworld is nourished through the contributions of communicative action, while the latter simultaneously is nourished through the resources of the lifeworld. However, the structures of possible mutual understanding, characterized by a fractured intersubjectivity, prohibit us from in turn inflating this circular process into a totality. To the degree that the reproduction of the lifeworld is no longer merely channeled through the medium of action oriented toward reaching understanding but, with the increasing rationalization of the lifeworld, is a *burden* placed on the interpretive achievements of the actors themselves, the *universal* structures of the lifeworld stand out increasingly sharply from the *particular* configurations of forms of life that simply overlap with one another. In the face of such totalities, which it reduces to a merely empirical status, the approach taken by the theory of intersubjectivity restores to favor the distinction between form and content discredited by Hegel.[21]

There is, however, another insight of Humboldt's that Taylor may indeed use against me justifiably. In *The Theory of Communicative Action*, I failed to treat properly the world-disclosing (*welterschließend*) function of language. In contrast to theories of meaning oriented toward ideas of denotation and representation, Taylor himself has developed an expressivist theory of language that goes back to the work of Herder, Hamann, and Humboldt.[22] He frees the linguistic constitution of worldviews from a foreshortening through a semantic ontology interested solely in a grammatically regulated preunderstanding of reality as a whole. Using Humboldt's work, Taylor demonstrates how every language opens up a grammatically prestructured space, how it allows what is within the world to appear there in a certain way, and also at the same time makes possible legitimate orders of interpersonal relationships and the spontaneous self-presentation of creative-expressive subjects. "World-disclosure" means for Taylor, as for Humboldt, that language is the constitutive organ not only of thought, but also of social practices and of experience, of the formation of ego and group identities. And yet Taylor here again tends to totalize this world-disclosing function of language. In so doing, he succumbs to an epistemological perspectivism that Humboldt himself avoids.

Humboldt conceives of the different linguistic worldviews as *converging* rays that illuminate one and the same world as "the sum of the knowable." This convergence is possible due to innerworldly learning processes in which the world-disclosing force of an interpreting language has first *to prove its worth* within the world. Of course, as the system of rules for a given language changes, so too do the conditions of validity for the sentences that can be formulated in that language. But whether such conditions of validity are actually satisfied to such an extent that the sentences can function within their language games depends not only on the world-disclosing power of language but also on the innerworldly effects of the practices that it for its part makes possible. Because all other functions of language (that is, the representation of states of affairs, the taking up of interpersonal relations, and the expressive self-presentation of speakers) are intimately connected with criticizable validity claims, everyday communicative practices—and also the cultures of experts that emerge out of them—can develop an independent logic (*Eigensinn*) that transcends all local boundaries. Thus, the modes of action constituted by a linguistic worldview operate in the light of a communicative rationality that imposes on the participants an orientation toward validity claims, and in this way triggers learning processes with possible reactive effects on the antecedent understanding of the world. Taylor is wrong to allow this problem-solving capacity of language to disappear behind its capacity for world disclosure.[23]

Problems in the Theories of Meaning and Action

Proponents of formal semantics are challenged by the proposition that reaching understanding in language terminates in the intersubjective recognition of criticizable validity claims and is therefore a phenomenon that cannot be grasped by a semantic analysis of the meaning of sentences, but rather necessitates a pragmatic analysis of *successful* utterances. Rolf Zimmermann has criticized the theory of communicative action from this point of view.[24] He believes that I have been led, through overgeneralizing the special case of action oriented toward reaching understanding, into carrying the *social* aspect of the orientation toward validity into the theory of meaning, and falsely making it into the central aspect of language itself.[25] Zimmermann fails to see that formal pragmatics provides solutions to problems that have arisen in the theoretical tradition dating back to Frege. If my proposals are conceived of as an internally motivated development of formal semantics, this might help to overcome certain barriers to their being understood and accepted.[26] I shall subsequently discuss a difficulty in the analysis of imperatives that has in the meantime prompted me to amend my theory.

To start with, a few key words concerning the most important stages on the path from formal semantics to formal pragmatics.[27] The point of departure is Frege's theory, which emerges out of a double critique of psychologism and reference semantics. Meanings are to be analyzed on the basis of the formal properties of their linguistic expression as something objective and publicly accessible. It is no longer the designation of an object by a name that is the model for linguistic meanings, but rather the relation between sentences and states of affairs. In this context, the sentence forms the most elementary unit constituting meaning. The decisive step then is to link meaning and validity in the sense of truth (*Wahrheitsgeltung*). Taking a simple assertoric sentence, Frege develops the thesis fundamental for truth-conditional semantics: one understands the meaning of a sentence if one knows the conditions under which the sentence is true. In this regard, Frege distinguishes the assertoric force that makes a sentence an assertion from the propositional content of what is stated in it. *What* has been asserted can be completely explicated with reference to the truth conditions; all the assertoric force adds to this is *that* these conditions are considered to be satisfied. The propositional sentence "*p*" expresses both at once.

For this reason, the analysis of linguistic meanings can confine itself to analyzing sentences and can abstract from the pragmatic rules concerning the use of sentences. In addition to this semantic abstraction, Frege also makes a less conspicuous cognitivist abstraction, whereby he reduces all meanings to propositional contents and, indirectly, to the meaning of assertoric sentences or propositions. A third abstraction is due to the objective conception of truth, which Davidson will later explain with the help of Tarski's theory of truth, stripping it of the Platonist connotations prevalent in Frege's work. The truth conditions, which are construed purely semantically, explain what makes a sentence true, and do not, for instance, extend epistemically to a knowledge of truth conditions attributable to a speaker or a hearer. As a result of these abstractions, the sphere of application of formal semantics is initially pretty restricted.[28] The further development of the theory of meaning is driven forward by attempts to relax these abstractions and ultimately to overcome them. Let me remind you (in reverse order) of Dummett's verificationist theory, which gives up the restriction to an objective conception of truth, of the modal theories from Stenius to Searle, which expand Frege's approach to include the analysis of nonassertoric forces, and of Austin's speech-act theory, which drops the semantic abstraction once and for all. Finally, I understand formal pragmatics as a theory that succeeds in overcoming even the barriers of the empiricist ontology within which all three of the aforementioned developments of formal semantics still move.

Dummett links truth conditions to the knowledge that speakers and hearers have of them. Truth conditions would remain ineffective for understanding the meaning of sentences if they were not known as such conditions. Now, this turn away from the objective conditions that make a sentence true in favor of the epistemic conditions under which the speaker and hearer are able to identify and recognize truth conditions is supposed not only to explain the understanding of sentences. It is intended at the same time to extend the sphere of application of formal semantics to include types of sentences that had hitherto eluded analysis. If, namely, the reasons that the speaker can provide for the possible truth of a sentence are constitutive for its meaning, and if in this way the meaning of a sentence is linked by way of potential justifications to its validity, in the sense of truth, then counterfactual statements, modalized statements, statements with a temporal index, and so forth are all opened up to an investigation based on truth-conditional semantics. With this move, Dummett has not yet done anything about the cognitivist abstraction, let alone the semantic one. For the verificationist procedure that he proposes in order to establish truth conditions can be carried out monologically and is geared solely to the truth conditions of assertoric sentences. Verification cannot yet be equated with the intersubjective putting into effect of a discursive vindication of *different* validity claims.

The post-Wittgensteinian modal theories that nonetheless link up with Frege's ideas, such as those put forward by Stenius, Kenny, Tugendhat, and others, can be understood as attempts to relax the cognitivist abstraction: the intention here is to make accessible the "forces"—now understood as illocutionary forces—to a purely semantic analysis. The simple ontological model of Austin's two "directions of fit" underlies this approach; the assertoric force represents the agreement between sentences and states of affairs, and the imperative force represents the adjustment of states of affairs to fit sentences. This model has the advantage of introducing each of the fundamental modes with reference to "conditions of satisfaction." However, although these conditions are now differentiated in terms of truth conditions and success conditions, respectively, they nonetheless continue to be based on the ontological presuppositions of language as a reflection of the world, and thus remain restricted to the fundamental relation between sentences and states of affairs. On this conception, illocutionary forces do not have to be conceived of as modes of using sentences, that is, pragmatically, with the result that the semantic abstraction remains untouched. This also, of course, explains the limited explanatory potential of this approach. For the whole breadth of illocutionary forces can in no way be derived from the assertoric-imperative double mode. Even the most elaborately worked out taxonomy[29] does not succeed in embracing even the most important modes or classes of speech act: normative obligations, orders, and declarations all evade—as do expressive utterances—an attempt at classification that operates using exactly two relations between language and the objective world, and in so doing, remains bound to the logocentrism of Frege's semantics.[30]

In the end it is Austin who, following the later Wittgenstein, takes the decisive step toward an analysis of speech acts and overcomes the semantic abstraction. He resolutely replaces truth semantics with a use theory of meaning and replaces the analysis of sentences with an analysis of the use of sentences in utterances. This provides him with the scope to uncouple the illocutionary forces from the proto-typical case of an assertoric sentence. Austin begins to free himself from an ontology that is geared exclusively toward the objective world as a totality of existing states of affairs and that results in special emphasis being placed on assertoric sentences and proposi-tional truth. His concept of an illocutionary act opens up the *entire* spectrum of speech to linguistic analysis. Wittgenstein's thesis that meaning is to be sought not in the relation of sentences to some-thing in the world, but rather in the conventionally regulated use of these sentences had directed the attention of linguistic analysts to the wealth of language games that regulate "grammatically" the use of sentences in the context of forms of life. Yet, this liberating turn away from the world of existing states of affairs back to the contexts of the lifeworld did not only push to one side all the abstractions of Frege-Davidsonian semantics; in giving up the reference to the ob-jective world, it also renounced any *internal* relation between mean-ing and validity—or rather, it assimilated a form of validity that had been equated with validity, in the sense of truth, to the social validity of cultural practices. That may have been sufficient for an investiga-tion motivated solely by a therapeutic interest. Yet anyone who main-tained an interest in explanation and wished to elaborate a use theory of meaning in the form of a theory of speech acts without at the same time surrendering linguistic analysis to the task of ethnolin-guistic description of family resemblances—in the wider sense of ethnolinguistic—was faced with the objection that, for every sen-tence, there are innumerable context-dependent ways of using it. Because Austin did not in any way wish to sacrifice to contextualism the orientation toward theory, he had to search for a systematically motivated classification of speech acts—for *general* rules for the typi-cal use of sentences in utterances. With this, the program of formal pragmatics was born, at least.

Admittedly, Austin's own analyses of types of language use, which he carried out inductively, did not lead to theoretical generaliza-tions. In contrast, the systematics of language functions, developed by Roman Jakobson following Karl Bühler, was motivated by an interest in theory; despite this, however, it remained entrenched in the framework of an empirical pragmatics, which could not match the insights provided by formal semantics or linguistic phenomenology. Language games, and speech acts as their elementary units, could be subjected once again to formal analysis only when a point of reference was successfully secured for speech-act theory that was as objective as that attained by formal semantics with its linking of meaning and validity in the sense of truth. Searle returned to formal semantics for this reason. As we have seen, an alternative is available to us if we follow Humboldt's theoretical approach to the constitution of language, for this retains the idea of a relation between the various linguistically constituted worldviews and an objective world. In his transcendental pragmatics, Karl-Otto Apel has always energetically articulated this universalist core in the face of the pluralism of Wittgenstein's language games.

Taking Apel as my point of departure, I then forged a link to Austin (and the early Searle) by

a. providing justification for Bühler's language functions in terms of a theory of validity;

b. generalizing the objective conception of truth conditions to an idea of validity conditions in general (including normative rightness and subjective truthfulness (*Wahrhaftigkeit*)), while renouncing the ontology of one world;

c. taking further the epistemic turn inaugurated by Dummett through connecting these conditions of validity with an intersubjective conception of justification through argumentation; in order finally to

d. recognize the illocutionary component of speech acts as the linguistic expression of the raising of validity claims that can be redeemed in discourse.

I have elaborated this idea in the shape of a formal-pragmatic theory of meaning.

It proceeds from the simple notion that we understand a speech act if we know the conditions that make it acceptable. What is at issue here are objective conditions of validity that may not be inferred directly from the semantic content of the linguistic expressions used, but only as mediated by the epistemic claim raised by the speaker for the validity of her utterance in the performance of her illocutionary act. This validity claim rests on a reservoir of potential reasons with which it can, if necessary, be redeemed in discourse. The reasons interpret the validity conditions and, to this extent, are themselves part of the conditions that render the validity claim worthy of intersubjective recognition and make a corresponding utterance acceptable. Only with this step is the turn away from formal semantics to pragmatics—initiated by Wittgenstein and Austin—truly effected, and furthermore in such a way that the cognitivist and objectivist abstractions, too, can be overcome completely. This in turn necessitates a revision of the basic ontological concepts that have become established in philosophy, but I do not want to go into this here.

This brief review of the history of the theory of language was intended merely to show that the comprehension of linguistic expressions already requires an orientation toward validity claims and that a rationally motivating force is already inherent in linguistic processes of reaching understanding as such. If understanding a speech act depends on knowing the conditions for its acceptability, then the speaker's illocutionary aim of being understood points to the further aim that the hearer should accept her speech-act offer. Acceptance or agreement on the part of the hearer is equivalent to recognition of a validity claim raised by the speaker. It is based on the good reasons that the speaker offers in order to redeem the validity claim in discourse (or else on a credible warranty issued by the speaker that she could provide such reasons, if necessary). And the hearer, with his "yes" to a validity claim he has accepted as worthy of recognition—that is, with his acceptance of the speech-act offer—also takes upon himself, as a rule, certain obligations relevant for the sequel of interaction, such as obligations to meet a request, to trust a confession, to believe a statement, to rely on a promise, or to obey an order. For this does have consequences for the further course of the interaction—whether with the speaker or with other participants or persons affected; and it explains why linguistic acts of reaching understanding—which have as their core a speech-act offer and a "yes" or "no" position—are *able* to take on functions of action coordination in the first place. What distinguishes the approach taken by formal pragmatics from that of formal semantics is the insight into the internal connection between understanding (*Verstehen*) and reaching understanding (*Verständigung*). This does not mean, however, as Jeffrey Alexander has contended,[31] that I in any way confuse linguistic understanding (*Verstehen*) and agreement (*Einverständnis*).

To understand an expression, however, means to know how one can make use of it in order to reach understanding with someone about something. One can already see from the conditions for *understanding* linguistic expressions that the speech acts that can be carried out with the help of such expressions are oriented toward *reaching understanding,* that is, toward achieving a rationally motivated agreement between participants in communication about something in the world. One would have utterly failed to grasp what it is to understand the meaning of an utterance if one did not know that this is supposed to serve the purpose of reaching understanding about something, that is, of bringing about agreement—and the concept of agreement involves its "being valid" for the participants. The dimension of validity is inherent in language. I regard Zimmermann's view that the orientation toward validity claims is *carried into* the genuine sphere of speaking and linguistic understanding from the domain of social action as an empiricist misconception.[32] The orientation toward validity claims is part of the pragmatic conditions of the possibility of reaching understanding, that is, of understanding language itself.

Someone trained in formal semantics is likely to present simple imperatives as an incisive example disproving my thesis. For it appears to be the case that a foreigner who has just arrived in town already understands a child's (begging) request, "Give me some money," if he knows the conditions under which the action requested would be carried out successfully.[33] It looks as though a normative validity claim is not involved here at all, or rather that it only then comes into play when we take into account the pragmatic context within which the speech act—semantically analyzable as a request—can be characterized pragmatically as begging.[34] Against such a counterintuitive reading I want to stick by the analysis carried out in *The Theory of Communicative Action.*[35] Knowledge of the conditions of success, which are to be inferred from the propositional component of the imperative in question, is not sufficient in order to understand the illocutionary meaning, that is, the specifically imperative character of the request. Rather, the hearer must understand the normative context that authorizes the speaker to make the demand, thereby legitimating her expectation in the first place that the addressee has reasons to carry out the action demanded of him. Otherwise the hearer lacks any knowledge of the conditions for his agreement; it is this agreement which first justifies his taking on of obligations relevant for the sequel of interaction—in this case, handing over "some money." A knowledge of (a) the conditions of success must be accompanied by a knowledge of (b) the conditions under which the speaker has reasons to regard as valid (that is, as normatively justified) an imperative with the content (a)—for example, that children are allowed to beg from foreigners in the streets of Lima.[36]

Now, what is decisive here is that we cannot conceive of any situation in which a request would be understandable as such without it being authorized or backed up by *some kind of* normative background, however weak this may be; even if it is only the authorizing norm that one should help people or children in distress—or human beings as such—whereby "being in need of help" is itself one of the pragmatic presuppositions underlying a request. Admittedly there is the limit case of normatively nonauthorized imperatives, such as that of the bank robber who threatens the bank teller, commanding her to hand over money. In such cases, the conditions of normative validity must be *replaced* by sanction conditions that complete the acceptability conditions. The robber's "Hands Up!," exclaimed while pointing a revolver, shows that a validity claim has been replaced by a power claim and that the imperative is to be understood in the sense of a factual expression of will, whereby one person's will is simply imposed on the will of another. In this case, the reservoir of potential sanctions contingently linked with the imperative provides the speaker with certainty that the addressee has good reasons to conform.

My mistake was to treat this limit case of a pure imperative backed up by power as a class of speech acts in its own right. In doing so, as Zimmermann, Tugendhat, and Skjei point out, I got caught up in contradictions. I have already revised this position in my reply to Skjei:[37] I now regard simple or normatively nonauthorized imperatives as a parasitical case.[38] As a sociologist I ought to have known that a continuum obtains between power that is merely established as a matter of fact and power that has been transformed into normative authority. For this reason, *all* imperatives to which we attribute an illocutionary force can be analyzed according to the model of normatively authorized imperatives. What I wrongly took to be a difference in category now shrinks to a difference in degree. The bank robber's imperative, sanctioned by his "Hands Up!," belongs to those *limit cases* of a manifestly strategic use of speech acts in which the missing illocutionary force is replaced by an appeal to a reservoir of potential sanctions. This mode of language use is parasitical to the extent that understanding a speech act of this kind involves conditions that are derived from the conditions under which normatively authorized, nondegenerate imperatives can be used.[39]

In general, to be sure, the strategic use of illocutionary acts functions under conditions of latently strategic action: the speaker may not "admit to" perlocutionary effects that he wishes to *trigger* in the hearer in the form of obligations relevant for the sequel of interaction, as the side effects of a consensus that is seemingly achieved communicatively. However, the objections raised by Alexander in his essay have shown me yet again that my use of Austin's terms "perlocutionary" and "illocutionary," diverging as it does from established philosophical usage, leads to misunderstandings. This prompts me to provide some terminological clarifications.

To begin with, I want to distinguish more clearly between the *immediate* illocutionary aim (or, as the case may be, success) of the speaker—namely, that the hearer understands her utterance—and the more *far-reaching* aim that the hearer accepts her utterance as valid and thereby takes on obligations relevant for the sequel of interaction. Illocutionary success in the narrower sense consists in understanding (*Verstehen*), whereas illocutionary success in the broader sense consists in an agreement that has a coordinating effect, that is, in the success of the interaction. I had hitherto termed only those effects "perlocutionary" that are not related internally to the meaning of the sentences uttered, whereas this term usually applies to all those effects the speaker has on the hearer that go beyond the mere understanding of the communicative act. Given that, as we have seen above, the dimension of validity is already inherent in linguistic understanding, it would appear advisable to count not just understanding an utterance (on the basis of knowing its acceptability conditions) as part of the illocutionary aim (or, as the case may be, success) of the speaker, but also to include the agreement reached with the hearer, that is, the hearer's acceptance of the speech-act offer. This illocutionary aim in the broader sense is also achieved solely through the performance of the illocutionary act. I want to hold onto this. However, in order to bring my terminology more into line with established usage, I now want to call all effects that go beyond this "perlocutionary." For example, the conviction that forms in a hearer when he accepts that a statement is true could just as easily be prompted by a lie; in this case it would represent precisely the type of effect that a speaker with a strategic intention wishes to achieve. This terminological concession necessitates a differentiation within the class of perlocutionary effects: between effects that, in the course of obligations relevant for the sequel of interaction, result from the semantic content of what is said, and those effects that occur contingently independently of grammatically regulated contexts. With this I wish to correct the mistake I made of equating this distinction within the theory of meaning with the distinction within the theory of action between strategically and nonstrategically motivated perlocutionary effects.

I term those effects strategically motivated that come about only if they are not declared or if they are brought about by deceptive speech acts that merely pretend to be valid. Perlocutionary effects of this type indicate that the use of language oriented toward reaching understanding has been put at the service of strategic interactions. I have referred to this as "the use of language with an orientation toward consequences"[40]—a speaker's one-sided and latently undertaken subordination of illocutionary acts to conditions of action oriented toward success. In accordance with this terminological revision, it is no longer possible to assign *all* perlocutions to the class of latently strategic actions.[41] Against Jeffrey Alexander, however, I want to emphasize that *the distinction between communicative and strategic action* is not influenced by this revision.

I define communicative action, inter alia, by stating that action coordination must satisfy the condition of an agreement reached communicatively, without reservation. The requirement that illocutionary aims be pursued "without reservation" is intended precisely to exclude cases of latently strategic action. In strategic action, linguistic processes of reaching understanding are (generally) not used as a mechanism of action coordination. Here, we can no longer explain the coordination of different plans of action through reference to conditions for a communicatively achieved agreement that culminates in the intersubjective recognition of criticizable validity claims; instead, we may appeal only to the conditions for the reciprocal influence that opponents, acting in a purposive rational way and oriented respectively toward their own success, attempt to exert upon one another. My critics have on occasion overlooked the fact that *both* models of action attribute to the actors a capacity for setting goals and for goal-directed action, as well as an interest in executing their own plans of action.[42] Other critics, it is true, acknowledge the fact that in both models a teleological structure of action is presupposed; however, they identify the pursuit of illocutionary aims without reservation (as well as the pursuit of the perlocutionary aims that are mediated through the attainment of illocutionary success), as envisaged in the model of communicative action, with the egocentric pursuit of one's own interests and aims, as permitted in the model of teleological or strategic action, in such a way that one model merges with the other.[43] An identification of this kind is not permissible, even if the description of both cases is based on the same teleological language game of goal-setting actors who pursue aims, achieve results, and trigger effects. For the illocutionary "aims" of reaching understanding cannot be defined without reference to the linguistic means of reaching understanding: the medium of language and the telos of reaching understanding inherent within it constitute one another reciprocally. The relation between them is not one of ends and means. For this reason, the "aims" that an actor pursues *in* language and can realize only in cooperation with another actor cannot be described as though they resembled conditions that we can bring about by intervening causally in the world. For the actor, the aims of action oriented respectively toward success and toward reaching understanding are situated on different levels: either in the objective world or, beyond all entities, in the linguistically constituted lifeworld. I do not mean to imply that speaking is a self-sufficient action that bears its purpose within itself and that must be distinguished from actions aimed at purposes external to them. Nonetheless, we must in both cases distinguish between the ontological presuppositions as well as between the perspectives and attitudes of the actors; we must in each case conceive of the aims and the realization of these purposes in a different way.

For the speaker and hearer involved, in reaching understanding about something with one another, the illocutionary aims of understanding (*Verstehen*) and agreement (*Einverständnis*) lie *beyond* the world in which a purposively acting individual intervenes in order to achieve his goal. Illocutionary aims can, from the perspective of the participants, be achieved only within the dimension of world-disclosing language itself, and in such a manner that the intersubjective recognition of disputable validity claims depends on the autonomous agreement of a subject who is held to be accountable. Illocutionary success can thus be achieved only cooperatively and is never, as it were, at the disposal of an individual participant in interaction. Strategic action is also subject to conditions of the double contingency of actors equipped with freedom of choice. Yet these purposive actors, who condition one another with regard to their own respective successes, are accessible for one another only as entities *in the world*. They have to attribute successes and failures solely to themselves, namely, as the results of their own causal intervention in the supposedly law-governed nexus of *innerworldly* processes. The same also holds, of course, for collective actors who are only constituted as such in the first place through the cooperation of individual actors.

Furthermore, communicative and strategic action do not differ primarily in terms of the attitudes of the actors but rather with respect to structural characteristics. A formal-pragmatic analysis of successful speech acts is required precisely because, in communicative action, the structure of the use of language oriented toward reaching understanding is superimposed on the fundamental teleological structure of action and subjects the actors to precisely such constraints as compel them to adopt a performative attitude—an attitude that is more laden with presuppositions than is the objectivating attitude of the strategic actor. Interaction mediated through acts of reaching understanding exhibits both a richer and a more restrictive structure than does strategic action.

As game theory has shown, strategic action has had the effect of generating models. If one is not led astray by a semanticist theory of meaning, that is, if one does not split off the illocutionary binding and bonding effect (*Bindungswirkung*) from the speech act, relegating this effect to context-dependent ways of using language, one will have no difficulty in recognizing two limit cases of communicative action in the two other models of action known to us from sociological theory. Just as the normative and expressive modes of language use correspond to one function of language respectively, so too are normatively regulated and dramaturgical action tailored to fit one specific aspect of validity respectively: in the first case, the legitimacy of the permissible interpersonal relations and, in the second case, the authenticity of self-presentation. The above-mentioned models represent limit cases (and not, as I had incorrectly asserted, "pure types")[44] of action oriented toward reaching understanding, to the extent that in these cases the dynamics of reciprocally taking a position with regard to criticizable validity claims, which is essential to communicative action, is suspended: in the one case, by means of a presupposed value consensus and, in the other, by an empiricist reinterpretation, as impression management, of self-presentation oriented toward reaching understanding.[45]

In the light of these philosophical observations, a number of the general misgivings raised by Alexander, Berger, Dux, Joas, and others with respect to the basic assumptions of my theory of action can be disposed of. I in no way identify the practice of speech with that of social action. I do not fail to recognize that social interactions of all types are mediated by language and that even strategic interactions require demanding feats of understanding and interpretation. However, because the structure of the use of language oriented toward reaching understanding imposes certain attitudes and perspectives on the communicative actor that are incompatible with exerting a causal influence over an opponent, which is oriented *directly*[46] toward one's own success, I do not distinguish between the two controversial types of action solely from an analytical point of view. The sociological observer, too, is in principle in a position to distinguish between communicative and strategic action on the basis of the attitudes that, from the perspective of the actor, present a complete alternative.[47]

This ideal-typical distinction, that is, one which is made on the basis of criteria unambivalent from the point of view of the pragmatics of language, and which is by no means merely analytic, does not in any way rob the complex concept of social cooperation—what Marx termed "labor"—of its relevance: something that is important in social reality must not also be fundamental conceptually. Moreover, the degree of rationality of strategic action can vary; seen empirically, it rarely meets the demands of game theory and decision theory.

It should now also be clear that approaching an analysis of action oriented toward reaching understanding from the vantage point of speech-act theory by no means implies an assimilation of this action to the model of discourses—which serve to relieve action.[48] Action oriented toward validity is not (as Dux believes) assimilated to the treatment in argumentation of validity claims that have become problematic. Nevertheless, I want to hold on to the thesis that, with the action-coordinating role of factually raised and recognized validity claims, a moment of unconditionality enters into everyday communicative practices. Criticizable validity claims are Janus-faced: as claims they transcend, at least from the perspective of the participants, all merely local agreements and rely on a subversive, ever-flexible reservoir of potential, disputable reasons; on the other hand, they must be raised *here and now* within specific contexts, with coverage provided by an unquestioned cultural background, and accepted (or rejected) with regard to nonreversible action sequences—the social reality of the lifeworld consists of such action sequences, which are intermeshed by way of criticizable validity claims. Apel uses the vivid image of the interlocking of the ideal and the real communication community; but this sounds almost too Kantian. The doctrine of the "two realms" has been completely overcome. The structure of the use of language oriented toward reaching understanding demands idealizing suppositions on the part of the communicative actors; however, these suppositions function as social facts and are, as is language itself, constitutive for the form in which sociocultural life reproduces itself.

Alexander maintains that, in the concept of communicative action, I conflate "ideological" questions with methodological and empirical ones. I am supposed to have tacitly smuggled in "value postulates" by way of the definitions of reaching understanding and action oriented toward reaching understanding, instead of declaring them openly. The identification of linguistic understanding (*Sprachverstehen*) with a communicatively achieved agreement supposedly serves this purpose. Even if we leave this misinterpretation aside, however, what Alexander overlooks is the point of the entire project. I would never have tackled a formal-pragmatic reconstruction of the rational potential of speech if I had not harbored the expectation that I would in this way be able to obtain a concept of communicative rationality from the normative content of the universal and unavoidable presuppositions of the *noncircumventable* practice of everyday processes of reaching understanding. It is not a matter of this or that preference, of "our" or "their" notions of rational life; rather, what is at issue here is the reconstruction of a voice of reason, a voice that we have no choice but to allow to speak in everyday communicative practices—whether we want to or not. Perhaps I have deviously obtained through definitions what I claim to have found through reconstructions—this, at any rate, is the claim on which criticism should focus.

Those who reproach me for neglecting materialist components suspect me of another type of idealization. This objection occurs in several versions. Johannes Berger suspects that lurking behind my conceptual strategy is the intention to divide up, as Durkheim did, all social actions into moral and immoral actions from the point of view of altruism and egoism. Johannes Weiss also maintains that communicative action owes its integrative achievements in the first instance to the moral force of normative validity claims.[49] Apart from anything else, these reservations do not apply for the simple reason that I introduce normatively regulated action merely as a limit case of communicative action: the rationally motivating binding and bonding effect of speech acts spreads across the whole spectrum of illocutionary forces, which are differentiated according to the particular language involved, and appear in different constellations depending on the particular linguistic worldview and form of life. It is precisely this internal differentiation of the spectrum of validity and the interplay of cognitive, expressive, and aesthetic validity claims with conventional, moral, and legal ones that accords everyday communicative practices their autonomy vis-à-vis (and their clear distinction from) normative contexts (which, moreover, comprise only one of three components of the background of the lifeworld).

Weiss and others have rendered their objections more specific in that they argue that the concept of communicative action suggests the rationalist illusion that language could engender from within itself illocutionary binding and bonding effects; they maintain that, in fact, the binding and bonding effect of communicative acts can arise only "if certain social and institutional constellations as well as psychological dispositions are presupposed;" and "it is toward these empirical conditions for the development and binding character of rationality that the explanations offered by an empirical theory of society must be directed."[50] This is precisely my contention. However, the pragmatic concept of language permits another, nonempiricist description of the same thing. I have never left any room for doubt that the concept of action oriented toward reaching understanding developed in "Intermediate Reflections: Social Action, Purposive Activity, and Communication"[51] must be supplemented by a complementary concept of the lifeworld as elaborated in "Intermediate Reflections: System and Lifeworld."[52] It would be completely impossible to explain how everyday processes of consensus formation repeatedly succeed in overcoming the hurdle posed by the risk of disagreement built into practices of reaching understanding in the form of criticizable validity claims were we not able to take into account the *massive preunderstanding* of participants in communication; this preunderstanding resides in the self-evident features of an intuitively present, prereflexively known form of life that is presupposed as unproblematic—features that have become culturally habitualized for the participants in communication and into which they have been socialized. Subjects acting communicatively, in their superficially autonomous achievements in reaching understanding, are dependent on the resources of a background knowledge of the lifeworld that is not at their disposal. What is important here is the double—philosophical and sociological—point of view in terms of which the lifeworld can be analyzed more accurately. It is not I who blend both analytical levels "into one another in a way that is, for all the convergence of approaches to the problem, inadmissible" (Weiss).[53]

Notes

1. [Editor's note:] Charles Taylor, "Language and Society," in A. Honneth and H. Joas, eds., *Communicative Action* (Cambridge, Mass., 1991).

2. Cf. Wilhelm von Humboldt, "Über den Nationalcharakter der Sprachen," in *Schriften zur Sprachphilosophie. Werke*, vol. 3 (Darmstadt, 1963), p. 81: "A lively, engaged conversation in which the speakers truly exchange ideas, feelings, and perceptions is in itself the central point of language, as it were, the essence of which can only be conceived as both echo and re-echo, as address and response, which, in its origins as in its transformations, never belongs to one but always to all, and which lies in the lonely depths of each person's spirit yet comes to the fore only in sociality."

3. [Editor's note:] The word "*Gespräch*" implies not only dialogue or discussion but also conversation. I have translated it here as "dialogue" because Habermas himself focuses on these more structured forms of speech rather than on conversations. Nonetheless, it may be useful to bear in mind that *Gespräch* has a broader interpretation than I have given it here.

4. W. von Humboldt, "Über die Verschiedenheit des menschlichen Sprachbaus und ihren Einfluß auf die geistige Entwicklung des Menschengeschlechts," *Werke*, vol. 3, p. 438: "Language has an objective effect and is independent precisely in so far as it is subjectively effected and dependent. . . . Its dead part, as it were, must always be generated anew in thought, become alive in speech or understanding (*Verständnis*) and therefore completely merge with the subject. . . . In this manner it on each occasion experiences the full influence of the individual upon it; yet this influence is already in itself bounded by what it (language as a system) effects and has effected."

5. Ibid., p. 439.

6. W. von Humboldt, "Über den Dualis," *Werke*, vol. 3, pp. 138f.:

An unalterable dualism resides in the original essence of language, and the possibility of speech is determined by someone speaking and someone replying. Thought itself is already substantially accompanied by a proclivity for social existence, and human beings long for . . . a You that accords with the I; concepts appear to them [human beings] to become determinate and certain only by being reflected back by an alien capacity for thought. . . . The objectivity appears even more perfected, however, if this division does not occur solely within the subject, but rather when the person imagining can truly perceive the thought outside him, which is possible only if perceived in another being imagining and thinking like himself. There is, however, no mediator other than language between one capacity for thought and another.

7. Von Humboldt, *Werke*, vol. 3, pp. 80f.

8. [Editor's note:] The word "*unvertretbar*" expresses a particular interpretation of the idea of irreplaceability—the idea that only I can speak on behalf of myself, in other words, the idea of *unrepresentability;* for a brief discussion of this, see M. Cooke, "Selfhood and Solidarity," *Constellations* 1 (1995): 3.

9. Von Humboldt, *Werke*, vol. 3, p. 208.

10. Von Humboldt, "Über den Dualis," pp. 113ff., and "Über die Verschiedenheit des menschlichen Sprachbaus," pp. 191ff., in particular, pp. 200ff.

11. [Editor's note:] The word "*Verständnis*" has connotations beyond mere comprehension, suggesting that two or more people see the world (or some aspect of it) in the same way.

12. Von Humboldt, "Über die Verschiedenheit," p. 60.

13. Von Humboldt, *Werke*, vol. 3, p. 150.

14. Ibid., p. 160.

15. Von Humboldt, "Über den Nationalcharakter der Sprachen," *Werke*, vol. 3, pp. 64ff.

16. Von Humboldt, *Werke*, vol. 3, p. 20: "[T]he sum of all that is knowable, as the field to be processed by the human spirit, lies in the middle . . . between all languages."

17. Ibid., p. 419.

18. Ibid., pp. 147–148: "If there is one idea visible throughout history that has gained ever increasing validity . . . then it is the endeavor to overcome all barriers that prejudices and one-sided views of all sorts inimically erect between humans, and to treat all humanity, without consideration of religion, nation, and colour, as one great, almost fraternal tribe."

19. Cf. J. Habermas, *Moral Consciousness and Communicative Action*, trans. C. Lenhardt and S. W. Nicholsen (Cambridge, Mass., 1990), pp. 105f., 175f.

20. Cf. a similar argument by Rüdigier Bubner in "Rationaliät als Lebensform. Zu J. Habermas' *Theorie des kommunikativen Handelns*," in *Handlung, Sprache und Vernunft* (Frankfurt, 1982), pp. 295ff. On p. 312: "It is precisely this, however, which practical philosophy has always regarded as a major problem, namely how consistent behavior

can follow from valid insight. . . . Aristotle insists that the eudaimonia of a successful life is not the object of intersubjectively mediated knowledge but is rather the final horizon of meaningful practices that is given directly with the human disposition to act." I have attempted to show why this position, which Bubner has since developed fully in *Geschichtsprozesse und Handlungsnormen* (Frankfurt, 1984), is inconsistent if one attempts to follow it through: see my essay in H. Schnädelbach, ed., *Rationalität* (Frankfurt, 1983), pp. 218ff.

21. Cf. J. Habermas, *Philosophical Discourse of Modernity*, trans. F. Lawrence (Cambridge, Mass., 1987), pp. 341ff.

22. C. Taylor, "Theories of Meaning," in his *Human Agency and Language* (*Philosophical Papers*, vol. 1) (Cambridge, 1985), pp. 215ff.

23. I have put forward this argument with respect to Heidegger, Derrida, and Castoriadis in *Philosophical Discourse of Modernity*, pp. 153ff., 179ff. (see chapter 9 below), and 318f., respectively.

24. Rolf Zimmermann, *Utopie–Rationalität–Politik* (Freiburg, 1985).

25. Cf. also M. Bartels, "Sprache und soziales Handeln. Eine Auseinandersetzung mit Habermas' Sprachbegriff," *Zeitschrift für philosophische Forschung*, vol. 36 (1982): 226–233.

26. Cf. E. Tugendhat, "J. Habermas on Communicative Action," in G. Seebaß and R. Tuomela, eds., *Social Action* (Dordrecht, 1985), pp. 179ff.

27. Here I draw on some of James Bohman's reflections; cf. the second chapter in his doctoral dissertation *Language and Social Criticism* (Boston University, 1985), pp. 139ff.

28. Davidson himself lists the categories of sentences that cannot initially be analyzed by means of the theory. Cf. "Truth and Meaning," in *Synthese* (1967): 310.

29. Cf. John Searle's "Taxonomy of Illocutionary Acts" in his *Expression and Meaning* (Cambridge, 1979), pp. 1–29; cf. also J. Searle and D. Vanderveken, *Foundations of Illocutionary Logic* (Cambridge, 1985).

30. Cf. my critique of Searle in chapter 2 in the present volume, pp. 156ff.

31. [Editor's note:] J. Alexander, "Habermas and Critical Theory: Beyond the Marxian Dilemma?," in Honneth and Joas, *Communicative Action*, pp. 49ff.

32. Zimmermann, *Utopie*, p. 373: "Habermas hereby expands his conceptualization of the illocutionary sense of speech acts in such a way that it already includes an understanding of their social function."

33. See Tugendhat's example in "Habermas on Communicative Action," p. 184.

34. Zimmermann speaks of the "social deployment" of the same illocutionary forces in different contexts. Here, the illocutionary meaning of a normative prescription is "superimposed" on the illocutionary meaning of the request.

35. [Editor's note:] See chapter 2 in the present volume, pp. 131ff.

36. That this second set of conditions belongs to the very meaning of the request that has been uttered can be seen from what it would mean to turn down the request. With his "no," the foreigner can negate the existential presuppositions on which the propositional component rests ("I have no money on me") or the sincerity of the speaker ("You must be joking"), that is, the implicit claims to truth or truthfulness. But only with a "no" that challenges the normative context ("People should no longer be begging in this day and age") does the hearer dispute the validity of the explicitly raised claim.

37. J. Habermas, "A Reply to Skjei's 'A Comment on Performative, Subject, and Proposition in Habermas's Theory of Communication,'" *Inquiry,* 28 (1985): 87–122.

38. [Editor's note:] See also chapters 4 and 6 in the present volume, pp. 223ff. and 301ff., respectively.

39. Formal semantics is able to stylize this limit case as the normal case all the more easily because imperatives, in the course of ontogenesis, are learned initially as simple imperatives reinforced by sanctions, and only later as imperatives that have normative "backing."

40. [Editor's note:] See chapter 2 in the present volume, pp. 126ff.

41. See chapter 2 in the present volume, pp. 125ff. and p. 164.

42. Misunderstandings may have been caused by the fact that, in earlier publications, I introduced action types *first* in terms of criteria for the action orientations ascribed to the actor, and not from the sociological standpoint of the combination of actor attitudes (orientation toward success vs. orientation toward reaching understanding) with types of coordination of different plans of action (influence vs. consensus). The fundamental teleological structure of all action, including all social interactions, was thus lost from view.

43. For example, M. Baurmann, "Understanding as an Aim and Aims of Understanding," in Seebaß and Tuomela, eds., *Social Action,* pp. 187ff. Cf. also J. Berger, "The Linguistification of the Sacred and the Delinguistification of the Economy," in Honneth and Joas, *Communicative Action,* p. 172. "One can reach an understanding successfully and achieve success in an understanding manner (*verständnisvoll*). The two figures of action cannot be disentangled as easily as Habermas imagines."

44. [Editor's note:] See chapter 2 in the present volume, p. 164.

45. Zimmermann, *Utopie,* p. 379, nonetheless raises the justifiable objection that "conversation" cannot be construed as a limit case of communicative action from the same point of view as are, respectively, normatively regulated and dramaturgical action. The fact that, in conversation, the interest in communication gains independence from the interest in pursuing one's own plans of action suggests that it should rather be considered from a functional point of view as a special case.

46. [Editor's note:] The German word here is *unvermittelt,* which literally means "without mediation."

47. This does not exclude combinations such as those considered by Max Weber under the heading "Social Action": in the case of economic action regulated by civil law, for example, the conflicting action orientations are situated at a level different from the normative consensus regarding the framework of legal conditions involved. It equally does not exclude hybrid forms such as a politician's rhetorical behavior, which cannot be analyzed point by point in terms of the model of latently strategic action. Overall, indeed, the hierarchization of levels of action must be taken into account whenever both types of action are entwined. Communicative action is always embedded in the teleological action contexts of the individuals respectively participating in it. Admittedly, the situation of someone guilelessly pursuing a random action goal, or one not declared explicitly due to specific circumstances, must be distinguished from the situation of someone cunningly pursuing a deliberately concealed (because it could not be declared openly) action goal that, as the likely side effect of a communicatively achieved consensus, he strives for with a strate- gic intention. Conversely, the strategic deployment of communicative means can be subordinated to the goal of consensus formation if, for example, the situation permits no more than a "giving the other person to understand something" (*Zu- Verstehen-Geben*) in an indirect way. I assume that the corresponding attitudes of the actors similarly can form a hierarchy; attitudes oriented respectively toward success and reaching understanding are incompatible only with reference to one and the same level of action.

48. [Editor's note:] For a discussion of the various "relief mechanisms" that compensate for the ever-increasing complexity of communicative action in developed societies, see J. Habermas, *The Theory of Communicative Action*, vol. 2, trans. T. McCarthy (Boston, 1987), esp. pp. 179ff.

49. J. Weiss, "Verständigungsorientierung und Kritik," *Kölner Zeitschrift für Soziologie und Sozialpsychologie* 1 (1983): 108ff.

50. Ibid., p. 113.

51. [Editor's note:] See chapter 2 in the present volume, pp. 105ff.

52. [Editor's note:] In *Theory of Communicative Action*, vol. 2, pp. 113ff.

53. Weiss, "Verständigungsorientierung," p. 113.

4

Actions, Speech Acts, Linguistically Mediated Interactions, and the Lifeworld (1988)

It will facilitate a perspicuous overview of the multiple interconnections between action and speech if we start with the clearest and simplest examples possible.[1] I shall exemplify "action" by means of everyday or practical activities such as running, handing things over, hammering, or sawing; I shall exemplify "speech" by means of speech acts such as commands, avowals, and statements. In both cases we may speak of "actions" in a broader sense. However, so as not to blur the differences that are important for my argument, I shall choose from the outset two different descriptive models. First, I shall describe actions in the narrower sense—simple nonlinguistic activities of the aforementioned sort—as purposive activities (*Zweck-tätigkeiten*); with these, the actor intervenes in the world in order to achieve his intended goals through the choice and implementation of appropriate means. Second, I shall describe linguistic utterances as acts by means of which a speaker wishes to reach understanding (*sich verständigen*) with another person about something in the world.

Descriptions of linguistic utterances are possible from the perspective of the actor, that is, in the first person. They may be contrasted with descriptions from the perspective of a third person who observes how an actor, by means of purposive activity, attains a goal or how he, by means of a speech act, reaches understanding about something with another person. In the case of speech acts, descriptions from the perspective of the second person are always possible

("You order me (he orders me) to drop my weapon"); in the case of purposive activities, such descriptions are possible only when the activities are incorporated into contexts of cooperation ("You hand over (he hands over) the weapon to me").

Speech versus Action

To begin with, one can appeal to the difference between descriptive perspectives in order to explain why the two types of nonlinguistic and linguistic actions respectively rely on specific conditions of understanding (*Verstehen*). When I observe a friend hurrying past at a run on the other side of the road, I can, of course, identify her hurrying past as an action. For some purposes, the sentence "She hurries down the road" will also suffice as a description of the action; with this, we attribute an intention to the actor, namely, that she wishes to get to somewhere down the road as quickly as possible. But we cannot *infer* this intention from the observation; rather we presuppose a general context that justifies our conjecture of such an intention. To be sure, even then the action remains curiously in need of further interpretation. It might be the case that our friend does not want to miss her train, does not want to be late for a lecture, or wants to keep an appointment; it might equally be the case that she thinks she is being followed and is fleeing, that she has just escaped attack and is running away, that she has panicked for some other reason and is simply wandering about, and so forth. Although, from the perspective of the observer, we can identify an action, we cannot describe it with certainty as the execution of a specific plan of action; for to do so, we would have to know the intention accompanying the action. We can, by means of indicators, deduce what the intention is and attribute it hypothetically to the actor; in order to be certain of it, however, we would have to be able to take up the perspective of the participant. Nonlinguistic activity does not of itself afford us such an insight in any way—it does not *of its own accord* make itself known as the action that it is planned to be. Speech acts, by contrast, do satisfy this condition.

If I understand the command that my girlfriend gives me (or someone else) when she tells me (or that other person) to drop my gun, then I know fairly well what action she has carried out: she has uttered this specific command. This action does not remain in need of interpretation in the same sense as does the running past of my hurrying friend. For in the standard case of literal meaning, a speech act makes the intention of the speaker known; a hearer can infer from the semantic content of the utterance how the sentence uttered is being used, that is, what type of action is being performed with it. Speech acts interpret themselves; they have a self-referential structure. The illocutionary element establishes, as a kind of pragmatic commentary, the sense in which what is said is being used. Austin's insight that one does something by saying something has a reverse side to it: by performing a speech act, one also says what one is doing. Admittedly, this performative sense of a speech act reveals itself only to a potential hearer who, in adopting the stance of a second person, has given up the perspective of an observer in favor of that of a participant. One has to speak the same language and, as it were, enter the intersubjectively shared lifeworld of a linguistic community in order to benefit from the peculiar reflexivity of natural language and to be able to base the description of an action carried out with words on understanding the implicit self-commentary of this speech act.

Speech acts differ from simple nonlinguistic activities not only by virtue of this reflexive characteristic of self-interpretation but also by virtue of the kind of goals that can be intended through speaking, as well as the kind of successes that can be achieved. Certainly, at a general level, *all* actions, linguistic and nonlinguistic ones, can be conceived of as goal-oriented activity. However, as soon as we wish to differentiate between *action oriented toward reaching understanding* and *purposive activity,* we must heed the fact that the teleological language game in which actors pursue goals, are successful, and produce results takes on a different meaning in the theory of language than it does in the theory of action—the same basic concepts are interpreted in different ways. For our present purposes, it suffices to describe purposive activity in a general way as a goal-oriented and causally effective intervention in the objective world. Corresponding to the goal, which is selected from a standpoint that is value laden, is a state in the world that is to be brought into existence through the choice and application of apparently appropriate means. Underlying the plan of action here is an interpretation of the situation in which the goal of action is determined (a) independently of the means of intervention (b) as a state to be brought about causally (c) in the objective world. It is interesting to note that speech acts cannot be subsumed without difficulty under this model of purposive activity; at any rate, the speaker himself cannot intend his illocutionary aims in terms of this description (a–c).

If we conceive of a speech act as a means whose end is reaching understanding (*Verständigung*) and divide up the general aim of reaching understanding into the subcategories of, first, the aim that the hearer should *understand* the meaning of what is said and, second, the aim that she should *recognize the validity* of the utterance, then the description of how the speaker can pursue these aims does not fulfill any of the three conditions mentioned above.

a. Illocutionary goals cannot be defined independently of the linguistic means of reaching understanding. Grammatical utterances do not constitute instruments for reaching understanding in the same way as, for example, the operations carried out by a cook constitute means for producing enjoyable meals. Rather, the medium of natural language and the telos of reaching understanding interpret one another reciprocally: the one cannot be explained without recourse to the other.

b. The speaker cannot intend the aim of reaching understanding as something that is to be brought about causally, because the kind of illocutionary success that goes beyond mere understanding of what is said depends on the hearer's rationally motivated agreement. The hearer must, as it were, of her own free will give approval to agreement on a given matter by recognizing (the validity of) a criticizable validity claim. Illocutionary goals can be attained only cooperatively; they are not, unlike causally produced effects, at the disposal of the individual participant in communication. A speaker cannot attribute illocutionary success *to himself* in the same way that someone acting purposively is able to attribute to himself the result of his intervention in the nexus of innerworldly processes.

c. Finally, from the perspective of the participants, the process of communication and the result to which this is supposed to lead do not constitute innerworldly states. Persons acting purposively encounter one another solely as entities in the world, despite the freedom of choice they mutually attribute to each other; they are accessible for one another only as objects or opponents. Speaker and hearer, by contrast, adopt a performative attitude in which they encounter one another as members of the intersubjectively shared lifeworld of their linguistic community, that is, in the second person. In reaching an understanding with one another about something in the world, the illocutionary aims they pursue reside, from their perspective, beyond the world to which they can refer in the objectivating attitude of an observer and in which they can intervene purposively. To this extent, they also remain in a transmundane position for one another.

We have distinguished speech acts from simple nonlinguistic activities on the basis of two characteristics: first, that the former are self-interpreting actions with a reflexive structure; and second, that they are directed toward illocutionary goals that cannot have the status of a purpose to be achieved in an innerworldly way, cannot be realized without the freely given cooperation and agreement of an addressee, and can be explained only with recourse to the concept of reaching understanding that is inherent in the linguistic medium itself. The conditions for understanding both types of action are different, as are the basic concepts in terms of which the actors themselves could describe their goals.

The relative independence of these two types of action is also confirmed by the different respective criteria for success. Purposive interventions and speech acts satisfy different conditions of rationality. Rationality has less to do with the possession of knowledge than with how subjects capable of speech and action use knowledge. Now, it is certainly true that a propositional knowledge is embodied in nonlinguistic activities just as much as it is in speech acts. It is the specific way in which such knowledge is used, however, that determines the sense of rationality according to which the success of the action is assessed. If we take as our point of departure the noncommunicative use of propositional knowledge in teleological actions, we encounter a concept of purposive rationality—as it has been elaborated in the theory of rational choice. If we start with the communicative use of propositional knowledge in speech acts, we encounter a concept of communicative rationality (*Verständigungs-rationalität*) that can be explicated in the theory of meaning with the help of the conditions for the acceptability of speech acts. Intuitively underlying the concept of communicative rationality is the experience of the noncoercively unifying, consensus-promoting force of argumentative speech. Whereas purposive rationality refers to the conditions for causally effective interventions in the world of existing states of affairs, the rationality of processes of reaching understanding is assessed with reference to the interconnections between (a) the conditions of validity for speech acts, (b) the validity claims raised with speech acts, and (c) the reasons provided for the vindication of these claims in discourse. The conditions for the rationality of successful speech acts are of a different caliber than the conditions for the rationality of successful purposive activity.

These observations are intended merely to serve as initial evidence in favor of the more far-reaching contention that purposive and communicative rationality may not be substituted for one another. On this premise, I regard purposive activity and action oriented toward reaching understanding as elementary types of action, neither of which may be reduced to the other. In the following, we shall be concerned with the associations into which both of these types of action enter in linguistically mediated interactions. What I call communicative action emerges out of one of these associations.

Communicative versus Strategic Action

I use the term "social action" or "interaction" as a complex concept that can be analyzed with the aid of the elementary concepts of action and speech. In linguistically mediated interactions (and our discussion will deal only with these from now on), both these types of action are entwined. To be sure, they occur in different constellations, depending on whether the illocutionary forces of speech acts assume an action-coordinating role, or whether the speech acts for their part are subordinated in such a way to the extralinguistic dynamics of the exertion of influence of actors who affect one another purposively that the specifically linguistic binding and bonding energies (*Bindungsenergien*) remain *unused*.

An interaction may be understood as the solution to the problem of how the action plans of several actors can be coordinated in such a way that the actions of Alter can be connected up with those of Ego. Here, "connecting up" means in the first instance merely the reduction in scope of contingently colliding possibilities for choice to a degree that makes possible the radial interlocking of topics and actions in social spaces and historical time. If we adopt the perspective of the participants, the need for connection already arises out of the interest each has in pursuing her own action plans. A teleological action can be described as the realization of a plan that relies on the actor's interpretation of the situation. In carrying out a plan, the actor comes to grips with a situation, whereby the action situation forms a segment of the environment interpreted by the actor. This segment is constituted in light of the options for action considered relevant by the actor with respect to the success of a plan. The problem of action coordination occurs as soon as an actor can carry out her plan only interactively, that is, with the help of the action of at least one other actor (or of his refraining from action). Depending on how Alter's plans and actions are connected up to those of Ego, different types of linguistically mediated interactions result.

The two types of interaction can, to begin with, be distinguished from one another according to the respective mechanism of action coordination—in particular, according to whether natural language is employed solely as a medium for transmitting information or whether it is also made use of as a source of social integration. In the first case I refer to strategic action and in the second to communicative action. In the latter case, the consensus achieving force of linguistic processes of *reaching understanding* (*Verständigung*)—that is, the binding and bonding energies of *language itself*—becomes effective for the coordination of actions. In the former case, by contrast, the coordinating effect remains dependent on the *influence*—functioning via nonlinguistic activities—exerted by the actors on the action situation and on each other. Seen from the perspective of the participants, the two mechanisms—that of reaching understanding, which motivates convictions, and that of exertion of influence, which induces behavior—must be mutually exclusive. Speech acts cannot be carried out with the simultaneous intentions of reaching an agreement with an addressee with regard to something and of exercising a causal influence on him. From the point of view of speakers and hearers, agreement cannot be imposed from without, that is, cannot be forced upon one side by the other, either by direct intervention in the action situation or indirect exertion of influence (again, calculated in terms of one's own success) on the propositional attitudes of one's opponent. What comes about *manifestly* through gratification or threat, suggestion or deception, cannot count intersubjectively as an agreement; an intervention of this sort violates the conditions under which illocutionary forces arouse convictions and bring about "connections."

Because communicative action is dependent on the use of language oriented toward reaching understanding, it has to fulfill more stringent conditions. The participating actors attempt to attune their respective plans *cooperatively* within the horizon of a shared lifeworld and on the basis of common interpretations of the situation. Furthermore, they are prepared to achieve these indirect goals of defining the situation and harmonizing their aims in the role of speakers and hearers *via processes of reaching understanding*—that is, by pursuing illocutionary aims without reservation. Reaching understanding linguistically functions in such a way that the participants in interaction come to an agreement with one another about the validity claimed for their speech acts or, as appropriate, take into consideration disagreements that have been ascertained. With speech acts, criticizable validity claims are raised that have a built-in orientation toward intersubjective recognition. A speech-act offer gains a binding and bonding force in that the speaker, in raising a validity claim, issues a credible warranty that he would be able to redeem this claim with the right sort of reasons, if required. Communicative action can thus be distinguished from strategic action in the following respect: the successful coordination of action does not rely on the purposive rationality of the respective individual plans of action but rather on the rationally motivating power of feats of reaching understanding, that is, on a rationality that manifests itself in the conditions for a rationally motivated agreement.

To be sure, speech-act offers can develop an action-coordinating effect only because the binding and bonding force of a speech act that is both understandable and has been accepted by the hearer also extends to the consequences for the sequel of interaction that result from the semantic content of the utterance—whether asymmetrically for the hearer or speaker or symmetrically for both parties. Whoever accepts a command feels herself obliged to carry it out; whoever makes a promise feels himself bound to make it come true if need be; whoever accepts an assertion believes it and will direct her behavior accordingly. I have subsumed the understanding and acceptance of speech acts under illocutionary success; all goals and effects that go beyond this are to be termed "perlocutionary." I now want to distinguish between perlocutionary effects$_1$, which arise from the meaning of the speech act, and perlocutionary effects$_2$, which do not arise as grammatically regulated effects from what has been said itself but rather occur in a contingent way, although they are conditional on illocutionary success. Consider the following example: H understands (illocutionary success$_1$) and accepts (illocutionary success$_2$) the request that she give Y some money. H gives Y "some money" (perlocutionary effect$_1$) and thus gives pleasure to Y's wife (perlocutionary effect$_2$). This latter sort of effect, which is not regulated by grammar, usually will be a public component of the interpretation of the situation, or at least will be of a kind that could be declared openly without impairing the course of the action. This is not the case if the speaker by means of his request wishes to get the addressee to enable Y to make preparations for a burglary with the money he has received, whereby the speaker assumes that H would not approve of such a criminal act. Here, carrying out the planned criminal act would be a perlocutionary effect$_3$, which would not come about if the speaker were to declare it as his aim from the beginning.

This case of *latently strategic action* is an example of how the mechanism of reaching understanding works in the construction of interactions that is deficient in an interesting way: the actor can reach his strategic aim of aiding and abetting a criminal act in the form of a nonpublic perlocutionary effect$_3$ only if he achieves illocutionary success with his request. He will, in turn, succeed in this only if the speaker professes to be pursuing unreservedly the illocutionary aim of his speech act, that is, if he leaves the hearer in the dark as to the actual violation of the presuppositions of action oriented toward reaching understanding by one of the parties involved. The latently strategic use of language lives parasitically on normal language usage because it functions only if at least one of the parties involved assumes that language is being used with a built-in orientation toward reaching understanding. This derivative status points to the independent logic underlying linguistic communication—a logic that is effective for coordination only to the extent that it subjects the purposive activities of the actors to certain constraints.

Of course, even in communicative action, the teleologically structured sequences of action of the individual actors pervade the processes of reaching understanding; it is, after all, the purposive activities of the participants in interaction that are linked up with one another via the medium of language. However, the linguistic medium can fulfill this linking-up function only if it *interrupts* the plans of action—each respectively monitored in terms of the actor's own success—and temporarily changes the mode of action. This communicative shift by way of speech acts performed unreservedly subjects the action orientations and action courses—egocentrically geared toward the requirements of each actor involved—to the structural constraints of an intersubjectively shared language. These constraints force the actors to change their perspective: they must shift perspective from the objectivating attitude of an actor oriented toward success who wants to realize some purpose in the world, to the performative attitude of a speaker who wants to reach understanding with a second person with regard to something in the world. Without this switch to the conditions for the use of language oriented toward reaching understanding, the actors would be denied access to the potential inherent in the binding and bonding energies of language. This is why a latently strategic action fails as soon as the addressee discovers that her counterpart has only apparently broken off his orientation toward success.

The constellation of speech and action changes in strategic action. Here, the illocutionary binding and bonding forces wane; language shrinks to a medium of information. We can see this clearly if we look at the example just mentioned:

(1) *S:* I request that you give *Y* some money.

Under the presuppositions of communicative action, the person to whom an order or a demand is addressed must know the normative context that authorizes the speaker to make his demand, thereby justifying the expectation that the addressee has reasons to carry out the required action. Knowledge of the conditions of success (for handing over the money), which can be inferred from the propositional content of (1), does not suffice in order to understand the illocutionary meaning of this speech act—that is, its specific character *qua* imperative. Knowledge of the conditions of success must be supplemented by knowledge of those conditions under which the speaker can have reasons to regard request (1) as a valid imperative, which means in this case, as normatively justified: for example, that *S* is addressing a friend, a colleague known to be generous in money matters, a creditor, or an accomplice. For it is of course also a normative validity claim that the addressee may reject for some reason or other.

(1′) *H:* No, you have no right to ask that of me.

In contexts of manifestly strategic action it is precisely these validity claims—claims to propositional truth, to normative rightness, and to subjective truthfulness (*Wahrhaftigkeit*)—that are undermined. The presupposition of an orientation toward validity claims is suspended here.

A bank robber's cry of "Hands up!" while pointing a gun at a cashier whom he orders to hand over money demonstrates in a drastic fashion that, in such a situation, the conditions of normative validity have been replaced by sanction conditions. The acceptability conditions for an imperative that has been stripped of any normative backing must be supplemented by such sanction conditions. So too in the case of request (1). If the law-abiding addressee knows that *Y* wishes to use the money she is to give him in order to make preparations for a crime, then *S* will have to supplement his request by pointing to possible sanctions. He may, for example, say:

(2) *S:* I request that you give *Y* some money—otherwise I will tell the police how deeply you are already involved in the whole affair.

The disintegration of the normative background is shown symptomatically in the "if-then" structure of the threat, which replaces the validity claims presupposed in communicative action with power claims; from this we can see the changed constellation of speech and action. In *manifestly strategic action,* the speech acts (whose illocutionary forces have been weakened) relinquish the role of coordinating action, passing it on to forms of exerting influence that are external to language. Stripped in this way of its potency, language now fulfills only those information functions remaining once linguistic feats of reaching understanding have been robbed of their consensus-forming function, and once the validity of utterances—now suspended in communication—can be deduced only indirectly. Speech act (2) is a request only on the surface; it is in fact a threat:

(2a)   *S:* If you do not give *Y* money, I will tell the police that . . .

Threats are examples of speech acts that play an instrumental role in contexts of strategic action, have forfeited their illocutionary force, and derive their illocutionary meaning from other contexts of employment in which the same sentences are normally uttered with an orientation toward reaching understanding. Acts of this kind—acts that have become independent as perlocutionary acts—are not illocutionary acts at all, for they are not aimed at the rationally motivated position of an addressee. This can be seen from the way in which threats are repudiated:

(2a′)   *H:* No, you have nothing you can use against me.

The "no" refers to empirical conditions under which the threat alone could achieve the desired perlocutionary effect. The hearer contests the reasons that were supposed to motivate her to act in the manner predicted by *S.* Unlike illocutionary acts, threats do not rely on general, addressee-independent reasons that could convince anyone. Their "then-component" points rather to particular reasons that could provide specific addressees in particular circumstances with an empirical motive to act in a certain way.

Like simple imperatives, insults, too, often have an ambiguous character. They may have normative backing, and express, for instance, moral condemnation; however, they may also become independent as perlocutionary acts, serving, for instance, to instill fear and terror in the addressee.

The concept of communicative action provisionally introduced here is based on a particular conception of language and reaching understanding; it has to be developed in the context of theories of meaning. I cannot attempt to do this in detail here. Nonetheless, I wish at least to introduce and explicate the basic assumption of the formal-pragmatic theory of meaning, which refers to the internal connection between meaning and validity. This, as yet, says nothing about the fruitfulness of such a theoretical approach for the social sciences. The concept of communicative action must prove its worth within the sociological theory of action. The latter is supposed to explain how social order is possible. In this respect, the analysis of the presuppositions of communicative action may be helpful. It opens up the dimension of the background of the lifeworld, which enmeshes and stabilizes interactions to form higher-level aggregates.

The Pragmatic Turn in the Theory of Meaning

The concept of communicative action develops the intuition that the telos of reaching understanding is inherent in language. Reaching understanding is a normatively laden concept that goes beyond the mere understanding of a grammatical expression. A speaker reaches understanding with another with regard to some matter. Such an agreement (*Einverständnis*) can be achieved by both parties only if they accept the utterances involved as correct (*sachgemäß*). Agreement with regard to something is measured in terms of the intersubjective recognition of the validity (*Gültigkeit*) of an utterance that can in principle be criticized. Of course, understanding the meaning of a linguistic expression and reaching understanding about something with the help of an utterance held to be valid are two different things; an equally sharp distinction must be made between an utterance that is held to be valid and one that is valid. Nonetheless, questions of meaning cannot be separated completely from questions of validity. The basic question of meaning theory—namely, what it is to understand the meaning of a linguistic expression—cannot be isolated from the question of the context in which this expression may be accepted as valid. One simply would not know what it is to understand the meaning of a linguistic expression if one did not know how one could make use of it in order to reach understanding with someone about something. One can see from the very conditions for understanding linguistic expressions that the speech acts that can be formed with their help have a built-in orientation toward a rationally motivated agreement with regard to what is said. To this extent, an orientation toward the possible validity of utterances is part of the pragmatic conditions, not just for reaching understanding but, prior to this, for linguistic understanding itself. In language, the dimensions of meaning and validity are internally connected.

Truth-conditional semantics has made use of this insight ever since Frege: one understands an assertoric sentence if one knows what is the case if it is true. It is, however, no coincidence that it is a sentence and not a speech act—moreover, a propositional sentence rather than a nonassertoric sentence—that serves here as the prototype. According to this theory, the problem of validity is located exclusively in the relation of language to the world conceived as the totality of facts. Because validity is equated with assertoric truth, a relationship between the meaning and the validity of linguistic expressions is produced only in the modes of speech in which facts are established. However, as Karl Bühler already observed, the representational function is only one of three equiprimordial (*gleichursprünglich*) functions of language. Sentences that are used communicatively serve simultaneously to express the intentions or subjective experiences (*Erlebnisse*) of a speaker, to represent states of affairs (or something occurring in the world), and to enter into relations with an addressee. The three basic aspects of a speaker reaching understanding/with another/about something are reflected in these three functions. A threefold relation exists between the meaning of a linguistic expression and (a) what is *intended* (*gemeint*) with it, (b) what is *said* in it, and (c) the *way in which it is used in a speech act*.

Curiously enough, each of the three best-known approaches to meaning theory proceeds from just one of these three rays of meaning that are bundled together, as it were, in the focal point of language; each approach then aims to explain the entire spectrum of meaning in terms of this single function of language. Intentionalist semantics (from Grice to Bennett and Schiffer) takes as fundamental what the speaker means (*meint*), or wishes to give to understand, with an expression used in a given situation; formal semantics (from Frege via the early Wittgenstein to Dummett) takes as its point of departure the conditions under which a sentence is true (or, as the case may be, rendered true); and the use theory of meaning inaugurated by the later Wittgenstein refers everything in the final instance to the habitualized contexts of interaction in which linguistic expressions fulfill practical functions. Each of these three competing theories of meaning connects up with precisely one aspect of the process of reaching understanding. They wish to explain the meaning of a linguistic expression either from the perspective of what is meant as intended meaning, or from the perspective of what is said as literal meaning, or from the perspective of its use in interaction as utterance meaning. The stylization in each case of just one of the three aspects simultaneously taken account of in Bühler's schema of language functions has led to bottlenecks that I cannot go into here. The theory of speech acts (as developed by Searle, following Austin) came on the scene in response to these difficulties.

Speech-act theory accords the speaker's intention a proper place without, as in Gricean semantics, simply reducing linguistic processes of reaching understanding (*Verständigung*) to strategic action. In emphasizing the illocutionary component, speech-act theory also takes into consideration the interpersonal reference of speech, as well as its character as action; however, it does so without, as in Wittgensteinian pragmatics, excluding all validity claims that point beyond the provincial horizon of particular, in principle equally legitimate language games. For with the concept of satisfaction conditions, speech-act theory also ultimately respects the relation between language and world, between sentence and states of affairs. By virtue of this one-dimensional definition of validity as the satisfaction of conditions of propositional truth, however, speech-act theory remains bound to the cognitivism of truth-conditional semantics. It is precisely here that I see the deficit that has to be made good as soon as one recognizes that all language functions, and not only the function of representation, are imbued with validity claims.

The sentence "I give *Y* some money" is ambiguous with regard to its mode; this ambiguity disappears when, depending on the context, the sentence functions as a promise, as a confession, or even as a prediction:

(3) *S:* I promise you that I will give *Y* some money.

(4) *S:* I would like to divulge to you that I am going to give *Y* some money.

(5) *S:* I can predict to you that *X* (another person) will give *Y* some money.

The type of validity claim that a speaker connects with promises, confessions, and predictions emerges from the corresponding negations with which the hearer could reject these speech-act offers:

(3′) *H:* No, you've always been unreliable in such matters.

(4′) *H:* No, you just want to lead me up the garden path.

(5′) *H:* No, he doesn't have any money.

With (3) the speaker raises the normative claim that he is entering into an obligation, with (4) the claim to subjective truthfulness (*Wahrhaftigkeit*)—to mean what he says, with (5) a claim to propositional truth. Moreover, a speech act may be negated from several points of view and not just from the aspect of validity dominant in a given situation. The imperative

(1) *S:* I request that you give *Y* some money.

can be turned down not only with

(1′) *H:* No, you have no right to do so.

but also by casting doubt on the truthfulness of the speaker or on the existential presuppositions of the propositional content:

(1″) *H:* No, you don't mean that seriously—you are pulling my leg.

(1‴) *H:* No, I won't be meeting *Y* and will have no opportunity to hand over money to him.

The same holds true *mutatis mutandis* for constative and expressive speech acts. Whether an utterance fulfills its representational function is measured, of course, in terms of the truth conditions; but the fulfillment of the interactive and expressive functions of language is assessed in terms of truth-analogous conditions of authorization and truthfulness. Every speech-act can, as a whole, always be criticized as invalid from three points of view: as untrue with respect to the statement made (or the existential presuppositions of its propositional content); as incorrect with respect to established normative contexts (or the legitimacy of the norms presupposed); or as lacking in truthfulness with respect to the speaker's intention. Let us assume for the moment that this trichotomous extension of the concept of validity, here merely sketched, could be developed in detail. What would be the implications of this for the basic question addressed by meaning theory?

Dummett already takes the first step toward a pragmatic reinterpretation of the problem of validity. He demonstrates that truth-conditional semantics can abstract from the circumstances in which a hearer is in a position to *recognize* when the truth conditions of an assertoric sentence have been satisfied at the very most only in the case of simple predicative observation sentences. Relying on the pragmatic distinction between "truth" and "assertibility"—between the truth of a sentence and the entitlement to make an assertion by means of that sentence—Dummett replaces knowledge of the truth conditions with an indirect sort of knowledge. The hearer must know the kinds of reasons with which the speaker could, if necessary, redeem her claim that certain truth conditions have been satisfied. One understands a propositional sentence if one knows what kinds of reasons a speaker would have to provide in order to convince a hearer that she is entitled to raise a truth claim for that sentence. The conditions of understanding, as they have to be satisfied in everyday communicative practices, thus point to the supposition of a game of argumentation in which the speaker, as the proponent, might convince the hearer, as the opponent, that a possibly problematic validity claim is justifiable. Following this *epistemic turn* in truth-conditional semantics, the question of the validity of a sentence can no longer be considered as a question—detached from the process of communication—of the objective relation between language and the world.

This suggests, however, that the claim to truth should no longer be defined semantically and solely from the perspective of the speaker. Validity claims constitute the point of convergence for intersubjective recognition by all those involved. They play a pragmatic role in the dynamics of speech-act offer and the hearer's taking a position with his "yes" or "no." This *pragmatic turn* in truth-conditional semantics calls for a reevaluation of the concept of "illocutionary force." Austin conceived of this force as the irrational component of the speech act, the actually rational part being monopolized by the propositional content. On a pragmatically enlightened reading, the modal component determines the validity claim that, in the standard case, the speaker raises with the help of a performative sentence. The illocutionary component thereby becomes the locus of a rationality that presents itself as a structural interconnection between validity conditions, validity claims that refer to these, and reasons by means of which they may be vindicated in discourse. Thus, the conditions of validity no longer remain fixated on the propositional component; room is made for the introduction of further validity claims that are not directed toward conditions of truth (or success), that is, that are not geared toward the relation between language and the objective world.

Once propositional truth has been supplemented by normative rightness and subjective truthfulness, it is possible, in a final step, to generalize Dummett's explanation. We understand a speech act when we know the kinds of reasons that a speaker could provide in order to convince a hearer that he is entitled in the given circumstances to claim validity for his utterance—in short, when we know *what makes it acceptable.* A speaker, with a validity claim, appeals to a reservoir of potential reasons that he could produce in support of the claim. The reasons interpret the validity conditions and to this extent are themselves part of the conditions that make an utterance acceptable. In this, the acceptability conditions point to the holistic character of natural languages; every single speech act is linked via logical-semantic threads to numerous other, potential speech acts that could take on the pragmatic role of reasons. Knowledge of a language is therefore entwined with knowledge of what is actually the case in the linguistically disclosed world. Perhaps knowledge of the world merely hangs on a longer chain of reasons than does knowledge of a language. That each cannot sharply be distinguished from the other confirms the basic idea from which we started: to understand an expression is to know how one can make use of it in order to reach understanding with someone with regard to something.

If this approach to a formal-pragmatic theory of meaning can be elaborated sufficiently, and rendered plausible, then it provides an explanation for why the medium of natural language can draw on a reservoir of potential binding and bonding forces that can be used for purposes of action coordination. In that a speaker, with his criticizable validity claim, issues a warranty to provide reasons for the validity of the speech act, if necessary, the hearer—who knows the acceptability conditions and thus understands what has been said—is challenged to take up a rationally motivated position; if the hearer recognizes the validity claim, thereby accepting the speech-act offer, she assumes her share of the obligations relevant for the sequel of interaction arising for all those involved from what is said.

From Social Action to Social Order

I have treated communicative and strategic action as two variants of linguistically mediated interaction. It holds only for *communicative action* that the structural constraints of an intersubjectively shared language impel the actors—in the sense of a weak transcendental necessity—to step out of the egocentricity of a purposive rational orientation toward their own respective success and to surrender themselves to the public criteria of communicative rationality. The transsubjective structures of language thus suggest a basis for answering, from the point of view of action theory, the classical question of how social order is possible.

The atomistic concept of *strategic* action does not itself provide us with any equivalent answer. If it nonetheless is to serve as the basic concept in a sociological theory of action, then it has to be explained how contexts of interaction that emerge solely from the reciprocal exertion of influence upon one another of success-oriented actors can establish themselves as stable orders. Ever since Hobbes, the attempt has repeatedly been made to explain how norms with trans-subjectively binding normative validity claims can develop out of the interest positions and individual profit calculations of actors who make decisions in a purposive rational way and who encounter each other only haphazardly. Today, this "Hobbesian problem" (Parsons) is being tackled using game theory. However, to the extent that I have been able to follow the debates (from Amartya Sen to Jon Elster), I have not gained the impression that the question of how social order can emerge from the double contingency of actors who make decisions independently of one another can be answered more convincingly today than by Hobbes in his time.

More promising than the attempt to renew with modern means the classical concept of an instrumental order is the introduction of a medium of communication through which behavior-steering information flows are conducted. Insofar as this concept is defined according to the model of a market exchange steered by money, strategic action geared toward rational choice can be retained as the conception of action suitable for a steering medium. For example, information conveyed via the money code conditions—on account of a built-in structure of preferences—decisions regarding actions without recourse to more demanding and higher-risk feats of communication that are oriented toward validity claims. The actor assumes a success-oriented attitude—in the extreme case, a purposive rational one. However, for the actor, the switch to *media-steered interactions* results in an objective inversion of setting goals and choosing means. The medium itself now transmits the system-maintenance imperatives of the system in question (here the market system). This inversion of means and ends is experienced by the actor, as Marx observed, as the reifying character of objectified social processes. To this extent, media-steered interactions no longer embody an instrumental reason located in the purposive rationality of decision makers, but rather a functionalist reason inherent in self-regulating systems. This approach, however, which is elaborated in economics and organization theory, covers only specific domains of action; it does not meet the standard of an explanatory theory that would be sufficiently general in scope to explain social action as a whole in terms of strategic action. Since behavior-steering communication media such as money merely branch off as special codes from a more richly structured everyday language, media theory points toward the broader framework of a theory of language (cf. my *The Theory of Communicative Action*, vol. 2, pp. 256ff).

The only alternative that remains is to dispense with any attempt to develop a concept of social order in general from the point of view of action theory. The transsubjective structures of language entwined with everyday practices are replaced in the work of Parsons and Luhmann by *boundary-maintaining and autopoetic systems* introduced at a more general level than are actors and linguistically mediated interactions. Actions and interactions can then for their part be understood as psychological and social systems that form environments for and reciprocally observe one another. In cutting loose from action theory, however, systems theory must pay the price for its objectivistic approach. Systems functionalism cuts itself off from the intuitive knowledge of the lifeworld and its members. Hermeneutic access to this reservoir of knowledge proceeds by way of (at least virtual) participation in everyday communicative practices. Of course, in the face of complex societies, the social sciences must be prepared to extract even counterintuitive insights from their object domain. Yet society, woven from webs of linguistically mediated interactions, simply is not encountered in the form of an external nature accessible only to observation. The meaning that is sedimented in society's symbolic contexts and self-interpretations discloses itself only to a hermeneutic approach. Whoever does not want to block off this path for himself, but wishes rather to open up the sociocultural context of life *from within*, has to take as his point of departure a conception of society that can be connected up with the perspectives on action and interpretive efforts of the participants in interaction. For this first step, the concept of *lifeworld,* which formal-pragmatic analysis of the presuppositions of communicative action already comes upon prior to all sociological theorizing, presents itself.

That social order is supposed to produce and reproduce itself by way of processes of consensus formation might seem at first glance to be a trivial notion. The improbability of this idea becomes clear, however, as soon as one reminds oneself that every communicatively achieved agreement depends on the taking up of "yes"/"no" positions with regard to criticizable validity claims. In the case of communicative action, the double contingency that has to be absorbed by all interaction formation takes the particularly precarious shape of an ever-present risk of disagreement that is built into the communicative mechanism itself, whereby every disagreement has a high cost. In this regard, various options are available: simple repair work; leaving open or bracketing controversial validity claims with the result that the common ground of shared convictions shrivels; the transition to discourses costly in terms of time and effort, with uncertain outcomes and disruptive effects; breaking off communication; or finally, switching over to strategic action. If one considers that every explicit agreement to a speech-act offer rests on a double negation, namely the repudiation of the (always possible) rejection of it, then the communicative processes operating by way of criticizable validity claims hardly recommend themselves as reliable rails along which social integration might run. Rational motivation, which rests on the fact that the hearer can say "no," constitutes a maelstrom of problematization that makes linguistic consensus formation appear more like a disruptive mechanism. For the risk of disagreement receives ever new sustenance from experiences. Experiences disrupt the routinized and taken-for-granted aspects of life and constitute a wellspring of contingency. Experiences frustrate expectations, run counter to habitual modes of perception, trigger surprises, make us conscious of new things. Experiences are always new experiences and provide a counterbalance to everything with which we have grown familiar.

With this we have gained a first pointer in the direction of the complementary phenomena of *the surprising* and *the familiar.* A preunderstanding sedimented in a deep-seated stratum of things that are taken for granted, of certainties, and of unquestioned assumptions, could explain how the risk of disagreement inherent in linguistic communication (*Verständigung*)—and lurking everywhere—is absorbed, regulated, and kept in check in everyday practices. As is well known, Husserl in his later work, under the heading of "lifeworld," endeavored to explore the terrain of the immediately familiar and the unquestionably certain. He attempted with phenomenological means to shed light on this realm of implicit knowledge, of the prepredicative and the precategorial, of the forgotten foundations of meaning underlying everyday life-practices and world experience. Here, I shall neither go into Husserl's method nor the context in which he introduced his concept of the lifeworld; rather, I shall appropriate the material content of his investigations by assuming that communicative action, too, is embedded in a lifeworld that provides risk-absorbing coverage in the form of a massive background consensus. The explicit feats of communication achieved by communicative actors take place within the horizon of shared, unproblematic convictions; the disquiet that arises through experience and critique crashes against the—as it seems—broad and imperturbable rock projecting out from the deep of agreed-upon interpretive patterns, loyalties, and proficiencies.

With his concept of unthematic knowledge, Husserl has also already indicated a path along which we can uncover these foundations on which meaning rests. Here, however, we must take two delimitations into account. The prereflective knowledge that accompanies processes of reaching understanding without itself being thematized must first be distinguished from the knowledge that is *concomitantly thematized* in speech acts. In a speech act Mp, the propositional content of the sentence is the carrier (*Träger*) for thematic knowledge. The performative sentence gives expression to a validity claim and specifies in which sense the sentences are being used. This self-referential commentary is declared performatively—through the carrying-out of an action—and is not, as in the case of the commented-upon propositional content, presented explicitly as knowledge. In order to make the merely concomitantly thematized meaning of the illocutionary act available in the same way as the thematic knowledge, Mp has to be transformed into a description of Mp:

(1) *S:* I request that you give *Y* some money.

must be reformulated as

(1a) In uttering (1), *S* has requested *H* to do "*p*."

Unthematic knowledge is to be distinguished from merely *concomitantly thematized knowledge* on the basis that it cannot be made accessible through a simple transformation of the participant's perspective into the observer's perspective; unthematic knowledge requires, rather, an analysis of presuppositions. For what is unthematic are those presuppositions that the participants in communication must make if a speech act in a given situation is to be able to take on a specific meaning and if it is to be capable of being valid or invalid at all.

Not all unthematic knowledge is constitutive for a *particular* lifeworld, however. Of no relevance in this respect is the universal generative knowledge that enables competent speakers to use grammatical sentences in utterances properly in the first place. Equally irrelevant is the knowledge of how one fulfills the general pragmatic presuppositions of communicative action—for example, the knowledge of how one orients oneself toward validity claims and reciprocally imputes accountability to one another; how one identifies objects, thus establishing contact between language and the world; how one distinguishes between illocutionary and perlocutionary aims; how one separates the subjective and the social worlds from the objective world; how one moves from action to argumentation. All of this is implicit knowledge that is mastered only intuitively and requires the reflexive work of rational reconstruction in order to be transformed from a "know-how" into a "know-that."

However, this *universal, prereflexive unthematic knowledge*—which is part of linguistic competence—serves the production of speech acts in general; it generates communicative action but does not serve to complement and supplement it. In the remaining section I shall focus on that other sort of unthematic knowledge that complements, supplements, and accompanies communicative action and provides the context within which this is embedded. What is at issue here is the concrete knowledge of language and the world that dwells persistently in the penumbra of the prepredicative and the precategorial and that forms the unproblematic ground for all thematic and concomitantly thematized knowledge.

To be sure, the phenomenological concept of lifeworld suggests a conception of world constitution borrowed from epistemology that cannot straightforwardly be taken over into sociology. In order to avoid the difficulties connected with social phenomenology, social theory must from the very outset detach itself from a constitution theory of knowledge and allow itself to be guided by a pragmatic theory of language that applies itself intrinsically to linguistically mediated interactions. "Lifeworld" shall therefore be introduced as a complementary concept to communicative action. However, a formal-pragmatic investigation, which investigates the background of the lifeworld by way of an analysis of presuppositions, is carried out from the reconstructively obtained perspective of a participating speaker. The use of the concept of lifeworld in the social sciences requires a switch over in method from the (performative) attitude of the [first and] second person to the (theoretical) attitude of the third person.

The Formal-Pragmatic Concept of Lifeworld

In *The Crisis of European Sciences,* Husserl introduced the concept of lifeworld within the framework of a critique of reason. From beneath the reality that the natural sciences take as the only one, he pulls out the antecedently existing context of prereflective life-practices and world experience as the ousted foundation of meaning. To this extent, the lifeworld forms a counterconcept to those idealizations that first constitute the object domain of the natural sciences. In opposition to the idealizations of measurement, imputed causality, and mathematicization, as well as to the tendency toward technologization operative within these, Husserl sues for the recovery of the lifeworld as the immediately present realm of originary accomplishments; from the perspective of the lifeworld, he criticizes the idealizations—oblivious of their own existence—of natural scientific objectivism. However, since the philosophy of the subject is blind to the independent logic (*Eigensinn*) of linguistic intersubjectivity, Husserl is not able to recognize that the very ground of everyday communicative practices itself rests on idealizing presuppositions.

With validity claims that transcend all merely local standards of evaluation, the tension between transcendental presuppositions and empirical facts now moves into the facticity of the lifeworld itself. The theory of communicative action detranscendentalizes Kant's realm of the Intelligible by revealing the idealizing force of anticipation in the unavoidable pragmatic presuppositions of speech acts, that is, at the heart of everyday communicative practices themselves—idealizations that simply emerge more visibly in the extraordinary forms of communication that argumentations constitute. The idea of vindicating criticizable validity claims requires idealizations that, having descended from the transcendental heavens down to the earth of the lifeworld, develop their effectiveness in the medium of natural language; the power of resistance of a—cunningly operating—communicative reason to the cognitive-instrumental deformations of selectively modernized forms of life is also manifested in these idealizations.

Since the idealizations are due to a linguistic competence that the speakers possess prereflectively in the form of an implicit knowledge, the conflict between, on the one hand, the explicit knowledge dependent on idealizations and, on the other hand, the risk-absorbing background knowledge takes place *within* the domain of unthematic knowledge—it does not appear only for the first time, as Husserl maintained, in the competition between the expert knowledge of the empirical sciences and pretheoretical everyday convictions. Most of what is said in everyday communicative practices remains unproblematic, escapes criticism, and avoids the pressure of surprise exerted by critical experiences, because it draws in advance on the validity of antecedently agreed-upon certainties, in other words, the certainties of the lifeworld.

The burden of rendering validity claims plausible is assumed prima facie by an unthematically concurrent, relatively *foregrounded knowledge* on which the participants rely in the form of pragmatic and semantic presuppositions. What is at issue here is (a) a situation-specific horizontal knowledge (*Horizontwissen*) and (b) a topic-dependent contextual knowledge.

a. The perceived environment, which is embedded in concentrically arranged spatiotemporal horizons that are not perceived, constitutes the center of the speech situation. The participants may usually suppose that they interpret, from coordinated perspectives, the more trivial components of the speech situation and of their surroundings (becoming ever more diffuse the more distant they are) more or less in the same way. They also assume that their divergent perspectives, resulting from their differing life-histories, converge here and now and, at most, accord different relevance to a shared interpretation of the situation. This *horizontal knowledge* is actualized concomitantly yet implicitly when something is said; it renders an utterance unproblematic and lends support to its acceptability. If I mention in the course of small talk in a park in Frankfurt that it is snowing in California, my partner in conversation will refrain from questioning me further only if he knows that I have just returned from San Francisco or, for example, that I work as a meteorologist.

b. An equally important role in stabilizing validity is played by the *topic-dependent contextual knowledge* that a speaker can presuppose within the framework of a common language, the same culture, similar schooling, and so forth—that is, within the framework of a common milieu or horizon of subjective experience. The speaker who addresses a particular topic implicitly summons up factual contexts in the light of which what is said appears as trivial or surprising, informative or implausible. From this concomitantly present contextual knowledge, information and reasons can be mobilized as required. This will be necessary whenever the supposition that the unthematically concurrent knowledge is intersubjectively shared and agreed upon turns out to be wrong. My attempt to introduce the concept of lifeworld from the point of view of the theory of communication in the way that I am doing here will provoke different questions and objections from an audience of academic colleagues in Madrid or Paris than, for example, in Berkeley.

This sort of unthematic knowledge easily gets drawn into the maelstrom of problematization. The horizon of the situation, or the topic, need only shift marginally. If I exceed the usual length of a lecture by even ten minutes or digress to an impending holiday trip when dealing with the topic of lifeworld in an academic context, then attention will focus on the violated pragmatic presuppositions that we had until then tacitly shared. In this respect, the (a) situation-related horizontal knowledge and (b) topic-dependent contextual knowledge are to be distinguished from (c) the *background knowledge of the lifeworld*. The latter is subject to different conditions of thematization. It cannot intentionally be brought to consciousness in the same way as is possible with the first two, and it forms a deep stratum of unthematized knowledge in which the situation-related horizontal knowledge and topic-dependent contextual knowledge—which are both still relatively in the foreground—have their roots.

c. This *deep-seated background knowledge* has a greater stability since it is to a large extent immune to the pressure of problematization exerted by contingency-generating experiences. This can be seen by the fact that this layer of elliptical and always already-presupposed knowledge can be extricated from the inaccessible mode of providing an unquestioned background and thematized only by *methodical effort* and, even then, only piece by piece. Husserl proposed that a procedure of eidetic variation be used for this purpose, namely, the unrestrained imagining of modifications of the world or the projecting of contrasting worlds, which sheds light on our expectations of normality—as unconscious as they are unshakable and unavailable— and which may bring to light how the foundations of our everyday practices depend on a *Weltanschauung*. John Searle's examples also recall Husserl's method. With the help of these examples, Searle demonstrates that the meaning of speech acts remains indeterminate until their semantically fixed validity conditions have been supplemented by intuitively known, implicit background assumptions that remain unthematic and are presumed to be completely unproblematic. Thus, Searle transposes "the cat is on the mat" into outer space in order to make us aware by means of this modification that, normally, when we imagine a body upon some surface, we imagine it only as affected by the force of gravity. Similarly, Homo sapiens must have had an intuitive knowledge of how levers work ever since they started to use certain tools for survival; yet the law of levers was discovered as a law and given the form of explicit knowledge only in the course of methodical questioning by modern science of our pretheoretical knowledge.

However, the method of free variation of unavoidable presuppositions soon meets its limits. The background of the lifeworld is just as little at our disposal as we are in a position to subject absolutely everything to abstract doubt. Rather, Charles S. Peirce, with his pragmatic doubt about this Cartesian doubt, has reminded us that problems that severely unsettle lifeworld certainties come to meet us with the objective power of historical contingencies. Husserl himself had already linked his analysis of the lifeworld with the crisis motif. It is a crisis arising from the consequences of modern science that shakes Husserl out of a state of objectivistic oblivion of both world and self. The problematizing pressure brought to bear by such crisis situations, whether of a world-historical or a life-historical type, objectively transforms the conditions for thematization, and only thus creates an illuminating distance from what is most familiar and most taken for granted. An example of this is the thrust toward moral universalism that sets in with the prophetic world religions, disrupting naive familiarity with the substantive ethical life (*Sittlichkeit*)—commanding reverence from those within it—of the clan or tribal association, a thrust, incidentally, that has sparked off so many regressions that it had to be renewed at intervals right up until this century—until the death camps opened their doors.

Like all unthematic knowledge, the background of the lifeworld is implicitly and prereflectively present. It is distinguished, first, by its mode of *immediate certainty*. This lends a paradoxical character to this knowledge from within which—without any distance—we live our lives, undergo experiences, speak, and act. The insistent yet at the same time imperceptible presence of this background appears as an intensified, although nonetheless deficient, form of knowledge. Such background knowledge lacks an internal relation to the possibility of becoming problematic for it comes into contact with criticizable validity claims, thereby being transformed into fallible knowledge, only at the moment in which it is expressed in language. Absolute certainties remain unshakable until they suddenly disintegrate; for, in lacking fallibility, they do not constitute knowledge in the strict sense at all.

This deep-seated background knowledge is distinguished, secondly, by its *totalizing power.* The lifeworld constitutes a totality with a center and indeterminate, porous borders that recede rather than permit themselves to be transcended. The two other forms of unthematic knowledge mentioned—which are, relatively speaking, in the foreground—derive their world-constituting function, in the dimension of perception as well as in that of meaning, from the background in which they are rooted. The common speech situation constitutes the center—and not, for instance, my body, as an anthropologizing phenomenology has claimed—in which social spaces (staggered concentrically according to depth and width) and historical times (arranged three-dimensionally) converge prior to any objectivation through measuring operations. The spaces and times experienced are the coordinates of *our respective shared world;* these coordinates are always concretely interpreted or embodied, for instance, as village community, region, state, nation, world society, and so forth, or as the succession of generations, epochs, world historical ages, life-histories individuated in the eyes of God, and so forth. I, in my body, and I, as my body, find myself always already occupying an intersubjectively shared world, whereby these collectively inhabited lifeworlds telescope into each other, overlap, and entwine like text and context.

A third feature, connected with immediacy and totalization, is the *holism* of this kind of background knowledge that, despite the latter's apparent transparency, renders it impenetrable; the lifeworld may be described as a "thicket." Components are fused together here that can be split up into different categories of knowledge only under the pressure of problematizing experiences. Indeed, the formal-pragmatic analyst casts his gaze back into the lifeworld from the vantage point of a thematic knowledge already differentiated into facts, norms, and subjective experiences. Only the ricocheting of this differentiating gaze leads him to conclude that, in the background knowledge of the lifeworld, convictions about something are alloyed with a relying-on-something, with a being-moved-by-something, with a knowing-how-to-do-something. The things we simply assume, the things on which we rely and the things with which we are familiar, the things that move us, and the things that we can do—all of which are intermeshed in this background knowledge—are prereflective prefigurations of something that must first be thematized in speech acts before it can branch out and take on the meaning of propositional knowledge, of an interpersonal relationship produced through illocutionary means, or of the speaker's intention.

The three attributes of immediacy, totalizing power, and holistic constitution belonging to this unthematically presupposed knowledge may perhaps explain the lifeworld's paradoxical function as "ground" (*Boden*): how it keeps contingency in check through proximity to experience. Using sureties that we obtain only from experience, the lifeworld erects a wall against surprises that themselves originate from experience. If knowledge of the world is defined on the basis that it is acquired a posteriori, whereas linguistic knowledge, relatively speaking, represents an a priori knowledge, then the paradox may be explained by the fact that, in the background of the lifeworld, knowledge of the world and knowledge of language are integrated.

The problematizing force of critical experiences separates the background of the lifeworld from the foreground. Such experiences are themselves differentiated according to the various ways in which what is encountered in the world—things and events, persons, and stories in which people are involved—is dealt with practically. The *world of things* (*Zeugwelt*) and pragmatic contexts of explanation are constituted through our handling of things and events; the *solidary world* and historical contexts of meaning are constituted through our interactive dealings with persons to whom we relate—the former within the framework of communities of cooperation, the latter within the framework of linguistic communities. Ontogenetically, the empirical world in which we deal with external nature in a technical-practical way separates only gradually from the world in which we deal with others within society in a moral-practical way. Finally, experiences with our inner nature, with our body, needs, and feelings are of an indirect kind; they are *reflected* against our experiences of the external world. When experiences of inner nature then gain independence as aesthetic experiences, the ensuing works of autonomous art take on the role of objects that open our eyes, that provoke new ways of seeing things, new attitudes, and new modes of behavior. Aesthetic experiences are not forms of everyday practice; they do not refer to cognitive-instrumental skills and moral ideas, which develop in innerworldly learning processes, but rather are bound up with the world-constituting, world-disclosing function of language.

This structuring of experience reflects the architecture of the lifeworld insofar as it is linked to the trichotomous constitution of speech acts and of the background knowledge of the lifeworld. To be sure, these general structures of the lifeworld become visible only when we shift perspective with regard to method. The terminology of "background," "foreground," and "situationally relevant segment of the lifeworld" is meaningful only so long as we adopt the perspective of a speaker who wishes to reach understanding with someone about something in the world and, in this, can base the plausibility of her speech-act offer on a mass of intersubjectively shared, unthematic knowledge. The lifeworld as a whole comes into view only when we, as it were, stand behind the back of the actor and view communicative action as an element of a circular process in which the actor no longer appears as the initiator but rather as the product of the traditions within which she is situated, of solidary groups to which she belongs, of socialization and learning processes to which she is subjected. Only after this initial objectivating step does the network of communicative actions constitute the medium through which the lifeworld reproduces itself.

Society as Symbolically Structured Lifeworld

Every speech act with which a speaker reaches understanding/with another person/with regard to something situates the linguistic expression in relation to the speaker, in relation to the hearer, and in relation to the world. From the point of view of constructing interactions, we have been concerned above all with the second of these three aspects—the interpersonal relationship. With their speech acts, participants in interaction accomplish feats of coordination by establishing such relationships. However, they do not achieve this simply by fulfilling precisely one linguistic function. Speech acts serve generally to coordinate actions through making possible a rationally motivated agreement between several actors; the two other functions of language—representation and expression—are also involved in this. The viewpoint of action coordination is thus situated at a more abstract level than the actor's directly intended establishing of a particular interpersonal relationship. Action coordination in general serves the purpose of the social integration of a lifeworld shared intersubjectively by its members. To be sure, such a description already presupposes the shift in perspective that allows us to pose questions about the contribution of communicative actions to the reproduction of the lifeworld. Once we have methodologically carried out this shift in perspective, we can make a similar observation with regard to reaching understanding about what is said or with regard to the socialization of participating persons; these roles, too, are fulfilled by speech acts in all their functions. From the point of view of reaching understanding, they serve to transmit and further develop cultural knowledge; from the point of view of socialization, they serve to form and maintain personal identities.

One can now imagine the components of the lifeworld—cultural paradigms, legitimate orders, and personality structures—as condensed forms of, and sediments deposited by, the following processes that operate by way of communicative action: *reaching understanding, action coordination,* and *socialization.* What enters into communicative action from the resources of the background of the lifeworld, flows through the sluice gates of thematization, and permits the mastery of situations, constitutes the stock of knowledge preserved within communicative practices. This stock of knowledge solidifies, along paths of interpretation, into interpretive paradigms that are handed down; the knowledge becomes compressed, in the network of interactions of social groups, into values and norms; and it condenses, by way of socialization processes, into attitudes, competencies, modes of perception, and identities. The components of the lifeworld result from and are maintained through the continuation of valid knowledge, the stabilization of group solidarities, and the formation of accountable actors. The web of everyday communicative practices extends across the semantic field of symbolic contents just as much as in the dimensions of social space and historical time, constituting the medium through which culture, society, and personality structures develop and are reproduced.

Culture is what I call the stock of knowledge from which the participants in communication, in reaching understanding with one another with regard to something, supply themselves with interpretations. *Society* consists of the legitimate orders by way of which the participants in communication regulate their affiliations to social groups and safeguard solidarity. In the category of *personality structures,* I include all motives and competencies that enable a subject to speak and act and thereby to secure her own identity. Whereas for the communicative actors culture constitutes the cone of light within which entities can encounter one another and can be represented or dealt with as something, such actors encounter norms and subjective experiences as something in the social world or something in a subjective world to which they can refer, respectively, in a norm-conformative or expressive attitude. In order to prevent a widespread misunderstanding, I now want to explain why, in the transition from communicative to strategic action, this scenario changes all at once for the participating subjects, although not for the social scientist who uses this concept of lifeworld.

If we consider society in the broader sense as a symbolically structured lifeworld, it is certainly true that society develops and reproduces itself only via communicative action. It does not follow from this, however, that for the social scientific observer no strategic interactions can occur in lifeworlds constituted in this way. To be sure, such interactions have a different status here than they have for Hobbes or in game theory. These theories conceive of strategic action as a mechanism for the generation of society as an instrumental order. From the vantage point of communication theory, by contrast, strategic interactions can occur only within the horizon of lifeworlds already constituted elsewhere, more precisely, as an alternative option in case of the failure of communicative actions. They occupy, retrospectively, as it were, social spaces and historical times— segments within dimensions of an already existing lifeworld constituted through communicative action. The strategic actor, too, keeps the background of his respective lifeworld behind him and the institutions or persons within his lifeworld before him, but in each case their shape has been transformed. The background of the lifeworld is neutralized in a peculiar way in order to permit the mastery of situations that have been subjected to the imperatives of success-oriented action; it loses its action-coordinating power as a resource that guarantees consensus. And like all other entities in the (now no longer intersubjectively shared) lifeworld, the other participants in interaction are now also encountered only as social facts—as objects that the actor can influence (if need be with the help of perlocutionary effects), as objects in which he can spark off particular reactions. However, in the objectivating stance of the strategic actor, he can no longer reach an understanding with them as he can with a second person.

For the social scientific observer, therefore, sequences of action (and, in certain circumstances, systems of action) can occur in the lifeworld she analyzes that are integrated not by way of values, norms, and processes of reaching understanding but, at most, by way of the reciprocal exertion of influence—for instance, through market or power relations. It then remains an empirical question whether this approach based on the concept of lifeworld is more realistic than an approach of the Hobbesian type. At first glance, there are a number of points in the former's favor. Market and power relations, too, are normatively—as a rule, legally—regulated, that is, they are set within an institutional framework. Even military conflicts remain embedded within normative contexts. Civil wars—and genocide even more so—leave behind them traces of moral distress that support the view that intersubjectively shared lifeworlds constitute the indispensable ground even for strategic interactions.

The components of the lifeworld—culture, society, and personality structures—form complex contexts of meaning that communicate with one another, although they are embodied in different substrata. Cultural knowledge is embodied in symbolic forms—in objects of utility and technologies, in words and theories, in books and documents—just as much as in actions. Society is embodied in institutional orders, in legal norms, or in webs of normatively regulated practices and customs. Finally, personality structures are embodied—in a literal sense—in the substratum of human organisms. What is thus embodied are semantic contents that can also be liquidated and put into circulation in the currency of normal language. All meaning comes together in the marketplace of everyday communicative practices. Nonetheless, the various components of the lifeworld constitute distinct quantities; this can be seen ontologically from the spatiotemporal aspects of their embodiments.

Cultural traditions are diffused across the boundaries of collectivities and linguistic communities and in their life span are not tied to the identity of societies, let alone persons. The world religions are the best example of this. Societies, for their part, occupy a larger social space and longer historical periods than a person and her life-history, but have less diffuse and more narrowly circumscribed boundaries than traditions. Finally, personality structures, which adhere to their organic substrata, are defined most sharply from a spatiotemporal point of view. For individuals, culture and society appear first of all in the shape of an overarching generational interrelationship.

Nonetheless, these components of the lifeworld should not be conceived of as systems constituting environments for one another; they remain entwined with one another via the common medium of everyday language. So long as no special codes such as money or administrative power become differentiated and split off from this medium—codes by way of which, in turn, functionally specific systems of action become differentiated and split off from the society component of the lifeworld—everyday language (which is always multifunctional) sets a limit to the differentiation of the lifeworld. Even systems of action that are specialized to a high degree in cultural reproduction (school) or social integration (law) or socialization (family) do not operate on the basis of sharp distinctions. Via the common code of everyday language they also concurrently fulfill the other respective functions alongside their own particular ones, thus maintaining a relation to the totality of the lifeworld. The lifeworld, as a symbolically structured context of meaning that extends through these various functions and forms of embodiment, comprises three components *entwined with one another in an equiprimordial way.*

The concept of lifeworld thus explicated does not only provide an answer to the classical question of how social order is possible. With the idea of the intermeshing of the lifeworld components, this concept also answers the other question of classical social theory: that of the relationship between individual and society. The lifeworld does not constitute an *environment* against whose contingent influences the individual has to assert herself. Individual and society do not constitute systems existing in their respective environments that would relate to one another externally as observers. Equally, however, the lifeworld is not some kind of *receptacle* in which individuals might be contained like parts of a whole. The latter figure of thought, which comes from the philosophy of the subject, is just as deficient as that of systems theory.

From the perspective of the philosophy of the subject, society has been conceived of as a whole composed of parts, whether as the state made up of political citizens or as the association of free producers. The concept of lifeworld also breaks with this figure of thought. For communicatively socialized subjects would not be subjects without the network of institutional orders and of the traditions of society and culture. Of course, communicatively acting subjects experience their respective lifeworlds as an intersubjectively shared totality in the background. But this totality, which would have to disintegrate *for them* at the moment of thematization and hypostatization, is constituted by the motives and competencies of socialized individuals as much as by cultural traditions and group solidarities. The lifeworld is structured by cultural traditions and institutional orders no more and no less than it is by identities that arise out of socialization processes. For this reason, the lifeworld does not constitute an organization to which individuals belong as members, nor an association in which individuals join together, nor a collective comprised of individual participants. Rather, the everyday communicative practices in which the lifeworld is centered are nourished by means of an *interplay* of cultural reproduction, social integration, and socialization that is in turn rooted in these practices.

Organisms fall under the description of persons only if, and to the extent that, they are socialized, that is, invested with and structured by social and cultural contexts of meaning. Persons *are* symbolic structures, whereas the symbolically structured nature-like substratum, although experienced as one's own body, nonetheless, as nature, remains just as external to individuals as does the material natural basis of the lifeworld as a whole. Whereas internal and external nature constitute external boundaries—delimitations with respect to an environment—for socialized individuals and their lifeworlds, these persons remain internally linked—via grammatical relationships—with their culture and their society.

The content of culturally handed-down traditions is always a knowledge acquired by persons; without the hermeneutic appropriation and further development of cultural knowledge through persons, no traditions can develop or be maintained. To this extent, persons accomplish something for culture by way of their interpretive achievements. However, culture for its part also represents a resource for persons. For persons are not "carriers" (*Träger*) for traditions in the sense in which the organic substratum can be described as a carrier for personality structures. Every cultural tradition is at the same time a process of education (*Bildung*) for subjects capable of speech and action who are formed within this, just as much as they for their part keep culture alive.

In a corresponding manner, normative orders, whether they solidify into institutions or remain free floating as fleeting contexts, are always orders of interpersonal relationships. The networks of interaction of more or less socially integrated, of more or less united groups, are constituted only through the feats of coordination of communicatively acting subjects. But, once again, it would be wrong to describe persons as "carriers" for these networks of interaction. Once again, society and the individual constitute one another reciprocally. Every process of social integration of action contexts *is* simultaneously a process of socialization for subjects capable of speech and action who are formed in this process and who for their part in equal measure renew and stabilize society as the totality of legitimately ordered interpersonal relationships (cf. figure 4.1).

Processes of socialization and education are learning processes that are dependent on persons. They must be distinguished from the suprasubjective learning effects that manifest themselves as cultural

Actions, Speech Acts, Linguistically Mediated Interactions, and Lifeworld

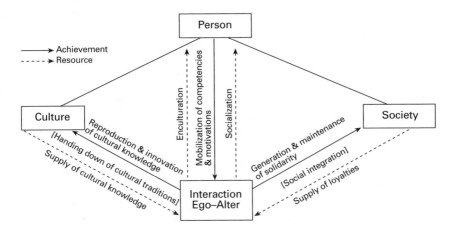

Figure 4.1
Entwining of personality structures with culture and society

and social innovations and find expression in the forces of production or structures of moral consciousness. These innerworldly learning processes are connected with problems of material reproduction, with which we are not concerned in the present context. Situated at another level than these innerworldly learning processes are processes whereby the lifeworld itself is structurally differentiated. The dynamic here can be explained, from an internal perspective, in terms of an interaction between innovative linguistic processes of world disclosure and innerworldly learning processes. To conclude, I would like to consider once more, with the help of a language-pragmatic reminder, the logic of this interplay.

From the theory of meaning, we are already acquainted with the internal connection between meaning and validity: we understand the meaning of a speech act if we know the conditions under which it may be accepted as valid. Semantic rules thus lay down the conditions of validity for the sentences or speech acts possible in a linguistic system. With such contexts of meaning language opens up a horizon of possible actions and experiences for those who belong to the linguistic system. World-disclosing language, as Heidegger says, allows something to be encountered as something in the world. It is a different question, however, whether these linguistically projected possibilities also *prove their worth* (*sich bewähren*)[2] in their inner-worldly dealings. Whether or not the semantically established conditions of validity are actually satisfied to the extent that the sentences and utterances possible in a given linguistic system find their place within functioning language games does not only depend on the world-disclosing power of language; it also depends on the success of innerworldly practices that are, however, made possible through the linguistic system. Creative innovations in the linguistic worldview should not be hypostasized, as Heidegger and Foucault have done, as a cryptic history—dating back to time immemorial—of ontology or forms of knowledge. As the linguistic horizon of meaning changes, only the *conditions* for the validity of utterances change with it; an altered preunderstanding must *prove its truth* (*sich bewähren*) in its dealings with what is actually encountered within the now shifted horizon. Furthermore, the spectrum of validity claims inscribed in communicative action provides for the feedback of learning processes to innerworldly practices. The worldview structures that make innerworldly practices possible through a preexisting understanding of meaning do not renew themselves only by virtue of a poetic bestowing of meaning; they also in turn react upon the learning processes that they have made possible and whose results find expression in changes in worldview structures.

On the other hand, neither should the restrictions on the environment—contingent and exerting influences externally—that become visible when dealing with the problematizing pressure brought to bear by critical experiences be hypostasized as an all-dominating imperative of the self-assertion of systems in over-complex environments. In this way, systems functionalism grants independence to a single aspect, one that is in itself legitimate. Viewed as systems, societies present themselves merely from the side of what Marx referred to metaphorically as the metabolism between society and external nature. The constitutive feature of system formation is the differentiation between an internal and an external perspective, whereby the system is attributed with the maintenance of the system–environment difference as its own achievement. However, this attribution should not be undertaken from the perspective of an observer who now superimposes a systems model on the lifeworld as well. If the initially hermeneutically appropriated lifeworld, made accessible from the perspective of a participant and reconstructively grasped in its general structures, is to be objectified one further time in the shape of a boundary-maintaining system, then the profit yielded for social scientific inquiry through an analysis of the lifeworld should not be gambled away in the process. In order to avoid a confusion of paradigms, I have elsewhere attempted (in *The Theory of Communicative Action,* vol. 2) to bring together action theory and the basic concepts of systems theory, guided by the thread of the twin concepts of social integration and system integration. This model permits explanation of why systemic elements emerge only as the result of historical processes. The dynamics of dissociation from complex environments, which characterizes society as a whole in its capacity as system, enters into the very *interior* of society only with the media-steered subsystems.

Notes

1. The absence of references is due to the nature of this essay, which is meant to provide a rough sketch of my pragmatic approach to language.

2. [Editor's note:] See my note 52 to chapter 8, p. 380.

5

Comments on John Searle's "Meaning, Communication, and Representation" (1988)

1

Every analysis of linguistic processes of communication (*Verständigung*) is guided by intuitions. We think we know what it means to perform a speech act successfully. My comments serve indirectly to compare two intuitions of this kind.

The intentionalist view assumes that a speaker S successfully performs a given speech act if, with the aid of a sign x, he gets an addressee A to recognize an intention or a meaning (*Meinung*) intended by him (intention$_1$). S achieves his goal by making this communicative intention (intention$_2$), too, known to A. The model according to which the process of communication is analyzed is that of the transmission of ideas possessed by S to an addressee who is to acquire possession of them with the help of a sign x employed by S with a communicative intent: S gives A to understand something by means of x.

The intersubjectivist view assumes that S successfully performs a speech act if he reaches understanding (*sich verständigen*) with an addressee about something in the world. Here, the intentionalist description is replaced not only by a more complex (and thus vaguer) conceptualization, but by a *different* one. With an utterance x, S allows an addressee the possibility of taking a position with a "yes" or a "no" to something concerning which he wishes to reach agreement with her. The model in this case is not that of transmitting ideas but that of bringing about a consensus with regard to some (in principle, disputed) matter. Language is not conceived as a means for transmitting subjective contents but as a medium in which the participants intersubjectively share an understanding of a given matter. The sign *x* is not a tool that an individual can use, and with which *S* gives *A* to understand something by prompting her to recognize his meaning or intention; rather, the sign *x* is an element of a repertoire used in common that permits the participants to understand the same matter in the same way.

The intentionalist can, with more sparing assumptions, offer the prospect of a more elegant explanation because he wants to trace back the phenomenon of reaching understanding (*Verständigung*) to general conditions for the success of intentional actions. If he can show how a speaker realizes his communicative intent of making his intentions known to a hearer, then he can hope to explain something that the intersubjectivist always already presupposes in his description of the communication process: that is, the linguistic rule system, which establishes the meaning of a conventionally produced expression. I cannot deal with the critique of this program of explanation here.[1] I am interested only in the fact that John Searle—despite his earlier criticism of Grice—does not want to relinquish the explanatory power of the intentionalist approach. He has in the meantime given his speech-act theory an intentionalist turn.[2]

2

Searle had shown in 1969 that the comprehension of a speech act cannot be described as a perlocutionary effect.[3] A speech act cannot adequately be analyzed according to the model of purposive activity because the meaning content of what the speaker wishes to give an addressee to understand is not exhausted by the subjective content of a speaker's intention. Following Austin, Searle had described the understanding of a speech act as the illocutionary goal that results primarily from what is said itself and not from the speaker's intention. The goal intended by the speaker consists in the addressee recognizing that the conditions for the validity of a correctly executed speech act are satisfied in the given instance. Understanding a speech act requires knowledge of these conditions.

Searle at that time had analyzed such conditions with the help of the sentences used in standard speech acts; to this extent, he *presupposed* that S and A speak the same language—that is, that they already have at their disposal a prior understanding of the same language. However, since then he holds the view that he can dispense with this strong presupposition and can treat the common language itself as the phenomenon in need of explanation. For this reason, he renews the intentionalist approach; in doing so, however, he does not in any way reverse the—initially semantically inspired—uncoupling of the meaning of a linguistic expression from the speaker's intention.[4] To all appearances, Searle radicalizes his earlier critique of Grice by tracing the concept of meaning back to cognitive intentions, which are not only prelinguistic but are also independent of the situation of interaction. Like Husserl, he conceives of "meaning" as the content of a mental representation (*Vorstellung*). To be sure, in contrast to Husserl, meanings for Searle are analyzed in terms of so-called satisfaction conditions, because the representations in which meanings are rooted are tailored fundamentally to the representation of states of affairs, that is, they have a propositional structure. This mentalist conception of meaning allows Searle to retain Grice's model in a modified form.

The speaker has the intention$_2$ of getting an addressee to recognize his intention$_1$ with the help of a sign x. According to Searle's revision, however, the intention$_1$ has the structure of a representation (*Vorstellung*) "p," which is true if "p" exists. Thus, the speaker can impose on the sign x the conditions for the existence of a state of affairs represented a fortiori; he can measure the success of communicating this representation according to whether the addressee, with the help of the truth conditions imposed on x, recognizes the state of affairs represented by the speaker.

From my point of view, by contrast, a speech act, which the speaker uses in order to reach understanding with an addressee about something, expresses simultaneously (a) the speaker's intention, (b) a state of affairs, and (c) an interpersonal relationship. According to the original intentionalist view, this whole process of communication is supposed to be able to be explained from the perspective of the speaker and his intention, that is, in such a way that (c) and (b) are reduced to (a). Searle expands this model because he sees that with the representation of states of affairs, a relation to the world and a dimension of validity come into play and provide the criteria for the successful execution of a communicative intention in the first place. While retaining the intentionalist claim to be able to explain meaning, Searle modifies the intentionalist strategy of explanation to the effect that communicative success is now traced back to the successful representation of states of affairs—which means that (c) and (a) are reduced to (b). This strategy requires, inter alia, the justification of two important theses:

1. The mental representation of states of affairs is, in the sense of an analysis of conditions, more primordial (*ursprünglicher*) than the linguistic representation of states of affairs.

2. Illocutionary types can be characterized according to the kind of representation of states of affairs and corresponding propositional attitudes of the speaker.

I shall use one of Searle's own examples in order to discuss the first thesis: that linguistic notions can be analyzed in terms of intentional notions. With this reductionist thesis, Searle wants to ground the theory of language in the philosophy of mind. The question here is whether representational content is prior to language or whether it in turn borrows its own propositional structure from the grammatical form of assertoric sentences (section 3). I shall then proceed with a discussion of the second thesis: that the theory of intentionality provides a conceptual frame for the classification of speech acts. The question here is whether the meaning of a speech act is determined by the satisfaction conditions of a representational content imposed on the linguistic expression or whether it has to be explained in terms of validity conditions that are determined by a process of interpretation terminating in the intersubjective recognition of corresponding validity claims (section 4). This will be followed by a brief exposition of an alternative approach (section 5). Finally, I shall elucidate this intersubjectivist view of communication with reference to Searle's recent analysis of performatives (section 6).

3

The sentence "The crankshaft of this engine is broken" reports the state of affairs that the crankshaft of this engine is broken. This linguistically represented state of affairs can be distinguished from the communication of the represented state of affairs in a similar way to how the aforementioned sentence can be distinguished from a constative speech act in which a speaker uses this sentence with a communicative intent. Searle now suggests replacing the assertoric sentence by a drawing, thereby replacing the linguistic representation by a graphic representation of the same state of affairs. He imagines that a motorist who does not know the language of the country in which he finds himself could in this way convey to a mechanic which part of his car needs to be repaired. Now the drawing that represents a broken crankshaft can also be completed without any intention of using it for the purpose of conveying this kind of information. The graphic representation of the object can be complete quite independently of any communicative intention or use, provided only that it is accurate enough to permit recognition of the represented state of affairs. The same holds good when S replaces his drawing with other expressions, for instance, with gestures or word symbols: "We may say that whenever S produces x with the intention that it represents a state of affairs A, then it must be the case that S produces x with the intention that a criterion of success of his action should be that A obtains, independently of the uttering" (p. 215).

Of course, Searle would not have chosen the example of a graphic representation if he were concerned only with the trivial contention that we can also conceive of a linguistically available state of affairs independently of actual communicative intentions. Clearly, the example is supposed to support the less trivial contention that we can make present a state of affairs to ourselves *in mente* without using any language—whether for purposes of representation or communication. Thesis (1) can then be interpreted as the contention that we are able to do this not only when we do not *use* any language but even when we have no *command* of any language. However, the conclusion drawn in the excerpted passage does not provide any argument in support of this thesis. For here, Searle already presupposes that *S* produces (or chooses) his drawing (or some other *x*) with the intention that it should permit recognition of a certain state of affairs, *A*. And, indeed, the drawing of a broken crankshaft can be interpreted in this way by a linguistically proficient observer. Drawings, however, do not intrinsically represent states of affairs. As Searle himself observes, the relation between the depicted object and the object itself is of a different kind. The drawing reproduces a broken crankshaft; its usefulness depends on whether it is sufficiently similar to the object being depicted. Similarity is, however, merely a necessary and not a sufficient condition for the interpretation in question—namely, that the depicted crankshaft expresses the fact that the crankshaft is broken.

Considered on its own terms, the relation of similarity between the representation and the original fulfills, perhaps, the role of a deictic gesture or a designation. It points to a certain *object,* serving to highlight this particular object amidst the multitude of all possible objects, and thereby to identify it. However, the drawing does not of its own accord represent a *state of affairs*. It is not equivalent to a statement, which could be true or false. The cartographic representation of a mountain range may be more or less accurate; but only the interpretations that we base on our reading of the map—that we infer from it, so to speak—are true or false, for example, that the mountain ranges are separated by wide valleys or that the highest peak lies 3,000 meters above sea level. In the same way, we can *infer* from the drawing of a broken crankshaft the proposition that the represented crankshaft is broken. However, only an interpreter who knows *in advance* what the representation of states of affairs means in general is able to understand the representation of a broken crankshaft as a designation with the propositional content that the crankshaft is broken. The interpreter could not even *see* that the drawing, by imitating a certain object, represents a state of affairs if he did not already have command of a language and know, on the basis of his linguistic practices, how states of affairs are represented linguistically.[5]

Comments on Searle's "Meaning, Communication, and Representation"

4

Even if, contrary to the foregoing reflections, it proved possible to defend thesis (1), the intentionalist explanatory program would require the justification of thesis (2). Because the success of a speech act ultimately is supposed to be measured according to the conditions for the representation of a state of affairs, the different modes of speech acts must be analyzable as just so many ways of referring to the satisfaction conditions for—originally mentally represented—states of affairs: "Different kinds of illocutionary acts, insofar as they have propositional contents, can be regarded as different modes in which utterances represent reality. . . . If we see the basic form of the illocutionary act as $F(p)$ . . . then the illocutionary points will determine the different ways in which p's are related to the world" (p. 219).

On the presupposition that utterances owe their meanings to the representation of states of affairs, one understands the uttered sentence if one knows the conditions that make it true. This holds to begin with for assertoric sentences that are used in constative speech acts. However, in the case of most speech acts, what is at issue is not the existence of states of affairs. If, nonetheless, the relation of representation is supposed to be constitutive for the meaning of nonconstative speech acts as well, the illocutionary types must be distinguishable on the basis of the attitudes adopted in each case by the speaker to the represented state of affairs, as well as on the basis of the *sense in which* his utterances represent something: "The basic idea here is the old one, that the meaning of a statement is somehow given by its truth conditions; the meaning of a command is given by its obedience conditions; the meaning of a promise is given by its fulfillment conditions, a.s.o." (p. 220).

Thus, the mode of a speech act changes with the propositional attitude of the speaker and with the type of satisfaction conditions for the state of affairs represented in the propositional component.

However, the relation of representation allows only two specifications in the sense of Austin's "directions of fit": truth conditions are satisfied when the words (*Worte*) fit the asserted states of affairs (or the world) ($\downarrow$), and success conditions are satisfied when the desired states of affairs (or the world) are made to fit the words ($\uparrow$). Searle therefore explains the first three of his five basic modes as follows: An utterance x belongs to the class of "assertives," "directives," or "commissives" if its success is measured according to whether the state of affairs "p" represented by x

• exists even independently of the speaker and his utterance, and

• comes into existence on the basis of the fact that the speaker or his addressee regard x at least in part as a reason for bringing about "p."

I would like to show by way of a few counterexamples that propositional attitude and direction of fit (together with the relation to speaker and to the hearer) do not suffice to determine the illocutionary type. Let us consider first of all an imperative which, depending on the context, can be interpreted as a request, supplication, command, and so forth (but also, as we shall see, as a threat):

(1) I request you to hand over the required sum of money to Y.

Whoever understands (1) can paraphrase the illocutionary meaning of this speech act roughly as follows: S gives the addressee to understand that she should make sure that "p" occurs. However, for this it is not sufficient to know the conditions under which the desired state "p" would be brought about. The hearer understands the speech act only when, in addition to these success conditions, she also knows the conditions that *authorize* the speaker to issue his imperative so that he may expect the addressee to carry out the required action. This requirement already follows from the fact that a speaker who utters (1) without being able, in his role as supplicant, friend, neighbor, or commander, to rely on *any* normative context *whatsoever* must instead draw on a reservoir of potential sanctions in order to replace the missing normative validity claim with a power claim. In the case of negative sanctions, the imperative turns, for example, into a threat:

(2) I request you to hand over the required sum of money to Y— otherwise I will notify the police that . . .

The sanction conditions specified in the appositive expression now take the place of the missing authorization conditions that—in contrast to (1)—can no longer be inferred from the illocutionarily weakened preceding clause. (2) has to be understood as an indirect speech act whose literal meaning expresses an illocutionary meaning from which the speaker's intention deviates. The threat actually intended by the speaker would have to be conveyed literally roughly in the following form:

(2a) If you don't hand over the required sum of money to Y, I will notify the police that . . .

In the present context it is important to note that, in the case of (1) and (2) (where (2) is interpreted as (2a)), we are clearly not dealing with speech acts of the same type, even though they both meet the same conditions specified by Searle for determining illocutionary type. They satisfy the same success conditions for "p" (with the same direction of fit) and require the same propositional attitude of the speaker; nonetheless, they do not have the same illocutionary meaning. As we shall see, threats do not have proper illocutionary force at all.[6] Searle might object that orders as well as imperatives deprived of their normative backing and threats do belong to the same class of directives and that they are distinguished only by having different modes of achieving the same illocutionary purpose.[7] While orders appeal to a position of authority or to some (intersubjectively recognized) normative context, naked imperatives and explicit threats invoke sanctions. Granting this much, it should be clear, however, that there is still a difference in illocutionary meaning. The illocutionary aim of an order "p" is that the hearer, in recognizing the corresponding conditions of success, realizes that she is supposed to bring about "p" in a specific way, namely, through obeying, which means meeting the normative expectation of the speaker. For him, the expected behavior falls under the description of "following a previously established and intersubjectively recognized norm." In the case of naked imperatives or threats the expected behavior does not fit this description, at least not from the viewpoint of the actor. It has quite a different meaning: that of avoiding negative consequences that the hearer would have to suffer otherwise.

With Searle we may say that the hearer is intentionally caused to perform the required action by orders as well as by imperatives and threats; but then in each case we mean something different by "intentional causation." It is true that in both cases speech acts constitute for the hearer at least partially a reason to bring about a certain state of affairs, but the types of reasons they constitute are distinct in an interesting way. The reasons vindicating the validity claim raised with an order are reasons for everybody, or at least for all the parties who recognize the authorizing norms or institutions. By contrast, reasons for submitting to a power claim connected with naked imperatives or threats do not belong to this set of general reasons; they are specific in the sense that they count as reasons only for the more or less rational choice of a particular person with particular preferences in a particular situation. This difference becomes obvious when the hearer rejects the respective speech-acts. In the case of an order, a hearer who rejects the speech-act offer disputes that the speaker is authorized to expect the behavior commanded of her:

(1′) No, you cannot order me to do anything.

In the second case, the hearer challenges only certain existential presuppositions pertaining to the reservoir of potential sanctions on which the speaker draws:

(2′) No, you have nothing you can use against me.

Whereas general reasons can facilitate an uncoerced agreement between speaker and hearer, specific reasons, in the sense illustrated by the latter case, mediate an influence that the speaker exerts on the attitude of the hearer.

　　To this objection Searle could respond by drawing attention to his distinction between successful and successful but defective speech acts. Everything then hinges on what kind of deficiency we mean. If we describe the lack of authorizing conditions as a failure in preparatory conditions, as Searle has suggested, we would miss the point. Illocutionary acts owe their motivating force to the validity claims they carry, since these claims—like truth claims—are capable of being intersubjectively recognized to the extent that they are based on reasons that count as reasons for all parties involved. Naked imperatives and threats are deprived of this illocutionary force; there

Comments on Searle's "Meaning, Communication, and Representation"

is no claim to validity associated with them but rather a power claim; they are oriented not toward the possibility of common agreement but toward the causal effect of the speaker's influence on the hearer.[8]

5

Before drawing some conclusions, let us return to the issue of classification. The analysis that I have proposed for normatively authorized directives also applies to commissives.

(3) I promise you I will hand over the required sum of money to Y.

An addressee can understand the utterance as a promise only when she knows the conditions under which an accountable (*zurechnungsfähig*) actor can bind his own will—that is, take on an obligation to do something. Here, too, the negative response is aimed at these autonomy conditions, which, as in (1), supplement the conditions of success for "*p*." For instance:

(3') No, you are far too unreliable for me to take such a promise seriously.

In order to understand a directive or commissive speech act, the hearer must know not only the satisfaction conditions for the state of affairs represented in it, but also the conditions under which it can be regarded as legitimate or as binding. This view is due to a formal-pragmatic generalization of a basic insight of truth-conditional semantics. This is all the more reason to expect that it may be confirmed through reference to constative speech acts as well.

In this respect, however, an asymmetry is initially striking: the validity of constative speech acts appears to depend only on the satisfaction of the truth conditions for the assertoric sentence "*p*" used in it; by contrast, however, as our analysis so far has shown, the satisfaction of the corresponding success conditions for the state of affairs "that *p*" expressed in the propositional component is in fact not sufficient for the validity of orders or promises. This asymmetry disappears as soon as one realizes that, even in the case of constative speech acts, the speaker must intend something more and something different than what is expected from him on the intentionalist reading, namely, to get the hearer to recognize that he holds "p" to be true (intention₁) and that he wishes to let her know this (intention₂). The speaker wants to communicate to the hearer not only the intention₁ that *he* has (that he believes "that p"), but he also wants to communicate to her the fact "p" (so that the addressee *herself* believes "that p"). The illocutionary aim does not consist simply in the addressee becoming aware of the speaker's intention (*Meinung*); rather, she herself is supposed to arrive at the *same* view as that of which the speaker is convinced. In short, the addressee is supposed to accept the speaker's assertion as valid. This is what the communication of facts is all about. The intentionalist description according to which the speaker intends to produce in the hearer the belief that the speaker is committed to the existence of a certain state of affairs comes close to a distortion. In order to achieve his illocutionary aim, it is not sufficient that the speaker impose truth conditions for a mentally represented state of affairs on a sign x and that he makes the addressee aware of these by uttering x (the assertoric sentence), which is impregnated, as it were, with the truth conditions. Rather, the speaker must confront the addressee with his *claim* that the conditions that make the asserted sentence true are indeed satisfied.

Just as with orders and promises, therefore, the speaker with a constative speech act also raises a criticizable validity claim that the hearer is supposed to accept. In contrast to nonconstative speech acts, however, this claim refers to the satisfaction of the conditions that make the assertoric sentence employed true. Against this, the validity claims linked to orders and promises refer *directly* to the normative conditions that entitle one party to expect that the other party will bring about the represented state of affairs. The claim to propositional truth refers to the existence of a state of affairs, in other words to the fact "p." By contrast, the claim to normative validity refers to the legitimacy of the expectation that one or other of the parties concerned should bring about a represented state of affairs "that p."

Comments on Searle's "Meaning, Communication, and Representation"

My main point in the present context is the inadequacy of the intentionalist model. It condemns the hearer to a peculiar passivity. It deprives her of the possibility of taking the speaker's utterance *seriously*—that is, of accepting it as valid or of rejecting it as invalid. Without the *possibility* of taking a position with a "yes" or "no," however, the process of communication remains incomplete.

With a speech act, the speaker not only provides the hearer with the opportunity to become aware of his own intention; he further claims to have reasons that can move the hearer to accept an assertion as true, an order as legitimate, a promise as binding, or—as I would like to add at this point—an avowal as sincere. The speaker cannot achieve his illocutionary aim of conveying a fact, giving an order, making a request or a promise, or revealing a subjective experience (*Erlebnis*) if he does not at the same time make known the conditions under which his utterance could be accepted as valid; and, indeed, he must do so in such a way that, in claiming that these conditions are satisfied, he implicitly also offers to provide reasons in support of this claim, if necessary. The hearer must be able to have reasons for accepting an assertion as true, an order as legitimate, a promise as binding, an avowal as authentic or sincere (or, alternatively, for questioning such claims). The hearer does not understand the speech act if she does not know the conditions for taking such a "yes" or "no" position. The illocutionary meaning of an assertion, an order, a promise, or avowal remains concealed from the hearer if she becomes aware only that the speaker has a certain intentional state: that he believes "that p"; that he wants the hearer to bring about "p" or that he himself has the intention of bringing about "p"; or that he wants to reveal the propositional content of a belief, a feeling, a desire, an intention, and so forth.

6

Understanding the meaning of a linguistic expression is certainly not the same as *reaching understanding* about something with the help of an utterance held to be valid. An equally clear distinction must be made between a valid utterance and one that is merely held to be valid. Nonetheless, questions of meaning can not be separated completely from questions of validity.[9] The basic question of what it is to understand the meaning of a linguistic expression cannot be isolated from the question of the context in which this expression can be accepted as valid. One simply would not know what it is to understand the meaning of a linguistic expression if one did not know how one *could* make use of it in order to reach understanding with someone about something. It can be seen from the very conditions for understanding linguistic expressions that the speech acts that can be formed with their help have a built-in orientation toward a rationally motivated agreement about what is said. To this extent, the orientation toward the possible validity of utterances is part of the pragmatic conditions not just for reaching understanding but, prior to this, of the conditions for linguistic understanding itself. In language, the dimensions of meaning and validity are internally connected.

If we start from this intersubjectivist conception of language, illocutionary types may be identified according to the validity claims associated with them.[10] In order to identify the validity claims themselves, the following heuristic question may be useful: In what sense can the speech act as a whole be negated? We arrive at precisely three validity claims if we consider from which points of view an illocutionarily ambiguous sentence such as

(4)   I will hand over the required sum of money to Y.

can be negated.

(4′)   No, you are far too unreliable in such matters.

(4″)   No, you don't really mean what you say.

(4‴)   No, it will never come to this.

In the first case, the hearer understands the utterance as a promise and disputes that the speaker is sufficiently autonomous to uphold such an obligation. In the second case, the hearer understands the utterance as a declaration of intention and doubts the seriousness or sincerity of the intention uttered. In the third case, the hearer understands the utterance as a prediction and disputes the truth of the statement about the future. Any illocutionary act at all can be challenged from the points of view of normative rightness, truthfulness (*Wahrhaftigkeit*), and truth. For example, an imperative such as (1) can be negated not only with respect to the authorization of the speaker but also with respect to the sincerity of the speaker's intention expressed in it, or with respect to the truth of the existential presuppositions of the propositional content it expresses.[11]

If one considers Searle's analysis of the conditions for speech acts as a whole, the three aforementioned validity claims can be found in his schema of analysis under a different description. In a discussion, Searle proposed analyzing the claim to normative rightness in terms of his "preparatory conditions," the claim to truthfulness in terms of his "sincerity conditions," and the claim to truth in terms of his "essential conditions." The fact that such a translation is possible speaks for the sharpness and complexity of Searle's analyses. John Searle was the first to grasp clearly the structure of speech acts. However, his pioneering insights point beyond a framework of analysis that is based on the intentionalist model. The concept of a validity claim would lose its point if it were brought back inside that model. Truth conditions and satisfaction conditions are semantic concepts for which mentalist correlates may also be specified. However, private access to validity conditions—whether prelinguistic or simply monological—can be defended only at the price of what I regard as an untenable correspondence theory of truth. I propose, therefore, that validity conditions should be considered not in isolation from, but in pragmatic connection with, validity claims and potential reasons for the vindication of such claims.

Criticizable validity claims, which have a built-in orientation toward intersubjective recognition, are necessary for a speech act to achieve the illocutionary aim of the speaker.

In a recent paper on performatives,[12] Searle comes fairly close to recognizing the intersubjective nature of meaning and validity. The analysis of performatives leads to the very center of a theory that takes as its starting point Austin's insight into the peculiar character of a speech act whereby we do something by saying it. In the standard form of a speech act $F(p)$, the performative sentence makes explicit the illocutionary force F of an utterance containing "p."

With regard to the question of how performatives work we find two competing interpretations. One of these treats performatives as simple statements, while the other maintains that performatives do not admit of truth and falsity and therefore lack meaning in any proper sense. Both interpretations are strongly counterintuitive.

Performative sentences such as "I state that . . .," "I promise you . . .," or "I confess that . . ." in fact constitute performances that can neither be confirmed nor falsified like fully fledged assertions. They do not operate by way of a claim to truth. This is revealed by the fact that they first have to undergo a transformation from the speaker's first-person (performative) perspective [toward a second person] into the third-person perspective of an observer before they themselves can be true or false. This transformation shows, however, that performative sentences have a meaning, too. Obviously, the following sentences

(5)   I order you to come.

(5′)   He orders her to come.

have the same meaning, if references are preserved. But, at the same time, the illocutionary force switches over into the propositional content and thereby loses, if not its meaning, at least its force: it is included in the topic of another—constative—speech act. Uttered in the first-person attitude [toward a second person], performative sentences have a meaning (a) only in connection with some other proposition or propositional content, and (b) only as a kind of escort in the background, which is articulated in an unthematic and implicit way. These and other features can be explained as soon as we realize that performative sentences (like other illocutionary indicators) are self-referential and executive expressions for the act of raising a validity claim for a sentence with propositional content. Searle states the problem clearly. The difficulties into which his own proposal runs are instructive; they disclose an underlying intuition close to my own.

Searle explains the meaning of sentences, the performance of which constitutes the act they say they are, through recourse to declarations—a class of speech acts we have not yet discussed. Uttering a sentence such as "I hereby order you to leave" functions, according to Searle, "as a performative, and hence as a declaration because (a) the verb 'order' is an intentional verb, (b) ordering is something you can do by manifesting the intention to do it, and (c) the utterance is both self-referential and executive, as indicated by the word 'hereby.'"[13]

Without going into detail, I shall now explain—and question—the declarative character of performatives. Searle has introduced declaratives as speech acts that both express a propositional content and make it true. In concluding a contract or closing a meeting, I let what I say be the case by saying it. Within the limits of this model, Searle somewhat paradoxically postulates of declarations that they simultaneously satisfy both directions of fit: they both state a fact and produce it. The paradox disappears with the observation of how the authorizing or legitimizing conditions of contract law or business procedures normatively back these speech acts. It is because of this legal or institutional—in any case normative—background that declarations can produce a change in the domain of legitimate interpersonal relationships and thereby create new social facts. Compared with directives and commissives, declaratives display features of both types: like orders they rely on a normative context and like promises they draw from the normative resource of the speaker's responsibility.

Searle, however, makes a further move; he now interprets the performative character of all classes of illocutionary acts in light of the illocutionary force of declarations. This proposal faces two major difficulties. First, it explodes the architecture of the classification of speech acts; this is because declarations would lose their distinctive place within this classification if they were to explain the performative character of *all* speech acts. Of greater interest is the second difficulty. Since many performatives do not appeal to or rely on a normative backing, the illocutionary point of declarations would lose its specificity. Consequently, Searle is pushed in the direction of redifferentiating the illocutionary meaning of declaratives. Apart from "extralinguistic declaratives"—such as pronouncing a couple husband and wife or declaring war—Searle introduces another category of "linguistic declarations," which are neither attached to particular institutions like marriage or warfare nor supported by some informal value consensus in the background. However, once *all* illocutionary acts gain a declarative force so that this force extends to requests, promises, and avowals as well as statements, what meaning then remains for the force of such "linguistic declarations"? Strictly speaking, there cannot be any declaration without dependence on authorizing or legitimizing conditions of the sort that have the power to create new social facts. If, nonetheless, his analysis leads Searle to refer to some declarative force inherent in speech itself, the intuition behind this peculiar force might well match what I prefer to call the rationally motivating force of validity claims that are in need of intersubjective recognition. Searle elucidates the intrinsically linguistic force of the very act of raising a validity claim through the force of an institution that enables a speaker, via his social roles, literally to call something into existence. In order to turn the elucidation into an explanation, Searle has to assimilate language to institutions. Language, however, is an institution only in a metaphorical sense. Thus Searle's explanation of how performatives work reaches no further than this metaphor.

Notes

1. Cf. chapter 6 in this volume, pp. 286ff., especially notes 18 and 19, p. 305.

2. Cf. K.-O. Apel, "Is Intentionality More Basic than Linguistic Meaning?" in E. Lepore and R. Van Gulick, eds., *John Searle and His Critics* (Oxford, 1993), pp. 31–55.

3. J. Searle, *Speech Acts* (Cambridge, 1969), pp. 49ff.

4. In the following I refer to J. Searle, "Meaning, Communication, and Representation," in R. E. Grandy and R. Warner, eds., *Philosophical Grounds of Rationality* (Oxford, 1986). Page references in the text refer to this essay. Searle worked out his conception in *Intentionality* (Cambridge, 1983).

5. The history of the philosophy of consciousness from Descartes to Husserl teaches us that it is no coincidence that the basic concepts of mentalism were oriented toward the representation of objects, that is, toward the subject–object relation. It was the linguistic turn initiated by Frege that first led to the insight that, analogous to sentences, our representations (*Vorstellungen*), too, have a propositional structure; cf. E. Tugendhat, *Traditional and Analytical Philosophy*, trans. P. A. Gorner (Cambridge, 1982).

6. J. Searle, "Intentionality and Method," *Journal of Philosophy* 78 (1981): 720–733.

7. I am grateful to Chris Latiolais for indicating this to me.

8. Naked imperatives and threats are examples of perlocutionary acts that play an instrumental role in the context of success-oriented acts. They have lost their illocutionary *force* and derive their illocutionary *meaning* from other contexts of use in which the utterance of the same sentences is mainly determined by communicative goals. Such speech acts, which have gained perlocutionary independence, are not oriented toward the rationally motivated attitude of an addressee; insofar as they are not motivated in this way, they do not rely on a reservoir of potential reasons that are unspecific with regard to the addressee.

9. Cf. K.-O. Apel, "Sprachliche Bedeutung, Wahrheit und normative Gültigkeit," in *Archivio di Filosofia* 55 (1987): 51ff.

10. Cf. my classificatory schema in chapter 2 in the present volume, pp. 154ff.

11. If the class of expressive speech acts is demarcated from the point of view of the claim to truthfulness (*Wahrhaftigkeit*) raised by the speaker for the expression of a subjective experience to which he has privileged access, avowals present themselves as the prototype. Unlike avowals, acts such as saying "thank you," congratulating, or making excuses are *not* expressive speech acts, for these can succeed even when the speaker does not mean what he says. As in the case of bets and christenings, the illocutionary meaning of such regulative speech acts is determined by a normative context. If this normative context is not violated, an act of saying "thank you" can be valid, for instance, even when it does not come from the heart.

12. J. Searle, "How Performatives Work," *Linguistics and Philosophy* 12 (1989): 535–558.

13. Ibid., p. 552.

6

Toward a Critique of the Theory of Meaning (1988)

Three Approaches to a Theory of Meaning

A theory of meaning should answer the question of what it is to understand the meaning of a well-formed symbolic expression. In 1934, Karl Bühler proposed a schema of language functions that placed the linguistic expression in relations to the speaker, to the world, and to the hearer (figure 6.1).[1] This schema of how linguistic signs are used proves useful if one releases it from the context of the specific psychology of language in which it arose, extends the semiotic approach, and gives a charitable interpretation to the three functions mentioned. The diagram then yields the general thesis that language represents a medium—Bühler spoke of the organon model of language—that simultaneously serves three different, although internally related, functions. Expressions that are employed communicatively serve to express the intentions (or subjective experiences (*Erlebnisse*)) of a speaker, to represent states of affairs (or something the speaker encounters in the world), and to establish relations with an addressee. The three aspects of a *speaker* reaching understanding/with *another person*/about *something* are reflected here. In linguistic expressions, three converging rays of meaning are focused. What the speaker wants to say with the expression connects up with what is literally said in it, as well as with the action as which it should be understood. There exists a threefold relation between the meaning of a linguistic expression and what is *intended* (*gemeint*)

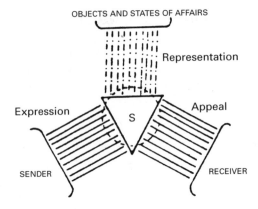

Figure 6.1
Bühler's schema of language functions

by it, what is *said* in it, and the way in which it is *used* in the speech act. Normally, linguistic meaning is not exhausted by any one of these three relations.[2]

Despite this, intentionalist semantics (from Grice to Bennett and Schiffer)[3] treats as fundamental only what the speaker intends by the expression he employs in a given situation; formal semantics (from Frege via the early Wittgenstein to Dummett)[4] begins with the conditions under which a sentence is true; and the use theory of meaning (inaugurated by the later Wittgenstein)[5] has recourse to the habitualized contexts of interaction in which linguistic expressions serve practical functions. Once linguistic behaviorism (from Bloomfield via Morris to Skinner)[6] had failed to explain three fundamental phenomena[7]—namely, the identity of linguistic meanings, the situation-independence of the meaning of expressions employed with reference to specific situations,[8] and the acquisition of the competence to generate innumerable linguistic expressions—the discussion has essentially been dominated by these three theories, for each of them has been able to appeal to a fundamental intuition. Bühler brings these intuitions together in his threefold schema of language functions.

a. Intentionalism shares with Bühler a conception in which language has the character of a tool. The speaker uses the signs and concatenations of signs produced by him as a vehicle for informing his addressee about his beliefs or intentions. In this conception, the premises of the modern philosophy of consciousness are still presupposed as unproblematic. *The representing subject (das vorstellende Subjekt)* stands over and against a world of things and events, and asserts at the same time his sovereignty in the world as a purposively *acting subject.* From the same perspective, he encounters other subjects who, in turn, assert themselves. As subjects capable of action, they influence each other in the way in which they generally intervene causally in innerworldly processes. That their interactions are mediated by language appears as something secondary in comparison to the representational and purposive activity of the individual subjects. Representations (*Vorstellungen*) connect up with the substratum of linguistic signs in a conventional way, so as to be capable of emerging from the inwardness of a particular individual subjectivity and taking on external form. In turn, the signs, as instruments for influencing an alien subjectivity, are accorded a place within the context of teleological action.

Once language has been assimilated in such a way to the physical means of purposive interventions, the explication of the meaning of linguistic expressions can be treated as a special task within a general theory of action. A speaker *S* intends to call forth an effect *r* in a hearer *H* by uttering "*x*" in a particular context, whereby "*x*" does not yet have a conventionally regulated meaning content but has its meaning *conferred* by *S* in the given situation in a way recognizable for *H*. According to the proposal of H. P. Grice, the effect intended by the speaker resides in the hearer's being induced by the utterance of "*x*" to recognize the intention of the speaker and to accept it (at least in part) as a reason either for thinking that *S* intends (*meint*) something specific or for regarding the fact that *S* intends something specific as occasioning her (the hearer's) intention to do something specific.[9] The effect *r*, which is produced by "*x*" and triggered in *H* by *S*, is a specific belief (*Meinung*) or the intention to carry out a specific action. Two functions of the sign that Bühler had separated, namely, expression and appeal, fuse consistently into one and the same accomplishment: to allow a hearer to infer the intention of the speaker and thereby to motivate her to form the corresponding belief or intention.

The point of this strategy of explanation is that what is meant (*gemeint*) is in no way determined by what is said. The meaning of an utterance "*x*" by *S* is supposed to be explained solely by the intention with which *S* utters the expression "*x*" in a given context. This strategy is guided by the intuition that language usage is only one specific manifestation of the general sovereignty of purposively acting subjects—a sovereignty that, with respect to the medium of language, reveals itself, for example, in the fact that we can assign to objects any names we choose, as well as arbitrarily bestow meanings on signs. Under the same premises drawn from the philosophy of consciousness, Husserl was able to speak in this context of meaning-conferring acts. If language derives its meaning exclusively from the intentions of the purposive users of language, then it loses the autonomy of having its own internal structure.

b. Formal semantics follows a different intuition. It attends to the grammatical form of linguistic expressions and ascribes to language a status independent of the intentions and ideas of speaking subjects. In comparison to the rule system of language itself, the practice of language usage and the psychology of linguistic understanding occupy a status that is merely secondary. First of all, the object of the theory of meaning is constituted by linguistic expressions and not by the pragmatic relations between speakers and hearers that can be read off from the process of communication. The correct use and correct understanding of an expression do not result from the intentions of the speaker or from the conventions agreed upon by users of language, but from the formal properties of the expressions themselves and the rules whereby they are constituted. In this way, the theory of meaning is detached from action-theoretic contexts and reserved for linguistic analysis in the narrower sense. A dimension is thereby revealed that Bühler failed to take into consideration in his semiotically foreshortened model: that of the logical-semantic construction of language. Admittedly, from Bühler's point of view, formal semantics pays for this advantage by limiting its analysis to the representational function of language.

This explains both the methodological abstraction of the meaning of the sentence from the meaning of the utterance and the choice of the sentence as the smallest unit of semantic analysis. For, with the emphasis on the representational function, the relationship between language and the world, between an assertoric sentence and a state of affairs, moves to the center of analysis. Only with sentences is a speaker able to say something specific or, according to Frege, to express a "thought." Only in relation to a sentence and its thought is a hearer able to take a position with a "yes" or "no." When the croupier says "red" after the ball has come to a stop, the word takes on a specific sense only if the roulette player, on the basis of the context, tacitly expands it to the sentence "Red has won."

The approach of propositional semantics revolutionizes the older and long-dominant viewpoint of reference semantics, according to which language is related to reality as a name is related to its object. The relation of the signified (the meaning) to the signifier (the sign) was thought to be explicable in terms of the relation of the symbol (the meaningful sign) to the designatum (the signified object). This basic semiotic notion was suited to the object-centered theory of knowledge in the philosophy of consciousness.[10] In fact, names or designations, indeed all terms that we use to identify objects, do, as it were, establish contact between language and reality. A false picture arises, however, if this part is taken for the whole. In the case of a simple predicative sentence, a singular term must first be expanded to a sentence by means of a universal predicate expression before we can represent an elementary state of affairs. The predicate should "apply" to the object for which the subject expression "stands." But the relationship of the whole sentence to the state of affairs that is expressed in it may not then be conceived according to the model of "standing for an object." And if assertoric sentences are representative of language as a whole, then the relationship between language and the world must be explained in terms of a model different from that of the relation to an object: it is facts that *make* assertoric sentences *true*.

This, then, is the key to answering the fundamental question of the theory of meaning. If the meaning of an assertoric sentence is the state of affairs that it represents, and if this sentence is true precisely when the expressed state of affairs exists or is the case, then we understand the sentence only if we know the conditions under which it is true. The truth conditions of an assertoric sentence serve as an explanans for its meaning: "To understand a proposition means to know what is the case if it is true."[11]

This crucial insight by Frege into the internal connection between meaning and validity is based upon an intuition that, to anticipate, can be elucidated from a pragmatic perspective, which Frege himself did not adopt. Participants in communication reach understanding (*sich verständigen*) by using sentences about something in the world; if, however, the validity of the sentences uttered by the speaker could not be judged by the hearer, they would be completely inadequate as the smallest units of communication. Mutual understanding (*Verständigung*) with regard to the contested existence of states of affairs can be reached by participants only on the basis of the evaluation of sentences that are capable of being true.

c. Yet a different intuition underlies the use theory of meaning, which Wittgenstein developed from his critique of the truth-conditional semantic conception he himself once shared. Wittgenstein uncovers the action character of linguistic utterances.[12] From his perspective, the representational function, amidst the multiplicity of ways of using language, loses its privileged position. The medium of language does not serve first and foremost to describe or establish facts; it equally serves to issue commands, solve riddles, tell jokes, give thanks, curse, send greetings, and pray.[13] Later on, Austin uses these performative verbs to analyze the dual accomplishment of speech acts, with which a speaker, in saying something, simultaneously does something.[14]

Wittgenstein's formula—that the meaning of a word is its use in the language—is admittedly in need of interpretation, for the famous example of the builders in the second paragraph of *Philosophical Investigations* suggests an intentionalist reading. The assistant learns to bring "pillars," "slabs," and "beams" to the master when he calls; as soon as the participants intuitively master the cooperative context, they can assign objects to words through implicit definitions. The habitualized work practices are thereby determined by the purpose of building a house as well as by the relationship of authority between the master and the apprentice. For the speaker who issues the directives, the words that are called out and the feats of cooperation that are steered by them function as tools for the realization of his intentions. The words appear to derive their meaning from the purposes and the activities of the speaking subjects.

Formulations such as, "To understand a language means to be master of a technique," come close to the viewpoint of intentionalist semantics.[15] Nonetheless, there is a decisive difference. Wittgenstein conceives of the practice of the language game, which determines the use of the linguistic expressions, not as the result of individual teleological actions on the part of isolated, purposive subjects but as the "common behavior of mankind."[16] "Language game" is his name for the totality of the intermeshed linguistic utterances and nonlinguistic activities. It is the prior agreement in an intersubjectively shared form of life or the preunderstanding of common practices regulated by institutions and customs that constitute the interrelationship of activities and speech acts. Learning to master a language or learning how expressions in a language should be understood requires habitualization into a form of life. The form of life *antecedently* regulates the use of words and sentences within a network of possible purposes and possible actions.

Unlike the intentionalist approach, the use-theoretical approach does not emphasize the tool character of language but rather the intermeshing of language with interactive practices in which a form of life is simultaneously reflected and reproduced. With this, the relation to the world of linguistic expressions retreats once again, this time behind the relationships between speakers and hearers. These relationships are not interpreted intentionalistically from the perspective of the speaker but as reflections of antecedently established habitualized practices. With the grammar of language games, the dimension of an intersubjectively shared background knowledge of the lifeworld that carries (*trägt*) the multiple functions of language is disclosed.

The example of the builders seems to lend itself rather to concealing the real point of the use theory of meaning: in a competently mastered language game, the speech acts *carry* (*tragen*) interactive practices in a completely different way than the activities that are coordinated through them in the first place. Communicative acts owe this primacy to a property to which Austin drew attention with his investigation of the illocutionary character of speech acts. An observer can understand a nonlinguistic action only when she knows the intention that is supposed to be satisfied by means of it. Speech acts, by contrast, identify themselves.[17] Because the speaker, in carrying out an illocutionary act, simultaneously says what he is *doing*, a hearer who understands the meaning of what is said can straightforwardly identify the performed act as some specific action. Thus, the use-theoretical approach is already based on an intuition, the full import of which has been recognized only since Wittgenstein. The acts carried out in a natural language are always self-referential. They say both how what is said is to be used and how it is to be understood. This reflexive structure of everyday language becomes tangible in the grammatical form of the individual speech act. The illocutionary component establishes the sense in which the propositional content is being used and the sort of action as which the utterance should be understood.

The Limits of Semantics and of Speech-Act Theory

Each of the three competing theories of meaning takes up exactly one aspect of the process of reaching understanding. They seek to explain the meaning of a linguistic expression from the perspective of what is meant (as intended meaning), or from the perspective of what is said (as literal meaning), or from the perspective of use (as utterance meaning). By introducing each of these theories as stylizations of just one of the aspects that Bühler's schema of language functions takes into consideration *simultaneously*, I have already implicitly suggested their one-sidedness. I now want to go through the theories once more in order (a) to discuss the limits of what they are capable of achieving and then (b) to test the problemsolving potential of a fourth approach, namely, that of the theory of speech acts.

a. The intentionalist program sets itself the task of tracing the conventional meaning of a random grammatical expression "*x*" (*x*-meaning timeless) back to the nonconventional meaning of the speaker's intention connected with the utterance of "*x*" in a particular context (*S*-meaning occasional). Grice selects his premises in such a way that communication can be explained in terms of the purposive-rational influence of *S* upon *H*. The model is set up in such a way that strategic action can serve as a functional equivalent for reaching understanding linguistically. Given this preliminary decision, however, only such phenomena can come into view as are categorially different from those supposedly to be reconstructed. For, even in the most complex cases, what is reconstructed is only the meaning of an utterance "*x*" by *S* that, on the presupposition that a common language is not available, is capable of *inducing H* to believe or to intend to do something specific—that is, to *understand something indirectly* by way of inferences. But giving someone something to understand indirectly is a borderline case that, for its part, refers back to the normal case of reaching an understanding directly in a common language by way of utterances that identify themselves.

This parasitic status reveals itself in the type of counterexamples introduced by Strawson and dealt with by S. R. Schiffer, in which *S* can achieve the desired effect only so long as the intention that *H* is supposed to take as *S*'s intention does not coincide with the strategic ulterior intention that *S* is actually pursuing.[18] Through this asymmetry, however, an infinite regress is set in motion that could be prevented only if the participants were allowed to have recourse to shared knowledge, indeed in the final instance to the natural meaning of signals established through a causal chain (for example, that smoke means fire). Yet this recourse functions only on the condition that both sides, speaker and hearer, already understand the natural meaning of such a signal in a way analogous to understanding language, that is, in the manner of an intersubjectively known, nonnatural meaning of a conventionally regulated sign. Schiffer makes an illegitimate leap from the natural evidence of a signal like smoke (accessible from the perspective of an observer) to the comprehension (possible only in the performative attitude) of a communicatively used sign (that is, one recognizably used for the purpose of imparting information) with the corresponding propositional content that smoke means fire.[19] He thereby smuggles in precisely what is supposed to be explained, namely, the reflexivity of a self-identifying utterance and the intersubjective knowledge made possible by the comprehension of that utterance. Certainly, interactions among purposively acting subjects (which are mediated solely through observations, the strategic deployment of signs, and inferences) can lead to the reciprocally reflected attribution of propositional attitudes and contents; they cannot, however, lead to something like intersubjective knowledge in the strict sense.

Truth-conditional semantics allows the rationality and internal structure of the linguistic medium, disregarded by the intentionalist approach, to come into its own. The clear articulation of thoughts and intentions is made possible only through grammatical language, which constitutes a reality of its own kind and with its own dignity; states of affairs can be mirrored only in sentences. Yet this also bestows a privileged position on the validity, in the sense of truth, of assertoric sentences. The diverse functions served by language are susceptible to analysis only by way of the form of the sentences employed, ultimately, indeed, only by way of the form of assertoric sentences that serve representational functions. For even the meaning of nonassertoric sentences is elucidated through recourse to the conditions that make assertoric sentences true. Frege himself had already divided assertoric sentences into two components: the assertoric force or the mode of assertion must join up with the propositional content "that p" in order to yield the statement "p," whereby "that p" signifies a state of affairs and "p" signifies a fact, that is, an existing state of affairs. Only the modal component distinguishes imperative and interrogative sentences from assertoric sentences with the same content.

In order to explicate such distinctions between modes in terms of truth-conditional semantics, Stenius and Kenny make use of an idea of Austin's, who had assumed two opposing "directions of fit" between sentences and states of affairs.[20] They begin with statements and imperatives as the two basic modes, whereby true statements represent existing states of affairs and imperatives require that states of affairs be brought into existence. The conditions that make statements true correspond to the conditions under which imperatives are successfully carried out. In both cases, what is at issue are the conditions for states of affairs, either for the existence of recognized states of affairs or for the bringing about of desired states of affairs. However, this strategy of analysis founders on the asymmetry between truth conditions and success conditions that assertoric and imperative sentences, respectively, are supposed to "satisfy." For the force of imperatives cannot be differentiated adequately from the force of assertions on the basis of the opposed "directions of fit" in which a speaker takes up, with imperatives or assertions, respectively, a relation to (the same) state of affairs from different perspectives. A hearer is able to understand a sentence *qua* imperative only when she knows the conditions under which the speaker may expect that he could impose his will upon a hearer, even a reluctant one. The sense of the imperative demand for compliance cannot be explained in terms of the semantically analyzable knowledge of success conditions; it can be explained only pragmatically, specifically with reference to the authority standing behind it.[21]

Admittedly, a purely semantic approach to analysis meets its limits even in the case of assertoric sentences themselves. In its classical form, truth-conditional semantics believed it possible to ignore altogether the circumstances under which a hearer *is in a position to recognize* when the truth conditions of a sentence are satisfied in a given case. But the knowledge of truth conditions is, at most, unproblematic only in the case of simple predicative observation sentences, whose truth can be tested in easily surveyable contexts with the help of readily accessible perceptual evidence. At any rate, there are no correspondingly simple tests for predictions, counterfactual conditional sentences, nomological statements, and so forth. Assertoric sentences of these kinds quantify dimensions that are infinite or are inaccessible to observation. Michael Dummett correctly points out that simple rules of verification for these and similar sentences are not at our disposal. It is therefore not sufficient to render the Fregean thesis more precise to the effect that one understands an assertoric sentence when one knows its rules of verification. Relying on the pragmatic distinction between "truth" and "assertibility"—that is, between the truth of a sentence and the entitlement to make an assertion with that sentence—Dummett replaces knowledge of the truth conditions (or knowledge of the verification rules of a justification game geared toward observation situations[22]) with indirect knowledge: the hearer must know the kinds of reasons with which the speaker could, if necessary, vindicate his claim that particular truth conditions are satisfied. In short, one understands an assertoric sentence when one knows the kinds of reasons a speaker must provide in order to convince a hearer that the speaker is entitled to raise a truth claim for the sentence.[23]

Just as Dummett implicitly makes reference to the game of argumentation in which the speaker *qua* proponent is able to convince a hearer *qua* opponent of the entitlement for his truth claim, so Wittgenstein comes upon the presuppositions underlying a similar distribution of roles in his analysis of the concept of following a rule.[24] Following a rule means following the *same* rule in each case; the meaning of a rule is interwoven with the use of the word "same." *A* cannot be certain whether she is following a rule at all unless a situation exists in which she exposes her conduct to the judgment of a critic *B* who is able to ascertain deviations from the rule. Identical meaning and the validity of a rule are conceptually connected. For the identity of a rule in the multiplicity of its realizations does not rest upon *observable* invariances but upon the validity of a criterion according to which rule-conformative behavior can be judged. Rule-guided conduct is fallible and therefore requires two simultaneous, interchangeable roles: one for *A,* who follows a rule and thereby seeks to avoid mistakes, and one for *B,* who is able critically to judge the correctness of the rule-guided conduct of *A.* The point of this consideration is that a linguistic expression can have an identical meaning only for a subject who is capable, together with at least one other subject, of following a rule that is valid *for both of them.* A monadically isolated subject can no more use an expression in a way that maintains identity of meaning than a rule can be followed privately.

In this way, Wittgenstein introduces the internal connection between meaning and validity independently of language's relation to the world; he therefore does not link up the rules for the meaning of words with the validity, in the sense of truth, of sentences. Instead, he compares the validity of meaning conventions with the prevailing social validity of customs and institutions and assimilates the grammatical rules of language games to social norms of action. Of course, he thereby surrenders any relation to validity that transcends the context of a given language game. Utterances are valid or invalid only according to the standards of the language game to which they belong. Thus, almost imperceptibly, even the relation to truth of fact-ascertaining speech is lost. For Wittgenstein, the representational function is just one among many other functions of language that have developed, as it were, as part of the natural history of a diversity of interlocking (and in principle, equally legitimate) language games.

b. Following on from the later Wittgenstein, Austin investigated more closely, on the basis of individual illocutionary acts, how language is bound up with interactive practices in a form of life. In addition, however, and unlike Wittgenstein, Austin does not want to ignore the relationship brought out by truth-conditional semantics between language and the objective world, between a sentence and a state of affairs. Austin takes the first steps en route to a theory of speech acts that combines the insights of truth-conditional semantics with those of language-game pragmatics. At first, this leads him to a dualistic conception that in a general way opposes illocutionary acts to the ascertaining of facts. In so-called constative utterances, assertoric sentences are used to represent states of affairs. Austin also speaks of locutionary acts here: the speaker uses locutionary acts in order to say something (say what is the case). Against this, illocutionary acts as such are not supposed to have any propositional content, not even a meaning. With such an act, the speaker does not say anything that could be true or false but instead performs a social action. "Hello!" does not *mean* anything; rather, it *is* a greeting, which the speaker can perform with this expression. Of course, such an act can be infelicitous, if, for example, it is carried out with the wrong words, in an inappropriate context, or without the correct emphasis. Instead of having a meaning, an illocutionary act gives expression to a particular force—a power of a kind with the binding character of promises. While locutionary acts make possible a cognitive use of language that is, as it were, turned toward the world, speakers and hearers are able to establish relations among each other with illocutionary acts; the latter serve the interactive use of language.

Initially Austin proposed the following classifications:

Locutionary Act—Assertoric Sentence—Meaning—True/False

Illocutionary Act—Performative Sentence—Force—Felicitous/ Infelicitous

This dualism could not be maintained.[25] Austin saw from the beginning, of course, that most illocutionary acts do not appear independently but incorporate clauses with propositional content. In general, the speaker carries out an illocutionary act by saying *something*. The illocutionary component establishes only the mode of a sentence that is used as a promise, a recommendation, an avowal, and so forth. The notation Mp indicates that we execute two acts in one, acts that can be separated only analytically. But then it is no longer clear why the contrast between "force" and "meaning," familiar from truth-conditional semantics, ought to be retained in a theory of speech acts. Performative sentences obviously have just as clear a meaning as assertoric sentences. And constative speech acts exhibit the same illocutionary-propositional double structure as all other speech acts. Assertions, descriptions, or narratives can, completely independently of their truth value, be infelicitous in a way similar to other illocutionary acts: one can make such a mess of telling a tale that "it is no longer a good story," or discuss a delicate matter so bluntly that those present "will not tolerate any further discussion of it."

If, however, *all* speech acts can be analyzed in the form Mp, then locutionary acts lose the special status that was initially claimed for them. They are, so to speak, absorbed into the propositional component of any and every speech act, and hand over their monopoly on the claim to truth to a particular class of speech acts, the constative. This then gives rise to the interesting question of whether only constative speech acts can be valid or invalid (true or false) or whether other speech acts, too, might exhibit an equivalent dimension for that of truth. If the latter were the case, we would have to work out a conception of language that attributes no essential importance to the fact that what is said in a language *always* transcends the boundaries of that language and refers to something in the world. But both Austin and Searle give an affirmative answer to this question, albeit significantly different ones.

Austin corrects his position to the effect that he now understands the two dimensions of evaluation, which he had initially correlated, respectively, with locutionary and illocutionary acts (truth vs. success), as aspects that are merely analytically separable. *Every* speech act can be evaluated according to whether it is "right" as well as whether it is "in order."[26] To be sure, Austin does not fill the dimension of "rightness"—to which the validity, in the sense of truth, of constative speech acts is now generalized—with a specific number of well-defined validity claims; rather, his "loosening up of the ideas of truth and falsity" is supposed to open up a whole spectrum of aspects of validity, ranging from propositional truth via goodness and appropriateness to normative rightness. Out of a wealth of evaluative viewpoints, the linguistic analyst is supposed in each case to be able to identify the relevant criterion of assessment and to capture it descriptively. By contrast, Searle wants to avoid the difficulties that necessarily result from this kind of subsumption of validity, in the sense of truth, and normative validity under a diversity of "values." In the dimension of the validity of speech acts, he admits only the one clear-cut universal validity claim that had already been privileged by truth-conditional semantics. In this respect, Searle takes a step backward from Austin and the later Wittgenstein to Frege.

We are nonetheless indebted to Searle for the version of speech-act theory that has been most precisely explicated up to now.[27] He takes Austin's conditions of felicity and renders them more precise as "preparatory conditions;" these refer to standardized contexts that must obtain if certain kinds of speech acts are to be performed meaningfully and with the prospect of success. He then adds comprehensibility and sincerity conditions; these refer on the one hand to the availability of a common linguistic medium and the suitability of the speech situation, and on the other hand to the corresponding intention of the speaker. He further specifies conditions for the semantic form that the clauses with propositional content must obey, and finally faces the task of specifying the "essential conditions" according to which different illocutionary forces or modes of using language can be demarcated. The five basic modes distinguished by Searle (constative, directive, commissive, expressive, and declarative speech acts) are open to more precise surface differentiations using pragmatic criteria (such as the direction of interest of the speaker and hearer, the degree of intensity in bringing out the illocutionary point, or the institutional ties of the speech act).

However, the differentiation of the basic modes themselves—moreover, in a validity dimension geared solely toward propositional truth (which permits variation only according to the direction of fit between language and the world)—is the problem on which Searle labors in vain. In both directions (from "word to world" and from "world to word"), the relation of language to the objective world provides a basis that is too narrow for distinguishing the five proposed classes of speech acts. Indeed, for Wittgenstein, the fact that the rich variety of illocutionary forces could not be brought to order from the viewpoint of truth-conditional semantics had already been a sufficient reason for giving up all attempts at classification in favor of describing an unordered collection of language-game grammars. Only constative speech acts can be characterized—and only partially—according to the direction in which sentences and facts can be brought into agreement.[28] Assertoric force means that S presents to H a truth claim for "p" and thereby issues a warranty that the truth conditions of "p" are satisfied—or, simply, that the proposition fits the facts.

Even the illocutionary force of authorized imperatives is incapable of being explained solely through recourse to the satisfaction of success conditions, that is, in terms of H effecting that "p" becomes true. H understands an imperative sentence as a command, directive, a request, or the like only when knowledge of the success conditions (given in the clause with propositional content) is augmented by knowledge of those conditions (contained in the illocutionary component) under which S could justify why he regards an imperative with the content "p" as legitimate or enforceable. With this, a validity claim of a normative kind, which cannot be reduced to a truth claim, comes into play. The same holds for the illocutionary force of commissive speech acts, with which the speaker binds his own will in the sense of a normative obligation. The conditions for the binding character of obligating declarations of intention are of a different kind from the success conditions, which the speaker fulfills as soon as he translates his intention into action—that is, makes it come true.

The illocutionary force of expressive speech acts, with which S expresses a subjective experience (*Erlebnis*) to which he has privileged access, can be defined neither through the cognitive nor through the interventionistic relation of a subject to the world of existing states of affairs. Searle is thus consistent in using a neither-nor sign in such cases in order to indicate the inapplicability of the perspective of truth-conditional semantics. In expressive speech acts, a claim to truthfulness (*Wahrhaftigkeit*) comes into play—a claim, moreover, that Searle has already employed in an unspecific way for the sincerity condition that *all* comprehensible speech acts are supposed to satisfy. A similar objection can be made to his definition of the illocutionary force of declarative speech acts.[29]

These problems are avoided when one does not respond to the validity problems bequeathed by Austin in the way Searle does— namely, with a truth-conditional-semantic weakening of speech-act theory—but instead interprets Bühler's language functions in terms of the corresponding validity claims.

Speech Acts, Communicative Action, and Strategic Interaction

An interpretation of Bühler's schema of language functions from the point of view of a theory of validity suggests itself as a way out of the difficulties of speech-act theory because it does justice to all three aspects of a *speaker* reaching understanding/with *another* person/about *something*. It incorporates within itself the truth contained in the use theory of meaning and at the same time overcomes the specific one-sidedness of intentionalist and formal semantics, respectively. The resulting formal-pragmatic analysis of speech acts provides a basis for the concept of communicative action. Communicative action constitutes an alternative to strategic action, yet it remains linked to the teleology of the various individual plans of action that come together in it.

a. Following the transition from the semantic to the pragmatic point of view, the question of the validity of a sentence no longer poses itself as a question—detached from the process of communication—about the objective relation between language and the world. Nor can the validity claim, with which the speaker refers to the validity conditions of his utterance, be defined solely from the perspective of the speaker. Validity claims have a built-in orientation toward intersubjective recognition by speaker and hearer; they can be vindicated only with reasons, that is, discursively, and the hearer reacts to them with rationally motivated "yes" or "no" positions. The smallest independent unit of explicitly linguistic processes of reaching understanding is composed of the elementary speech act Mp, with which S raises at least one criticizable validity claim for her utterance, and of the "yes" or "no" position that determines whether H understands and accepts the speech-act offer from S. Reaching understanding aims at consensus formation. The attempt by S to reach understanding with H about something in the world terminates in the agreement brought about between them; this agreement is then sealed by the acceptance of a comprehensible speech act. For this reason, understanding (*Verstehen*) a speech act already points to the conditions for a possible agreement (*Einverständnis*) about what is said.

Of course, the pragmatic reinterpretation of the problem of validity also requires a complete reevaluation of what was originally meant by the "illocutionary force" of a speech act. As we saw, Austin had conceived of the illocutionary force as the literally irrational component of the speech act, whereas the rational content was monopolized by the content of the assertoric sentence (or its nominalized form). Meaning and understanding were concentrated solely on this rational component. By contrast, the consistent execution of the pragmatic turn makes validity claims into the stewards of a rationality that presents itself as the structural interconnection of validity conditions, validity claims referring to these conditions, and reasons for the vindication of these validity claims. The individual speech act is bound to this structure primarily through its modal component. That is, the mode is defined according to the type of claim raised by the speaker with her misleadingly named "illocutionary" act, in the standard case through the utterance of a performative clause (and also according to the way in which this validity claim is referred to). The locus of rationality is thereby transferred from the propositional to the illocutionary component, and at the same time the validity conditions no longer remain fixated on the proposition. Room is thus made for the introduction of validity claims that are *not* directed toward truth conditions—that is, are not geared toward the relation of language to the objective world.

Bühler's schema of language functions had already placed the linguistic expression in relation to the intention of the speaker, to the objective world, and to the addressee. And each of the three theories of meaning discussed in the foregoing claimed that it could explain the comprehensibility of linguistic expressions through some one of these relations—whether through the function of expressing intentions, or of representing states of affairs, or of actualizing and establishing interactive relationships. What we are looking for is a theory of speech acts that takes account of the kernel of truth in all three of these theories of meaning. However, from Searle's classification of speech acts it has once again become apparent that the way in which truth-conditional semantics conceives the internal relation between truth and meaning is *too specialized.*

Certainly, whether or not an utterance fulfills its representational function is measured against truth conditions; however, the fulfillment of the expressive and the interactive functions is also measured against conditions that are *analogous to truth.* I therefore want to introduce subjective truthfulness and normative rightness as truth-analogous concepts for the validity of speech acts. The relations of the speech act to speakers' intentions and to addressees can also be conceived in terms of the model of a relation to the objective world. That is, there exists simultaneously a relation to the subjective world (of the speaker), as the totality of experiences (*Erlebnisse*) to which he has privileged access, and a relation to the social world (of the speaker, the hearer, and other members), as the totality of interpersonal relations held to be legitimate. These world-concepts formed *through analogy* must not, of course, be misunderstood as partial regions (in Popper's sense) of the one objective world.[30] The subjective experiences that *S* externalizes in expressive speech acts (prototypically in avowals and revelations) should no more be understood as a particular class of *entities* (or inner episodes) than should the norms legitimating an interpersonal relationship established between *S* and *H* by means of regulative speech acts (prototypically through commands and promises). From the perspective of the participants, the first-person experiential sentences employed in expressive speech acts can be uttered *truthfully* or *untruthfully,* according to whether the speaker means what he says. But they cannot be true or false unless experiential sentences are to be assimilated to assertoric sentences. In the same way, the imperative sentences (commands or requests) or intentional sentences (promises) that are employed in the attitude of the first person [toward a second person] in regulative speech acts can be *right* or *not right,* according to whether they satisfy or violate recognized normative expectations or whether they have a binding character or merely create the illusion of being binding. But they, too, cannot be true or false. With their speech acts, participants in communication relate to something in the subjective world or to something in the social world in ways that are *different* from the way in which they relate to something in the objective world. That these world-concepts should be used only in an analogous sense is shown by these differences in the *type of reference:* objects are identified in a different way than subjective experiences (which, in an expressive attitude, I reveal or disguise as "in each case mine"), and also in a different way than the norms acknowledged in each case "by us" (which, in a norm-conformative attitude, we follow or contravene).

Furthermore, an interpretation of Bühler's schema of language functions from the point of view of a theory of validity leads to the assumption that, with a speech act Mp, S relates *simultaneously* to something in the objective world, to something in the subjective world, and to something in a shared social world. Every speech act as a whole can always be criticized as invalid from three perspectives: as untrue with respect to a statement made (or with respect to the existential presuppositions underlying the propositional content), as untruthful with respect to the expressed intention of the speaker, and as not right with respect to the existing normative context (or with respect to the legitimacy of the presupposed norms themselves). To be sure, no more than one of these three validity claims can be emphasized thematically in an explicit speech act. Finally, it is in terms of these thematized validity claims (modified on the basis of surface distinctions according to the particular language and context in question) that the illocutionary forces are defined; these illocutionary forces must be capable of being traced back to three basic modes: they belong to the class of either constative, expressive, or regulative speech acts.

Now, if every speech act is thematically linked with some one validity claim, then Dummett's proposal for explicating the meaning of the assertoric sentences employed in constative speech acts can be generalized. We understand a speech act when we know what makes it acceptable. Of course, this is a matter of objective conditions of validity that the hearer cannot infer directly from the semantic content of the expressions used, but only indirectly through the epistemic claim that the speaker raises for the validity of his utterance in performing his illocutionary act. With his validity claim, the speaker appeals to a reservoir of potential reasons that could be provided in support of it. The reasons interpret the conditions of validity, and to this extent they themselves are part of the conditions that make an utterance acceptable. In this way, the acceptability conditions point to the holistic constitution of natural languages. In a language, every individual speech act is connected by way of logical-semantic threads to many other potential speech acts, which can take on the pragmatic role of reasons. Naturally, depending on the structure and content of a speech act, the reasons standing latently at the ready and suitable for the discursive vindication of the validity claim raised in that speech act will be more or less complex as regards type and scope. When the speaker makes an assertion with a simple predicative observation sentence in the present indicative, the reasons that interpret the truth conditions of the sentence are normally easy to survey. By contrast, when a court passes judgment on a complicated matter or when a physicist explains a natural event with the help of an empirical theory, the evaluation of the validity—and thus also the *comprehension*—of the court verdict or of the scientific explanation will require knowledge of more demanding kinds of reasons. Otherwise we simply do not understand what is said—not even if we were to understand the individual words because they have occurred frequently prior to this in *other* sentences.

We understand a speech act when we know the kinds of reasons that a speaker could provide in order to convince a hearer that she is entitled in the given circumstances to claim validity for her utterance. For this reason, knowledge of a language is bound up with knowledge of what is actually the case in the (linguistically disclosed) world. Perhaps knowledge of the world merely hangs upon a longer chain of reasons than knowledge of language. That they cannot be separated sharply from one another becomes plausible when one realizes the basic idea of the formal-pragmatic explanation of meaning (already contained within Bühler's schema). To understand an expression is to know how one can make use of it in order to reach understanding with somebody about something. Therefore, it can already be discerned from the conditions for understanding linguistic expressions that the speech acts that can be performed with their help have a built-in orientation toward reaching understanding, that is, toward a rationally motivated agreement about what is said. One simply would not know what it is to understand the meaning of an utterance if one did not know that the utterance can and should serve to bring about an agreement; moreover, it is part of the concept of agreement that it "holds" (*gilt*) for the participants. The dimension of validity is thus inherent in language. The orientation toward validity claims is part of the pragmatic conditions of possible mutual understanding (*Verständigung*)—and of linguistic understanding (*Sprachverstehen*) itself.

b. With the concept of a mutual understanding oriented toward validity claims, formal pragmatics finds a connection with action theory, albeit in a way completely different from the attempt of intentionalist semantics to explain processes of reaching understanding using concepts of action theory. A teleological action can be described as the realization of a plan of action that is based on the actor's interpretation of the situation. By carrying out a plan of action, an actor comes to grips with a situation, whereby the action situation constitutes a segment from the environment as interpreted by the actor. This segment is constituted in light of possibilities for action that the actor regards as relevant with respect to the success of her plan. The problem of coordinating action arises with regard to interaction between several actors: how can Alter's plans and actions be "linked up" with Ego's plans and actions? Types of interaction can be distinguished according to the various mechanisms for this linking-up. I speak either of "communicative action" or of "strategic action," depending on whether the actions of different actors are coordinated by way of "reaching understanding" or "exerting influence," respectively.[31] From the perspective of the participants, these two mechanisms and their corresponding types of action mutually exclude one another. Processes of reaching understanding cannot be undertaken with the dual intention of reaching an agreement about something with a participant in interaction and simultaneously causally exerting some effect on him. From the perspective of the participants, an agreement cannot be imposed from without, cannot be foisted by one party upon the other—whether instrumentally, through direct intervention into the action situation, or strategically, through indirect influence (again, concerned only with one's own success) on the propositional attitudes of the other actor. Whatever manifestly comes about through external influence (gratification or threat, suggestion or deception) cannot count intersubjectively as an agreement; an intervention of this sort forfeits its effectiveness for coordinating action.

Communicative or strategic action is required when an actor can carry out his plans of action only interactively, that is, with the help of the actions of another actor (or of his refraining from action). Over and above this, communicative action must satisfy certain cooperative and communicative conditions:

a. The participating actors must conduct themselves cooperatively and attempt to harmonize their plans with one another (within the horizon of a shared lifeworld) on the basis of common (or sufficiently overlapping) interpretations of the situation.

b. The participating actors must be prepared to achieve the indirect goals of a common definition of the situation and of action coordination in the roles of speakers and hearers by way of processes of reaching understanding, that is, by way of the unreserved and sincere pursuit of illocutionary aims.

This means specifically that:

• They pursue their illocutionary aims with the help of speech acts in a performative attitude, which demands an orientation toward reciprocally raised, criticizable validity claims.

• In doing this, they make use of the binding and bonding effects (*Bindungseffekte*) of speech-act offers, which come about when the speaker, with his validity claim, issues a credible warranty for the validity of what is said.

• The binding and bonding effect of a comprehensible and accepted speech act is carried over to the obligations relevant for the sequel of interaction arising out of the semantic content of the speech act—whether asymmetrically for the hearer or the speaker, or symmetrically for both sides.

Thus, communicative action distinguishes itself from strategic action through the fact that successful action coordination cannot be traced back to the purposive rationality of action orientations but to the rationally motivating force of achieving understanding, that is, to a rationality that manifests itself in the conditions for a communicatively reached agreement. The way in which linguistic processes of reaching understanding function as a mechanism for coordinating action is that the participants in interaction agree about the validity claimed for their speech acts—that is, they recognize criticizable validity claims intersubjectively. What gives rationally motivating force to speech-act offers is, in turn, the structural connection between the meaning of an utterance on the one hand, and on the other its validity conditions, the validity claim raised for what is said, and the reasons that can be mobilized for the discursive vindication of this claim.

Like all action, communicative action is purposive. But here, the teleology of the individual action plans and of the operations for carrying them out is *interrupted* by the action-coordinating mechanism of reaching understanding. Orientations and action processes are initially egocentrically geared toward a particular actor, but the communicative "switch" by way of illocutionary acts carried out without reservation places them under the structural constraints of an intersubjectively shared language. The telos of reaching understanding inherent in the structures of language compels the communicative actors to alter their perspective; this shift in perspective finds expression in the necessity of going from the objectivating attitude of the success-oriented actor, who seeks to *effect* something in the world, to the performative attitude of a speaker, who seeks to *reach understanding* with a second person about something.[32]

In their standard form, illocutionary acts are carried out using performative sentences. For the formation of the predicate expression, these sentences require performative verbs; for the subject expression, they require the first person in the present indicative; for the position of the direct object, they require the second person. This grammatical form of the performative sentence mirrors the attitude of a speaker who takes up an interpersonal relation with a hearer in order to reach understanding with her about something, whereby the speaker is reflexively oriented toward the possibility that the hearer may dispute the validity of what is said. Such a *performative attitude* of an actor oriented toward reaching understanding can be differentiated conceptually from the objectivating attitude of a success-oriented actor on the basis of the world-relations that each permits: with our speech acts, we *simultaneously* relate, with varying thematizations, to something in the objective, the subjective, and the social worlds, whereas in acting purposively we intervene solely in the objective world.

If, however, the attitude toward reaching understanding and that oriented toward success are not merely to be distinguished from one another analytically, but rather correspond to two different types of interaction, then from the perspective of the actors themselves they must be mutually exclusive. Against this, the objection has been raised that (i) any speech act whatsoever can also be strategically deployed, and that (ii) simple imperatives, which are not embedded in normative contexts, do not express validity claims but rather power claims, and therefore fall into the category—paradoxical on our account—of illocutionary acts that are carried out with an orientation toward success.

i. Whether conventionally regulated or not, perlocutionary effects that are striven for *openly* within the framework of a common definition of the situation are of a kind that, *mutatis mutandis,* could also be effected through purposive intervention alone. But such nonlinguistically produced effects cannot be described as perlocutionary effects because the latter are always illocutionarily mediated. Admittedly, there is the case of the latently strategic speech act that aims at perlocutionary effects that are not conventionally regulated. The perlocutionary effects come about only if the speaker does not declare his aims to the hearer within the framework of a common definition of the situation. Thus, for example, a speaker who wants to persuade his audience of something proceeds in this way, perhaps because in the given situation he lacks convincing arguments. Such nonpublic perlocutionary effects can be achieved only parasitically, namely, on condition that the speaker feigns the intention of *unreservedly* pursuing his illocutionary aims and leaves the hearer in the dark as to his actual violation of the presuppositions of action oriented toward reaching understanding.[33] The latently strategic use of language is parasitic because it functions only when at least one party assumes that language is being used with an orientation toward reaching understanding. Whoever acts strategically in this way must violate the sincerity condition of communicative action *inconspicuously*.

The use of language that is manifestly strategic also has a derivative status; in this case, all participants are aware that reaching understanding linguistically is subject to conditions of strategic action—and therefore remains deficient. They know and reckon with the fact that they must supplement the illocutionarily mediated perlocutionary effects of their speech acts with empirical effects that are triggered purposively. For, in the end they remain dependent on indirect communication: only the proverbial shot across the bows is able, for example, to demonstrate to an opponent the seriousness of a threat.

This case of the manifestly strategic use of language is to be distinguished, in turn, from cases of an indirect communication that remains *subordinated* to the aim of communicative action. In unstructured preliminary situations, a common definition of the situation is first of all constructed, as, for example, when in an accidental meeting in a bar, a young man indirectly gives an attractive young woman to understand something. In the same way, the pedagogically sensitive teacher instills self-confidence in her pupil by means of compliments, so that the pupil learns to take his own ideas seriously.[34] In cases such as these, in which communicative action has first of all to establish its own presuppositions step by step, the *terminus ad quem* is an agreement that is ultimately also communicatively available, and not a perlocutionary effect that would be destroyed by being admitted or declared.

ii. I analyze simple or nonauthorized imperatives according to the model of the derivative manifestly strategic use of language. The addressee of a command or a request must as a rule be familiar with the normative context that authorizes a speaker to make her demand, and that thereby legitimates her expectation that the addressee has reasons to carry out the action demanded. Knowledge of success conditions, which can be derived from the propositional component "p" of the imperative Ip, is not sufficient in order to understand the illocutionary meaning of this speech act, that is, its specific character as an imperative. Knowledge of the success conditions (a) must be augmented by knowledge of those conditions (b) under which the speaker has reasons to regard an imperative with the content (a) as valid, that is, normatively justified—for example, that children in the streets of Lima may beg from visiting foreigners.[35] Of course, the speaker may connect a validity claim with Ip only so long as she knows her imperative to be secured by *some or other* normative context, be this ever so weak.

From the perspective of a sociological observer, there is a continuum between merely de facto habitualized power relations and power relations that have been transformed into normative authority. However, from the perspective of participants in communication—so long as their lifeworlds are sufficiently interwoven—it is possible to understand *all* imperatives (against the background of such an intersubjectively shared lifeworld) according to the model of normatively authorized imperatives. Even strangers who encounter one another in foreign lands will, in emergencies, expect from each other a readiness to help. Even such weak normative contexts are sufficient to authorize a speaker to expect a certain kind of behavior, which the hearer can criticize if need be. Only in the borderline case of manifestly strategic action does the normative validity claim shrivel into a pure power claim based upon a reservoir of potential sanctions that is contingent and is no longer conventionally regulated or grammatically readable. The "Hands up!" of a bank robber who at pistol point demands of the threatened bank teller that she hands over the money demonstrates in a drastic way that the conditions of normative validity have been replaced by sanction conditions.

The dissolution of the normative background appears in a symptomatic way in the "if-then" structure of the threat, which in strategic action takes the place of the sincerity or earnestness of the speaker presupposed in the case of communicative action. Imperatives or threats that are deployed purely strategically and robbed of their normative validity claims are not illocutionary acts—that is, acts with a built-in orientation toward reaching understanding—at all. They remain parasitic insofar as their comprehensibility must be derived from the employment conditions for normatively secured illocutionary acts.

In latently strategic action, the perlocutionary effects are dependent upon the illocutionary effects of a use of language that is oriented toward reaching understanding, however much it may be feigned on one side. In manifestly strategic action, illocutionarily weakened speech acts, if they are to be comprehensible, continue to refer to the meaning they owe to a use of language that is antecedently habitualized and originally oriented toward reaching understanding.

Notes

1. K. Bühler, *Sprachtheorie* (Jena, 1934), p. 28.

2. K.-O. Apel, *Die Idee der Sprache in der Tradition des Humanismus von Dante bis Vico* (Bonn, 1963).

3. G. Meggle, ed., *Handlung, Kommunikation und Bedeutung* (Frankfurt, 1979).

4. M. Dummett, *Frege: Philosophy of Language* (London, 1973).

5. W. P. Alston, *Philosophy of Language* (Englewood Cliffs, N.J., 1964).

6. C. W. Morris, *Signs, Language, Behavior* (Englewood Cliffs, N.J., 1946).

7. N. Chomsky, "A Review of B. F. Skinner's 'Verbal Behaviour,'" in J. Fodor and J. Katz, eds., *The Structure of Language* (Englewood Cliffs, N.J., 1964), pp. 547ff.

8. E. Tugendhat, *Traditional and Analytical Philosophy*, trans. P. A. Gorner (Cambridge, 1982), pp. 163ff.

9. H. P. Grice, "Utterer's Meanings and Intentions," in *Studies in the Ways of Words* (Cambridge, Mass., 1989), pp. 86ff., "Utterer's Meaning, Sentence-Meaning and Word-Meaning," in ibid., pp. 117ff., and "Meaning Revisited," in ibid., pp. 283ff.

10. Tugendhat, *Traditional and Analytical Philosophy*, pp. 207ff.

11. L. Wittgenstein, *Tractatus Logico-Philosophicus*, trans. D. F. Pears and B. F. McGuinness (London, 1961), 4.024.

12. K.-O. Apel, "Wittgenstein and the Problem of Hermeneutic Understanding," in *Towards a Transformation of Philosophy*, trans. G. Adey and D. Frisby (London, 1980), pp. 1ff.

13. L. Wittgenstein, *Philosophical Investigations*, trans. G. E. M. Anscombe (London, 1958), §§23ff.

14. J. L. Austin, *How to Do Things with Words* (Oxford, 1962).

15. Wittgenstein, *Philosophical Investigations*, §199.

16. Ibid., §206.

17. D. S. Shwayder, *Stratification of Behavior* (London, 1965), pp. 47ff.

18. S. R. Schiffer, *Meaning* (Oxford, 1972); cf. J. Habermas, "Intentionalistische Semantik," in *Vorstudien und Ergänzungen zur Theorie des kommunikativen Handelns* (Frankfurt, 1984), pp. 332ff.

19. This argument is developed by C. B. Christensen, "On the Mechanism of Communication," Ms. (Frankfurt, 1987).

20. E. Stenius, "Mood and Language Game," *Synthese* 17 (1964), pp. 254ff.; A. Kenny, *Will, Freedom and Power* (Oxford, 1975); cf. also Tugendhat, *Traditional and Analytical Philosophy*, pp. 398ff.

21. J. Habermas, *The Theory of Communicative Action*, vol. 1, trans. T. McCarthy (Boston, 1984), pp. 298ff.

22. Tugendhat, *Traditional and Analytical Philosophy*, pp. 207ff.

23. M. Dummett, "What Is a Theory of Meaning?," in G. Evans and J. McDowell, eds., *Truth and Meaning* (Oxford, 1976), pp. 67ff.

24. Wittgenstein, *Philosophical Investigations*, §§380ff.; cf. P. Winch, *The Idea of a Social Science* (London, 1958); Habermas, *The Theory of Communicative Action*, vol. 2, trans. T. McCarthy (Boston, 1987) pp. 15ff.

25. On the development of Austin's position, see chapter 1 in the present volume, especially pp. 72ff.

26. Austin, *How to Do Things with Words*, pp. 145ff., and "Performative-Constative," in C. E. Caton, ed., *Philosophy and Ordinary Language* (Urbana, Ill., 1963), pp. 22–33.

27. J. Searle, *Speech Acts* (Cambridge, 1969), *Expression and Meaning* (Cambridge, 1979), *Intentionality* (Cambridge, 1983), and *Minds, Brains, and Science* (Cambridge, Mass., 1984).

28. For the following, cf. chapter 2, pp. 157ff. and chapter 5 in the present volume.

29. Searle's own explanation already makes it apparent that the use of a double arrow to characterize the declarative mode expresses an embarrassment: Searle, *Expression and Meaning*, p. 19. Cf. also chapter 5 in the present volume.

30. Cf. the discussion of Popper's doctrine of three worlds in *Theory of Communicative Action,* vol. 1, pp. 76ff.

31. J. Habermas, "Remarks on the Concept of Communicative Action," in G. Seebaß and R. Tuomela, eds., *Social Action* (Dordrecht, 1985).

32. In "Communicative Competence and Normative Force," *New German Critique* 35 (1985): 133ff., J. Culler claims that through a tendentious choice of examples, I smuggle a normatively laden conception of "reaching understanding" (*Verständigung*) into the analysis: "When I am reading the instructions for my word processing program I assume that statements are correct descriptions of the system's capabilites and that the manual has been checked for errors, but there seems no interesting sense in which I presuppose the sincerity of any individual communicator" (p. 140). The impersonal form of the written instructions for the use of a computer is, however, no obstacle to drawing on the model of face-to-face communication in order to analyze the illocutionary meaning—and the obligations arising out of it—of such technical instructions. Through the conditions of the sales contract, a normative context is established that appears to justify the normative expectation, mentioned by Culler, that the user has toward the computer firm.

33. 3. Cf. chapter 3 in the present volume pp. 203ff. In an incisive article ("Habermas's Defence of Rationalism," *New German Critique* 25 (1985): 145ff.), Allen Wood has criticized my attempt to justify the primacy of the use of language oriented toward reaching understanding with the help of the opposition between illocutionary and perlocutionary acts. I admit that (in *Theory of Communicative Action,* vol. 1, see pp. 119ff. in this volume) I over-hastily conflated this meaning-theoretic distinction with the action-theoretic distinction between action oriented toward reaching understanding and action oriented toward success. It is sufficient to justify the primacy of the use of language oriented toward reaching understanding through the theory of meaning as proposed here, and to distinguish communicative from strategic action on the basis of the fact that the former is mediated by illocutionary acts that are carried out without reservation, and is therefore subject to the performative constraints of the action-coordinating mechanism of reaching understanding. This mechanism interrupts, as it were, the teleology of the individual chains of action that are connected up by way of consensus formation, whereas the speech acts that are instrumentalized for strategic action are robbed of their illocutionary binding and bonding power. Perlocutionary effects, which are intially demarcated from illocutionary effects in purely meaning-theoretic terms, can then be described in various ways in action-theoretic terms, depending on whether they appear openly and as susceptible to consensus within the framework of common situation definitions or whether they are pursued strategically and may not be declared.

34. The example is taken from Wood, "Habermas's Defence of Rationalism," p. 161.

35. Cf. the example in E. Tugendhat, "J. Habermas on Communicative Action," in Seebaß and Tuomela, eds., *Social Action,* pp. 179ff. (referred to in chapter 3 of the present volume pp. 199f).

7

Some Further Clarifications of the Concept of Communicative Rationality (1996)

Herbert Schnädelbach has raised a serious objection to my attempt to analyze the concept of rationality in terms of the justifiability and criticizability of expressions, and to thereby attribute a key role to the procedural rationality embodied in argumentative practices. As he sees it, one may concede that all rational expressions

can in principle be defended in response to queries (through linking up argumentatively with their linguistic mode of representation); it doesn't follow from this, however, that that with which the argumentation links up must itself take the form of argumentation in order for it to be capable of being deemed rational; argumentative or discursive rationality (Habermas) is simply one *component* of reason. The fixation on the justificatory model of rationality seduces us into regarding everything as irrational so long as it is not completely argumentatively or discursively vindicated—which means that the field of the irrational would assume just about gigantic proportions. Other rational capacities include the capacity for testing reality (Freud), for learning from mistakes and errors (Popper), for solving problems in feedback-controlled action contexts (Gehlen), for purposively selecting means (Weber)—many other prominent examples could be added to the list; those I have mentioned simply cannot be accommodated in a schema of "justification" or of "the discursive vindication of validity claims" (Habermas).[1]

Schnädelbach himself understands rationality as a disposition for reason on the part of subjects capable of knowledge, speech, and action that can be captured descriptively.[2] What he sets up against discursive rationality is not simply a (generically ascribed) rationality of the person, identifiable with the help of corresponding expressions, but rather the "reflexive character"[3] of these expressions. For, of course, what we know, do, and say is rational only if we are at least implicitly aware of why our beliefs are true, our actions right, and our linguistic utterances valid (or showing promise of success from an illocutionary point of view, or effective from a perlocutionary one): "[T]he trope of 'reflexivity' as the fundamental characteristic of rationality in general, can thus be rendered more precise with the help of the self-referential thematization of . . . performances in the perspective of the first person singular or plural; only she who is capable of saying 'I' or 'we,' and of thematizing what she is or does, and of attributing it to herself, is rational."[4] With this Schnädelbach places himself in the tradition of the philosophy of consciousness. Since the linguistic turn, however, we have good reasons for following a suggestion of G. H. Mead and explaining the self-relation of the knowing, acting, and speaking subject—that is, the relation of the first person "to herself"—on the basis of the adoption of the perspective of a *second* person "on me." Correspondingly, the *reflected* self-relation distinguished by Schnädelbach as the fundamental characteristic of rationality would be dependent on the relationship between participants in argumentation: there would be no reflection that could not be reconstructed as an inner discourse. The reflexive attitude to one's own expressions takes place according to the model of the attitude of other participants in argumentation to the problematic validity of one's expressions. Reflection, too, is due to a prior dialogical relation and does not float in the vacuum of an inwardness constituted free from communication.[5] The discursive thematization of validity claims, in terms of which the rationality of our expressions is measured, and the reflexive character of these expressions stand in a complementary relation: they *refer to one another.* I do not consider the proposal to reduce rationality to a disposition of rational persons promising.

However, this does not invalidate Schnädelbach's objection to my privileging of the discursive rationality embodied in argumentative practices. I will accept Schnädelbach's point of criticism and, in the following, assume that we use the predicate "rational" in the first instance to refer to beliefs, actions, and linguistic utterances be-

309

Some Further Clarifications of the Concept of Communicative Rationality

cause, in the propositional structure of knowledge, in the teleological structure of action, and in the communicative structure of speech, we come upon *various roots of rationality*. These do not for their part appear to have common roots, at least not in the discursive structure of justificatory practices, nor in the reflexive structure of the self-relation of a subject participating in discourses. It is more probably the case that the structure of discourse establishes an interrelation among the entwined structures of rationality (the structures of knowledge, action, and speech) by, in a sense, *bringing together* the propositional, teleological, and communicative roots. According to such a model of *intermeshed* core structures, discursive rationality owes its special position not to its foundational but to its integrative role.

If, to begin with, we allow ourselves to be guided by this picture, a noteworthy consequence results. Since argumentative practices are, so to speak, a reflexive form of communicative action, the justificatory rationality embodied in discourse does indeed rest to a certain extent on the communicative rationality embodied in everyday action; nonetheless, communicative rationality remains on a level with epistemic and teleological rationality. Communicative rationality does not constitute the *overarching* structure of rationality but rather one of three core structures that are, however, interwoven with one another by way of the discursive rationality that emerges out of communicative rationality. This picture should not, however, be misunderstood in a mentalist way. Just as communicative rationality may not be equated with linguistically embodied rationality in general, epistemic and teleological rationality are not of a prelinguistic nature.

I would first of all like to elucidate this complex of rationality structures, which I have introduced in an intuitive way, by means of some further remarks. I will then explain how various rationality structures intermesh within the linguistic medium through reference to different modalities of language use and to corresponding types of action. Finally, I will deal with the complex relation between language and communicative rationality. As an appendix, I will indicate two implications for a pragmatic theory of meaning that result from these considerations.

Three Roots of Rationality

In order to provide a provisional overview, I will discuss the complementary relationship between discursive structure and reflection (or self-reference as a condition for the rationality of persons), proceeding then to deal with the rational core structures of knowledge, purposive activity, and communication.

Discursive Rationality and Reflection

The rationality of a person is proportionate to his expressing himself rationally and to his ability to give account for his expressions in a reflexive stance. A person expresses himself rationally insofar as he is oriented performatively toward validity claims: we say that he not only behaves rationally but is himself rational if he can give account for his orientation toward validity claims. We also call this kind of rationality *accountability* (*Zurechnungsfähigkeit*).

Accountability presupposes a reflected self-relation on the part of the person to what she believes, says, and does; this capacity is entwined with the rational core structures of knowledge, purposive activity, and communication by way of the corresponding self-relations. The epistemic self-relation implies a reflexive attitude on the part of the knowing subject to her own beliefs and convictions; the technical-practical self-relation implies a reflexive attitude on the part of the acting subject to his own purposive activity, be it to his own instrumental interventions in the objective world or to his success-oriented dealings with other subjects encountered as opponents in the objective world. (I understand "objective world" as the totality of entities concerning which true propositions are possible.) The moral-practical self-relation of the communicatively acting actor demands a reflexive attitude to her own norm-regulated actions; the existential self-relation requires from the actor a reflexive attitude to her own life-project in the context of an individual life-history which is, of course, interwoven with pregiven collective forms of life. Moreover, a person's ability to distance himself in this way in these various dimensions from himself and his expressions is a necessary condition of his *freedom*.

Freedom is differentiated according to the different self-relations of the knowing and acting subject. Reflexive freedom in the sense of cognitive openness (*Unbefangenheit*) requires liberation from the egocentric perspective of a participant deeply involved in action contexts; this is the freedom we traditionally associate with the theoretical stance. Freedom of choice (*Willkürfreiheit*) consists in the capacity for rationally choosing to act in one way or another, or for making a new start in the chain of events. With Kant, we refer to the capacity for binding one's own will on the basis of moral insight as freedom of will (*Willensfreiheit*), or autonomy. Finally, ethical freedom makes possible a deliberate life-project and the stabilization of an ego-identity. Certainly, these forms of freedom are dispositions that can be ascribed to a person; but the accompanying self-relations are due in each case to the adoption and internalization of the perspective on me of other participants in argumentation: in the epistemic self-relation and in the various practical self-relations I, as a first person, adopt the second-person perspective in which interlocutors—that is, other participants in (empirical or theoretical, pragmatic, moral, or ethical) discourses—focus on my expressions. Thus, in the reflection of the rational person who distances himself from himself, the rationality inherent in the structure and in the procedure of argumentation is *mirrored* in a general way. However, it becomes clear at the same time that on the integrative level of reflection and discourse, the three rationality components—knowing, acting, and speaking—combine, that is, form a syndrome.

Epistemic Rationality

Our knowledge is built up from propositions or judgments—those elementary units that can be true or false; on account of its propositional structure, knowledge is intrinsically of a linguistic nature. This structure can be analyzed with the help of propositional sentences. However, I will not deal here with the semantics of propositional sentences or with the pragmatic meaning of acts of reference and predication.

In order to know something in an explicit sense, it is not, of course, sufficient merely to be familiar with facts that could be represented in true judgments. We *know* facts and have a knowledge of them at our disposal only when we simultaneously know why the corresponding judgments are true. Otherwise we speak of intuitive or implicit knowledge—of a "practical" knowledge of how one does something. One can know very well how to do something without knowing what it is that goes to make up these competencies. By contrast, the explicit "knowing what" is bound up implicitly with a "knowing why" and insofar points toward potential justifications. Whoever believes that he has knowledge at his disposal assumes the possibility of a discursive vindication of corresponding truth claims. Put differently, it is part of the grammar of the expression "knowing" that everything we know can be criticized and justified.

This does not mean, of course, that rational beliefs or convictions always consist of true judgments. Whoever shares views that turn out to be untrue is not *eo ipso* irrational. Someone is irrational if she puts forward her beliefs dogmatically, clinging to them although she sees that she cannot justify them. In order to qualify a belief as rational, it is sufficient that it can be held to be true on the basis of good reasons in the relevant context of justification—that is, that it can be accepted rationally. In posttraditional societies, or under conditions of postmetaphysical thinking, all knowledge—from the stance of a third person—is deemed fallible (this, too, is part of the grammar of the word "knowing" nowadays), even though in the performative stance, that is, from the perspective of a participant, we cannot avoid *unconditionally* regarding the asserted knowledge as true. Despite this "Platonic" nature of knowledge, the rationality of a judgment does not imply its truth but merely its justified acceptability in a given context.

Of course, the reflexive character of true judgments would not be possible if we could not *represent* our knowledge, that is, if we could not express it in *sentences,* and if we could not correct it and expand it; and this means: if we were not able also to *learn* from our practical dealings with a reality that resists us. To this extent, epistemic rationality is *entwined* with action and the use of language.[6] I speak of an epistemic *core* structure because the propositional structure is dependent on its embodiment in speech and action: it is not a *self-*

supporting structure. It is the linguistic representation of what is known, and the confrontation of knowledge with a reality against which a justified expectation can shatter, that first make it possible to deal with knowledge in a rational way.

On the one hand, we can deal with our knowledge operatively—that is, render it more precise, elaborate it, reconstruct it, systematize it, test it for consistency and coherence—only if it takes on a shape that can be grasped symbolically. (On the reflexive level of science, where it is a matter of constructing theories, the necessity for organizing knowledge linguistically—as the case may be, using a formal language—is striking.) On the other hand, as Peirce and pragmatism correctly emphasize, we have to make use of our knowledge in practices, implementing it in goal-directed actions controlled in terms of success, in order to be able to learn from negative experiences. We learn from disappointments by processing surprises by means of abductive judgment, and by revising the knowledge that has been rendered problematic. (On the reflexive level of science, disappointments of this sort, which are to be processed productively, are generated methodically; the relation to action of the falsifying evidence—that is, of the disappointments—is revealed, in particular, in experimental action.)[7]

Teleological Rationality

All action is intentional; an action may be understood as carrying out the intention of a freely choosing and deciding actor. Action has a teleological structure, for every action-intention aims at the realization of a set goal. Once again, the rationality of an action is proportionate not to whether the state actually occurring in the world as a result of the action coincides with the intended state and satisfies the corresponding conditions of success, but rather to whether the actor has *achieved* this result on the basis of the deliberately selected and implemented means (or, in accurately perceived circumstances, could normally have done so). A successful actor has acted rationally only if he (i) knows why he was successful (or why he could have realized the set goal in normal circumstances) and if

(ii) this knowledge motivates the actor (at least in part) in such a way that he carries out his action for reasons that can at the same time explain its possible success.

In the simplest case, the considerations that can simultaneously justify and motivate a rational action take the form of a practical inference. Given certain preferences, A intends in situation S to bring about the state p; in given circumstances A regards the implementation of the means M as the satisfaction of a necessary—or even sufficient—condition in order to bring about p with a certain probability; for this reason A carries out the action that deploys the selected means.[8] We have seen that knowledge in the strict sense requires a reflexive "having" of knowledge that refers to possible justifications; correspondingly, purposive-rational action requires a reflexive "having"—suitable for possible justifications—of the decisive action-intention, that is, a calculation of the success of the action. Once again, there is a relationship of mutual reference between the rationality of the action and the forum of a discourse in which an actor's decisive reasons for making his decision—determined *ex ante*—could be tested. The theory of rational choice deals with those aspects of the decision-making problems of acting subjects, who are guided in an egocentric way by their respective personal preferences and expectations of success, that can be used to construct models.

The rationality of purposive activity, too, is entwined with the two other core structures of knowledge and speech. For the practical considerations by means of which a rational plan of action is carried out are dependent on the input of reliable information (about expected events in the world, or about the behavior and the intentions of other actors)—even if, in general, the actors acting in a purposive-rational way have to be satisfied with highly incomplete information. On the other hand, such information can be processed intelligently—that is, referred to decision-making maxims and goals that for their part have been selected in light of personal preferences—only in the medium of linguistic representation. This is obvious in the case of the theoretical treatment of complex decision-making problems. But elementary action-intentions and simple practical inferences, too, are linguistically structured. Just as propositional knowledge is dependent on the use of propositional sentences, so too is intentional action essentially dependent on the use of intentional sentences.

Communicative Rationality

There is a peculiar rationality, inherent not in language as such but in the communicative use of linguistic expressions, that can be reduced neither to the epistemic rationality of knowledge (as classical truth-conditional semantics supposes) nor to the purposive-rationality of action (as intentionalist semantics assumes). This *communicative rationality* is expressed in the unifying force of speech oriented toward reaching understanding, which secures for the participating speakers an intersubjectively shared lifeworld, thereby securing at the same time the horizon within which everyone can refer to one and the same objective world.

The communicative use of linguistic expressions serves not only to give expression to the intentions of a speaker but also to represent states of affairs (or to presuppose their existence) and to establish interpersonal relations with a second person. Here, the three aspects of (a) an actor reaching understanding (b) with someone (c) about something are reflected. What the speaker wants to say with an expression is connected both with what is literally said in it and with the action as which it should be understood. Thus, a threefold relation exists between the meaning of a linguistic expression and (a) what is *intended* (*gemeint*) by it, (b) what is *said* in it, and (c) the *way in which it is used* in the speech act. With his speech act, the speaker pursues his aim of reaching understanding with a hearer about something. This illocutionary aim, as we will refer to it, is two-tiered: the speech act is first of all supposed to be understood by the hearer and then—so far as possible—accepted. The rationality of the use of language oriented toward reaching understanding then depends on whether the speech acts are sufficiently comprehensible and acceptable for the speaker to achieve illocutionary success with them (or for him to be able to do so in normal circumstances). Once again, we do not call only valid speech acts rational but rather all comprehensible speech acts for which the speaker can take on a *credible* warranty in the given circumstances to the effect that the validity claims raised could, if necessary, be vindicated discursively. Thus here, too, there is an internal connection between the rationality of a speech act and its possible justification. Only in argumentations can the validity claims implicitly raised with a speech act be thematized as such and tested with reasons.

Illocutionary aims may not be described as states that can be brought about through interventions in the objective world. For this reason, we should not conceive of the illocutionary aims of reaching understanding (which are, so to speak, immanent to language) as perlocutionary effects that the speaker produces in the hearer with her speech act by way of a causal exertion of influence. Here, I would like to make three observations. First, the illocutionary aims cannot be defined independently of the linguistic means of reaching understanding; as Wittgenstein made clear, the telos of reaching understanding is inherent in the linguistic medium itself. Second, the speaker cannot intend her aim as something to be effected causally, because the "yes" or "no" of the hearer is a rationally motivated position; participants in communication enjoy the freedom of being able to say "no." Finally, speakers and hearers confront one another in a performative attitude as first and second persons, not as opponents or as objects within the world of entities *about* which they are speaking. In wanting to reach understanding with one another about something, their illocutionary aims lie beyond the objective world in which they can intervene purposively as observing actors. As events that are localizable in time and space, however, speech acts are simultaneously part of the objective world in which, like all teleological actions, they can *also* bring things about, that is, they can also produce perlocutionary effects.

The speaker would like the addressee to accept what is said as valid; this is decided by the addressee's "yes" or "no" to the validity claim for what is said that the speaker raises with his speech act. What makes the speech-act offer acceptable are, ultimately, the reasons that the speaker could provide in the given context for the validity of what is said. The rationality inherent in communication thus rests on the internal connection between (a) the conditions that make a speech act valid, (b) the claim raised by the speaker that these conditions are satisfied, and (c) the credibility of the warranty issued by the speaker to the effect that he could, if necessary, discursively vindicate the validity claim.

In order to cover the entire spectrum of possible validity claims, it makes sense to start by posing the heuristic question: in what sense can speech acts be negated *as a whole?* In answering this question we hit upon precisely three sorts of validity claims: truth claims in regard to facts that we assert with reference to objects in the objective world; claims to the truthfulness (*Wahrhaftigkeit*) of utterances that make manifest subjective experiences (*Erlebnisse*) to which the speaker has privileged access; and finally, claims to the rightness of norms and commands that are recognized in an intersubjectively shared social world.[9]

Modalities of Language Use

The illocutionary success of a speech act is proportionate to the intersubjective recognition accorded to the validity claim raised with it. Here, a communicative situation is presupposed in which the participants can take on the respective roles of speaker and hearer (and, if need be, the role of a third party present)—that is, can take on the roles of the first, second, and third person. This distribution of roles, which is built into the logic of the system of personal pronouns, is essential for the communicative rationality embodied in processes of reaching understanding. We can see this clearly if we compare the use of language oriented toward reaching understanding with a use of linguistic expressions that is not geared toward communication. Following on from this distinction between the communicative and noncommunicative use of language, I will undertake differentiations in the concept of "reaching understanding" (*Verständigung*) itself.

The Communicative Use of Language versus the Noncommunicative Use

The epistemic and teleological uses of language are not dependent on an interpersonal relationship between speaker and hearer in a communicative situation. *Illocutionary acts*—and the validity claims connected with them, which have a *built-in orientation toward intersubjective recognition*—do not play a fundamental role either in the epistemic use of language, which serves primarily to represent knowledge, or in the calculation of action effects; in these cases, the language users are not pursuing illocutionary aims. Although in every case language has to be acquired communicatively, the linguistic expressions *can* be used monologically in such instances—that is, without reference to a second person. That the pragmatic aspects are not relevant in the case of the purely epistemic or teleological use of language is clear from the structure of the propositional sentences and intentional sentences essentially used in each. Unlike, for example, questions or imperatives, propositional and intentional sentences are not fundamentally tied to addressees; their meaning content is independent of the illocutionary acts in which they can be embedded—which is why they can be analyzed exhaustively with the tools of formal semantics.[10]

One understands epistemically used propositional sentences if one knows their truth conditions, that is, if one knows when they are true; this is the special case to which the thesis of truth-conditional semantics applies. Moreover, it makes sense here to speak of assigning "truth values" (as is customary in logic), because the assertoric force of acts of assertion is not intrinsically connected with such monologically employed sentences. For purposes of pure representation we abstract from how the propositional *sentence* is embedded in a speech *act;* in other words, we disregard the possible communicative situation in which a speaker would *assert* the proposition "*p*" with the aim of finding agreement with an addressee.[11] An epistemically used propositional sentence serves to represent a state of affairs or a fact. For the purpose of this sort of *representation,* it is sufficient if the author gives (whomever) *to understand* that he is considering "*p*" or holds it to be true. By contrast, with the *assertion* of a fact, a communicating speaker would not merely wish to have an addressee know that he himself holds "*p*" to be true; rather, he would pursue the illocutionary aim of having the other *acknowledge* that "*p*" is true.

It is a similar matter with intentional sentences used for planning action monologically. One understands intentional sentences that structure purposive activities if one knows the conditions of success, that is, if one knows under which circumstances they are made true. Conditions of success are truth conditions that are interpreted in an actor-relative way. As in the case of epistemically used propositional sentences, the relation of the sentences to something in the objective world—that is, knowledge of the state of affairs and direction of fit—is sufficient for understanding such pragmatically used intentional sentences. An illocutionary force is not already connected with these per se; they acquire this force only when the actor *announces* her intentions in a communicative situation, that is, when the actor utters her intentions with the illocutionary aim of having others take them *seriously* and count on their being carried out.

However, the noncommunicative use of language for purposes of pure representation or for a plan of action played through mentally is due to a feat of abstraction that merely suspends the reference—which is *always present virtually*—of propositions to truth, or of intentions to the seriousness of what is resolved. This is evident as soon as representations or plans of action are called into question. When this happens, the author is expected to justify *to others* discursively what she has considered monologically—that is, in the public forum of argumentation. Certainly, such argumentations, too, can be conducted *in foro interno*, similar to the manner in which we can direct imperatives to ourselves. However, arguments and imperatives are by their very nature pragmatic and for this reason, unlike propositional and intentional sentences, can be internalized only *together with* the interpersonal relations that are inherent to their meaning. Propositions and intentions can be divested of the illocutionary meaning of acts of asserting and announcing without losing their meaning, whereas even *in foro interno* an imperative without an illocutionary component would no longer be an imperative (for even here, I, in the role of the first person, direct an imperative to myself as a fictive second person). Communicative rationality is first embodied only in a process of reaching understanding that operates by way of validity claims whenever speaker and hearer, in a performative attitude directed to second persons, (want to) reach understanding with one another about something in the world. The difference between this and the noncommunicative use of language results from the addition of a validity claim *with which the speaker confronts a hearer.* Here, his illocutionary aim does not consist in letting the addressee know his double intention, namely, that he (intention₁) holds "*p*" to be true (or would like to bring about "*p*") and that he wishes her to know this (intention₂); rather, he wishes to communicate the fact (or the intention) "*p*" to the addressee in such a way that she herself is convinced "that *p*" (or takes seriously the speaker's intention "to bring about *p*"). The illocutionary meaning of an utterance is not that the hearer should take note of *S*'s belief (or intention) but rather that she should come to hold the *same* view as *S* (or that she should take seriously *S*'s announcement). For *S* to achieve his illocutionary aim, it is not sufficient for *H* to know the truth conditions (or the success conditions) of "*p*;" *H* is also supposed to understand the illocutionary meaning of assertions (or declarations of intention) and, so far as possible, accept the corresponding validity claims.

In the case of an assertion, the speaker raises a truth claim for what is said. The hearer will take an affirmative position on this (no matter how implicitly) only if he holds what is said to be justified or, at least, regards the speaker's warranty as credible to the effect that she could, if necessary, convince the hearer of the asserted fact on the basis of good reasons. In the case of the validity claim raised with a declaration of intention, the hearer will take seriously the announced intention if he is convinced that the speaker means what she says and has good reasons for wanting to make her announcement true: he presumes that the utterance is serious if he holds *S*'s intention to be justified (from her point of view).

The Use of Language Oriented toward Agreement versus the Use of Language Oriented toward Reaching Understanding

Now, of course, it makes a difference whether agreement (*Einverständnis*) concerning a fact exists between participants or whether they both *merely* reach an understanding (*sich verständigen*) with one another concerning the seriousness of the speaker's intention. *Agreement* in the strict sense is achieved only if the participants are able to accept a validity claim for the *same* reasons, while *mutual understanding* (*Verständigung*) can also come about when one participant sees that the other, in light of her preferences, has good reasons in the given circumstances for her declared intention—that is, reasons that are good *for her*—without having to make these reasons his own in light of his preferences. Actor-independent reasons permit a stronger mode of reaching understanding than actor-relative reasons. In the following, I will compare (i) declarations of intention and simple imperatives with (ii) promises, declaratives, and commands in order to make a differentiation within the communicative use of language between a "weak" and a "strong" mode of reaching understanding.

i. As we have seen, the validity claim raised with an act of assertion for a proposition "*p*" achieves intersubjective recognition only if all participants are convinced "that *p*" for the same reasons. So long as the speaker and addressee accept the proposition "*p*" as true for different reasons respectively, and both know with regard to the other that these reasons constitute good reasons only for the one or the other of them, the truth claim raised for "*p*," which is dependent on *intersubjective* recognition, is not accepted *as such*. Since a *discursive* competition for the better argument has, for conceptual reasons, agreement and not compromise as its goal, the discursive vindication of the validity claim is left open until *actor-independent* reasons make the contested truth claim rationally acceptable in principle for all participants. It is a different matter with the one-sided announcement of an action based on arbitrary free choice ("I will leave tomorrow") or with simple imperatives ("Sit down"). Although these utterances are, without doubt, illocutionary acts, it would be counterintuitive to suppose that a speaker wishes to bring about any kind of "consensus" with them. The speaker cannot reckon with agreement for one-sided expressions of will. Nonetheless in such cases, too, it is permissible to speak in a weaker sense of "mutual understanding" between participants. For here, too, validity claims are involved that one participant raises and the other can accept or reject.

In the case of announcements or declarations of intention, the actor can gain assent by showing the intended action to be one that is *rational* in light of his preferences (in the given circumstances and with the given means). For this sort of mutual understanding, teleological rationality takes on a mediating role. In such cases, the hearer has good reasons for taking the announcement seriously, even if she does not *adopt as her own* the reasons for the declared intention. In general, one understands the propositional content of an announcement if one knows the conditions of success for "*p*"; however, one understands its illocutionary meaning only if one knows why one should take the declared intention seriously as an announcement, that is, why one should count on its being carried out. Certainly, a hearer, in a given case, may accept the announcement as an utterance to be taken seriously for the same reasons as the actor; however, it is assumed that these are *actor-relative* reasons that show the announced action to be rational for the actor *from his point of view*—and therefore, from the point of view of the addressee, likely to be carried out. There can be no question of "agreement" here because the reasons supporting the sincerity of the actor's intention can qualify as good reasons only according to premises that are valid for the actor but not for his addressee. We might call such reasons—to distinguish them from generally acceptable reasons—"publicly intelligible" reasons. What are good reasons for the actor to intend to carry out an action are good reasons for the addressee not to doubt his intention.

It is a different matter again—though in effect, similar—with imperatives. There is no noncommunicative use of imperative sentences, for imperatives are intrinsically of a pragmatic nature. Their illocutionary meaning consists in the fact that the speaker wants to motivate an addressee—that is, *another person*—to bring about "*p*." One understands the propositional content of an imperative if one knows the conditions of success for the corresponding action; in order to understand its illocutionary meaning, however, one has to know (as in the case of declarations of intention) why the speaker sincerely means what she says and, over and above this, why she believes she may expect the addressee to comply with her imperative. An imperative is rational only if (apart from its viability) the actor has good reasons for supposing that the addressee has reasons not to oppose her imperative. These additional reasons, too, are actor-relative: in this case, ones that the speaker (possibly wrongly) attributes to the addressee as good reasons for him; the speaker assumes the availability either of sanctions, should the desired action fail to be carried out, or of rewards, if it is carried out. As with declarations of intention, in the case of imperative acts, too, the rationally expectable action consequences count as part of the actor-relative reasons that speak for the rationality of such utterances (although now they are assessed positively or negatively from the point of view of the hearer).

Announcements and imperatives do not aim at agreement (in the strict sense). Nonetheless, they move within the horizon of a mutual understanding based on validity claims and thus still within the domain of communicative rationality. It is true that the acceptability of the validity claims is mediated via the purposive rationality that the resolve or the decision has for the actor whose attitude is success oriented; however, their illocutionary success is in turn measured in terms of claims to truth and truthfulness even if this is only with reference to the preferences of the speaker (or in connection with the preferences attributed by the speaker to the hearer). The hearer assumes that the speaker means what she says and holds it to be true. For this reason, declarations of intention and imperatives characteristically can be challenged under the two aspects of truthfulness (compare 1′ and 2′) and the accuracy or truth of existential presuppositions (compare 1″ and 2″).

(1)   I will sign the contract tomorrow in Tokyo.

(1′)   You are pulling my leg.

(1″)   You couldn't possibly be in Tokyo by tomorrow (due to the time difference).

(2)   Give me the money I need now.

(2′)   You aren't basically looking for money at all but for something quite different (namely affection).

(2″)   I couldn't get that amount of money together so quickly.

ii. Of course, the mode of language use would have to change as soon as the truth of the assertions presupposed with such announcements or imperatives is itself thematized. Such a change in topic would necessitate transition to an orientation toward an "agreement" that goes beyond mere "reaching understanding." Such a switch from the use of language oriented toward reaching understanding to one oriented toward agreement may also be illustrated in a different way with the help of the examples given, for in each case there is a further possible way in which it can be negated.

(1‴) You lack the good will necessary to take on such a strenuous commitment.

(1⁗) You don't have the legal authority for that.

(2‴) No, I don't owe you anything.

Here, however, the speech acts are presumed to have a different illocutionary meaning. For, now, the negation of (1) and (2) refers to *normative* validity claims that come into play only when intentional and imperative sentences are "embedded" in normative contexts and are "authorized" by a normative background. The announcement of the signing of the contract could be a commissive speech act—for instance, a promise with which the actor commits herself to something—or else a declarative speech act, with which the speaker discharges an institutional task (for example, the duty of a representative of the Board to inform the public). The imperative to hand over the money could imply a friend's request, a superior's command, a creditor's demand, and so forth.

Through backing of this kind, declarations of intention and imperatives are transformed into *normatively authorized* expressions of will such as promises, declarations, and commands. With this, the illocutionary meaning and validity basis of the utterances change. Normative reasons do not determine the prudential assessments of *arbitrarily choosing* decisionmaking subjects; they determine rather the decisions of subjects who *bind their wills* and are thus able to enter into obligations. In contrast to the case of "naked" declarations of intentions and "simple" imperatives, normative reasons are not actor-relative reasons for one's own (or another's) purposive-rational behavior but—as in the case of assertions—actor-independent reasons; however, unlike the reasons for assertions, they are not reasons for the existence of states of affairs but rather for the satisfaction of normatively binding expectations. Connected with regulative speech acts such as promises, declarations, and commands is a validity claim that has a built-in orientation toward vindication in practical discourses. In order to understand the illocutionary meaning of this sort of speech act, one has to know the normative context that explains why an actor feels authorized or obliged to perform a certain action or why, as far as the addressee is concerned, she may reckon with his compliance with the imperative. Insofar as the participants intersubjectively recognize a normative background (for example, within the framework of a shared lifeworld), they can accept regulative speech acts as valid for the *same* reasons.

In contrast to an epistemically achieved consensus, however, this normative background should be understood less as a result than as a point of departure. In the case of regulative speech acts, the presupposed normative background agreement serves as a reservoir for shared reasons, whereas in the case of constative speech acts, the reasons themselves serve as a vehicle for achieving a rationally motivated agreement. At any rate, this is how it is with a value consensus existing within the horizon of traditions handed down in a quasi-natural way. However, a certain analogy with an *achieved* epistemic agreement is established on the posttraditional level of justification where a consensus of the above kind can no longer be taken for granted, with the result that the justifying norms themselves require justification. (At this point, I would like simply to mention that what we normally deal with under the heading "practical reason" is not an elementary phenomenon but rather goes back to an entwinement—effected within the framework of social interactions—of epistemic and teleological rationality with communicative rationality.)

Communicative versus Strategic Action

I have compared "naked" or "simple" announcements and imperatives with normatively embedded ones in order to undertake a differentiation within the dimension of reaching understanding and to cast light on two kinds of communicative language use. We now have to see how this distinction affects the function of action coordination. Up to now we have considered only speech acts, that is, linguistic expressions, including the aspect from which they *themselves* represent actions. However, the communicative rationality embodied in illocutionary acts extends beyond verbal utterances to social actions or interactions as well. (A special class of these—normatively regulated social actions—has already been looked at anyhow in connection with the illocutionary forces of regulative speech acts.) With Max Weber, we can define social actions generally as actions whereby actors, in pursuing their personal plans of action, are also guided by the expected action of others. We will speak of *communicative action* where actors coordinate their plans of action with one another by way of linguistic processes of reaching understanding, that is, in such a way that they draw on the illocutionary binding and bonding powers (*Bindungskräfte*) of speech acts for this coordination. In strategic action, this potential for communicative rationality remains unexploited, even where the interactions are linguistically mediated. Because the participants in strategic action coordinate their plans of action with one another by way of a reciprocal exertion of influence, language is used not communicatively, in the sense elucidated, but with an *orientation toward consequences*. For analysis of the latter use of language, so-called perlocutions provide a suitable key.

Two Sorts of Communicative Action

I will speak of communicative action *in a weak sense* whenever reaching understanding applies to facts and to actor-relative reasons for one-sided expressions of will; I will speak of communicative action *in a strong sense* as soon as reaching understanding extends to the normative reasons for the selection of the goals themselves. In the latter case, the participants refer to intersubjectively shared value orientations that—going beyond their personal preferences—*bind* their wills. In weak communicative action the actors are oriented solely toward claims to truth and truthfulness; in strong communicative action they are oriented toward intersubjectively recognized rightness claims as well; in the case of strong communicative action, not just arbitrary freedom of choice but autonomy in the sense of the capacity to bind one's will on the basis of normative insights is presupposed.

In the case of both of the examples considered of expressions of will that are not embedded normatively, intentional and imperative sentences are already being used communicatively, that is, with the illocutionary aim of bringing the hearer to a rationally motivated agreement. In such cases, however, the actors, who are oriented toward success, can coordinate their plans only if one of them accepts the *seriousness* of the intentions or imperatives uttered by the other (as well as the *truth* of the beliefs implied by them). Two validity claims are involved: the sincerity of the resolve or the decision, and the truth of what is believed. On this level, reaching understanding does not yet extend to normative validity claims. Characteristic for action coordination in the weak sense of an orientation toward reaching understanding is the limited nature of the agreement, which cannot be reached with regard to the motivating intentions and preferences themselves, but merely with regard to their purposive rationality. In this respect, reaching understanding here means merely that the hearer understands the content of the declaration of intention or imperative and does not doubt its seriousness (and viability). The basis for the mutual understanding effective in action coordination is solely the acceptance of the claim to truthfulness raised for a declaration of intention or for an imperative, to which the discernible rationality of the resolve or of the decision attests.

This common basis restricts the free choice of the actors acting communicatively in an attitude oriented toward success only insofar as they expect each other to renounce all intentions to deceive (which are permissible in strategic action). In *weak communicative action* the actors do not as yet expect each other to be guided by common norms or values and to recognize reciprocal obligations. I will speak of *strong communicative action* only when an illocutionary act can be criticized with regard to all three validity claims, regardless of whether the normative validity claim is raised explicitly, as in regulative speech acts (commands, promises), or remains unthematized. Even assertions and confessions, with which explicit claims to truth and truthfulness are raised, can be criticized with respect to the normative context of the utterance as "out of place," "brazen," "embarrassing," and so on—in short, as normatively inappropriate. In such cases, they violate the legitimately regulated interpersonal relationships of a social world to which the participants in communication belong.

From normative contexts such as these, regulative speech acts derive the conditions under which the speaker may regard himself as authorized for directives, commands, imperatives, advice, requests, promises, contracts, negotiations, announcements, and so forth. To this extent rightness claims, with which illocutionary acts of this sort are connected, rely on something in a social world in a manner analogous to the way in which the truth claims connected with constative speech acts rely on something in the objective world (even if norms are "controversial" in a different way than facts and are by no means independent of the acting subjects in the same way as the entities to which we refer when we state facts about them). At any rate, under conditions of postmetaphysical thinking, claims to the normative rightness of utterances—like truth claims—may be discursively vindicated, which means on the basis of reasons that are the *same* reasons for all members of the social world in question. The aim in such cases is a normative agreement; unlike a mutual understanding concerning the seriousness (and viability) of resolutions and decisions, such a normative agreement extends not only to the actor-relative premises of the pursuit of action goals selected on the basis of arbitrary free choice, but also to the actor-independent mode of selecting legitimate goals. In strong communicative action, the participants presume not only that they are guided by facts and say what they hold to be true and what they mean, but also that they pursue their action plans only within the boundaries of norms and values deemed to be valid.

Underlying communicative action in the weak sense is the presupposition of an objective world that is the same for all; in strong communicative action the participants over and above this count on a social world that is shared by them intersubjectively. Certainly, agreement is reckoned with in the case of assertoric statements just as much as it is in the case of normative statements; statements of fact and "ought" sentences have to be capable of being made intelligible for all participants for the same reasons. However, a cognitive agreement about facts requires the participants in communication only to take these agreed-upon facts into consideration in the subsequent course of their interaction. In contrast to a normative agreement, a cognitive agreement does not affect the way in which the actors select and pursue their action goals; it does not affect whether they are guided exclusively by their personal preferences or whether they are also guided by binding norms (and values held in esteem by all members). Whereas in weak communicative action only constative speech acts and normatively nonauthorized expressions of will come into play, strong communicative action demands a use of language that also refers to something in a social world. Incidentally, this also holds for those expressive speech acts that—unlike declarations of intention and imperatives—do not refer to (future) actions, for example, expressions of feeling.

Perlocutions, the Use of Language Oriented toward Consequences, and Strategic Action

Communicative rationality is embodied in language games in which the participants take a position on criticizable validity claims. In the "weak" forms of the communicative use of language and communicative action, communicative rationality is entwined with the purposive rationality of actors in an attitude oriented toward success—although still in such a way that the illocutionary aims *dominate* the "perlocutionary" effects that in certain circumstances may be striven for as well. "Perlocutionary" is, of course, the name we give to the effects of speech acts that, if need be, can also be brought about causally by nonlinguistic actions. In the following, I am interested in (i) those speech acts and (ii) those interactions in which the relationship of dependency normally existing between illocutionary and perlocutionary aims and effects is reversed. In such cases, communicative rationality retreats, leaving gaps that constitute a kind of contrast or foil for the peculiar binding and bonding power of illocutionary acts.

i. I would like to begin by distinguishing three classes of perlocutionary effects. Perlocutionary effects$_1$ result grammatically from the content of a successful illocutionary act—as when a valid command is executed, a promise is kept, a declared intention is realized, or when assertions and confessions consistently fit with the subsequent course of the interaction. Here, the illocutionary aims rule the perlocutionary ones. By contrast, perlocutionary effects$_2$ are grammatically nonregulated, that is, contingent, consequences of a speech act that, however, occur only as a result of an illocutionary success—as when a piece of news, depending on the context, delights or startles the receiver, or when an imperative encounters resistance, a confession awakens doubt, and so forth. Finally, perlocutionary effects$_3$ can be achieved only in a manner that is *inconspicuous* as far as the addressee is concerned; the success of this kind of *strategic* action—a kind that remains latent for the other party—is also dependent on the manifest success of an illocutionary act.

The so-called *perlocutions* constitute a special case that is interesting for analytic purposes. These, too, require successful illocutionary acts as their vehicle; however, in the case of perlocutions, even the *apparent* dominance of the illocutionary aim—still necessary for the last class of perlocutionary effect I mentioned—disappears.[12]

The illocutionary act of asserting

(3) You are behaving like a swine.

takes on a different meaning in light of the *openly* pursued perlocutionary aim of offending the hearer, for then the assertion counts as slander, or as a reproach, or as an insult. In a similar way, any illocutionary act whatsoever can, according to the context, count as an expression of mockery or derision because the literally expressed illocutionary meaning is blotted out and reinterpreted by the set perlocutionary aim of showing up the addressee (or by the already occurring effect of this).

Threats represent a special sort of perlocution. The illocutionary act of announcing a conditional negative sanction acquires the sense of a threat through the explicit reference to the intended perlocutionary effect$_2$ of deterring the addressee. Its perlocutionary meaning as a deterrent overshadows its illocutionary meaning as an announcement. For this reason, a threat such as

(4)   If you don't give Peter the money I'll inform your superior that . . .

may be challenged not only as a literally meant "naked" announcement from the two points of view of the lack of truthfulness of the declaration of intention and the lack of truth of the existential presupposition; it can also be challenged with respect to the contextual conditions of the intended perlocutionary effect$_2$. (4) may be negated not only with the help of the validity claims expressly raised with this illocutionary act, as in

(4′)   You don't really mean what you are saying.

(4″)   You don't have anything you can use against me.

In addition, the context presupposed by the speaker, within which (4) first becomes a threat for a specific addressee, can also be contested:

(4‴)   You can't threaten me with that—he has already known it for a long time.

In such a case the speech act is not strictly speaking *contested;* rather it is simply explained why the intended effect will not occur and why the perlocution remains *ineffective.* Only illocutionary acts that can be *valid* or *invalid* may be contested.

(However, perlocutions of this kind can be re-embedded in a normative context in a secondary way because, of course, the condemnation of misdemeanors in a moral or a legal sense appeals to a normative background consensus and to this extent, despite its pejorative connotation, is directed toward agreement. For this reason, such *normatively embedded* reproaches—unlike actions that do not really aim to say anything but, in saying something, aim to offend someone—can be rejected on the basis of reasons. Something similar to what holds for moral reproaches, condemnations, and so on also holds, for example, for legal threats of punishment; due to the legitimating background consensus about the norms of punishment themselves, the threatened punishment is regarded as a consequence of a legal system for which agreement is presupposed).

ii. In strategic action contexts, language functions in general according to the pattern of perlocutions. Here, linguistic communication is *subordinated* to the prerequisites of purposive-rational action. Strategic interactions are determined by the decisions of actors in an attitude oriented toward success who *reciprocally observe* one another. They confront one another under conditions of double contingency as opponents who, in the interest of their personal plans of action, *exert influence* on one another (normally on the propositional attitudes of the other). They suspend the performative attitudes of participants in communication insofar as they take on the participating speaker and hearer roles from the perspective of third persons. From the latter vantage point, illocutionary aims are now relevant only as conditions for perlocutionary effects. Thus, unlike in the communicative use of language, strategically acting subjects who communicate with one another do not pursue their illocutionary aims unreservedly.

With this, even the narrow basis of reciprocally assumed truthfulness now disappears: *all* speech acts are robbed of their illocutionary binding and bonding power. Not only—as in weak communicative action—are the shared normative contexts and the corresponding claims to normative rightness lacking here; even the claims to truth and truthfulness raised with nonregulative speech acts are no longer aimed directly at the rational motivation of the hearer but at getting the addressee to draw his *conclusions* from what the speaker indirectly gives him to understand. Naturally, this is possible only if the participants understand one another, that is, if they feed parasitically on a common linguistic knowledge (that they have learned in contexts of communicative action). Because the presuppositions of communicative action are suspended, however, they now make use of this competence only indirectly to give each other to understand what they believe or want. Certainly, strategically acting subjects presume of each other that, insofar as they make decisions rationally, they base their decisions on beliefs that they *themselves* hold to be true. However, the truth values that guide each of them from the point of view of their respective personal preferences and goals are not transformed into truth *claims,* which have a built-in orientation toward intersubjective recognition, and which they therefore raise publicly, with a claim to discursive vindication. (We are familiar with this form of indirect communication from diplomatic intercourse between mutually mistrustful parties or from military contexts: in the Cuban missile crisis, for example, the proverbial shot across the bows [of the Russian ships] had to replace the missing illocutionary force of the verbal announcement with a signal from which the opponent could infer the seriousness of American intentions.)

Communicative Rationality and Linguistic World-Disclosure

A glance at the results of our reflections so far shows that the relationship between communicative rationality and language should not be construed over-eagerly. Not every use of language is communicative (see the first entry in the following schema) and not every linguistic communication serves to reach understanding on the basis of intersubjectively recognized validity claims (see the last line of the schema):

Exemplary types	Modes of language use
Propositional and intentional sentences used "mentally" ("pure" representation and "monological" action planning)	Noncommunicative
Normatively nonembedded expressions of will	Oriented toward reaching understanding (*Verständigung*)
Completely illocutionary acts (expressive, normative, constative)	Oriented toward agreement (*Einverständnis*)
Perlocutions	Oriented toward consequences (indirect mutual understanding—*Verständigung*)

The modalities of language use specify, in connection with various actor's attitudes, four different types of linguistically structured action of which, however, only two embody communicative rationality (see the second and third entries in the following schema).

	Modes of language use	Types of action/actor's attitude	
		Objectivating	Performative
Nonsocial action	Noncommunicative	Intentional action	—
Social interactions	Oriented toward reaching understanding (*Verständigung*)	—	Weak communicative action
	Oriented toward agreement (*Einverständnis*)	—	Strong communicative action
	Oriented toward consequences	Strategic interactions	—

Clearly, the linguistic medium extends further than communicative rationality. With the epistemic rationality of knowledge, the teleological rationality of action, and the communicative rationality of reaching understanding we have become acquainted with three autonomous aspects of rationality that are interwoven by way of the *common* medium of language. Furthermore, these core structures are internally related to discursive practices (and, as Schnädelbach correctly emphasizes, to a corresponding reflexivity of the consciously conducted life of persons). Their relation to the level of argumentation and reflection is as corroborative authorities. But what does language *as such* have to do with the rationality of beliefs, actions, communicative utterances, and persons?

A first indication is derived from the fact that these expressions are embedded in the context of a lifeworld that is in turn linguistically constituted. We speak of "rationalization" not only (like Freud) in the sense of a retrospective justification of wishes and actions but (like Weber) with respect to the life-conduct of persons and the forms of life of collectives. Such forms of life consist of practices and a web of traditions, institutions, customs, and competencies that may be called "rational" to the degree that they are *conducive* to the solution of problems that arise. To this extent, although forms of life qualify as candidates for the term "rational," they do so only in the indirect sense that they constitute the more or less "congenial" background for establishing discursive procedures and for developing reflexive capacities. In this way, they can promote capacities for problemsolving that for their part enable rational beliefs, actions, and communication.

With its categorial organization and grammatical prestructuring of the background consensus of the lifeworld, language makes a contribution to this *enabling* of rational behavior. In reaching understanding with one another about something in the objective world, communicative actors always already operate within the horizon of their lifeworld. No matter how high they climb, the horizon retreats before them, with the result that they can never bring the lifeworld *as a whole before them*—as is possible with the objective world—and survey it as a whole. It is no coincidence that this Being-in-the-World, as analyzed by Heidegger, can be illustrated by the strange semitranscendence of a language that, although we can use it as a means of communication, is nonetheless never at our disposal: we always operate through the medium of language and can never performatively—so long as we speak—objectify it as a whole. In this way, the lifeworld, which is itself articulated in the medium of language, opens up for its members an interpretive horizon for everything that they experience in the world, about which they reach understanding, and from which they can learn.

We have presumed up to now that language has a structure-forming power with regard to beliefs, actions, and communicative utterances. However, such a global reference to "language" conceals the genuine contribution that language makes with its world-disclosing productivity.[13] Certainly, the epistemic core structure of the proposition is part of the logical semantics of natural languages. The propositional attitudes of the competent speaker constitute the structural core of rational action. Moreover, communicative rationality is expressed in practices of speech that, with their dialogue roles and communicative presuppositions, are geared toward the illocutionary aim of intersubjective recognition of validity claims. The various aspects of rationality analyzed in the foregoing are *reflected* in linguistic structures. However, this entire rationality complex, on which a society's capacities for interpretation and learning in all its dimensions depend, obviously does not, as it were, stand on its own two feet but rather needs a lifeworld background whose *substance* is articulated in the medium of language: a lifeworld background that forms more or less suitable contexts, and provides resources, for attempts to reach understanding and to solve problems.

The question of the sense in which forms of life can be "rational" directs attention to the circular process that takes place between, on the one hand, the linguistically prior interpretive knowledge that discloses the world for a linguistic community in a more or less productive way and, on the other hand, the more or less innovative innerworldly learning processes that are made possible by means of this, through which knowledge of the world is acquired and expanded, and impetus is given for revision of the antecedent interpretive knowledge. Here we should distinguish three levels: the level of linguistic articulation of the lifeworld background, the level of practices of reaching understanding within such an intersubjectively shared lifeworld, and the level of the objective world, formally presupposed by the participants in communication, as the totality of entities about which something is said. The interaction between world-disclosure and innerworldly learning processes—an interaction that expands knowledge and alters meanings—takes place on the middle level where, within the horizon of their lifeworld, communicatively acting subjects reach understanding with one another about something in the world.

The world-disclosing function of language allows us to see everything that we encounter in the world not merely from the point of view of specific aspects and relevant properties but also as elements of a whole, as parts of a categorially organized totality. Although it does have a *relation* to rationality, it itself is, in a certain sense, a-rational. This does not mean that it is irrational. Even a linguistically creative renewal of our view of the world as a whole that allows us to see old problems in a completely new light does not fall out of the blue—it is no "Destining of Being" (*Seinsgeschick*). For world-disclosing interpretive knowledge must continuously prove its truth; it must put acting subjects in a position to come to grips with what happens to them in the world, and to learn from mistakes. On the other hand, the retrospectively produced revisions of this world-interpreting linguistic knowledge are just as little an automatic result of successful problemsolving. It is more a matter of *stimulating* the linguistic imagination—Peirce spoke of abductive fantasy—through failed attempts to solve problems and faltering learning processes.

The world-disclosing power of language is neither rational nor irrational; as an enabling condition for rational behavior it is itself a-rational. Throughout the history of philosophy this a-rational character has repeatedly failed to be recognized. At any rate, philosophical idealism from Plato through Kant to Heidegger has always discerned *Logos* at work in the totalizing power of the substantive linguistic interpretation of the world. Philosophical idealism singled out this "reason" (*Vernunft*) as the capacity for knowledge of the totality and accorded it an *overriding* importance vis-à-vis "understanding" (*Verstand*), conceived as the capacity for dealing rationally with problems that are posed for us in the world. In the ontological paradigm, reason was deemed to be the capacity for contemplatively grasping the order of being as a whole. On the Kantian reading of the mentalist paradigm, reason continued to be seen as the capacity for ideas, although the world-constituting power of these ideas was now conceived as the totalizing accomplishment of the transcendental subject. How difficult it is, even in the linguistic paradigm, to break free from idealism, can be seen in the case of Heidegger who still conceived epochal world-disclosures as the "Happening of Truth" (*Wahrheitsgeschehen*). Only a soberly conducted, pragmatic-linguistic turn permits us to relieve the world-constituting and articulating power of language of the burden of claims to *knowledge*.

Linguistic world-disclosure stands in a complementary relation to the rational accomplishments of subjects in the world who are fallible, though capable of learning. Seen in this way, reason can withdraw into the idealizations of validity claims and the formal-prag-matic presupposition of worlds; it renounces every form of totalizing knowledge, no matter how concealed, while nonetheless requiring of the communication communities—set in their contingent life-world contexts—a universalist anticipation of a muted "transcen-dence from within" that does justice to the irrefutably unconditional character of what is held-to-be-true and what ought-to-be.

Appendix on a Pragmatic Theory of Meaning

Some implications for a pragmatic theory of meaning result from the distinction between the above-mentioned different modalities of language use. Such a theory of meaning modifies the basic thesis of truth-conditional semantics as developed by Frege and Wittgenstein in the following way: one understands an illocutionary act when one knows what makes it acceptable. This thesis starts from the premise that the addressee's recognition of the validity claim raised for what is said is to be won by means of an acceptable speech-act offer, so that she is brought to accept the speech act itself as valid.[14] At first glance, however, expressions of will that are not embedded norma-tively, such as imperatives and declarations of intention (also speech acts specific to conflict situations such as insults and threats), present counterexamples. Clearly, illocutionary acts of this kind have no built-in orientation toward a consensual acceptance. Indeed, the assumption that linguistic communication aims fundamentally at agreement seems completely counterintuitive for, if that were the case, it would have to be possible to distinguish the communicative use of language as an original mode of language use, whereas all indirect forms of communication, in which one party gives another to understand something, would have a derivative status. I want to (i) begin by recalling the basic features of the pragmatic conception of meaning, and then (ii) undertake two revisions.

i. The pragmatic theory of meaning sets out to explain what it is to understand a speech act. In the performance of speech acts, sentences are used with "communicative intent." In order for this intention to be realized, the following conditions of communication, at least, must be satisfied:

- A speaker and an addressee who have command over a common language (or who could establish a common language by way of translation)
- A speech situation that can be scrutinized by both parties
- An intersubjectively shared (or sufficiently "overlapping") background understanding
- A locally situated utterance of a speaker, with a "yes" or "no" position on it by an addressee

To explain this I rely on two assumptions:

1. Linguistic communication essentially exists in order for one person to reach understanding with another about something in the world.

2. Reaching understanding implies that the hearer recognizes a validity claim raised by the speaker for a proposition.

These specifications of explanandum and explanans lead to the explanation:

- To understand a linguistic expression is to know how one could use it in order to reach understanding with someone about something in the world.

Naturally, understanding a linguistic expression is not the same as reaching understanding about something with the help of an utterance held to be valid. Nonetheless, as has already been observed by truth-conditional semantics, in language the dimensions of meaning and validity are internally connected; moreover, they are connected in such a way that one understands a speech act when one knows the conditions under which it may be accepted as valid. An orientation toward the *possible* validity of utterances is part of the pragmatic conditions not just of reaching understanding but of linguistic understanding itself. (Incidentally, this explains why we can learn to speak only under conditions of communicative action, that is, in practices from which it *emerges* when the given linguistic community accepts what as valid.)

Not "truth" but an epistemically inflected, generalized concept of "validity" in the sense of "rational acceptability" is the key concept for a pragmatic theory of meaning. This approach has, of course, the consequence that the validity conditions of a speech act are interpreted with the help of the reasons that, under standard conditions, can serve to vindicate a corresponding validity claim. Knowing the *kinds of reasons* with which a speaker could vindicate the validity claim raised for what is said is part of understanding a speech act. (This explains the holistic constitution of linguistic knowledge as well as the interpenetration of linguistic knowledge and knowledge of the world.)

ii. Previously, I had presumed that the acceptability of speech acts depends on the knowledge of reasons that justify an illocutionary success and can rationally motivate an agreement between speaker and hearer. I now have to revise this formulation in view of my differentiation within the concept of reaching understanding, and in view of the status of speech acts such as insults and threats.

To understand a speech act is to know the conditions for the illocutionary or perlocutionary success that the speaker can achieve with it (with this, we take account of perlocutions whose success, however, presupposes comprehension of the illocutionary act employed in a given case).

One knows the conditions for the illocutionary or perlocutionary success of a speech act when one knows the kinds of actor-independent or actor-relative reasons with which the speaker could vindicate her validity claim discursively. Mutual understanding between actors in an attitude oriented toward success is also possible (in a weak sense) if the seriousness (and viability) of an announcement or an imperative (or threat) can be proven with the help of actor-relative reasons for the rationality of a corresponding resolve. Here, those reasons "relative to a given actor" are valid that, from the point of view of the addressee, can be understood as good-reasons-for-the-given-actor.

These revisions take account of the fact that speech acts are illocutionary acts even when they are connected only with claims to truth and truthfulness, and when these claims to the seriousness (and viability) of intentions and decisions can be justified only through reference to the preferences of the speakers in an attitude oriented toward success (and, thus, from their perspective). Even perlocutions, which ride on the backs of illocutionary acts, can be criticized from the point of view of the truth of the assumptions implied in a given case (about conditions for context-dependent perlocutionary effects). Of course, since perlocutions *as such* do not represent illocutionary acts and are not geared toward rational acceptability, this kind of negation can have the sense only of an *explanation* as to why the perlocutionary aim cannot be attained in the given circumstances.

Notes

1. H. Schnädelbach, "Über Rationalität und Begründung," in *Zur Rehabilitierung des animal rationale* (Frankfurt, 1992), p. 63.

2. H. Schnädelbach, "Philosophie als Theorie der Rationalität," in *Zur Rehabilitierung*, pp. 47f.

3. [Editor's note:] Schnädelbach (as quoted by Habermas) speaks of the "reflexive having" of expressions, knowledge, actions, intentions, utterances, and so on. Since it is not possible in English to speak of "having" expressions, actions, or utterances, "reflexive character" or "reflexivity" has been used as appropriate.

4. Schnädelbach, *Zur Rehabilitierung*, p. 76.

5. J. Habermas, "Individuation through Socialization," in *Postmetaphysical Thinking*, trans. by W. M. Hohengarten (Cambridge, Mass., 1990), pp. 149–204.

6. This explains the wealth of ways of using the term "rational" in academic language; cf. the various "types of rationality" identified in H. Lenk and H. F. Spinner, "Rationalitätstypen, Rationalitätskonzepte und Rationalitätstheorien im Überblick," in H. Stachowiak, ed., *Handbuch pragmatischen Denkens* (Hamburg, 1989), pp. 1–31.

7. H. I. Brown, *Rationality* (London, 1988); cf. also the early work of H. Schnädelbach, "Über den Realismus," *Zeitschrift für allgemeine Wissenschaftstheorie* 111 (1972): 88ff.

8. G. H. von Wright, *Explanation and Understanding* (London, 1991), pp. 83–132.

9. See chapter 5 in the present volume, pp. 270ff.

10. E. Tugendhat, *Traditional and Analytical Philosophy*, trans. P. A. Gorner (Cambridge, 1982), pp. 391ff.

11. Cassirer assigned the "meaning function" to the epistemic use of language, which in science is specified as the mathematical representation of regularities or as

Fregean "thoughts;" see E. Cassirer, *The Philosophy of Symbolic Forms,* vol. 3, trans. R. Manheim (New Haven, 1957), pp. 279ff.

12. F. Hundschnur, "Streitspezifische Sprechakte," *Protosoziologie* 4 (1993): 140ff.

13. On the world-disclosing function of language, cf. Cristina Lafont, "Welterschließung und Referenz," *Deutsche Zeitschrift für Philosophie* 41 (1993): 491–505; also Martin Seel, "Über Richtigkeit und Wahrheit," ibid.: 509–524.

14. See chapters 2 and 6 in the present volume, pp. 116ff. and pp. 278–306, respectively.

Richard Rorty's Pragmatic Turn (1996)

In "Trotsky and the Wild Orchids" Richard Rorty casts a romantic eye back over his development as a philosopher.[1] Using the form of a "narrative of maturation," he presents his intellectual development as a progressive distancing of himself from his adolescent dream; this was the dream of fusing in a single image the extraordinary beauty of wild orchids and the liberation from profane suffering of an exploited society: the desire "to hold reality and justice in a single vision" (Yeats). The existential background to Rorty's neopragmatism is his rebellion against the false promises of philosophy: a philosophy that pretends to be able to satisfy aesthetic and moral needs in satisfying theoretical ones. Once upon a time, metaphysics wanted to instruct its pupils in spiritual exercises involving a purifying contemplation of the good in the beautiful. But the youthful Rorty, who had allowed himself to be filled with enthusiasm by Plato, Aristotle, and Thomas Aquinas, painfully comes to realize that the prospect of contact with the reality of the extraordinary held out by theory—a contact at once *desirable* and *reconciliatory*—although possibly attainable in the more definite forms of prayer, cannot be achieved along the path of philosophy. As a result, Rorty remembers Dewey—scorned by McKeon, Leo Strauss, and Mortimer Adler—who had not yet been completely forgotten in the Chicago of the 1940s. The realization that everyday reality conceals no higher reality, no realm of being-in-itself to be disclosed ecstatically, and that everyday practices leave no room for a *redemptory* vision, cures the sobered Rorty of his Platonic sickness. To be sure, the memory of the exotic sight and the overpowering smell of the wild orchids in the mountains of his childhood in the northwest of New Jersey cannot be extinguished completely.

It is roughly thus in terms of his own life-history that Rorty today explains to us the motives for his view of the dual dominance of Dewey and Heidegger developed in *Contingency, Irony, and Solidarity*. Strangely enough, this self-presentation contains no reference to the paramount role played by Wittgenstein, the third party in the alliance. Rorty's report on the experiences of his own philosophical development breaks off with his reading of Hegel as his student days in Yale draw to a close and his work as a professional philosopher is only about to begin. His training in analytic philosophy with his real teacher, Wilfrid Sellars, his basic conviction of the truth of physicalism, his successful career as a young analytic philosopher—these steps in his development are not mentioned at all. However, it is solely his ambivalence toward the tradition of *analytic* philosophy— the only tradition in whose language Rorty has learned to argue and using which he continues to expound his exciting teachings brilliantly—that can explain why he attributes a culturally critical significance to his anti-Platonic turn, a significance that is supposed to extend far beyond his own person and his private switch of philosophical allegiance.

I will deal briefly with this motivation for a kind of philosophizing that wants to bid farewell to itself as such before confining myself to discussion of the justification for the neopragmatic conception itself. From the pragmatic radicalization of the linguistic turn Rorty obtains a nonrealist understanding of knowledge. In order to test whether he radicalizes the linguistic turn in the right way, I will then compare the contextualist approach with the epistemological doubt of the modern skeptic. In doing so I will recall a problem that was always connected with coherence conceptions of truth: the problem of how truth is to be distinguished from rational acceptability. In responding to this question, there is a parting of philosophical ways. Whereas Rorty assimilates truth to justification at the expense of everyday realist intuitions, others attempt to take account of these intuitions even within the linguistic paradigm, whether with the help of a deflationary strategy as regards the problem of truth or through an idealization of the process of justification itself. On the one hand, I will take issue with the deflationary strategy that relies on a semantic conception of truth, emphasizing instead the advantages of a pragmatic viewpoint. On the other hand, again from a pragmatic perspective, I will criticize a kind of epistemization of the idea of truth that I myself once proposed. In doing so I will develop an alternative to the liquidation of unconditional claims to truth. It is this liquidation that has ultimately compelled Rorty to effect a problematic naturalization of linguistified reason—or, at any rate, one that leads to further problems.

A Platonically Motivated Anti-Platonist

Richard Rorty is one of the most outstanding analytic philosophers, consistently arguing in an informed and astute way. But his program for a philosophy that is to do away with all philosophy seems to spring more from the melancholy of a disappointed metaphysician, driven on by nominalist spurs, than from the self-criticism of an enlightened analytic philosopher who wishes to complete the linguistic turn in a pragmatist way. In 1967, when analytic philosophy (in both its versions) had achieved widespread recognition comparable to that enjoyed by Neo-Kantianism in the period before the First World War, Rorty edited a reader with the demandingly laconic title, *The Linguistic Turn*. This reader, as we can see in retrospect, marks a break in the history of analytic thought. The texts collected in the reader are meant to serve a double purpose. In summing up a triumphant progression, they are intended at the same time to signal its end. At any rate, notwithstanding his laudatory gesture, the metaphilosophical distance from which the editor comments on the texts betrays the Hegelian message that every manifestation of Spirit that achieves maturity is condemned to decline. At that time Rorty gave the starting signal to a discourse that has since given itself the name "postanalytic." In his introduction to the reader, he speculates on the "future" of analytic philosophy—a future that relegates it to the past tense. In the face of a still intact orthodoxy, Rorty points to three approaches that concur in their contradiction of the general basic assumption that "there are philosophical truths still waiting to be discovered that can be justified on the basis of arguments." Rorty links these anti-Platonic approaches with the names Heidegger, Wittgenstein, and Waismann (whose philosophical program Rorty even then described in terms similar to his later description of Dewey's pragmatism).

This distanced gaze on analytic philosophy in no way conceals the immense respect of the initiate who here steps outside of his *own* tradition: "Linguistic philosophy, over the last thirty years, has succeeded in putting the entire philosophical tradition, from Parmenides through Descartes and Hume to Bradley and Whitehead, on the defensive. It has done so by careful and thorough scrutiny of the ways in which traditional philosophers have used language in the formulation of their problems. This achievement is sufficient to place this period among the great ages of the history of philosophy."[2] Only the irresistibility of analytic philosophy's arguments explains Rorty's *real* grief. This irresistibility leads him to bid farewell to the alluring promises of metaphysics so irrevocably that, even *post* analytic philosophy, there can be no alternative to postmetaphysical thinking. Nonetheless, Rorty, then as now, is in search of some mode of thinking that, as Adorno puts it at the end of *Negative Dialectics,* shows solidarity with metaphysics at the moment of its fall.[3] There is melancholy in the strained irony propagated today by Rorty: "Rorty's post-philosophical intellectual is ironic because he realizes that truth is not all he would like it to be. Irony depends essentially on a kind of *nostalgie de la verité.*"[4] Even the romantic division of labor between irony and seriousness, Heidegger and Dewey, cannot ease the pain. Because metaphysics has command only over the language of knowledge, the aestheticization of its claim to truth amounts to an anaestheticization of the philosophical tradition as mere cultural heritage. The reality of the ideas with which Platonic theory promised to bring us into contact is not the same as the extraordinary appeal of aesthetic experience. What once aspired to be "true" in an emphatic sense cannot be preserved in the mode of the "edifying." In forfeiting the binding power of its judgments, metaphysics also loses its substance.[5]

When one is faced with this dilemma it is possible to understand the move Rorty finally makes in order to give back to philosophy, even today, something of a "doctrine," something of that inimitable combination of wild orchids and Trotsky: his imitation of the gesture, at least, of insight that is at once *stimulating* and *rich in practical consequence*. However, the metaphysical need to liberate philosophy from the sterility of a pusillanimous postmetaphysical thinking can now be satisfied only postmetaphysically. The farewell to analytic philosophy cannot lead back to a devalued metaphysics. For this reason, the only remaining option is to dramatize the farewell to philosophy in general. Only if the act of leave-taking itself were to release a shock and intervene into everyday life would philosophy "at the moment of its fall" be able to acquire a more than purely academic significance. But how is a separation from analytic philosophy carried out with analytic means supposed to achieve significance of a kind that would allow analytic thought to be illuminated one last time in the brilliance of its great tradition? As I understand his naturalistically refracted impulse toward great philosophy, Rorty wants to give an answer to this question.

Rorty begins by showing that analytic philosophy shares a fundamental premise with the tradition it has devalued. This is the conviction that "there are philosophical truths still waiting to be discovered." Thanks to a very German idea that he borrows from Heidegger, Rorty then attributes a dramatic weightiness to this *proton pseudos* of Western metaphysics. According to this Heideggerian thesis, the profane destinies of the West are supposed to have been fulfilled only within the scope of an epochal understanding of being; moreover, one governed by metaphysics. Of course, unlike Heidegger, Rorty can no longer stylize postmetaphysical thinking post analytic philosophy as a sacral "Commemoration of Being" (*Andenken des Seins*). Rorty understands the deconstruction of the history of metaphysics as a deflationary diagnosis in Wittgenstein's sense. Anti-Platonism draws its eminently practical significance only from the severity of the sickness that it is supposed to cure. The unmasking of Platonism is aimed, beyond scholasticism, at a culture that is alienated from itself platonistically. If, finally, the act of leave-taking is not to exhaust itself in negation, Rorty has to open a perspective that will enable a new self-understanding that can take the place of the old, deflated one. With this end in view, he adapts Dewey's Hegelianism for his own purposes in such a way that a perspective is opened on everyday practices that are no longer distorted by Platonist prejudices. In this way, like Hegel, even the "last" philosophers capture their own time once more in thought.

Rorty knows, of course, that such metaphilosophical reflections cannot transform the self-understanding of philosophy on their own.[6] He cannot get outside of philosophy without using philosophy to claim validity for his thoughts. Rorty would not be the scrupulous and sensitive, suggestive, and stimulating philosopher that he is were he to insist solely on the rhetorical role of the reeducator. The diagnosis of a false self-understanding, too, remains a matter for theory. Rorty has to provide arguments if he is to convince his colleagues that the "Platonic" distinction between "convincing" and "persuading" makes no sense. He has to prove that even analytic philosophy remains captivated by the spell of the metaphysics against which it is battling.

The Pragmatic Turn

Rorty's important book *Philosophy and the Mirror of Nature* (1979) pursues a number of aims. By carrying through to its conclusion the deconstruction of the philosophy of consciousness, he wants to complete a not yet completed linguistic turn in such a way that the Platonist self-misunderstanding deeply rooted in our culture becomes obvious. My doubts relate to the second step. Does the pragmatic turn, which Rorty rightly demands in the face of semantically fixated approaches, require an anti-realist understanding of knowledge?

a. The basic conceptual framework of the philosophy of the subject has, from Peirce to Wittgenstein and Heidegger, been subjected to a relentless critique. Rorty draws on contemporary arguments (among others those of Sellars, Quine, and Davidson) in order to expose the basic assumptions of mentalist epistemology with a view to a critique of reason. The ideas of "self-consciousness" and "subjectivity" imply that the knowing subject can disclose for itself a privileged sphere of immediately accessible and absolutely certain experiences (*Erlebnisse*) when it does not focus directly on objects but rather reflexively on its own representations (*Vorstellungen*) of objects. For classical epistemology, there is a constitutive separation between inner and outer—a dualism of mind and body—that appeals to the privileged access of the first person to her own experiences. The epistemic authority of the first person is sustained by the wellsprings of three paradigm-constituting assumptions:

1. that we know our own mental states better than anything else;

2. that knowing takes place essentially in the mode of representing objects; and

3. that the truth of judgments rests on evidence that vouches for their certainty.

Analysis of the linguistic form of our experiences and thoughts discovers in these assumptions three corresponding myths—the myth of the given, the myth of thought as representation, and the myth of truth as certainty. It is shown that we cannot circumvent the linguistic expression as the medium for the representation and communication of knowledge. There are no uninterpreted experiences (*Erfahrungen*) that are accessible only privately and elude public assessment and correction. Moreover, knowledge of objects is not an adequate model for the knowledge of propositionally structured states of affairs. Finally, truth is a property of criticizable propositions that cannot be lost; it can be justified only on the basis of reasons— it cannot be authenticated on the basis of the genesis of representations.

Rorty, of course, connects this critique of mentalism with the more far-reaching aim of radicalizing the linguistic turn. He wants to show "what philosophy of language comes to when purified of attempts to imitate either Kant or Hume."[7] So long as the subject-object relation is projected merely onto the sentence-fact relation, the resulting semantic answers remain tied to the mentalist mode of questioning. So long as the representation (*Darstellung*) of states of affairs—like the representation (*Vorstellung*) of objects[8]—is conceived as a two-place relation, the linguistic turn leaves the "mirror of nature"—as metaphor for knowledge of the world—intact.

Rorty wants to make full use of the conceptual scope that has been opened up by the philosophy of language. With Peirce he replaces the two-place relation between representing subject and represented object with a three-place relation: the symbolic expression, which accords validity to a state of affairs, for an interpretive community. The objective world is no longer something to be reflected but is simply the common reference point for a process of communication (*Verständigung*) between members of a communication community who come to an understanding with one another with regard to something. The communicated facts can no more be separated from the process of communication than the *supposition* of an objective world can be separated from the intersubjectively shared interpretive horizon within which the participants in communication always already operate. Knowledge no longer coincides with the correspondence of sentences and facts. For this reason, only a linguistic turn that is rigorously carried to its conclusion can, in overcoming mentalism, also overcome the epistemological model of the Mirror of Nature.

b. I am interested in the question of whether Rorty performs this plausible pragmatic radicalization of the linguistic turn in the right way. If we no longer refer epistemological questions only to language as the grammatical form of representation (*Darstellung*), relating them instead to language as it is used communicatively, an additional dimension is opened up. This is the dimension of interactions and traditions—the public space of a lifeworld shared intersubjectively by the language users. This expanded perspective allows the entwining of the epistemological accomplishments of the socialized individuals with their processes of cooperation and communication to become visible: "Once conversation replaces confrontation [of persons with states of affairs], the notion of the mind as Mirror of Nature can be discarded."[9] The "communication model" of knowledge highlights the point that we have no unfiltered access to entities in the world, independent of our practices of reaching understanding and the linguistically constituted context of our lifeworld: "Elements of what we call 'language' or 'mind' penetrate so deeply into what we call 'reality' that the very project of representing ourselves as being 'mappers' of something 'language-independent' is fatally compromised from the start."[10]

This is a quotation from Hilary Putnam with which Rorty agrees. Nonetheless, Rorty has something other than Putnam's "internal realism" in mind. Putnam's "internal realism" stresses that the conditions for the objectivity of knowledge can be analyzed only *in connection with* the conditions for the intersubjectivity of a mutual understanding with regard to what is said. On Rorty's view, "being in touch with reality" has to be translated into the jargon of "being in touch with a human community" in such a way that the realist intuition, to which mentalism wanted to do justice with its Mirror of Nature and its correspondence between representation and represented object, disappears completely. For Rorty, every kind of representation of something in the objective world is a dangerous illusion. Now, it is certainly the case that with the pragmatic turn the epistemic authority of the first person singular, who inspects her inner self, is displaced by the first person plural, by the "we" of a communication community in front of which every person justifies her views. However, it is only the empiricist interpretation of this new authority that leads Rorty to equate "knowledge" with what is accepted as "rational" according to the standards of our respective communities.

Just as Locke and Hume referred their mentalist reflections to the consciousness of empirical persons, Kant referred his to the consciousness of subjects "in general." Linguistic reflections, too, can be referred to communication communities "in general." But Rorty, the nominalist, stands in the empiricist tradition and refers epistemic authority to the received social practices of "our" respective communities. He regards the urge "to see social practices of justification as more than just such practices"[11] as nonsensical. Rorty himself makes the connection between, on the one hand, the contextualist interpretation of the pragmatic turn and the anti-realist understanding of knowledge and, on the other hand, the rejection of a Kantian strategy of analysis:[12] "If we see knowledge as a matter of conversation and of social practice, rather than as an attempt to mirror nature, we will not be likely to envisage a metapractice which will be the critique of all possible forms of social practice."[13] For Rorty, such a formal-pragmatic attempt would be a relapse into foundationalism. In the seventeenth century the basic concepts of subjectivity and self-consciousness had, with "the mental" and "introspection," respectively, secured for philosophy—which at that time had to find a new place *alongside* the new physics—an object domain and a method of its own. As a result, philosophy was able to understand itself as a foundational discipline that checked and justified the foundations of all other disciplines. Rorty now holds the view that this same foundationalist self-understanding takes possession of the philosophy of language when it stops short of a contextualist understanding of knowledge and justification. Universalist approaches within the philosophy of language—such as Rorty discerns in Dummett and others—come under suspicion here.

Contextualism and Skepticism as Problems Specific to Particular Paradigms

When Rorty regards contextualism as the necessary consequence of a fully executed linguistic turn, he is right in one respect: contextualism designates a problem that can occur only when we reckon on a reason embodied in linguistic practices. But he is wrong to see contextualism at the same time as the solution to the problem. This view has its roots, if I am correct, in a problematic understanding of philosophical paradigms.

Like, for example, Apel and Tugendhat, Rorty regards the history of philosophy as a succession of three paradigms. He speaks of metaphysics, epistemology, and the philosophy of language.[14] Of course, the philosophy of language has detached itself only half-heartedly from mentalism. Rorty believes that the linguistic turn can be carried through consistently to its conclusion only in the form of a critique of reason that takes its leave of philosophy as such.[15] It is not just the problems but the way of posing problems that changes with the leap from one paradigm to the next:

This picture of ancient and medieval philosophy as concerned with *things,* the philosophy of the seventeenth through the nineteenth centuries with *ideas,* and the enlightened contemporary philosophical scene with *words* has considerable plausibility. But this sequence should not be thought of as offering three contrasting views about what is primary, or what is foundational. It is not that Aristotle thought that one could best explain ideas and words in terms of things, whereas Descartes and Russell rearranged the order of explanation. It would be more correct to say that Aristotle did not have—did not feel the need of—a theory of knowledge, and that Descartes and Locke did not have a theory of meaning. Aristotle's remarks about knowing do not offer answers, good or bad, to Locke's questions, any more than Locke's remarks about language offer answers to Frege's.[16]

This *discontinuity* means that philosophical questions are not settled through finding the right answers; rather, they fall into disuse once they have lost their market value. This also holds for the question of the objectivity of knowledge.

On the mentalist view, objectivity is ensured when the representing subject refers to his objects in the right way. He checks the subjectivity of his representations against the objective world: "'subjective' contrasts with 'corresponding to what is out there,' and thus means something like 'a product only of what is in here.'"[17] On the linguistic view, the subjectivity of beliefs is no longer checked directly through confrontation with the world but rather through public agreement achieved in the communication community: "a 'subjective' consideration is one which has been, or would be, or should be, set aside by rational discussants."[18] With this, the intersubjectivity of reaching understanding replaces the objectivity of experience. The language–world relation becomes dependent on communication between speakers and hearers. The vertical world-relation of representations *of* something, or of propositions *about* something, is bent back, as it were, into the horizontal line of the cooperation of participants in communication. The intersubjectivity of the lifeworld, which subjects inhabit in common, *displaces* the objectivity of a world that a solitary subject confronts: "For pragmatists, the desire for objectivity is not the desire to escape the limitations of one's community, but simply the desire for as much intersubjective agreement as possible."[19] Rorty wants to say: the paradigm shift transforms perspectives in such a way that epistemological questions as such are passé.

The contextualist understanding of the linguistic turn from which this anti-realism emerges goes back to a conception of the rise and fall of paradigms that excludes continuity of theme between paradigms as well as learning processes that extend across paradigms. In fact, the terms in which we undertake a comparison of paradigms reflect our hermeneutic starting point—and, thus, our own paradigm. That Rorty selects for his comparison the frame of reference of objectivity, subjectivity, and intersubjectivity results from the basic conceptual perspective from which we now describe the linguistic turn of mentalism. On the other hand, the picture of a contingent succession of incommensurable paradigms does not in any way fit with this description. Rather, from the perspective of that frame of reference, a subsequent paradigm appears as an answer to a problem bequeathed to us by the devaluation of a preceding paradigm. Contrary to what Rorty supposes, paradigms do not form an arbitrary sequence but a dialectical relationship.

Nominalism robbed things of their inner nature or essence and declared general concepts to be constructions of a finite mind. Since then, comprehending that which is (*das Seiende*) in thought has lacked a foundation in the conceptual constitution of beings themselves. The correspondence of mind with nature could no longer be conceived as an ontological relation, the rules of logic no longer reflected the laws of reality. *Pace* Rorty, mentalism responded to this challenge by reversing the order of explanation. If the knowing subject can no longer derive the standards for knowledge from a disqualified nature, it has to supply these standards from a reflexively disclosed subjectivity itself. Reason, once embodied objectively in the order of nature, retreats to subjective spirit. With this, the being-in-itself (*das Ansich*) of the world is transformed into the objectivity of a world that is given for us, the subjects—a world of represented objects or *phenomena*. Whereas up to then, the constitution of the world of being-in-itself had enabled a correspondence of thought with reality—true judgments—the truth of judgments is now supposed to be measured against the certainty of evident subjective experiences (*Erlebnisse*). Representational thought leads to objective knowledge insofar as it comprehends the phenomenal world.

The concept of subjectivity introduced a dualism between inner and outer that seemed to confront the human mind with the precarious task of bridging a chasm. With this, the way was cleared for skepticism in its modern form. The private character of my particular subjective experiences, on which my absolute certainty is based, simultaneously provides reason to doubt whether the world as it appears to us is not in fact an illusion. This skepticism is anchored in the constitutive concepts of the mentalist paradigm. At the same time it conjures up memories of the comforting intuition that sustained the ontological paradigm: the idea that the truth of judgments is guaranteed by a correspondence with reality that is grounded in reality itself. This "residual" intuition, as it were, which had lost none of its suggestive power with the switch of paradigm, joined forces with the new skeptical question of whether—and if so, how—the agreement between representation and represented object is to be grounded on the basis of the evidence of our subjective experiences. It is this question that first provokes the epistemological quarrel between Idealism and Empiricism.[20] However, in light of this genealogy it becomes apparent—and this is my main point here—that contextualism is built into the basic concepts of the linguistic paradigm just as skepticism is built into mentalism. And once again, the intuitions regarding truth that carry over or stick with us from the preceding paradigms lead to an intensification of these problems.

Just as the dispute about universals at the end of the Middle Ages contributed to the devaluation of objective reason, the critique of introspection and psychologism at the end of the nineteenth century contributed to the shaking up of subjective reason. With the displacement of reason from the consciousness of the knowing subject to language as the medium by means of which acting subjects communicate with one another, the order of explanation changes once more. Epistemic authority passes over from the knowing subject, which supplies from within herself the standards for the objectivity of experience, to the justificatory practices of a linguistic community. Up to then the intersubjective validity of beliefs had resulted from the subsequent convergence of thoughts or representations. Interpersonal agreement had been explained by the ontological anchoring of true judgments or by the shared psychological or transcendental endowments of knowing subjects. Following the linguistic turn, however, all explanations take the primacy of a common language as their starting point. Description of states and events in the objective world, like the self-representation of experiences to which the subject has privileged access, is dependent on the interpreting use of a common language. For this reason, the term "intersubjective" no longer refers to the result of an *observed* convergence of the thoughts or representations of various persons, but to the prior commonality of a linguistic preunderstanding or horizon of the lifeworld—which, from the perspective of the participants themselves, is *presupposed*—within which the members of a communication community find themselves before they reach understanding with one another about something in the world. Finally, the contextualist question, which should not be confused with the epistemological doubt of skepticism, results from this primacy of the intersubjectivity of shared beliefs over confrontation with reality (a reality that is always already interpreted).

The pragmatic turn leaves no room for doubt as to the existence of a world independent of our descriptions. Rather, from Peirce to Wittgenstein, the idle Cartesian doubt has been rejected as a performative contradiction: "If you tried to doubt everything you would not get as far as doubting anything. The game of doubting itself presupposes certainty."[21] On the other hand, all knowledge is fallible and, when it is problematized, dependent on justification. As soon as the standard for the objectivity of knowledge passes from private certainty to public practices of justification, "truth" becomes a three-place concept of validity. The validity of propositions that are fallible in principle is shown to be validity that is justified *for* a public.[22] Moreover, because in the linguistic paradigm truths are accessible only in the form of rational acceptability, the question now arises of how in that case the truth of a proposition can still be isolated from the context in which it is justified. Unease with regard to this problem brings older intuitions about truth onto the scene. It awakens memory of a correspondence between thought and reality or of a contact with reality that is sensorially certain. These images, which are still suggestive despite having lost their bearings, are behind the question of how the fact that we cannot transcend the linguistic horizon of justified beliefs is compatible with the intuition that true propositions fit the facts. It is no accident that the contemporary rationality debates circle around the concepts of truth and reference.[23] Just as skepticism does not simply assimilate being to appearance but rather gives expression to the uneasy feeling that we *might* be unable to separate the one from the other convincingly, neither does contextualism, properly understood, equate truth with justified assertibility. Contextualism is rather an expression of the embarrassment that would ensue if we *did* have to assimilate the one to the other. It makes us aware of a problem to which cultural relativism presents a solution that is false because it contains a performative self-contradiction.

Truth and Justification

Even in the comprehension of elementary propositions about states or events in the world, language and reality interpenetrate in a manner that for us is *indissoluble.* There is no natural possibility of isolating the constraints of reality that make a statement true from the semantic rules that lay down these truth conditions. We can explain what a fact is only with the help of the truth of a statement of fact, and we can explain what is real only in terms of what is true. Being, as Tugendhat says, is veritative being.[24] Since the truth of beliefs or sentences can in turn be justified only with the help of other beliefs and sentences, we cannot break free from the magic circle of our language. This fact suggests an anti-foundationalist conception of knowledge and a holistic conception of justification. Because we cannot confront our sentences with anything that is not itself already saturated linguistically, no basic propositions can be distinguished that would be privileged in being able to legitimate themselves, thereby serving as the basis for a linear chain of justification. Rorty rightly emphasizes "that nothing counts as justification unless by reference to what we already accept," concluding from this "that there is no way to get outside our beliefs and our language so as to find some test other than coherence."[25]

This does not mean, of course, that the coherence of our beliefs is sufficient to clarify the meaning of the concept of truth—which has now become central. Certainly, within the linguistic paradigm, the truth of a proposition can no longer be conceived as correspondence with something in the world, for otherwise we would have to be able to "get outside of language" while using language. Obviously, we cannot compare linguistic expressions with a piece of uninterpreted or "naked" reality—that is, with a reference that eludes our linguistically bound inspection.[26] Nonetheless, the correspondence idea of truth was able to take account of a fundamental aspect of the

meaning of the truth predicate. This aspect—the notion of unconditional validity—is swept under the carpet if the truth of a proposition is conceived as coherence with other propositions or as justified
assertibility within an interconnected system of assertions. Whereas
well-justified assertions can turn out to be false, we understand truth
as a property of propositions "that cannot be lost." Coherence depends on practices of justification that let themselves be guided by
standards that change from time to time. This accounts for the
question: "Why does the fact that our beliefs hang together, supposing they do, give the least indication that they are true?"[27]

The "cautionary" use of the truth predicate[28] shows that, with the
truth of propositions, we connect an unconditional claim that points
beyond all the evidence available to us; on the other hand, the
evidence that we bring to bear in our contexts of justification has to
be sufficient to entitle us to raise truth claims. Although truth cannot be reduced to coherence and justified assertibility, there has to
be an internal relation between truth and justification. How, otherwise, would it be possible to explain that a justification of "p," successful according to our standards, points in favor of the truth of "p,"
although truth is not an achievement term and does not depend on
how well a proposition can be justified. Michael Williams describes
the problem as a dispute between two equally reasonable ideas:
"First, that if we are to have knowledge of an objective world, the
truth of what we believe about the world must be independent of
our believing it; and second, that justification is inevitably a matter
of supporting beliefs by other beliefs, hence in this minimal sense a
matter of coherence."[29] This leads to the contextualist question:
"Given only knowledge of what we believe about the world, and how
our beliefs fit together, how can we show that these beliefs are likely
to be true?"[30]

This question should not, however, be understood in a skeptical
sense, for the conception according to which we, as socialized individuals, always already find ourselves within the linguistically disclosed horizon of our lifeworld implies an unquestioned
background of intersubjectively shared convictions, proven true in
practice, which makes nonsense of total doubt as to the accessibility
of the world. Language, which we cannot "get outside of," should

not be understood in analogy to the inwardness of a representing subject who is as if cut off from the external world of representable objects. The relationship between justifiability and truth, although in need of clarification, signals no gulf between inner and outer, no dualism that would have to be *bridged* and that could give rise to the skeptical doubt as to whether our world *as a whole* is an illusion. The pragmatic turn pulls the rug from under this skepticism. There is a simple reason for this. In everyday practices, we cannot use language without *acting*. Speech itself is effected in the mode of speech acts that for their part are embedded in contexts of interaction and entwined with instrumental actions. As actors, that is, as interacting and intervening subjects, we are always already in contact with things about which we can make statements. Language games and practices are *interwoven*. "At some point . . . we have to leave the realm of sentences (and texts) and draw upon agreement in action and experience (for instance, in using a predicate)."[31] From the point of view of the philosophy of language, Husserl's phenomenological conclusion that we "are always already in contact with things" is confirmed.

For this reason, the question as to the internal connection between justification and truth—a connection that explains why we may, in light of the evidence available to us, raise an unconditional truth claim that aims beyond what is justified—is not an epistemological question. It is not a matter of being or appearance. What is at stake is not the correct representation of reality but everyday practices that must not fall apart. The contextualist unease betrays a worry about the smooth functioning of language games and practices. Reaching understanding cannot function unless the participants refer to a single objective world, thereby stabilizing the intersubjectively shared public space with which everything that is merely subjective can be contrasted.[32] This supposition of an objective world that is independent of our descriptions fulfills a functional requirement of our processes of cooperation and communication. Without this supposition, everyday practices, which rest on the (in a certain sense) Platonic distinction between believing and knowing unreservedly, would come apart at the seams.[33] If it were to turn out that we cannot in any way make *this* distinction, the result would be more of a pathological self-misunderstanding than an illusionary understanding of the world. Whereas skepticism suspects an epistemological mistake, contextualism supposes a faulty construction in the way we live.

Contextualism thus raises the question of whether and, as the case may be, how the intuition that we can in principle distinguish between what-is-true and what-is-held-to-be-true can be brought into the linguistic paradigm. This intuition is not "realist" in an epistemological sense. Even within pragmatism there is a parting of ways with regard to this question. Some are pragmatist enough to take seriously realist everyday intuitions and the internal relation between coherence and truth to which they attest. Others regard the attempt to clarify this internal relation as hopeless, treating everyday realism as an illusion. Rorty wants to combat this illusion by rhetorical means and pleads for *reeducation*. We ought to get used to replacing the desire for objectivity with the desire for solidarity and, with William James, to understanding "truth" as no more than that in which it is good for "us"—the liberal members of Western culture or Western societies—to believe. "[Pragmatists] should see themselves as working at the interface between the common sense of their community, a common sense much influenced by Greek metaphysics and by patriarchal monotheism. . . . They should see themselves as involved in a long-term attempt to change the rhetoric, the common sense, and self-image of their community."[34]

Before I deal with this proposal, I would like to examine whether the alternatives are as hopeless as Rorty assumes. Are there not plausible explanations for the fact that a justification successful in our justificatory context points in favor of the context-independent truth of the justified proposition? I am interested above all in two attempts at explanation: a deflationary one, which disputes that "truth" has any nature at all that could be explicated; and an epistemic one, which inflates the idea of a justified assertion to such an extent that truth becomes the limit concept of the justificatory process. Of course, deflationism is permitted to de-thematize the concept of truth only to the extent that this concept can continue to sustain realist intuitions, while the epistemic conception is allowed to idealize the justificatory conditions only to the extent that its idea of argumentation removed from everyday practices remains within the reach of "our" practices.[35]

The Semantic Conception of Truth and the Pragmatic Perspective

Tarski's Convention T—"'p' is true if and only if p"—relies on a disquotational use of the truth-predicate that can be illustrated, for instance, by the example of confirming another person's statements: "Everything that the witness said yesterday is true." With this, the speaker makes his own "everything that was said," in such a way that he could repeat the corresponding assertions in the stance of the first person. This use of the truth-predicate is noteworthy in two respects. For one thing, it permits a generalizing reference to subject matter that is mentioned but not explicitly reproduced. Tarski uses this property in order to construct a theory of truth that generalizes about all instances of "T." For another, the truth-predicate when used in this way establishes a relation of equivalence between two linguistic expressions—the whole point of the Tarskian strategy of explanation depends on this. For, through exploiting the disquotational function, the inaccessible "relation of correspondence" between language and world or sentence and fact can, it appears, be reflected onto the tangible semantic relation between the expressions of an object language and those of a metalanguage. No matter how one conceives of the representational function of statements, whether as "satisfaction" of truth conditions or as "fitting" the facts to the sentences, what is envisaged in every case are pictures of relations that extend beyond language. It now seems possible to clarify these pictures with the help of interrelations that are *internal to language*. This initial idea allows us to understand why weak realist connotations are connected with the semantic conception of truth— even if it is clear that this conception cannot sustain a strong epistemological realism in the manner of Popper.[36]

Now, it was already noticed at an early stage that the semantic conception of truth cannot vindicate its claim to be an explication of the full meaning of the truth-predicate.[37] The reason for this is that the disquotational function is not sufficiently informative because it already presupposes the representational function. One understands the meaning of Convention T when one knows what is *meant* (*gemeint*) with the right-hand side of the biconditional. The meaning of the truth-predicate in the sentence "Everything that the witness said yesterday is true" is parasitic on the assertoric mode of the witness's assertions. Before an assertion can be quoted it must be "put forward." This presupposed assertoric meaning can be analyzed in an exemplary way by looking at the "yes" and "no" positions of participants in argumentation who raise or refute objections; it can also be seen in the "cautionary" use of the truth-predicate, which recalls the experience of participants in argumentation that even propositions that have been justified convincingly can turn out to be false.

The truth-predicate belongs—though not exclusively—to the language game of argumentation. For this reason its meaning can be elucidated (at least partly) according to its functions in this language game, that is, in the *pragmatic dimension* of a particular employment of the predicate. Whoever confines herself to the semantic dimension of sentences and of metalinguistic commentaries on sentences comprehends only the reflection of a prior linguistic practice that, as remains to be shown, extends even into everyday practices. However, the deflationary treatment of the concept of truth, through its semantic dimming of the pragmatic meaning of truth, has the advantage of avoiding discussions about the "nature" of truth without having to forfeit a minimal orientation toward the distinction between knowing and believing, between being-true and being-held-to-be-true. This strategy aims at uncoupling these elementary distinctions from the dispute about substantial epistemological views. If it can be shown that the semantic conception of truth is sufficient to explain the usual methods of inquiry and theory selection—that is, sufficient also to explain what counts as "success" or "growth in knowledge" in the scientific enterprise—we can rescue the weak realist supposition of a world independent of our descriptions without boosting up the concept of truth in an epistemological-realist way.[38]

On the other hand, science is not the only sphere—and not even the primary one—in which the truth-predicate has a use. Even if a deflationary concept of truth were sufficient for elucidating the fact of science, for rendering the functioning of our practices of inquiry transparent, this would still not dissipate the contextualist doubt. For this doubt extends not only to the construction and selection of theories, indeed, not only to practices of argumentation in general: with respect to the pretheoretical orientation toward truth inherent in everyday practices, a semantic conception of truth simply does not help us at all.

What is at issue in the lifeworld is the pragmatic role of a Janus-faced notion of truth that mediates between behavioral certainty and discursively justified assertibility. In the network of established practices, implicitly raised validity claims that have been accepted against a broad background of intersubjectively shared convictions constitute the rails along which behavioral certainties run. However, as soon as these certainties lose their hold in the corset of self-evident beliefs, they are jolted out of tranquillity and transformed into a corresponding number of questionable topics that thereby become subject to debate. In moving from action to rational discourse,[39] what is initially naively held-to-be-true is released from the mode of behavioral certainty and assumes the form of a hypothetical proposition whose validity is left open for the duration of the discourse. The argumentation takes the form of a competition for the better arguments in favor of, or against, controversial validity claims, and serves the cooperative search for truth.[40]

With this description of justificatory practices guided by the idea of truth, however, the problem is posed anew of how the systematic mobilization of good reasons, which at best lead to justified beliefs, is supposed nonetheless to be adequate for the purpose of discriminating between justified and unjustified truth claims. To begin with, I simply want to keep hold of the picture of a circular process that presents itself to us from a perspective expanded by means of the theory of action: shaken-up behavioral certainties are transformed on the level of argumentation into controversial validity claims raised for hypothetical propositions; these claims are tested discursively—and, as the case may be, vindicated—with the result that the discursively accepted truths can return to the realm of action; with this, behavioral certainties (as the case may be, new ones), which rely on beliefs unproblematically held to be true, are produced once more. What still remains to be explained is the mysterious power of the discursively achieved agreement that *authorizes* the participants in argumentation, in the role of actors, to accept unreservedly justified assertions as truths. For it is clear from the description from the point of view of action theory that argumentation can fulfill the role of *troubleshooter* with regard to behavioral certainties that have become problematic only if it is guided by truth in a context-independent—that is, unconditional—sense.

Although when we adopt a reflexive attitude we know that all knowledge is fallible, in everyday life we cannot survive with hypotheses alone, that is, in a persistently fallibilist way. The organized fallibilism of scientific inquiry can deal hypothetically with controversial validity claims indefinitely because it serves to bring about agreements that are *uncoupled* from action. This model is not suitable for the lifeworld. Certainly, we have to make decisions in the lifeworld on the basis of incomplete information; moreover, existential risks such as the loss of those closest to us, sickness, old age, and death are the mark of human life. However, notwithstanding these uncertainties, everyday routines rest on an unqualified trust in the *knowledge* of lay people as much as experts. We would step on no bridge, use no car, undergo no operation, not even eat an exquisitely prepared meal if we did not consider the knowledge used to be safeguarded, if we did not hold the assumptions employed in the production and execution of our actions to be true. At any rate, the performative need for behavioral certainty rules out a reservation in principle with regard to truth, even though we know, as soon as the naive performance of actions is interrupted, that truth claims can be vindicated only discursively—that is, only within the relevant context of justification. Truth may be assimilated neither to behavioral certainty nor to justified assertibility. Evidently, only strong conceptions of knowledge and truth—open to the accusation of Platonism—can do justice to the unity of the illocutionary meaning of assertions, which take on different roles in the realms of action and discourse respectively. Whereas in everyday practices "truths" prop up behavioral certainties, in discourses they provide the reference point for truth claims that are in principle fallible.

The Epistemic Conception of Truth in a Pragmatic Perspective

The stubborn problem of the relation between truth and justification makes understandable the attempt to distinguish "truth" from "rational acceptability" through an idealization of the conditions of justification. This attempt proposes that a proposition justified according to "our" standards is distinguished from a true proposition in the same way that a proposition justified in a given context is distinguished from a proposition that could be justified in any context. A proposition is "true" if it could be justified under ideal epistemic conditions (Putnam)[41] or could win argumentatively reached agreement in an ideal speech situation (Habermas)[42] or in an ideal communication community (Apel).[43] What is true is what may be accepted as rational under ideal conditions. Convincing objections have been raised to this proposal, which dates back to Peirce. The objections are directed in part against conceptual difficulties with the ideal state adopted; in part they show that an idealization of justificatory conditions cannot achieve its goal because it either distances truth too far from justified assertibility or nor far enough.

The first kind of objection draws attention to the paradoxical nature of the notion of "complete" or "conclusive" knowledge— fixed as a limit concept—that, when its incompleteness and fallibility is taken away from it, would no longer be (human) knowledge.[44] Paradoxical, too, is the idea of a final consensus or definitive language that would bring to a standstill all further communication or all further interpretation, "with the result that what is *meant* as a situation of ideal mutual understanding stands revealed as a situation beyond the necessity for (and the problems connected with) linguistic processes of reaching understanding."[45] This objection is directed not just against an idealization that hypostatizes final states as *attainable* states in the world. Even if the ideal reference points are understood as aims that are not attainable in principle, or attainable only approximately, it remains "paradoxical that we would be obliged to strive for the realization of an ideal whose realization would be the end of human history."[46] As a regulative idea, the

critical point of the orientation toward truth becomes clear only
when the formal or processual properties of argumentation, and *not
its aims,* are idealized.

The second kind of objection leads to the same conclusion. These
objections are directed not against the incoherent results of the
idealization of the targeted states but against the operation of idealization itself. No matter how the value of the epistemic conditions is
enhanced through idealizations, either they satisfy the unconditional character of truth claims by means of requirements that cut
off all connection with the practices of justification familiar to us, or
else they retain the connection to practices familiar to us by paying
the price that rational acceptability does not exclude the possibility
of error even under these ideal conditions, that is, does not simulate
a property "that cannot be lost": "It would be apparent either that
those conditions allow the possibility of error or that they are so
ideal as to make no use of the intended connection with human
abilities."[47]

In his debates with Putnam, Apel, and me, Rorty makes use of
these objections not in order to discredit the epistemization of truth
but in order to radicalize it. With his opponents he shares the view
that the standards for the rational acceptability of propositions, although they change historically, do not always do so arbitrarily. At
least from the perspective of the participants, rationality standards
are open to critique and can be "reformed," that is, improved on the
basis of good reasons. Unlike Putnam, however, Rorty does not want
to take account of the fact of learning processes by conceding that
justificatory practices are guided by an idea of truth that transcends
the justificatory context in question. He completely rejects idealizing
limit concepts and interprets the difference between justification
and truth in such a way that a proponent is prepared in a given case
to defend her views not only here and now but even in front of
another audience. Whoever is oriented toward truth in this sense is
willing "to justify his convictions in front of a competent audience"
or "to increase the size or diversity of the conversational community."[48] On Rorty's view, every idealization that goes beyond this will
founder on the problem that in idealizing we must always take
something familiar as our point of departure; usually it is "us," that

is, the communication community as we are familiar with it: "I cannot see what 'idealized rational acceptability' can mean except 'acceptability to an ideal community.' Nor can I see, given that no such community is going to have a God's eye view, that this ideal community can be anything more than us as we should like to be. Nor can I see what 'us' can mean here except: us educated, sophisticated, tolerant, wet liberals, the people who are always willing to hear the other side, to think out all their implications, etc."[49]

Of course, it can be objected to this that an idealization of the justificatory conditions does not in any way have to take the "thick" characteristics of one's own culture as its point of departure; rather, it can start with the formal and processual characteristics of justificatory practices in general that, after all, are to be found in *all* cultures—even if not by any means always in institutionalized form. The fact that the practice of argumentation compels the participants themselves to make pragmatic assumptions with a counterfactual content fits in well with this. Whoever enters into discussion with the serious intention of becoming *convinced* of something through dialogue with others has to presume performatively that the participants allow their "yes" or "no" to be determined solely by the force of the better argument. However, with this they assume—normally in a counterfactual way—a speech situation that satisfies improbable conditions: openness to the public, inclusiveness, equal rights to participation, immunization against external or inherent compulsion, as well as the participants' orientation toward reaching understanding (that is, the sincere expression of utterances).[50] In these unavoidable presuppositions of argumentation, the intuition is expressed that true propositions are resistant to spatially, socially, and temporally unconstrained attempts to refute them. What we hold to be true has to be defendable on the basis of good reasons not merely in a different context but in all possible contexts, that is, at any time and against anybody. This provides the inspiration for the discourse theory of truth: a proposition is true if it withstands all attempts to refute it under the demanding conditions of rational discourse.[51]

However, this does not mean that it is also true *for this reason*. A truth claim raised for "*p*" says that the truth conditions for "*p*" are satisfied. We have no other way of ascertaining whether or not this is the case except by way of argumentation, for direct access to uninterpreted truth conditions is denied to us. But the fact that the truth conditions are satisfied does not itself become an epistemic fact just because we can only *establish* whether these conditions are satisfied by way of discursive vindication of the truth claim—whereby we have already had to interpret the truth conditions in light of the relevant sorts of reasons for the claim in question.

A consistently epistemic reading of the discourse-theoretical explanation of truth already founders on the problem that not all of the processual properties mentioned retain a "connection with human abilities." Nonetheless, with regard to the argumentative presuppositions of general inclusiveness, equal rights to participation, freedom from repression, and orientation toward reaching understanding, we can imagine *in the present* what an approximately ideal satisfaction would look like. This does not hold for anticipation of the future, of future corroboration (*Bewährung*).[52] To be sure, the orientation toward the future, too, *essentially* has the critical point of reminding us of the ethnocentric limitation and the fallibility of every actually achieved agreement, no matter how rationally motivated; that is, it serves as a reminder to us of the possible further decentering of the perspective of our justification community. Time, however, is a constraint of an ontological kind. Because all real discourses, conducted in actual time, are limited with regard to the future, we cannot know whether propositions that are rationally acceptable today will, even under approximately ideal conditions, assert themselves against attempts to refute them in the future as well. On the other hand, this very limitedness condemns our finite minds to be content with rational acceptability as *sufficient proof* of truth: "Whenever we raise truth claims on the basis of good arguments and convincing evidence we *presume* . . . that no new arguments or evidence will crop up in the future that would call our truth claim into question."[53]

It is not so difficult to understand why participants in argumentation, as subjects capable of speech and action, have to behave in this way if we look at a pragmatic description of their discourses, which are embedded in the lifeworld. In everyday practices, as we have seen, socialized individuals are dependent on behavioral certainties, which remain certainties only so long as they are sustained by a knowledge that is accepted unreservedly. Corresponding to this is the grammatical fact that, when we put forward the assertion "*p*" in a performative attitude, we have to believe that "*p*" is true unconditionally even though, when we adopt a reflexive attitude, we cannot rule out that tomorrow, or somewhere else, reasons and evidence could emerge that would invalidate "*p*." However, this does not yet explain why we are *permitted* to regard a truth claim explicitly raised for "*p*" as vindicated as soon as the proposition is rationally accepted under conditions of rational discourse. What does it mean to say that truth claims can be "vindicated" discursively?

The Pragmatic Conception of Truth

It is still unclear *what* it is that *authorizes* us to regard as true a proposition that is presumed to be justified ideally—within the limits of finite minds. Wellmer speaks in this regard of a "surplus" residing in the "anticipation of future corroboration." Perhaps it would be better to say that participants in argumentation who convince themselves of the justification of a controversial validity claim have reached a point where they have been brought by the unconstrained force of the better argument to a certain *shift in perspective*. When, in the course of a process of argumentation, participants attain the conviction that, having taken on board all relevant information and having weighed up all the relevant reasons, they have exhausted the reservoir of potential possible objections to "*p*," then all motives for continuing argumentation have been, as it were, used up. At any rate there is no longer any rational motivation for *retaining* a hypothetical attitude toward the truth claim raised for "*p*" but temporarily left open. From the perspective of actors who have temporarily adopted a reflexive attitude in order to restore a partially disturbed background understanding, the de-problematization of the disputed truth claim means that a license is issued for return to the attitude of actors who are involved in dealing with the world more naively. As soon as the differences in opinion are resolved between "us" and "others" with regard to what is the case, "our" world can merge once more with "the" world.

When this shift takes place we, who as participants in argumentation accept the truth claim for "*p*" as justified, reappoint the state of affairs "that *p*"—problematized up to now—with its rights as an assertion M*p* that can be raised from the perspective of the first person. An assertion that has been *disposed of* argumentatively in this way and returned to the realm of action takes its place in an intersubjectively shared lifeworld from within whose horizon we, the actors, refer to something in a single objective world. It is a matter here of a *formal* supposition, not one that prejudges specific content nor one that suggests the goal of the "correct picture of the nature of things" that Rorty always connects with a realist intuition. Because acting subjects have to cope with "the" world, they cannot avoid being realists in the context of their lifeworld. Moreover, they are allowed to be realists because their language games and practices, so long as they function in a way that is proof against disappointment, "prove their truth" (*sich bewähren*) in being carried on.

This pragmatic authority responsible for certainty—interpreted in a realist way with the help of the supposition of an objective world—is suspended on the reflexive level of discourses, which are relieved of the burdens of action and where only arguments count. Here, our gaze turns away from the objective world, and the disappointments we experience in our direct dealings with it, to focus exclusively on our conflicting interpretations of the world. In this intersubjective dimension of contested interpretations, an assertion "proves its truth" solely on the basis of reasons, that is, with reference to the authority responsible for possible refutation, not for practically experienced disappointment. Here, however, the fallibilist consciousness that we can err even in the case of well-justified beliefs depends on an orientation toward truth whose roots extend into the realism of everyday practices—a realism no longer in force within discourse. The orientation toward unconditional truth, which compels participants in argumentation to presuppose ideal justificatory conditions and requires of them an ever-increasing decentering of the justification community, is a reflex of that other difference—required in the lifeworld—between believing and knowing; this distinction relies on the supposition, anchored in the communicative use of language, of a single objective world.[54] In this way, the lifeworld with its strong, action-related conceptions of truth and knowledge projects into discourse and provides the reference point—transcending justification—that keeps alive among participants in argumentation a consciousness of the fallibility of their interpretations. Conversely, this fallibilist consciousness also reacts back upon everyday practices without thereby destroying the dogmatism of the lifeworld. For actors, who as participants in argumentation have learned that no conviction is proof against criticism, develop in the lifeworld, too, rather less dogmatic attitudes toward their problematized convictions.

This stereoscopic perception of processes of cooperation and communication, *layered* according to action-contexts and discourses, allows us recognize the *embeddedness* of discourses in the lifeworld. Convictions play a different role in action than in discourse and "prove their truth" in a different way in the former than in the latter. In everyday practices, a prereflexive "coping with the world" decides whether convictions "function" or are drawn into the maelstrom of problematization, whereas in argumentation it depends solely on reasons whether controversial validity claims deserve rationally motivated recognition. It is true that the question of the internal relation between justification and truth poses itself only on the reflexive level; however, only the interaction between actions and discourses permits an answer to this question. The contextualist doubt cannot be dissipated so long as we persist in remaining on the level of argumentation and neglect the transformation—secured by personal union, as it were—of the knowledge of those who act into the knowledge of those who argue, while equally neglecting the transfer of knowledge in the opposite direction. Only the entwining of the two different pragmatic roles played by the Janus-faced concept of truth in action-contexts and in rational discourses respectively can explain why a justification successful in a local context points in favor of the context-independent truth of the justified belief. Just as, on the one hand, the concept of truth allows translation of shaken-up behavioral certainties into problematized propositions, so too, on the other hand, does the firmly retained orientation toward truth permit the *translation back* of discursively justified assertions into reestablished behavioral certainties.

To explain this we have only to bring together in the right way the partial statements assembled here up to now. In the lifeworld actors depend on behavioral certainties. They have to cope with a world presumed to be objective and, for this reason, operate with the distinction between believing and knowing.[55] There is a *practical* necessity to rely intuitively on what is unconditionally held-to-be-true. This mode of unconditionally holding-to-be-true is reflected on the discursive level in the connotations of truth claims that point beyond the given context of justification and require the supposition of ideal justificatory conditions—with a resulting decentering of the justification community. For this reason, the process of justification can be guided by a notion of truth that *transcends justification* although it is *always already operatively effective in the realm of action.* The function of the validity of statements in everyday practices explains why the discursive vindication of validity claims may at the same time be interpreted as the satisfaction of a pragmatic need for justification. This need for justification, which sets in train the transformation of shaken-up behavioral certainties into problematized validity claims, can be satisfied only by a translation of discursively justified beliefs back into behavioral truths.

Because it is, in the end, this interaction that dissipates the contextualist doubt about everyday realist intuitions, the objection seems likely that the whole dispute is prejudiced by my tendentious description of the embedding of discourses in the lifeworld. Rorty would certainly not deny the connection between rational discourse and action. He would also agree with our establishing of a connection between the two perspectives: between the perspective of the participants in argumentation who seek to convince each other of the correctness of their interpretations, and the perspective of acting subjects involved in their language games and practices. However, Rorty would not distinguish these perspectives from each other in such a way that the one is relativized against the other. For the purpose of his description, he borrows from the perspective of participants in argumentation the imprisonment in dialogue that prevents us from breaking free from contexts of justification; at the same time, he borrows from the perspective of actors the mode of coping with the world. It is through the *blending into one another* of these opposing perspectives that the ethnocentric certainty is formed—a certainty that prompts Rorty to ask the question of why we should in the first place attempt to bring the contextualist knowledge obtained through reflexive experiences in argumentation into harmony with the everyday realism ascribed to the lifeworld. If the actors in the lifeworld—temporarily—cannot avoid being "realists," so much the worse for them. In that case it is up to the philosophers to reform the misleading commonsense conception of truth.

To be sure, deflationism, operating along the lines of Michael Williams with a semantic conception of truth, is still too strong for this purpose. Instead, Rorty rigorously carries through to its conclusion an epistemization of the concept of truth. Because there is nothing apart from justification, and because nothing follows for the truth of a proposition from its justified assertibility, the concept of truth is *superfluous*. "The difference between justification and truth is one which makes no difference except for the reminder that justification to one audience is not justification to another."[56] Even the only nonredundant use of the truth-predicate—the "cautionary" one—requires reinterpretation. It is a matter of inventing and implementing a new vocabulary that does without a concept of truth and eliminates realist intuitions (such as the supposition of an objective world, talk of representing facts, and so forth): "We simply refuse to talk in a certain way, the Platonic way. . . . Our efforts at persuasion must take the form of gradual inculcation of new ways of speaking, rather than of straightforward argumentation with old ways of speaking."[57]

The Naturalization of Linguistified Reason

Rorty's program of reeducation has provoked questions and objections.[58] In the first instance, Rorty himself must shoulder the burden of proof for his unwillingness to leave the language of common sense as it is. As a rule, pragmatists make substantial allowances for themselves on the basis that their views are at one with common sense. Strangely enough, neopragmatists boast of their role as "atheists in an overwhelmingly religious culture." Their therapy is supposed to reach through the pathological language games of philosophers to the distortions for which Platonism is responsible in daily life itself. In order to make plausible Platonism's idealist violence, Rorty has to let himself in for a diagnosis of the history of

Western metaphysics as a history of decline. However, what Heidegger or Derrida, for example, have to say in their own fairly metaphysical ways about the critique of metaphysics is, on Rorty's estimation, more part of the "edifying" literature that is supposed to be reserved for private perfection of the self and cannot, at any rate, serve the public critique of alienated living conditions.[59]

Of course, more important than the motivation for this enterprise is the question of its viability. I would like to conclude with just two questions in this regard:

a. Is the envisaged revision of our self-understanding compatible with the fact of an ability to learn that is not already constricted a priori?

b. What is to happen to the normative character of reason, and how counterintuitive is the proposed neo-Darwinist self-description of rational beings?

a. The program of a rational revision of deeply rooted Platonic prejudices presumes we are capable of a learning process that not only can take place within a given vocabulary and according to the standards prevailing in a given context but that seizes hold of the vocabulary and standards themselves. This reason alone requires Rorty to provide a suitable equivalent for an orientation toward truth that aims beyond the prevailing context of justification. If, however, the distinction between "true" and "justified" shrinks to the fact that the proponent is prepared to defend "*p*" even in front of a *different* audience, the reference point for such an anticipation [of truth] is missing. Rorty counters this objection by conceding a cautious idealization of justificatory conditions. He allows that what traditionally was called the "pursuit of truth" might just as well be described as the "pursuit of intersubjective, unforced agreement among larger and larger groups of interlocutors": "We hope to justify our belief to as many and as large audiences as possible."[60] Rorty, it is true, does not want this to be understood as an orientation toward an "ever-retreating goal," that is, as a regulative idea. Even the larger audience and the overarching context are supposed to be no more than a different audience and a different context. Nonetheless, Rorty adds to this description the qualifications mentioned: ever-expanding size and ever-increasing diversity—that is, conditions that hamper the possible success of argumentation in certain, not completely arbitrary, ways.

Rorty cannot explain this impediment to the success of argumentation that is unnecessary from a functional point of view. With the orientation toward "more and more," "larger and larger," and "increasingly diverse" audiences, Rorty brings a weak idealization into play that, on his premise, is far from self-evident. As soon as the concept of truth is eliminated in favor of a context-dependent epistemic validity-for-us, the normative reference point necessary to explain why a proponent should endeavor to seek agreement for "*p*" *beyond the boundaries of her own group* is missing. The information that the agreement of an increasingly large audience gives us increasingly less reason to fear that we will be refuted presupposes the very interest that has to be explained: the desire for "as much intersubjective agreement as possible." If something is "true" if and only if it is recognized as justified "by us" because it is good "for us," there is no rational motive for expanding the circle of members. No reason exists for the decentering expansion of the justification community especially since Rorty defines "my own ethnos" as the group in front of which I feel obliged to give an account of myself. There is, however, no normative justification for any further orientation toward the agreement of "strangers," merely an explanatory pointer toward the arbitrary features of a "liberal Western culture" in which "we intellectuals" adopt a more or less undogmatic attitude. But even we are assured by Rorty that, "we must, in practice, privilege our own group, even though there can be no noncircular justification for doing so."[61]

b. In losing the regulative idea of truth, the practice of justification loses that point of orientation by means of which standards of justification are distinguished from "customary" norms. The sociologizing of the practice of justification means a naturalization of reason. As a rule, social norms can be described not merely from the point of view of a sociological observer but also from the perspective of participants in light of the standards they hold to be true. Without a reference to truth or reason, however, the standards themselves would no longer have any possibility of self-correction and would thus for their part forfeit the status of norms capable of being justified. In this respect, they would no longer even be customary norms. They would be *nothing more than* social facts, although they would continue to claim validity "for us," the relevant justification community. If, despite this, the practice of justification is not to collapse, and if the predicate "rational" is not to lose its normative character—that is, if both are to continue to be able to function—the rationality standards valid for us have to be, if not justified, then at least explained.

For this Rorty falls back on a naturalist description of human beings as organisms that develop tools in order to adapt themselves optimally to their environment with the aim of satisfying their needs. Language, too, is such a tool—and not, for instance, a medium for representing reality: "No matter whether the tool is a hammer or a gun or a belief or a statement, tool-using is part of the interaction of the organism with its environment."[62] What appears to us as the normative dimension of the linguistically constituted human mind merely gives expression to the fact that intelligent operations are *functional* for the preservation of a species that, through acting, must "cope" with reality. This neo-Darwinist self-description demands an ironic price. For Rorty, in replacing the "correct description of facts" with "successful adaptation to the environment," merely exchanges one kind of objectivism for another: the objectivism of "represented" reality for the objectivism of instrumentally "mastered" reality. Although admittedly, with this, the direction of fit for interaction between human beings and world is changed, what remains the same is the reference point of an objective world as the totality of everything that we can, in the one case, "represent," in the other, "deal with."

The pragmatic turn was supposed to replace the representationalist model of knowledge with a communication model that sets successful intersubjective mutual understanding (*Verständigung*) in the place of a chimerical objectivity of experience. It is, however, precisely this intersubjective dimension that is in turn closed off in an objectivating description of processes of cooperation and communication that can be grasped as such only from the perspective of participants. Rorty uses a jargon that no longer permits any differentiation between the perspectives of the participant and the observer. Interpersonal relationships, which are owed to the intersubjective possession of a shared language, are assimilated to the pattern of adaptive behavior (or instrumental action). A corresponding dedifferentiation between the strategic and the nonstrategic use of language, between action oriented toward success and action oriented toward reaching understanding, robs Rorty of the conceptual means for doing justice to the intuitive distinctions between convincing and persuading, between motivation through reasons and causal exertion of influence, between learning and indoctrination. The counterintuitive mingling of the one with the other has the unpleasant consequence that we lose the critical standards operating in everyday life. Rorty's naturalist strategy leads to a categorial level- ing of distinctions of such a kind that our descriptions lose their sensitivity for differences that do make a difference in everyday practices.[63]

Notes

1. R. Rorty, "Trotsky and the Wild Orchids," *Common Knowledge* 3 (1992): 140–153.

2. R. Rorty, ed., *The Linguistic Turn. Recent Essays in Philosophical Method* (Chicago, 1970), p. 33.

3. T. W. Adorno, *Negative Dialectics*, trans. by E. B. Ashton (London, 1973), p. 408 (amended translation).

4. M. Williams, *Unnatural Doubts* (Princeton, N.J., 1996), p. 365 (n. 51). Cf. also R. Rorty, "Is Derrida a Quasi-Transcendental Philosopher?," *Contemporary Literature* (1995): 173–200.

5. Cf. The exchange between T. McCarthy and R. Rorty in *Critical Inquiry* 16 (1990): 355–370, 633–641.

6. Rorty, *Linguistic Turn*, p. 39.

7. R. Rorty, *Philosophy and the Mirror of Nature* (Princeton, N.J., 1979), p. 261.

8. [Editor's note:] Habermas notes that in English the word "representation" is used to refer to both *Darstellung* and *Vorstellung*.

9. Rorty, *Philosophy and the Mirror of Nature*, p. 170.

10. H. Putnam, *Realism with a Human Face* (Cambridge, Mass., 1990), p. 28; R. Rorty, "Putnam and the Relativist Menace," *Journal of Philosophy* 90 (1993): 443.

11. Rorty, *Philosophy and the Mirror of Nature*, p. 390.

12. Ibid., p. 179: "[The contexualist view] threatens the neo-Kantian image of philosophy's relation to science and to culture. The urge to say that assertions and actions must not only cohere with other assertions and actions but 'correspond' to something apart from what people are saying and doing has some claim to be called *the* philosophical urge."

13. Ibid., p. 171.

14. Cf. H. Schnädelbach, "Philosophie," in E. Martens and H. Schnädelbach, eds., *Grundkurs Philosophie* (Hamburg, 1985), pp. 37–76.

15. [Editor's note:] Habermas remarks that the subtitle to the German translation of *Philosophy and the Mirror of Nature* is *A Critique of Philosophy* (*Eine Kritik der Philosophie*).

16. Rorty, *Philosophy and the Mirror of Nature*, p. 263.

17. Ibid., p. 339.

18. Ibid.

19. R. Rorty, *Philosophical Papers I: Objectivity, Relativism, and Truth* (Cambridge, 1991), p. 23.

20. Only the empiricists were prepared to call "objective" the experience (*Erfahrung*) that "corresponds to what is there outside" (Rorty). The transcendental idealists, by contrast, reduce even the objectivity of experience to necessary subjective conditions of possible experience.

21. L. Wittgenstein, *On Certainty*, trans. by D. Paul and G. E. M. Anscombe (Oxford, 1969), §115, p. 125.

22. H. Schnädelbach, "Thesen über Geltung und Wahrheit," in *Zur Rehabilitierung des animal rationale* (Frankfurt, 1992), pp. 104–115.

23. With respect to a critique of Rorty's approach, I will confine myself in the following to the problem of truth. However, I would like to indicate, at least, that we would not be able to explain the possibility of learning processes without reference to the capacity for recognizing the same entities under different descriptions.

24. E. Tugendhat, *Traditional and Analytical Philosophy*, trans. P. A. Gorner (Cambridge, 1982), pp. 50ff.

25. Rorty, *Philosophy and the Mirror of Nature*, p. 178.

26. Cf. Williams, *Unnatural Doubts*, p. 232: "We need only ask whether or not the 'direct' grasping of facts on which such comparison depends is supposed to be a cognitive state with propositional content. If it isn't, it can have no impact on verification. But if it is, all we have been given is another kind of belief."

27. Ibid, p. 267.

28. R. Rorty, "Pragmatism, Davidson, and Truth," in E. Lepore, ed., *Truth and Interpretation* (Oxford, 1986), p. 343.

29. Williams, *Unnatural Doubts,* p. 266.

30. Ibid., p. 249.

31. F. Kambartel, "Universalität richtig verstanden," *Deutsche Zeitschrift für Philosophie* 44 (1996): 249.

32. It is no accident that I introduced the formal-pragmatic concept of the grammatical supposition of an objective world in the context of the theory of action. Cf. J. Habermas *The Theory of Communicative Action,* trans. T. McCarthy, vol. 1 (Boston, 1984), pp. 75–101; vol. 2 (Boston, 1987), pp. 119ff.

33. Cf. Williams, *Unnatural Doubts,* p. 238: "All that is involved in the idea of an objective world as 'what is there anyway' is that an objective proposition's being true is one thing and our believing it to be true, or being justified in believing it to be true, something else again."

34. R. Rorty, "Is Truth a Goal of Inquiry? Davidson vs. Wright," *Philosophical Quarterly* 45 (1995): 281–300 (here, p. 300).

35. D. Davidson pursues a third strategy that could be called "theoreticist" or, as he himself proposes, "methodological;" cf. D. Davidson, "The Folly of Trying to Define Truth," *Journal of Philosophy* 93 (1996): 263–278. Davidson uses the semantic conception of truth, understood in a nondeflationary way, as the undefined basic concept for an empirical theory of language. Both the concept of truth, which is used as a theoretical term in his theory of language, and the theory itself, which is supposed to explain the comprehension of linguistic expressions, can prove their truth (*sich bewähren*) at one and the same time. For this reason, Davidson's implicit "theory of truth" can be discussed only in connection with his theory as a whole. In general, I see the following difficulty: on the one hand, Davidson disputes that the concept of truth has a content capable of being explicated, to this extent allying himself with the deflationist polemic against attempts to explain the meaning of truth; on the other hand, he has to secure for the truth-predicate, over and above its disquotational function, a certain content as far as the theory of rationality is concerned in order to explain the veridical nature of beliefs. To this extent he joins forces with Putnam and Dummett, who insist that Tarski's Convention T says nothing about the actual meaning of truth. Standing between these two positions, Davidson, instead of merely using the concept, sees himself compelled to write learned treatises on a concept he declares to be "indefinable"—treatises in which he does, at least, in a metacritical way, isolate the realist intuitions bound up with truth. Cf. D. Davidson, "The Structure and Content of Truth," *Journal of Philosophy* 87 (1990): 279–328. Davidson holds onto the idea that we can know something of an objective world "which is not of our own making." This view separates him from Rorty who attempts in vain to pull Davidson over to his own side of an abolitionist understanding of truth. Cf. D. Davidson, "A Coherence Theory of Truth and Knowledge," in A. Malachowski, ed., *Reading Rorty* (Oxford, 1990), pp. 120–139; cf. also Rorty, "Pragmatism, Davidson, and Truth." For a comparison of Davidson's and my own approaches to the theory of language, see B. Fultner, *Radical Interpretation or Communicative Action* (Ph.D. dissertation, Northwestern University, 1995).

36. K. R. Popper, "Truth, Rationality and the Growth of Scientific Knowledge," in *Conjectures and Refutations* (London, 1963), pp. 215–250.

37. E. Tugendhat, "Tarskis semantische Definition der Wahrheit," *Philosophische Rundschau* 8 (1960): 131–159, reprinted in his *Philosophische Aufsätze* (Frankfurt, 1992), pp. 179–213.

38. I refer here to positions held by P. Horwich and A. Fine; cf. M. Williams, "Do We (Epistemologists) Need a Theory of Truth?," *Philosophical Topics* 14 (1986): 223–242.

39. I introduced this distinction in the Christian Gauss Lectures on founding sociology in the theory of language (1971); cf. J. Habermas, *Vorstudien und Ergänzungen zur Theorie des kommunikativen Handelns* (Frankfurt, 1984), pp. 1–126, esp. pp. 104ff.

40. Habermas, *Theory of Communicative Action,* vol. 1, pp. 22–42.

41. H. Putnam, "Introduction," in *Realism and Reason* (Cambridge, 1983).

42. J. Habermas, "Wahrheitstheorien," in Habermas, *Vorstudien und Ergänzungen zur Theorie des kommunikativen Handelns.*

43. K.-O. Apel, "Fallibilismus, Konsenstheorie der Wahrheit und Letztbegründung," in Forum für Philosophie, ed., *Philosophie und Begründung* (Frankfurt, 1987), pp. 116–211.

44. C. Lafont, "Spannungen im Wahrheitsbegriff," *Deutsche Zeitschrift für Philosophie* 42 (1994): 1007–1023; Williams, *Unnatural Doubts,* pp. 233ff.

45. A. Wellmer, "Ethics and Dialogue," in *The Persistence of Modernity,* trans. D. Midgley (Cambridge, Mass., 1991), p. 175 (amended translation).

46. A. Wellmer, "Wahrheit, Kontingenz, Moderne," in *Endspiele* (Frankfurt, 1993), p. 162. English translation as *Endgames: Essays and Lectures on the Irreconcilable Nature of Modernity* (Cambridge, Mass., 1998).

47. Davidson, "The Structure and Content of Truth," p. 307.

48. R. Rorty, "Sind Aussagen universelle Geltungsansprüche?," *Deutsche Zeitschrift für Philosophie* 6 (1994): 982f.

49. Rorty, "Putnam and the Relativist Menace," pp. 451f.

50. J. Habermas, "Remarks on Discourse Ethics," in *Justification and Application,* trans. C. Cronin (Cambridge, Mass., 1993), pp. 30ff., pp. 58f.

51. L. Wingert, *Gemeinsinn und Moral* (Frankfurt, 1993), p. 277.

52. [Editor's note:] The German term "*sich bewähren*" and its cognates have generally been rendered here as "prove to be true" (in the sense of "turn out to be true"), so as to preserve in translation its connection with "*wahr,*" true. *Sich bewähren* is proving to be true in the sense of standing the test, withstanding critical scrutiny. However, because it is the term that Albrecht Wellmer used to render "corroboration" in his influential discussion of Popper, where the reference is clearly to Wellmer's idea of "anticipating future *Bewährung,*" "corroboration" is used. See A. Wellmer, *Critical Theory of Society,* trans. J. Cumming (New York, 1974).

53. Wellmer, "Wahrheit," p. 163; cf. the corresponding reflections on "superassertibility" in C. Wright, *Truth and Objectivity* (Cambridge, Mass., 1992).

54. Cf. Lafont "Spannungen im Wahrheitsbegriff," p. 1021: "Only the presupposition of a single objective world . . . permits [us] to make the unconditional validity of truth compatible with a fallible understanding of knowledge."

55. I cannot in the present context deal with moral and other normative validity claims that have a built-in orientation toward discursive vindication. They lack the property of "transcending justification" that accrues to truth claims through the supposition of a single objective world built into the communicative use of language. Normative validity claims are raised for interpersonal relationships within a social world that is not independent of "our making" in the same way as is the objective world. The discursive treatment of normative claims is, however, "analogous to truth" insofar as the participants in practical discourse are guided by the goal of a commanded, permitted, or forbidden "single right answer." The social world is intrinsically historical, that is, ontologically constituted in a different way than the objective world. For this reason, in the case of the social world, the idealization of the justificatory conditions cannot include an "anticipation of future corroboration (*Bewährung*)," in the sense of an anticipated refutation of future objections (Wingert), but only in the critical sense of a proviso concerning approximation, that is, a proviso concerning the justification community's actually achieved state of decentering. The discursive vindication of a truth claim says that the truth conditions, interpreted as assertibility conditions, are satisfied. In the case of a normative validity claim, the discursively achieved agreement grounds the corresponding norm's worthiness to be recognized; to this extent the agreement itself contributes to the satisfaction of the norm's conditions of validity. Whereas rational acceptability merely indicates the truth of a proposition, it provides a constructive contribution to the validity of norms.

56. Rorty, "Is Truth a Goal of Inquiry?," p. 300.

57. R. Rorty, "Relativism: Finding and Making," Ms. (1995), p. 5.

58. T. McCarthy, "Philosophy and Social Practice: Richard Rorty's 'New Pragmatism,'" in *Ideals and Illusions* (Cambridge, Mass., 1991), pp. 11–34.

59. R. Rorty, "Habermas, Derrida, and the Functions of Philosophy," *Revue Internationale de Philosophie* 49 (1995), 437–460; cf. my reply in ibid., pp. 553–556.

60. Rorty, "Is Truth a Goal of Inquiry?," p. 298.

61. Rorty, *Philosophical Papers I*, p. 29.

62. Rorty, "Relativism: Finding and Making," pp. 11f.

63. The same objectivism and the same kind of insensitivity could be shown through reference to Rorty's egocentric or ethnocentric description of processes of interpretation, for example, of hard cases of intercultural understanding (*Verständigung*). Unlike Gadamer, Rorty does not have recourse to the symmetrical conditions for an adoption of perspectives learned by speakers and hearers in learning the system of personal pronouns and making possible a reciprocal convergence of interpretive

horizons that, initially, are far apart. Instead, he takes as his starting point an asymmetrical relationship between "us" and "them," so that we have to judge their utterances according to our standards and assimilate their standards to ours; cf. J. Habermas, *Postmetaphysical Thinking,* trans. W. M. Hohengarten (Cambridge, Mass., 1992), pp. 135ff. This assimilatory model of understanding (*Verstehen*) partially coincides with Davidson's model of interpretation. However, what for Davidson is the result of a methodological decision to view the interpretation of linguistic expressions as the application of the hypotheses of an empirically turned theory of truth, results for Rorty from the decision (of strategic significance for his theory) in favor of a naturalist descriptive vocabulary.

On the Distinction between Poetic and Communicative Uses of Language (1985)

1

From this complex discussion [between Jacques Derrida and John Searle],[1] Jonathan Culler selects as the central issue the question of whether John Austin succeeds in making what appears to be a totally harmless, provisional, and purely methodological move. Austin wants to analyze the rules intuitively mastered by competent speakers, in accordance with which typical speech acts can be executed successfully. He begins this analysis by focusing on sentences from *normal* everyday practices that are uttered seriously and used as *simply* and *literally* as possible. Thus, the unit of analysis, the standard speech act, is the result of certain abstractions. The theoretician of speech acts directs his attention to a sample of normal linguistic utterances from which all complex, derivative, parasitic, and deviant cases have been excluded. Underlying this demarcation is a conception of "customary" or normal linguistic practice—a concept of "ordinary language" whose harmlessness and consistency Derrida calls into question. Austin's intention is clear: he wants to analyze the universal properties of, for example, "promises" with respect to cases in which the utterance of corresponding sentences actually *functions* as a promise. Now, there are contexts in which such sentences lose the illocutionary force of a promise. Spoken by an actor on the stage, as part of a poem, or even within a monologue, a promise, as Austin tells us, becomes "peculiarly null and void." The same holds for a promise that occurs in a quotation, or for one that is merely mentioned. In such contexts, there is no *serious* or *binding* use, and sometimes not even a *literal* use, of the corresponding performative sentence, but rather a derivative or parasitic use. As Searle repeats insistently, fictional or simulated or indirect modes of use are "parasitic" in the sense that logically they presuppose the possibility of a serious, literal, and binding use of the sentences grammatically appropriate for promises. Culler extracts essentially three objections from Derrida's texts; these are aimed at showing the impossibility of such a use of language and are meant to demonstrate that the usual distinctions between serious and simulated, literal and metaphorical, everyday and fictional, and customary and parasitic modes of speech collapse.

   a. With his initial argument, Derrida posits a not very illuminating link between quotability and iterability, on the one hand, and fictionality, on the other. The quotation of a promise is only apparently something secondary in comparison with a directly made promise, for the indirect reporting of a performative utterance in a quotation is a form of repetition, and as quotability presupposes the possibility of repetition in accordance with a rule, that is, conventionality, it belongs to the essence of every conventionally generated utterance—and thus also to that of performative utterances—that it can be quoted and, in the broader sense, fictionally reproduced: "If it were not possible for a character in a play to make a promise, there could be no promises in real life, for what makes it possible to promise, as Austin tells us, is the existence of a conventional procedure, of formulas one can repeat. For me to be able to make a promise in 'real life,' there must be iterable procedures or formulas such as are used on stage. 'Serious' behavior is a special case of role-playing."[2]

   In this argument, Derrida obviously already presupposes what he wants to prove: that every convention that permits the repetition of exemplary actions intrinsically possesses not merely a symbolic but also a fictional character. But it would first have to be shown that conventions relating to play ultimately are indistinguishable from norms of action. Austin uses the quotation of a promise as an example of a derivative or parasitic form because the illocutionary force is removed from the quoted promise through the form of indirect speech: it is thereby taken out of the context in which it "functions," that is, in which it coordinates the actions of the various participants in interaction and gives rise to consequences relevant for action. Only the speech act actually performed in a given instance is *effective as action;* the promise mentioned in quotation, or reported, depends grammatically upon this. Such a setting depriving it of its illocutionary force constitutes the bridge between quotation and fictional representation. Even action on the stage rests on a basis of everyday actions (on the part of the actors, director, stageworkers, and theater employees); in the context of this framework, promises can function *in a different way* than they do "on stage," giving rise to obligations relevant for the sequel of action. Derrida makes no attempt to "deconstruct" this distinctive functional mode of everyday language within communicative action. In the illocutionary binding and bonding (*bindende*) force of linguistic utterances, Austin discovered a mechanism for coordinating action that subjects normal speech— speech that is part of everyday practices—to constraints different from those of fictional speech, simulation, and interior monologue. The constraints under which illocutionary acts develop an action-coordinating force and give rise to consequences relevant for action define the domain of "normal" language. They can be analyzed as those idealizing suppositions that we have to make in communicative action.

b. The second argument raised by Culler, with Derrida, against Austin and Searle relates to just such idealizations. Any generalizing analysis of speech acts has to be able to specify general contextual conditions for the illocutionary success of standardized speech acts. Searle, in particular, has taken on this task.[3] Linguistic expressions, however, change their meanings depending on shifting contexts; moreover, contexts are so constituted as to be open to ever-wider-reaching specification. It is one of the peculiarities of our language that we can release utterances from their original contexts and transplant them into different ones—Derrida speaks of "grafting." In this manner, we can, in relation to a speech act such as a "marriage vow," think of ever-new and more improbable contexts; the specification of general contextual conditions does not run up against any natural limits: "Suppose that the requirements for a marriage ceremony were met but that one of the partners were under hypnosis, or again that the ceremony were impeccable in all respects but had been called a 'rehearsal,' or finally, that while the speaker was a minister licensed to perform weddings and the couple had obtained a license, the three of them were on this occasion acting in a play that, coincidentally, included a wedding ceremony."[4] Such a variation of contexts producing changes in meaning cannot in principle be arrested or controlled, because contexts cannot be exhausted, that is, they cannot be mastered theoretically once and for all. Culler shows convincingly that Austin cannot escape this difficulty even by taking refuge in the intentions of speakers and hearers. It is not the thoughts of bride, bridegroom, or priest that decide the validity of the ceremony, but their actions and the circumstances under which they are carried out. "What counts is the plausibility of the description of the circumstances: whether the features of the context adduced create a frame that alters the illocutionary force of the utterances."[5]

Searle has reacted to this difficulty by introducing a qualification to the effect that the literal meaning of a sentence does not completely fix the validity conditions of the speech act in which it is employed; rather, it depends on tacit supplementation by a system of background assumptions regarding the normality of general conditions in the world. These prereflective background certainties are of a holistic nature; they cannot be exhausted by a countably finite set of specifications. Sentence-meanings, no matter how well analyzed, thus are valid only relative to a shared background knowledge that is constitutive of the lifeworld of a linguistic community. However, Searle makes clear that positing such a relation by no means brings with it the meaning-relativism that Derrida aims to show. So long as language games are functioning and the preunderstanding constitutive of the lifeworld has not broken down, participants reckon with conditions in the world—and clearly, rightly so—that are assumed as "normal" in their linguistic community. And in cases where individual background convictions do become problematic, they further assume that they could in principle reach a rationally motivated agreement. Both are strong, that is to say, idealizing suppositions; but these idealizations are not logocentric, arbitrary acts that theoreticians bring to bear on unmanageable contexts in order to give the appearance of mastering them; rather, they are presuppositions that the participants themselves have to make if communicative action is to be possible at all.

    c. The role of idealizing suppositions can also be clarified in connection with some other consequences of this same state of affairs. Because contexts are changeable and can be expanded in any direction whatsoever, the same text can be open to different readings; it is the text itself that makes possible its uncontrollable effective history (*Wirkungsgeschichte*). However, Derrida's deliberately paradoxical statement that every interpretation is inevitably a misinterpretation, and every understanding a misunderstanding, does not follow from this venerable hermeneutic insight. Culler justifies the statement "All readings are misreadings" as follows: "If a text can be understood, it can in principle be understood repeatedly, by different readers in different circumstances. These acts of reading or understanding are not, of course, identical. They involve modifications and differences, but differences which are deemed not to matter. We can thus say . . . that understanding is a special case of misunderstanding, a particular deviation or determination of misunderstanding. It is misunderstanding whose misses do not matter."[6] However, Culler leaves one thing out of consideration. The productivity of the process of understanding remains unproblematic only so long as all participants retain hold of the reference point of a possible, actually reached, mutual understanding (*Verständigung*) in which the *same* utterances are assigned the *same* meaning. As Gadamer has shown, even the hermeneutic endeavor, which aims to bridge temporal and cultural distances, remains oriented toward the idea of a possible, actually achieved, agreement.

    Under the pressure to make decisions inherent in everyday communicative practices, participants are dependent on an action-coordinating agreement. The more removed interpretations are from this kind of "serious situation," the more they can free themselves from the idealizing supposition of an achievable consensus. But they can never wholly free themselves from the idea that misinterpretations would in principle have to be criticizable in terms of an agreement aimed for in an ideal way. The interpreter does not impose this idea on her object; rather, in the performative attitude of a participating observer, she takes it over from those participating directly who can *act communicatively only on the presupposition of inter-subjectively identical ascriptions of meaning*. Thus, I do not wish to marshal a Wittgensteinian positivism of language games against Derrida's thesis. It is not any given habitualized practice that decides just what meaning is attributed to a text or an utterance.[7] Rather, language games work only because they presuppose idealizations that transcend any particular language game, idealizations that—as a necessary condition of possible mutual understanding—give rise to the perspective of an agreement that is open to criticism on the basis of validity claims. A language operating under these kinds of constraints is subject to an ongoing test. Everyday communicative practices, in which actors have to reach understanding about something in the world, stand under the need to prove their worth; such a proof of worth is made possible in the first place by these idealizing suppositions. It is on the basis of this need for everyday linguistic practices to prove their worth that one may distinguish, with Austin and Searle, between "customary" and "parasitic" uses of language.

Up to this point I have criticized Derrida's third and fundamental assumption only to the extent that (against Culler's reconstruction of Derridian arguments) I have defended the possibility of demarcating normal language from *derivative* forms. I have not yet shown how fictional speech can be demarcated from the normal (that is, everyday) use of language. This aspect is the most important one for Derrida. If "literature" and "writing" constitute the model for a universal insurmountable textual context within which all genre distinctions ultimately dissolve, they cannot be split off from other discourses as an autonomous realm of fiction. For the literary critics who follow Derrida in the United States, the thesis of the autonomy of the linguistic work of art is unacceptable for the further reason that they want to set themselves off from the formalism of New Criticism and from structuralist aesthetics.

The Prague Structuralists originally tried to distinguish poetic from ordinary language with respect to the relation of each to extralinguistic reality. Insofar as language occurs in *communicative functions,* it has to produce relations between the linguistic expression and speaker, hearer, and state of affairs represented. Bühler conceptualized this in his semiotic schema as the sign functions of expression, appeal, and representation.[8] To the extent that language fulfills a poetic function, however, it does so in the reflexive relation of the linguistic expression to itself. Consequently, reference to an object, informational content, and truth-value—validity conditions in general—are extrinsic to poetic language; an utterance is poetic to the extent that it is directed to the linguistic medium itself, to its own linguistic form. Roman Jakobson integrated this specification into an expanded schema of language functions. In addition to the basic functions, which go back to Bühler—expressing the speaker's intentions, establishing interpersonal relations, and representing states of affairs—and two further functions relating to making contact and to the code, he ascribes to linguistic utterances a poetic function, which directs our attention to "the message as such."[9] We are less concerned here with a closer characterization of the poetic function (in accordance with which the principle of equivalence is projected from the axis of selection to the axis of combination) than with an interesting consequence that is important for our problem of delimiting normal (from other kinds of) speech: "Any attempt to reduce the sphere of poetic function to poetry or to confine poetry to poetic function would be a delusive oversimplification. Poetic function is not the sole function of verbal art, but only its dominant, determining function, whereas in all other verbal activities it acts as a subsidiary, accessory constituent. This function, by promoting the palpability of signs, deepens the fundamental dichotomy of signs and objects. Hence, when dealing with poetic function, linguistics cannot limit itself to the field of poetry."[10] Poetic speech, therefore, is to be distinguished only by virtue of the primary and structure-forming force of a certain function that is always fulfilled together with other language functions.

Richard Ohmann makes use of Austin's approach in order to examine the specific features of poetic language in this sense. For him, the phenomenon in need of explanation is the fictionality of the linguistic work of art, that is, the generation of aesthetic appearance (*Schein*), with which a second arena, specifically removed from reality, is opened up on the basis of ongoing everyday practices. What distinguishes poetic language is its "world-generating" capacity: "A literary work creates a world . . . by providing the reader with *impaired* and incomplete speech acts which he completes by supplying the appropriate circumstances."[11] The peculiar *disempowerment* of speech acts, which generates fictions, consists in the fact that speech acts are robbed of their illocutionary force, retaining illocutionary meanings only as refracted by indirect reporting or quotation: "A literary work is a discourse whose sentences lack the illocutionary forces that would normally attach to them. Its illocutionary force is mimetic. . . . Specifically, a literary work purportedly imitates a series of speech acts, which in fact have no other existence. By doing so, it leads the reader to imagine a speaker, a situation, a set of ancillary events, and so on."[12] The bracketing of illocutionary force virtualizes the relations to the world in which the speech acts are involved thanks to their illocutionary force, and releases the participants in interaction from an obligation to reach understanding about something in the world on the basis of idealizing suppositions in such a way that they can coordinate their plans of action and thus enter into obligations relevant to the sequel of action: "Since the quasi-speech acts of literature are not *carrying on the world's business*—describing, urging, contracting, etc.—the reader may well attend to them in a nonpragmatic way."[13] Neutralizing their binding and bonding force relieves the disempowered illocutionary acts from the pressure to make decisions intrinsic to everyday communicative practices, removes them from the sphere of normal speech, and thereby empowers them for the playful creation of new worlds—or, rather, for the unmitigated demonstration of the world-disclosing force of innovative linguistic expressions. This specialization in the world-disclosing function of language explains the peculiar self-referentiality of poetic language to which Jakobson refers and that prompts Geoffrey Hartman to pose the rhetorical question: "Is not literary language the name we give to a diction whose frame of reference is such that the words stand out as words (even as sounds) rather than being, at once, assimilable meanings?"[14]

Mary L. Pratt refers to Ohmann's studies[15] in order to refute—admittedly by means of speech-act theory—the thesis of the independence of the literary work of art in Derrida's sense. She does not consider fictionality, the bracketing of illocutionary force, and the uncoupling of poetic language from everyday communicative practices to be decisive selective criteria, because fictional elements of language such as jokes, irony, fantasies, stories, and parables pervade our everyday discourse and in no way constitute an autonomous universe cut off from "the world's business." Conversely, works of nonfiction, memoirs, travel reports, historical romances, even *romans à clef* or thrillers that, like Truman Capote's *In Cold Blood,* adapt a factually documented case in no way create an unambiguously fictional world, even though we often count these productions, for the most part at least, as "literature." Pratt uses the results of studies in sociolinguistics by W. Labov[16] to prove that natural narratives, that is, the "stories" told spontaneously or on request in everyday life, obey the same rhetorical laws of construction as, and exhibit similar structural characteristics to, literary narratives. "Labov's data make it necessary to account for narrative rhetoric in terms that are not exclusively literary; the fact that fictive or mimetically organized utterances can occur in almost any realm of extraliterary discourse requires that we do the same for fictivity or mimesis. In other words, the relation between a work's fictivity and its literariness is indirect."[17]

Nonetheless, the fact that normal language is permeated with fictional, narrative, metaphorical—in general, with rhetorical—elements does not yet speak against the attempt to explain the autonomy of the linguistic work of art by the bracketing of illocutionary forces. For, according to Jakobson, fictionality is a distinguishing feature suited to demarcating literature from everyday discourses only to the extent that the world-disclosing function of language predominates over the other linguistic functions and determines the structure of the linguistic construct. In a certain respect, it is the refraction and partial sublation (*Aufhebung*) of illocutionary validity claims that distinguishes the story from the eyewitness statement, teasing from insulting, irony from misleading, hypothesis from assertion, fantasy from perception, the training maneuver from the act of warfare, and the imagined scenario from the report on an actual catastrophe. But in none of these cases do the illocutionary acts lose their action-coordinating binding and bonding force. Even in the cases adduced for the sake of comparison, the communicative functions of the speech act remain intact insofar as the fictional elements cannot be detached from contexts of life-practice. The world-disclosing function of language does not gain independence vis-à-vis the expressive, regulative, and informative functions. By contrast, precisely this may be the case in Truman Capote's literary treatment of a particular event, notorious in legal circles and carefully researched; for what grounds the *primacy* and the structuring force of the poetic function is not the deviation of a fictional representation from the documentary report of an event, but the exemplary way of dealing with it that takes the case out of its context and makes it the occasion for an innovative, world-disclosing, and eye-opening representation in which the rhetorical means of representation depart from communicative routines and take on a life of their own.

It is interesting to see how Pratt is compelled to work out this poetic function against her will. Her sociolinguistic counterproposal begins with an analysis of the speech situation that poetic speech shares with other discourses—that arrangement whereby a narrator or lecturer turns to a public and calls its attention to a text. The text is subjected to certain procedures of preparation and selection before it is ready for delivery. Finally, before a text can lay claim to the patience and capacity for judgment of the audience, it has to satisfy certain criteria of relevance: it *has to be worth telling*. The tellability is assessed in terms of the manifestation of some significant exemplary experience. In its content, a tellable text reaches beyond the local context of the immediate speech situation and is open to further elaboration: "As might be expected, these two features—contextual detachability and susceptibility to elaboration—are equally important characteristics of literary utterances."[18] Of course, literary texts share these characteristics with "display texts" in general. The latter are characterized with respect to their special communicative functions: they are designed to serve "a purpose I have described as that of verbally representing states of affairs and experiences which are held to be unusual or problematic in such a way that the addressee will respond affectively in the intended way, adopt the intended evaluation and interpretation, take pleasure in doing so, and generally find the whole undertaking worth it."[19] One sees how the pragmatic analyst of language stalks literary texts from outside, as it were. Of course, the latter have to satisfy a final condition; in the case of literary texts, tellability must gain predominance over other functional characteristics: "In the end, tellability can take precedence over assertibility itself."[20] Only in this case do the functional demands and structural constraints of everyday communicative practices (which Pratt defines by means of Grice's conversational postulates) lose their force. That everyone is concerned to present her contribution to the conversation informatively, to be relevant, straightforward, and to avoid obscure, ambiguous, and longwinded utterances are idealizing suppositions of *normal language* in communicative action, but not of poetic speech: "Our tolerance, indeed propensity, for elaboration when dealing with the tellable suggests that, in Gricean terms, the standards of quantity, quality, and manner for display texts differ from those Grice suggests for declarative speech in his maxims."[21]

In the end, the analysis leads to a confirmation of the thesis that it would like to refute. To the degree that the poetic, world-disclosing function of language gains primacy and structure-forming force, language escapes the structural constraints and communicative functions of everyday life. The space of fiction, which is opened up when linguistic forms of expression become reflexive, results from the fact that the illocutionary binding and bonding forces become ineffective—as do the idealizations that make possible a use of language oriented toward reaching understanding, thereby enabling a coordination of plans of action that operates via the intersubjective recognition of criticizable validity claims. One can also read Derrida's debate with Austin as a denial of this domain of everyday communicative practices, which is structured according to a logic of its own; the denial of such a domain corresponds to the denial of an autonomous realm of fiction.

2

Because Derrida denies both of the above, he is able to analyze any given discourse in accordance with the model of poetic language, and do so as though language in general were determined by the poetic use of language specialized in world-disclosure. From this viewpoint, language as such converges with literature or indeed with "writing." This *aestheticizing of language, which is purchased with the twofold denial of the independent logics of normal and poetic speech,* also explains Derrida's insensitivity toward the tension-filled polarity between the poetic, world-disclosing function of language and its prosaic, innerworldly functions; these functions are taken into account by a modified version of Bühler's schema of language functions.[22]

Linguistically mediated processes such as the acquisition of knowledge, the transmission of culture, the formation of personal identity, socialization, and social integration involve mastering problems posed in the world; they owe the independence of learning processes, which Derrida cannot acknowledge, to the independent logics of these problems and the linguistic medium tailored to deal with them. For Derrida, linguistically mediated processes in the world are embedded in a *world-constituting* context that prejudices everything; they are fatalistically at the mercy of the happenings of text creation beyond their control, overwhelmed by the poetic-creative transformation of a background designed by archewriting, and condemned to be temporally and spatially limited. An aesthetic contextualism blinds him to the fact that everyday communicative practices, by virtue of their built-in idealizations, make possible learning processes in the world, in relation to which the world-disclosing power of interpreting language has to *prove its worth.* These learning processes develop an independent logic that transcends all local barriers because experiences and judgments are formed only in the light of criticizable validity claims. Derrida neglects the potential for negation inherent in the validity basis of action oriented toward reaching understanding; he allows the capacity to solve problems to disappear behind the world-creating capacity of language; the former capacity is possessed by language as the medium through which those acting communicatively enter into relations to the world whenever they reach understanding with one another about something in the objective world, in their common social world, or in the subjective worlds to which each has privileged access.

Richard Rorty carries out a similar act of leveling. Unlike Derrida, however, he does not remain idealistically fixated upon the history of metaphysics as a transcendent happening (*Übergeschehen*) that determines everything within the world. According to Rorty, science and morality, economics and politics, are at the mercy of a process of language-creating protuberances in *just the same way* as art and philosophy. Like Kuhnian history of science, the flux of interpretations flows rhythmically between the revolutionizing and normalization of language. Rorty observes this back-and-forth movement between two situations in all domains of cultural life:

One is the sort of situation encountered when people pretty much agree on what is wanted, and are talking about how best to get it. In such a situation there is no need to say anything terribly unfamiliar, for argument is typically about the truth of assertions rather than about the utility of vocabularies. The contrasting situation is one in which everything is up for grabs at once—in which the motives and the terms of discussions are a central subject of argument. . . . In such periods people begin to toss around old words in new senses, to throw in the occasional neologism, and thus to hammer out a new idiom which initially attracts attention to itself and only later gets put to work.[23]

One notices how the Nietzschean pathos of a *Lebensphilosophie* that has made the linguistic turn beclouds the sober insights of pragmatism; in the picture painted by Rorty, the renovative process of linguistic world-disclosure no longer has a *counterpoise* in the processes of critical testing that are part of innerworldly practices. The "yes" and "no" of communicatively acting actors is prejudiced and rhetorically overdetermined by their linguistic contexts to such a degree that the anomalies occurring during the phases of exhaustion are presented only as symptoms of waning vitality, as aging processes, as processes analogous to natural ones—and are not seen as the result of *unsuccessful* solutions to problems and *invalid* answers.

Innerworldly linguistic practices draw their power of negation from validity claims that go beyond the horizons of the currently given context. But the contextualist conception of language, laden as it is with *Lebensphilosophie*, is insensitive to the actually existing force of the counterfactual, which makes itself felt in the idealizing presuppositions of communicative action. For this reason, Derrida and Rorty also fail to recognize the peculiar status of discourses, which are differentiated from everyday communication and tailored to a single validity dimension (truth or normative rightness), that is, to a single complex of problems (questions of truth or justice). In modern societies, the spheres of science, morality, and law have crystallized around these forms of argumentation. The corresponding cultural systems of action administer *problemsolving capacities* in a way similar to that in which the enterprises of art and literature administer *capacities for world-disclosure*. Because Derrida overgeneralizes this one linguistic function—the poetic—he no longer notices the complex relation between the normal language of everyday practices and the two noneveryday spheres, which are differentiated, as it were, in opposite directions. The polar tension between world-disclosure and problemsolving is held together within the cluster of functions of everyday language; but art and literature, on the one hand, and science, morality, and law, on the other, specialize in experiences and kinds of knowledge that develop and can be worked out within the catchment area of just *one* linguistic function and *one* dimension of validity, respectively. Derrida holistically levels these complicated relations in order to equate philosophy with literature and criticism. He fails to recognize the special status that both philosophy and literary criticism, each in its own way, assume as mediators between the cultures of experts and the everyday world.

On the one hand, literary criticism, institutionalized in Europe since the eighteenth century, contributes to the differentiation of art [from other value spheres]. It reacts to the increasing autonomy of linguistic works of art by means of discourses specializing in questions of taste. In such discourses, the claims with which literary texts appear are submitted to examination—claims to "artistic truth," aesthetic harmony, exemplary validity, innovative power, and authenticity. In this respect, aesthetic criticism is similar to the forms of argumentation specializing in propositional truth and normative rightness, that is, to theoretical and practical discourses. It is, however, not merely an esoteric component of a culture of experts but, over and above this, has the task of mediating between the cultures of experts and the everyday world.

This *bridging function* of art criticism is more clearly evident with regard to music and the plastic arts than with regard to literary works, which are, of course, already formulated in the medium of language, even if it is a poetic, self-referential one. In this second, exoteric respect, criticism accomplishes a process of translation of a unique kind. It draws the experiential content of the work of art into normal language; the innovative potential of art and literature for the forms of life and life-histories that reproduce themselves via everyday communicative action can be unleashed only in this maieutic way. This innovative potential then finds expression in the changed composition of an evaluative vocabulary—in the renovation of value-orientations and need interpretations—which alters the tincture of modes of life through altering modes of perception.

Like literary criticism, philosophy, too, takes up a position with two fronts—or at least this is true of modern philosophy, which no longer promises to vindicate the claims of religion in the name of theory. On the one hand, it directs its interest to the foundations of science, morality, and law and attaches theoretical claims to its statements. It distinguishes itself by posing problems with a universalist thrust and by its strong theoretical strategies, thereby maintaining an intimate relationship with the sciences. And yet philosophy is not simply an esoteric component of a culture of experts. It maintains just as intimate a relationship with the totality of the lifeworld and with sound common sense, even if it relentlessly and subversively shakes up the certainties of everyday practices. In the face of systems of knowledge differentiated according to particular dimensions of validity, philosophical thinking represents the lifeworld's interests in the totality of functions and structures that are clustered together and combined in communicative action. Admittedly, it maintains this relation to totality by means of a reflexivity lacking in the lifeworld's background, which is present intuitively.

If one becomes aware of this (here merely sketched) two-front position of [literary] criticism and philosophy—toward the everyday world, on the one hand, and toward the special cultures of art and literature, science, morality, and law, on the other—it becomes clear what the leveling of the genre distinction between philosophy and literature, and the assimilation of philosophy to literature and of literature to philosophy (as contended above), mean. Such a leveling mixes up the constellations in which the rhetorical elements of language take on *entirely different roles*. The rhetorical element occurs in its *pure form* only in the self-referentiality of poetic expression, that is, in the language of fiction, which specializes in world-disclosure. The normal language of everyday life, too, is ineradicably rhetorical; but here, within the cluster of multiple language functions, the rhetorical elements recede. In the routines of everyday practices, the world-constituting linguistic framework is nearly paralyzed. The same holds for the specialized languages of science and technology, law, morality, economics, political science, and so forth. They, too, are nourished by the illuminating power of metaphorical tropes; but the rhetorical elements—although by no means exterminated—are tamed, as it were, and enlisted for special purposes of problem-solving.

The rhetorical dimension plays a different and more important role in the languages of literary criticism and philosophy. Both are faced with tasks that are paradoxical in similar ways. They are supposed to feed the contents of expert cultures, in each of which knowledge is accumulated under just one aspect of validity, into everyday linguistic practices in which the various language functions and aspects of validity remain intermeshed, forming a syndrome. At the same time literary criticism and philosophy are supposed to accomplish this task of mediation using means of expression taken from particular languages specializing in questions of taste or truth. They can resolve this paradox only by rhetorically expanding and enriching their special languages to the extent required to link up—in a targeted way—indirect communications with manifest propositional contents. This explains the strong rhetorical strain characteristic of studies by literary critics and philosophers alike. Eminent critics and major philosophers are also writers of stature. In their rhetorical accomplishments, literary criticism and philosophy have a family relationship with literature—and to this extent, with one another as well. However, their family relationship does not extend beyond this. For, in each of these enterprises, the tools of rhetoric are subordinated respectively to the discipline of a *different* form of argumentation.

If, following Derrida's recommendation, philosophical thinking were to be relieved of the duty of solving problems and made to assume the function of literary criticism, it would be robbed not merely of its seriousness, but also of its productivity and capacity for achievement. Conversely, the literary-critical capacity for judgment loses its potency when, as envisioned by Derrida's disciples in literature departments, it switches from appropriating the content of aesthetic experience into a critique of metaphysics. The false assimilation of one enterprise to the other robs both of their substance. And so we return to the issue with which we started. Whoever transposes the radical critique of reason into the domain of rhetoric in order to defuse the paradox of self-referentiality also dulls the sword of the critique of reason. The false pretension of eliminating the genre distinction between philosophy and literature cannot lead us out of this aporia.[24]

Notes

1. [Editor's note]: Habermas is here referring to the 1970s debate between Jacques Derrida and John Searle. In his essay "Signature Event Context," in *Margins of Philosophy* (Chicago, 1982), pp. 307–330, Derrida devotes the last section to a discussion of Austin's theory. Searle refers to this in "Reiterating the Differences: A Reply to Derrida," *Glyph* 1 (1977): 198–208 (Derrida's essay also appeared in *Glyph* 1). Derrida's response appeared in *Glyph* 2 (1977): 162–254, under the title "Limited Inc abc. . . ." In his discussion of Derrida, Habermas draws on J. Culler, *On Deconstruction* (Ithaca, N.Y., 1982).

2. Culler, *On Deconstruction,* p. 119.

3. J. Searle, *Speech Acts* (Cambridge, 1969), and *Expression and Meaning* (Cambridge, 1979).

4. Culler, *On Deconstruction,* pp. 121ff.

5. Ibid., p. 123.

6. Ibid., p. 176.

7. Cf. ibid., pp. 130ff.

8. K. Bühler, *Sprachtheorie* (Jena, 1934), pp. 24ff.

9. R. Jakobson, "Linguistics and Poetics," in T. A. Sebeok, ed., *Style in Language* (Cambridge, Mass., 1960), pp. 350–377, here p. 356.

10. Ibid.

11. R. Ohmann, "Speech-Acts and the Definition of Literature," *Philosophy and Rhetoric* 4 (1971): 17.

12. Ibid., p. 14.

13. Ibid., p. 17.

14. G. Hartman, *Saving the Text* (Baltimore, 1981), p. xxi.

15. Cf. also R. Ohmann, "Speech, Literature and the Space Between," *New Literary History* 5 (1974): 34ff.

16. W. Labov, *Language in the Inner City* (Philadelphia, 1972).

17. M. L. Pratt, *A Speech Act Theory of Literary Discourse* (Bloomington, 1977), p. 92. I am grateful to Jonathan Culler for drawing my attention to this interesting book.

18. Ibid., p. 148.

19. Ibid.

20. Ibid., p. 147.

21. Ibid.

22. Cf. J. Habermas, *The Theory of Communicative Action,* vol. 1, trans. T. McCarthy (Boston, 1984), pp. 273ff.

23. R. Rorty, "Deconstruction and Circumvention," in his *Philosophical Papers II: Essays on Heidegger and Others* (Cambridge, 1991), pp. 85–107, here p. 88, and *Consequences of Pragmatism* (Minneapolis, 1982), esp. the introduction and chapters 6, 7, and 9.

24. At any rate, our reflections have brought us to the point from where we can see why Heidegger, Adorno, and Derrida get into this aporia at all. They continue to defend themselves as though, like the first generation of Hegelian disciples, they were still living in the shadow of the "last" philosopher. They are still battling against the "strong" conceptions of theory, truth, and system that have in fact belonged to the past for over a century and a half. They still think they have to arouse philosophy from what Derrida calls "the dream of its heart." They believe they have to tear philosophy away from the delusion of expounding a theory that has the last word. Such a comprehensive, closed, and definitive system of propositions would have to be formulated in a language that is self-explicating, that neither needs nor permits further commentary, and that thereby brings to a standstill the effective history (*Wirkungsgeschichte*) in which interpretation is heaped upon interpretation endlessly. Rorty speaks of the demand for a language "which can receive no gloss, requires no interpretation, cannot be distanced, cannot be sneered at by later generations. It is the hope for a vocabulary which is intrinsically and self-evidently final, not only the most comprehensive and fruitful vocabulary we have come up with so far" (Rorty, *Consequences of Pragmatism,* pp. 93f.).

If reason were bound, under penalty of demise, to hold on to these classical goals of metaphysics, pursued from Parmenides to Hegel; if reason as such (even after Hegel) stood before the alternative of either insisting on the strong conceptions of theory, truth, and system as they were customary in the great tradition or of renouncing itself, then an *adequate* critique of reason would have to be so very radical that it could scarcely avoid the paradox of self-referentiality. Nietzsche saw the matter in this way. And, unfortunately, Heidegger, Adorno, and Derrida, too, still seem to confuse the universalist *posing of questions* that continues to be part of philosophy with the long since abandoned *claims to universalist status* that philosophy once alleged its answers to have. Today, however, it is evident that the scope of universalist questions—for instance, the question of the necessary conditions for the rationality of utterances, or of the general pragmatic presuppositions of communicative action and argumentation—does indeed have to be reflected in the grammatical form of universal propositions; it does not, however, have to be reflected in any unconditional validity or "ultimate foundations" claimed for such universalist propositions or for their theoretical framework. The fallibilist consciousness of the sciences has long since caught up with philosophy as well.

With this kind of fallibilism, we, philosophers and nonphilosophers alike, do not in any way dispense with truth claims. Such claims cannot be raised in the performative attitude of the first person in any other way than as claims that—*qua* claims—transcend space and time. But we are also aware that there is no zero-context for truth claims. Truth claims are raised here and now and have a built-in orientation toward criticism. Hence we reckon with the trivial *possibility* that they will be revised at some future date or in some other context. Just as it always has, philosophy understands itself as the guardian of rationality in the sense of a claim of reason endogenous to our form of life. In its work, however, philosophy prefers a combination of strong propositions with weak status claims; this is so little totalitarian that there is no call for a totalizing critique of reason against it. On this point cf. J. Habermas, "Philosophy as Stand-In and Interpreter," in *Moral Consciousness and Communicative Action,* trans. C. Lenhardt and S. W. Nicholsen (Cambridge, Mass., 1990).

Questions and Counterquestions (1985)

1

I am happy to accept the editor's invitation to respond to the articles by Richard Rorty, Martin Jay, Thomas McCarthy, and Joel White-book.[1] Though critical, their friendly spirit reveals that we are all concerned, if not with the same problems, then at least with the same themes. At the same time, it is immediately apparent that there is some difference between us, for instance, between Rorty and myself. The gaps between the different universes of discourse become so wide at times that the mixture of reciprocal interpretations, suppositions, and misunderstandings suddenly also serves to reveal residual unconscious presuppositions, implications, and background assumptions. All this amounts to the quite normal confusion in conversation among friends who have sufficiently different points of view.

The confusion of lines of argument is much more drastic in controversies among adversaries who, feeling that their identity is threatened by the others' fundamental convictions, struggle with rhetorical weapons. Scarcely anyone would disagree that such distances and oppositions have increased and intensified in the modern age, which has itself become a philosophical topic of the first rank since the eighteenth century. Individuals, groups, and nations have drifted far apart as regards their backgrounds of biographical and sociocultural experience. This pluralization of diverging universes of discourse is part of specifically modern experience; the shattering of naive consensus is the impetus for what Hegel calls "the experience of reflection." We cannot now simply wish this experience away; we can only negate it. In the framework of our culture, invested as it is with reflection, the thrust of this experience has to be worked through not only politically but also philosophically. Today we can survey the spectrum of answers given by philosophers: roughly speaking, it extends all the way from historicism to transcendentalism.

On the one hand, Dilthey, Weber, Jaspers, and Kolakowski take an affirmative position on the growing pluralism of "gods and demons" (*Glaubensmächte*), existential modes of being, myths, value attitudes, and metaphysical or religious worldviews. A philosophy that treats forms of truth in the plural is supposed to leave to the sciences the job of providing an adequate reservoir of consensual knowledge. On the other hand, philosophers such as Husserl, the early Wittgenstein, Popper, and Apel all attempt to maintain, at a higher level of abstraction, the unity of reason, even if only in a procedural sense. They distill the common characteristics of rational activity that must implicitly be presupposed in the pluralism of "gods and demons" and in the argumentative collisions between universes of discourse. In this way, there arise what Rorty calls "metanarratives," that is, the theories of rationality that are supposed to account for why, and in what sense, we can still connect our convictions as well as our descriptive, normative, and evaluative statements with a transcending validity claim that goes beyond merely local contexts.

These are philosophical answers to the *unavoidable* experience of modernity; when they are sharpened into the opposition between relativism and absolutism, an *unmediated* confrontation emerges between pure historicism and pure transcendentalism. At that point, the failures of both positions become clear: the one side carries the burden of self-referential, pragmatic contradictions and paradoxes that violate our need for consistency; the other side is burdened with a foundationalism that conflicts with our consciousness of the fallibility of human knowledge. No one who reflects on this situation would want to be left in this bind.

In the context of our discussion here, this reading of the present situation is not really in dispute, although Rorty, Bernstein, and I react to it in different ways. Forcefully freeing himself from the straightjacket of analytic philosophy, Richard Rorty has undertaken the most ambitious project: he wants to destroy the tradition of the philosophy of consciousness—from its Cartesian beginnings—with the aim of showing the pointlessness of the entire discussion of the foundations and limits of knowledge. He concludes that philosophers, to be rid of the problem, need only recognize the hybrid character of their controversies and give the field over to the practitioners of science, politics, and daily life. Like the later Wittgenstein, Rorty sees philosophy itself as the sickness whose symptoms it previously and unsuccessfully tried to cure. But Rorty is still enough of a philosopher to give a reason for his recommendation that we avoid the *Holzweg* of philosophical justification; one shouldn't scratch where it doesn't itch. It is just this assumption that "it doesn't itch" that I find problematic.

Forms of life are totalities that always emerge in the plural. Their coexistence may cause friction, but this *difference* does not automatically result in their *incompatibility*. Something similar is the case for the pluralism of values and belief systems. The closer the proximity in which competing "gods and demons" have to live with each other in political communities, the more tolerance they demand; but they are not incompatible. Convictions can contradict one another only when those concerned with problems define them in a similar way, believe them to require resolution, and want to decide issues on the basis of good reasons.

To be sure, it is also a characteristic of modernity that we have grown accustomed to living with disagreement in the realm of questions that admit of "truth;" we simply put controversial validity claims to one side "for the time being." Nonetheless, we perceive *this* pluralism of contradictory convictions as an incentive for learning processes; we live in the expectation of *future* resolutions. As long as we retain the perspective of participants and do not merely look over our own shoulders as historians and ethnographers, we maintain precisely the distinctions that Rorty wants to retract: between valid and socially accepted views, between good arguments and those that are merely successful for a certain audience at a certain time.

In believing that he can consistently replace the implicitly normative conception of "valid arguments" with the descriptive concept of "arguments held to be true for us at this time," Rorty commits an objectivist fallacy. We could not even understand the meaning of what we describe from a third-person perspective as argumentative conduct if we had not already learned the performative attitude of a participant in argumentation, that is, what it means from the perspective of the first person to raise a validity claim that points beyond the provincial agreements of the specific local context. Only this capacity gives our *opinions* the character of *convictions*. (This is no less true for everyday communicative practices than for argumentative disputes about the hypothetical validity of statements.) Any mutual understanding produced in communication and reproduced in the lifeworld is based on a reservoir of potential reasons that may be challenged, reasons that force us to take a rationally motivated position of "yes" or "no." This calls for a *different* type of attitude from that which we bring to the claims of merely influential ideas. From the perspective of the participant, a moment of *unconditionality* is built into the *conditions* of action oriented toward reaching understanding. From the perspective of the first person, the question of which beliefs are justified is a question of which beliefs are based on good reasons; it is not a function of life-habits that enjoy social currency in some places and not in others.

And because in the modern age the gaps between competing convictions reach deep into the domain of questions that "admit of truth," there exists, contrary to Rorty, a philosophical interest "to see social practices of justification as more than just such practices."[2] The stubbornness with which philosophy clings to the role of the "guardian of reason" can hardly be dismissed as an idiosyncrasy of self-absorbed intellectuals, especially in a period in which basic irrationalist undercurrents are being transmuted once again into a dubious form of politics. In my opinion, it is precisely the neoconservatives who articulate, intensify, and spread this mood of the times via the mass media—with such an effect that "it itches."

2

In his latest book, Richard Bernstein gives us another answer: instead of bidding farewell to philosophy from the artificially alienated viewpoint of an ethnologist, he turns it toward the practical. While

Rorty absolutizes the perspective of the observer, Bernstein remains within the perspective of the participant and enters into a debate that today leads beyond the mistaken alternatives of historicism and transcendentalism, a debate going on between Gadamer, Arendt, Rorty, and me, among others.[3] Bernstein does not end his splendid reconstruction of the diverse paths of this discussion—a discussion that has not yet come to a close—with a proposal for a theoretical solution; he ends it rather with a practical recommendation: we ought to act under the presupposition of the unifying power of communicative reason. In order to make this argument more intelligible, let me cite a thesis of Herbert Schnädelbach with which Bernstein would probably agree: "that the difference between what we always claim for our rationality and what we are actually able to explicate as rational can in principle never be eliminated."[4] If I understand the conclusion of his book correctly, it is for this reason that Bernstein from the start locates the moment of unconditionality built into the universalist validity *claims* of our communicative practices in the horizon of *practical* reason; he finds in the communicative infrastructure of the lifeworld a practical postulate, one that is dictated by reason itself. He refuses to regard the procedural unity of rationality within the historical and cultural multiplicity of standards of rationality as a question that is accessible to *theoretical* treatment.

I suspect that behind Bernstein's argumentative strategy there lies an absolutizing of the perspective of the participant that is complementary to Rorty's absolutizing of that of the observer. I do not see why one could not, at least in a preliminary way, explore a *third* path—one that I have embarked upon with my theory of communicative action. According to this approach, philosophy surrenders its claim to be the sole representative in matters of rationality and enters into a nonexclusive division of labor with the reconstructive sciences. It has the aim of clarifying the presuppositions of the rationality of processes of reaching understanding that may be presumed to be universal because they are unavoidable. Then philosophy shares with the sciences a fallibilist consciousness in that its strong universalist suppositions require confirmation in an interplay with empirical theories.[5] This revisionary self-understanding of the role of philosophy marks a break with the aspirations of first philosophy (*Ursprungsphilosophie*) in any form, even that of the theory of knowledge; but it does not mean that philosophy abandons its role as the guardian of rationality. With its self-imposed modesty of method, a philosophy starting from formal pragmatics preserves the possibility of speaking of rationality in the singular. Unlike the sciences, it has to account reflectively for its own context of emergence and thus for its own place in history.[6] For this reason, "metanarratives," in the sense of foundational "ultimate groundings" or totalizing philosophies of history, could never even arise.

The most important achievement of such an approach is the possibility of clarifying a concept of communicative rationality that escapes the snares of Western logocentrism. Instead of following Nietzsche's path of a totalizing and self-referential critique of reason, whether it be via Heidegger to Derrida, or via Bataille to Foucault,[7] and throwing the baby out with the bath water, it is more promising to seek this end through the analysis of the *already* operative potential for rationality contained in everyday practices of communication. Here the validity dimensions of propositional truth, normative rightness, and subjective truthfulness (*Wahrhaftigkeit*) or authenticity are entwined with each other. From this network of a bodily and interactively shaped, historically situated reason, our philosophical tradition has selected out only the single thread of propositional truth and theoretical reason and stylized it into the monopoly of humanity. The common ground that unites both von Humboldt and pragmatism with the later Wittgenstein and Austin is their opposition to the *ontological* privileging of the world of entities, the *epistemological* privileging of contact with objects or existing states of affairs, and the *semantic* privileging of assertoric sentences and propositional truth. Logocentrism means neglecting the complexity of reason effectively operating in the lifeworld, and restricting reason to its cognitive-instrumental dimension (a dimension, we might add, that has been noticeably privileged and selectively utilized in processes of capitalist modernization).

Rorty takes Western logocentrism as an indication of the exhaustion of our philosophical discourse and as a reason to bid farewell to philosophy as such. This way of reading the tradition could not be maintained if philosophy were to be transformed in such a way as to enable it to cope with the entire spectrum of aspects of rationality—and with the historical fate of a reason that has been arrested again and again, ideologically misused and distorted, but that also stubbornly raises its voice in every inconspicuous act of successful communication. Such a transformation is possible only if philosophy does not remain fixated on the natural sciences. Had Rorty not shared this fixation, he might have entertained a more flexible and accepting relationship to the philosophical tradition. Fortunately, not all philosophizing can be subsumed under the paradigm of the philosophy of consciousness.

Rorty believes that the need in the modern age for self-reassurance is a capricious problem created by intellectuals—indeed, even a typically German problem. In his view it arises from the esoteric *Weltschmerz* of small intellectual circles, from the preoccupation with a world that was lost along with the religious beliefs of their fathers. But does it not remain an open question whether or not the socially integrative powers of religious tradition that have been shaken up by enlightenment can find an equivalent in the unifying, consensus-creating power of reason? This was indeed the motivation behind German Idealism; this type of idealism has found equally influential proponents in the tradition of Peirce, Royce, Mead, and Dewey, in which Rorty prefers to place himself. What is perhaps specifically German is the philosophical concept of alienation, both in the Hegelian-Marxist version and in the early Romantic version taken up by Nietzsche. The same theme resonates not only in poststructuralist France; since the 1960s, and I need not remind Rorty of this, the discussion of modernity in conflict with itself has nowhere been so lively as in the United States—admittedly, more so among social scientists and psychologists than among analytic philosophers. Carl Schorske even thought he could see intellectual affinities between the contemporary American scene and Weimar Germany. While the expression "postmodern" was not invented by American neoconservatives, they at least popularized it.

Do not these and similar signs indicate that intellectuals articulate shifts in mood, which they in no way invent but which have instead palpable social and often economic causes? As a good pragmatist, I hold the view that a philosopher's capacity to create problems through intentionally inciting doubt is quite limited. I share Peirce's doubt about any type of Cartesian doubt. Problems emerge in situations over which we are not in control; they are something that objectively happens to us. The slogan that leftist intellectuals are the cause of the misery they analyze has been bandied about for too long among rightist intellectuals in Germany to be credible. It is no more credible in the attractive packaging of a theory of the new class.

To me, the notion of intellectual "value elites" is absolutely worthless. Like Rorty, I have for a long time identified myself with the radical democratic mentality that is present in the best American traditions and articulated in American pragmatism. This mentality takes seriously what appears to so-called radical thinkers as so much reformist naïveté. Dewey's "attempt to concretize concerns with the daily problems of one's community" expresses both a practice and an attitude. It is a maxim of action about which it is in fact superfluous to philosophize.

Rorty puts in question the entire undertaking of the theory of communicative action. As opposed to this form of questioning, the reservations of Martin Jay, Thomas McCarthy, and Joel Whitebook concern particular steps in its execution. These authors direct their attention to complications in my attempt to work out the concept of communicative rationality. Jay points out an under-illuminated aspect; McCarthy touches upon a central difficulty; Whitebook deals with a problem that emerges as a consequence of the theory. Within the framework of a brief reply, I can respond only by alluding to how I have dealt with some of these problems in the past and how I would like to work on others in the future. An added difficulty here is that only McCarthy directs his remarks to my more recent works.

3

With a great deal of hermeneutic sensitivity, Martin Jay has collected and interpreted my scattered remarks on the question of aesthetic modernity. In every case these remarks had a secondary character to the extent that they arose only in the context of other topics and always in relation to the discussions among Adorno, Benjamin, and

Marcuse. In *The Theory of Communicative Action,* my discussion of Max Weber's theory of culture and his diagnosis of the times required understanding the autonomous art that emerged in modern Europe (together with art criticism institutionalized since the eighteenth century) as the product of a disintegration and as the result of a process of rationalization. Weber described the rationalization of worldviews as a process of decomposition and differentiation. On the one hand, the basic substantive concepts with which the world orders of "salvation history" and cosmology were constructed have dissolved; with this dissolution, ontic, moral, and expressive aspects are no longer fused into one and the same concept. Without the possibility of recourse to God and the cosmic order as an origin, theological and metaphysical forms of grounding lose their credibility. On the other hand, profane forms of "knowledge" that are relatively independent of one another have arisen alongside a subjectivized "faith." Philosophy, forced into the position of mediator, becomes dependent on these. As documented in the division of Kant's three *Critiques,* questions of truth are differentiated from questions of justice and these in turn from questions of taste.

Originating in the eighteenth century, idealist aesthetics strictly distinguished aesthetic pleasure from other "empirical" forms of satisfaction; that is, it separated the beautiful and the sublime, on the one hand, from the useful and the desirable, on the other. Art emerges with its own proper claim, as do science and technology, law and morality. Max Weber speaks of the internal or independent logic (*Eigensinn*) of each of these three cultural value spheres, which are also separated from one another institutionally in the form of functionally specified systems of action. Since the investigations of Arnold Hauser into the social history of modern art, this *institutional* differentiation of art has frequently been analyzed.[8]

There is no need here to go into the external aspects of the transformation of the forms of production of art, the purposes to which it was put, or the modes of its reception in the transition from sacrally bound art, through the art of the court and patron, to bourgeois commercialized art.[9] What is in dispute are the internal aspects of the independent logic of autonomous art since the eighteenth century. One of the two questions raised by Martin Jay is the extent to which one can speak of an aesthetic-practical *rationality,* or even of a *learning process,* in this sphere.

There is an unmistakable indicator for the fact that a certain type of "knowing" is objectified in art works, albeit in a different way than in theoretical discourse or in legal or moral representations. These objectivations of spirit, too, are fallible and hence criticizable. Art criticism arose at the same time as the autonomous work of art; and, since then, it has become an established insight that the work of art calls for the interpretation, evaluation, and even "linguistification" (*Versprachlichung*) of its semantic content. Art criticism has developed forms of argumentation that specifically differentiate it from the argumentative forms of theoretical and moral-practical discourse.[10] As distinct from merely subjective preference, the fact that we link judgments of taste to a criticizable validity claim presupposes nonarbitrary standards for the judgment of art. As the philosophical discussion of "artistic truth" reveals, works of art raise claims with regard to their unity or harmony (*Stimmigkeit*), their authenticity, and the success of their expressions, against which they may be assessed and in terms of which they may fail. For this reason I believe that a pragmatic logic of argumentation is the most appropriate guiding thread with the help of which the "aesthetic-practical" type of rationality can be differentiated over and against other types of rationality.

When we refer to learning processes, it is the works of art themselves, and not the discourses about them, that are the locus of directed and cumulative transformations. As McCarthy correctly notes, what accumulates are not epistemic contents but, rather, the effects of the differentiation, with its own independent logic, of a special sort of experience: precisely those aesthetic experiences of which only a decentered, unbound subjectivity is capable. Authentic experiences of this type are possible only to the extent that the categories of the patterned expectations of organized daily experience collapse, that the routines of daily action and conventions of ordinary life are destroyed, and the normality of foreseeable and accountable certainties are suspended. The ever-more radical uncoupling of this potential for experience, the purification of the aesthetic from admixtures of the cognitive, the useful, and the moral, is mirrored in the reflections of the early Romantic period (especially in Friedrich Schlegel's work), in the aestheticism of Baudelaire and the Symbolists, in the program of *l'art pour l'art,* in the surrealistic celebration of illumination through shock effects, with its ambivalence of attraction and repulsion, of broken continuity, of the shudder of profanization, of agitated disgust—in short, in the reflection of those moments in which the bewildered subject "transgresses his boundaries," as Bataille puts it. What is reflected in these interpretations and declarations is a transformation of the form of aesthetic experience, induced by avant-garde art itself, in the direction of the decentering and unbounding of subjectivity. At the same time, this decentering indicates an increased sensitivity to what remains unassimilated in the interpretive achievements of pragmatic, epistemic, and moral mastery of the demands and challenges of everyday situations; it effects an openness to the expurgated elements of the unconscious, the fantastic, and the mad, the material and the bodily—thus to everything in our speechless contact with reality that is so fleeting, so contingent, so immediate, so individualized, simultaneously so far and so near that it escapes our normal categorical grasp.

Benjamin called this style of experience "concentrated distraction" and set it off from the contemplative style of experience. The characteristics and tendencies of the development of avant-garde art, analyzed repeatedly since Benjamin and Adorno, point in the direction of the former style of experience. The loss of aura and the importance of allegory are continuous with the destruction of the organically unified work of art and its pretended totality of meaning; one can think here of the incorporation of the ugly, of the negative as such. By treating materials, methods, and techniques reflectively, the artist opens up a space for experiment and play and transfers the activity of the genius to "free construction" (*freie Arbeit*).[11] Forced novelty, dependence on the latest trends, and the accelerated pace of fads perpetuate the creative break with the tradition and serve to make all stylistic means equally accessible. Art becomes a laboratory, the critic an expert, the development of art the medium of a learning process—here, naturally, not in the sense of an accumulation of epistemic *contents,* of an aesthetic "progress," which is possible only in individual dimensions, but nonetheless in the sense of a concentrically expanding, progressive exploration of a realm of possibilities structurally opened up with the autonomization of art. (I do not know whether or not the results of Piaget's genetic psychology are as appropriate here for the analysis of this "level of learning" as they are for the analysis of the stages of postconventional conceptions of law and morality. I tend to be rather skeptical.)

Martin Jay's other question concerns the relation between the independence of art in a culture of experts and the cultural impoverishment of the lifeworld. Jay asks why I do not unambiguously decide between Adorno and Benjamin—between the esotericism of the exclusive, often hermetically sealed avant-garde work of art, and the hopes for profane illumination in exoteric mass art. He notes that I seem to find some truth in both positions.

Peter Bürger takes an unambiguous position. In his view, the impulse of several avant-garde movements to rebel against the institutionalization of art, against its being split off from the lifeworld, was correct despite the failure of the surrealist revolt.[12] I do not differ with this judgment per se. The intention of redeeming a promise of happiness, whose superabundance radiates beyond art, is part of art itself. But this intention cannot be realized in the way in which the surrealists wanted, through the liquidation of aesthetic appearance (*Schein*) as the medium of artistic representation. This false sublation (*Aufhebung*) of art into life certainly does not preclude the possibility of a correct mediation of art with the lifeworld. An aesthetic experience that is not simply to be transposed into judgments of taste by the professional arbiters, that is not merely to circulate in the realm of art alone, would entail a change in the status of an, as it were, experimentally unbound subjectivity.

If aesthetic experience is incorporated into the context of individual life-histories, if it is utilized to illuminate a situation and to throw light on individual life-problems—if it at all communicates its impulses to a collective form of life—then art enters into a language game that is no longer that of aesthetic criticism but belongs rather to everyday communicative practices. It then no longer affects only our evaluative language or merely renews the interpretation of needs that color our perceptions; rather, it reaches into our cognitive interpretations and normative expectations and transforms the totality in which these moments are related to each other. In this respect, modern art harbors a utopia that becomes a reality to the degree that the mimetic powers sublimated in the work of art find resonance in the mimetic relations of a balanced and undistorted intersubjectivity in everyday life. However, this does not require the *liquidation* of an art set off from life in the medium of aesthetic *appearance,* but rather a *changed constellation* of art and the lifeworld.

I developed these ideas earlier at the suggestion of Albrecht Wellmer.[13] In the meantime, Wellmer has elaborated them in such an ingenious way that I can here be content simply to refer to his treatment.[14] I do not wish to retrace Wellmer's subtle line of argument but only to repeat his main thesis in order to offer it as an answer to Martin Jay's question. The fact that we can dispute the reasons for evaluating a work of art in aesthetic discourse is, as we said, an unmistakable indication for a validity claim inherent in works of art. The aesthetic "validity" or "unity" that we attribute to a work refers to its singularly illuminating power to open our eyes to what is seemingly familiar, to disclose anew an apparently familiar reality. This validity claim admittedly stands for a *potential* for "truth" that can be released only in the whole complexity of life experience; therefore, this "truth potential" may not be connected to (or even identified with) just one of the three validity claims constitutive for communicative action, as I have previously been inclined to maintain. The one-to-one relationship that exists between the prescriptive validity of a norm and the normative validity claims raised in regulative speech acts is not a proper model for the relation between the potential for truth of works of art and the transformed relations between self and world stimulated by aesthetic experience.

Neither truth nor truthfulness (*Wahrhaftigkeit*) may be attributed unmetaphorically to works of art, if one understands "truth" and "truthfulness" in the sense of a pragmatically differentiated, everyday concept of truth. We can explain the way in which truth and truthfulness—and even normative rightness—are metaphorically interlaced in works of art only by appealing to the fact that the work of art, as a symbolic formation with an *aesthetic* validity claim, is at the same time object of an *experience,* in which the three dimensions of validity are *unmetaphorically* intermeshed.[15]

4

Thomas McCarthy raises two sorts of objections: first, against my systematic interpretation of Weber's diagnosis of the times; and second, against my analysis of interpretive understanding. Since I believe that the relationship established by McCarthy between the two problems is artificial, I will first deal separately with the problem of the objectivity of understanding.

In the field of meaning theory, I hold the view that we understand a literally meant speech act when we know the conditions under which it could be accepted as valid by a hearer. This pragmatically extended version of truth-conditional semantics is supported by the fact that we connect the execution of speech acts to various validity claims: claims to the truth of propositions (or of the existential presuppositions of their propositional content), claims to the rightness of an utterance (with respect to existing normative contexts), and claims to the truthfulness (*Wahrhaftigkeit*) of an expressed intention. With these claims we issue, as it were, a warranty for their vindication, should this be necessary—above all by offering, at least implicitly, reasons for the validity of our speech acts. A hearer knows the content of what is said when he knows what reasons (or what sorts of reasons) the speaker would give for the validity of her speech act (under appropriate circumstances). The interpreter (even the social scientific interpreter who deals with linguistically formed data), does not understand symbolically prestructured objects (in the normal case, communicative utterances) if he does not also understand the reasons potentially related to their validity claims.

Now the interesting point is that reasons are of a special nature. They can always be expanded into arguments that we then understand only when we *recapitulate* (*nachvollziehen*) them in the light of some standards of rationality. This "recapitulation" requires a reconstructive activity in which we bring into play our own standards of rationality, at least intuitively. From the perspective of a participant, however, one's own standards of rationality must always claim general validity, which can be restricted only subsequently from the perspective of a third person. In short, the interpretive reconstruction of reasons requires that we place "their" standards in relation to "ours," so that in the case of a contradiction we either revise our preconceptions or relativize "their" standards of rationality against "ours."

These preconceptions do indeed lead to the rather "strong" thesis that we *cannot* understand reasons without at least implicitly *evaluating* them. McCarthy argues that this conclusion is false, since, even if it is the case that it is necessary to take up a rationally motivated "yes" or "no" position on reasons in order to understand them, the interpreter cannot only agree or disagree with them but can also practice a kind of abstention; he has the option of "leaving to one side" the question of the validity of "their" rationality standards (and hence of the reasons themselves). However, I think that such an abstention is also a rationally motivated position, just as much as a "yes" or a "no," and in no way relieves us of the necessity of taking a position. Abstention in this context does not really signify a true declaration of neutrality but only signals that we are putting off problems for the time being and wish to suspend our interpretive efforts. For example, so long as we are unable to see a perspicuous internal relation between the categorial frameworks of Aristotelian and Newtonian physics, we do not know precisely in what sense Aristotle, in contrast to Newton, wanted to "explain" natural processes. Simply noting the competition between various paradigms comes close to confessing that we do not yet understand the physics and metaphysics of Aristotle as well as we do the basic assumptions about nature in classical mechanics.

The rational character of understanding, which Gadamer always emphasized, becomes especially clear in extreme cases such as, for example, the interpretation of mythical narratives. Undercutting or leaving to one side (or merely shaking one's head while accepting) the totalistic categories of a worldview within which the narrative interweaving and (as it appears to *us*) the categorical confusion of surface phenomena lay claim to explanatory power merely indicate that we are putting off—prematurely breaking off—the interpretive process. This is tantamount to confessing that we do not yet understand the point of mythical modes of thought. We understand them only when we can say why the participants had good reasons for their confidence in this *type* of explanation. But in order to achieve this degree of understanding, we have to establish an internal relation between "their" sort of explanation and the kind we accept as correct. We must be able to reconstruct the successful and unsuccessful learning processes that separate "us" from "them;" both modes of explanation have to be located within the same universe of discourse. So long as this is not achieved, the feeling remains that one does not understand something. It is this perplexity that finds its appropriate expression in the suspension of one's interpretive efforts.

But it does not follow from this that the sciences that must establish hermeneutic access to their object domain also have to renounce the objectivity of knowledge. I have criticized this hermeneutist position in various ways.[16] In principle, I do not see any difficulty in achieving some theoretical knowledge even in those domains of reality with which we have contact primarily through norm-conformative or expressive attitudes. My reservations concern only those theoretical positions that ignore the hermeneutic dimension of access to the object domain entirely.[17] If the sentence McCarthy criticizes is to be read as reporting my own view, "that nothing can be learned in the objectivating attitude about inner nature *qua* subjectivity,"[18] then it may be understood only in the sense of a rejection of *purely* objectivist approaches to psychology.

McCarthy is further interested in the question of whether the rationality complexes that have been differentiated in modern times and have achieved a certain autonomy do not, as it were, also communicate with one another and have their roots in one and the same reason. In my view, this topic can be treated independently of the problem of interpretive understanding. For this purpose, the schema reproduced by McCarthy is not really a fruitful point of departure. Its purpose was only to represent the content of Max Weber's famous *Zwischenbetrachtung.*[19] Unfortunately, in response to earlier objections, I made the mistake of referring to this schema in a systematic way.[20] And McCarthy does the same here. My previous carelessness thus makes it necessary in what follows to distinguish more carefully between my interpretation of Weber and my own views.

5

I first want to isolate those elements of Weber's theory of culture that I appropriated into my own view (a). In so doing, we then encounter McCarthy's concern for the costs of a process of disenchantment that now leaves open only the possibility of a procedural unity of reason cutting across different forms of argumentation (b). McCarthy finally treats the question of the synthesis of the differentiated moments of reason under three quite distinct aspects. He lists three problems that cannot be subsumed under the *same* analytic perspective (that is, the perspective of the various basic attitudes toward the objective, the social, and the subjective worlds) (c).

a. To begin with, let me turn to what I have appropriated from Weber's theory of culture. In Weber's view, the assertion of a differentiation of "value spheres" each with its own independent logic—which was inspired by the neo-Kantians Emil Lask and Heinrich Rickert—can plausibly be defended in regard to modern Europe on two levels: first, on the level of ideas that can be transmitted in traditions (scientific theories, moral and legal beliefs, as well as artistic productions); but also, second, on the level of cultural action systems, in which corresponding "discourses" and activities are given professionally and institutionally organized form. The differentiation of value spheres corresponds to a decentered understanding of the world, which is an important internal condition for the professionalized treatment of cultural traditions separated into questions of truth, justice, and taste. This modern understanding of the world makes possible a hypothetical approach to phenomena and experiences, which are isolated from the complexity of lifeworld contexts and analyzed under experimentally varied conditions. This is equally true for the states of an objectified nature, for norms and modes of acting, and for the reflective experiences of an "unbound" subjectivity (set free from the practical constraints of everyday life). The well-known distinction made by cognitive developmental psychology between structurally defined levels of learning, on the one hand, and the learning of contents, on the other, certainly may not be applied in the same way to science, morality, and art. In this respect, my formulations were not careful enough.

Compared to the growth of theoretical knowledge, described by McCarthy as the accumulation of contents across paradigm shifts, the trends in the development of art (discussed more extensively above) do not so much signify an accumulation of contents as the progressive constitution of a specific domain of autonomous art and aesthetic experience purified of cognitive and moral admixtures; they also signify expanding explorations that illuminate more and more of this realm of experience. Yet this concentric expansion is not accompanied by the familiar effect of a devaluation of formerly held insights that is typical for cumulative learning processes. Moral and legal theories occupy a middle position. Here, too, we can observe the constitution of a domain of autonomous morality and moral universalism that distills a class of rationally solvable problems under the single aspect of justice out of the complexity of the contexts of ethical life. Learning processes in this sphere are similar to a theoretical progress achieved within the limits of a single paradigm. Thus, in the modern age, the explication and justification of moral intuitions make a certain "progress" that is not exhausted in ever-new interpretations of the same moral principle.

However, the thesis that capitalist modernization can be grasped as a selective actualization of the rationality potential contained in modern structures of consciousness requires the counterfactual supposition of a nonselective model of societal rationalization.[21] In this connection, I have suggested that for the value spheres of science, morality, and art in modern Europe "we should be able to demonstrate plausible correspondences with typical forms of argumentation, each of which is specialized in accord with a universal validity claim."[22] Thus, the burden of proof is put on the theory of argumentation; leaving aside explicative discourse and therapeutic critique, this has to distinguish and clarify the systematic content of three different forms of argumentation: empirical-theoretical discourse, moral discourse, and aesthetic critique.[23] It was due to the context of Weber's diagnosis of the times that I did not introduce the three rationality complexes via argumentation theory but by way of a schema that was supposed to represent the characteristics of a decentered understanding of the world. Indeed, the modern understanding of the world structurally opens up the possibility of taking objectivating, norm-conformative, and expressive attitudes toward three different worlds (objective, social, or subjective—in short, to states of affairs, norms, or subjective experiences); it also allows us to vary these attitudes in relation to one and the same world. If we keep to the schema in figure 10.1 (originally figure 11 in volume 1 of *The Theory of Communicative Action*), but leave aside its application to Weber's diagnosis of the times and pursue instead a systematic line of thought, the three forms of argumentation corresponding to the modern complexes of rationality can, *to begin with,* be correlated with the formal-pragmatic relations along the diagonal (1.1, 2.2, 3.3).

b. Based on reflections in the theory of meaning, I take as my starting point the view that facts, norms, and subjective experiences have their *primary* locus in "their" corresponding worlds (objective, social, or subjective), and *in the first instance* are accessible, or identifiable, only from the perspective of an actor who adopts a corresponding attitude (be it objectivating, norm-conformative, or expressive). It is in connection with this linear ordering that the first of the three questions McCarthy treats at the end of his article arises.

How is it that we can talk in an objectivating attitude about something in the subjective or social worlds, that is, about those elements that we *first* experience as something subjective or that we *first* encounter as something normative? In theoretical discourse (for instance, scientific discourse) we can incorporate these elements only if we thematize subjective experiences and norms as states of affairs after having transformed them into components of the objective world. In everyday communication we certainly succeed, without much trouble, in transforming expressive utterances (or sentences in the first person) into equivalent statements in the third person, or in accurately reporting the content of normative utterances or imperatives from the point of view of the third person. On the level of scientific discourse, however, there is a tendency to delimit the object domains of, for example, psychology or sociology by neglecting their hermeneutic dimensions in such a way that the components of the social or subjective worlds are naturalistically assimilated to physical entities or to observable behavior. In each case, they are made into components of the objective world, inherently accessible only in the objectivating attitude; that is, they are forced into the

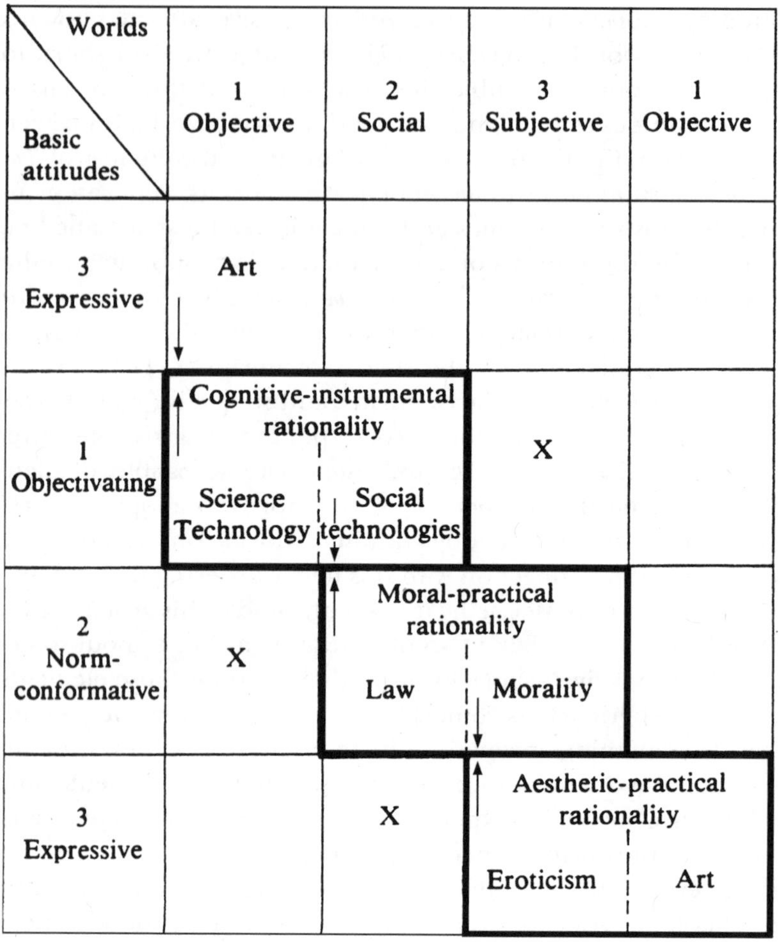

Worlds / Basic attitudes	1 Objective	2 Social	3 Subjective	1 Objective
3 Expressive	Art ↓			
1 Objectivating	↑ Cognitive-instrumental rationality Science Technology ┊ Social ┊technologies ↓		X	
2 Norm-conformative	X	↑ Moral-practical rationality Law ┊ Morality ↓		
3 Expressive		X	↑ Aesthetic-practical rationality Eroticism ┊ Art	

Figure 10.1
Rationalization complexes

basic conceptual framework of physicalism or behaviorism. As opposed to this naturalist reduction, the point here is simply to defend nonobjectivist approaches in psychology and the social sciences.

Mutatis mutandis, the same questions arise for moral-practical discourse and, indirectly, for aesthetic criticism. These forms of argumentation are also inherently related to components of one specific world, the social or the subjective. Here, too, elements of the other two worlds must be brought into play in such a way as to avoid the dangers of, respectively, *moralism* and *aestheticism,* just as previously the danger of *objectivism* had to be avoided. We can thus observe that science, morality, and art have not only been differentiated *from one another,* they also communicate *with one another.* But within the boundaries of each expert culture, the different moments of reason come into contact with each other in such as way as to avoid violating the independent logic of the dominant form of argumentation specialized either in truth, normative rightness, or aesthetic unity. This is one concern of the last chapter of *The Theory of Communicative Action.*[24]

At this point the motivation behind McCarthy's criticism becomes clear: an interest in the question of how the moments of reason can retain their unity within differentiation and of how this unity can be adequately expressed in philosophical analysis. Unfortunately, my schematic presentation of Weber's diagnosis of the times leads McCarthy to conflate three quite distinct questions under a single viewpoint. As has just been shown, formal-pragmatic relations play a role in the analysis of these interactions between the cognitive, moral, and expressive moments of reason. But the other two questions really have nothing to do with this problem: first, the question of how the knowledge produced in expert cultures can be mediated with everyday practices (which I have already touched upon above in relation to the constellation "art and life"); and second, the question of whether we can provide an equivalent for the meaning of traditional worldviews—for their meaning-bestowing function.

c. With the emergence of autonomous art and science, problems of mediation arise—such as the relation of art and life, or of theory and practice. Since Hegel, a corresponding problem has emerged that has to do with the relation of morality and ethical life (*Sitt-lichkeit*). This problem has less to do with an expressive attitude toward the social world than with the fact that the insights of a postconventional morality would remain without any impact on real life unless morality is anchored in concrete forms of ethical life. The deontological ethics developed in the Kantian tradition do indeed offer a solution to the problem of justification; they show how to choose between controversial norms of action with good reasons (in light of what could be willed by all). But they do not offer any solution for two resultant problems: first, that of the *application* of justified norms that are general and abstracted from any content; and second, that of the *efficacy* of pure moral insights that have been gained under the condition of abstracting from available motivations. Autonomous morality owes its gain in rationality to the transformation of questions of the good life into problems of justice. As a consequence of this deontological abstraction, it can provide only answers to questions lacking specific contexts. This necessary disregard for the complexity of concrete forms of life, in which moral moments are always interlaced with evaluative, cognitive, and expressive moments, calls for specific compensations that make good the deficits with regard to the application and realization of moral insights. I am not able to go further into this question here.[25]

The discussions of morality and ethical life, of theory and practice, and of art and life all center around the idea of nonreified everyday communicative practices, a form of life with structures of an undistorted intersubjectivity. Such a possibility must today be wrung from the professional, specialized, self-sufficient cultures of experts and from the functional imperatives of state and economy that destructively invade both the ecological basis of life and the communicative infrastructure of our lifeworld. This same intuition is expressed in Marx's utopian perspective on the realization of philosophy: to the extent that the reason expressed in Hegel's philosophy can be embodied in the forms of life of an emancipated society, philosophy somehow becomes pointless. For Marx, philosophy realized is philosophy sublated (*aufgehoben*). The theory of communicative action gives this idea another reading: the unity of reason cannot be reestablished on the level of cultural traditions in terms of a substantive worldview but only on this side of the expert cultures, in the non-reified communicative practices of everyday life. Indeed, in a certain way, the unity of reason is *a tergo* always already realized in communicative action—namely, in such a way that we have an intuitive knowledge of it. A philosophy that wants to bring this intuition to a conceptual level must retrieve the scattered traces of reason in communicative practices themselves, no matter how muted they may be. However, it cannot simply repeat the attempt, long since discredited, to project some theoretical picture of the world as a whole.

I think I have learned from the tradition of Hegelian-Marxism, from the history of critical social theory from Marx to Benjamin, Bloch, Marcuse, and Adorno, that any attempt to embed the perspective of reconciliation in a philosophy of history of nature, however indirectly it is done, must pay the price of dedifferentiating forms of knowledge behind whose categorial distinctions we can no longer retreat in good conscience. All this is not really an argument but more an expression of skepticism in the face of so many failed attempts to have one's cake and eat it too: to retain both Kant's insights and, at the same time, to return to the "home" (*Behausung*) from which these same insights have driven us. But, perhaps, McCarthy or others will someday succeed in formulating the continuities between human history and natural history so carefully that they are weak enough to be plausible and yet strong enough to permit us to recognize human beings' place in the cosmos (Scheler), at least in broad outlines.

6

The philosophical purpose behind Joel Whitebook's attempt to oppose to "linguistic idealism" the truth of the materialist tradition from Feuerbach through Marx and Freud to the later Frankfurt School accords with McCarthy's arguments against banning all substantive moments from the concept of a procedural rationality. The theoreticians of Western Marxism were relentless in their search for some Archimedian point between Kant and Hegel from which they might retrieve the materialist tradition without surrendering the justificatory achievements of formalist thought, on the one hand, or the meaning-bestowing capacity of holistic thought, on the other. These philosophers were in agreement on the goal; they differed as to how to attain it since they could not avoid paying some price for it, whether excising part of Kant, or Hegel, or Marx. McCarthy and Whitebook chastise me either for cutting too much from Hegel and totalizing forms of thought (McCarthy), or too much from Marx and materialism (Whitebook). In their common diagnosis of too much Kantianism, both agree with Rorty, who is disturbed less by the latter's formalism than by its supposed foundationalism.

Whitebook's analysis sheds light on the reception of Freudian id psychology by Horkheimer, Marcuse, and Adorno, as well as on their critique of ego psychology and the famous thesis of the "end of the individual." Whitebook himself retains a more or less orthodox interpretation of Freud; from a clinical perspective, he regards the contributions of ego psychology more as supplements to the classical Freud. In my view, however, the achievement of Heinz Hartmann and his allies lies in having demonstrated the need to revise metapsychology; the revision itself should come rather from cognitive developmental psychology. Piaget's approach can supplement assumptions about the psychodynamic development of the child with hypotheses about the development of cognitive structures, so as to give us a handle on, and make empirically testable, the implicitly normative content of such concepts as "ego strength," "conscious conflict resolution," and "the rational control of drives." I have proposed a communication-theoretical interpretation of approaches deriving from Piaget and Freud. To my mind, this proposal has a number of advantages: (i) It creates a common ground between Freud's therapeutic and metapsychological writings, by connecting the structural model of id, ego, and superego with the experiences gained in the communication between patient and analyst.[26] (ii) This version conceptualizes clinical intuitions about deviant and successful processes of ego development by making defense mechanisms comprehensible as inner-psychic communication disturbances and by relating the extremes of overly defined/deficient ego boundaries (isolation/diffusion) to the pragmatic presuppositions of intact intersubjectivity and undistorted communication.[27] (iii) Reading psychoanalysis in terms of communication theory also explains the central importance and individuating effects of the Oedipal conflict that remains decisive for the development of the structure of personality. Structurally described levels of interaction serve here as a conceptual bridge connecting developmental logic and developmental dynamics.[28] (iv) Finally, such a reading offers a categorial framework in which metapsychology can be connected up with the basic concepts of research on socialization and the family.[29] In Parson's version, the vocabulary of a theory of drives formulated in terms of energy loses its currency here.

As I see it, nothing of significance is lost in this reading. The hydraulic model and its reliance on a mechanics of instinctual energy has only a metaphorical character, even for Freud himself. In any case, one cannot have both the analytic instrument of a depth hermeneutics and a theory of drives formulated in quasi-physicalist concepts. The Freudo-Marxism of the earlier Frankfurt School could conceptually integrate psychology and sociology only through the mechanization of internalization; but, as Whitebook shows, this results in a false antagonism between the domain of the organism, which is described in biological terms, and the domain of the social apparatus, which invades the individual from the outside. It certainly makes more sense to attempt to integrate both disciplines from the beginning within the same conceptual framework. Such a framework would permit us to understand the development of personality as socialization (*Vergesellschaftung*), and to understand socialization as individualization.

If one is clear about the purely *methodological* character of this decision, one need not fear the consequences Whitebook has in mind. It is only from the point of view of a reifying theory of drives that the extralinguistic referent of both the structure and autonomy of "inner nature" gets lost along with the vocabulary of instinct and drive energy, cathexis, displacement, and so forth. But the essential difference actually consists only in replacing "drive energies" with "interpreted needs" and describing "instinctual vissicitudes" from the perspective of identity formation and processes of interaction. On this reading, inspired by the theory of communication, inner nature is not in any way vaporized into a culturalist haze.[30] It does not determine in advance that the substratum of inner nature has to fit harmoniously into linguistic structures, and even be utterly absorbed into them. But such a categorial framework does decide in favor of the perspective of a lifeworld intersubjectively shared by participants. One does give up biological or physicalist third-person descriptions of the organic substratum. This change in perspective does not entail the elimination of inner nature as an extralinguistic referent.

Whitebook is led astray by some of my remarks that belong to another context. They were made apropos the question of whether a theory of natural evolution could be projected from such an internal perspective. Naturally, I am enough of a materialist to take as my starting point that Kant is right only to the extent that his statements are compatible with Darwin. I have never had any doubts about the primacy of natural history over the history of the human species. Nonetheless, it is better not to try to resolve all problems with the same theory, or even with theories of the same type. The neo-Darwinian theory of evolution has a different status and form from Newtonian physics, on the one hand, and Romantic theories of nature, on the other. The three theories are not concerned with the same "nature." "Instinctual nature" as dealt with, respectively, in ethology and psychoanalysis is just as distinct. It seems to me that the single most important question here is whether that "inner nature" whose fateful entwinement in life-histories is the object of psychoanalysis can be better explained through interactional concepts or through concepts with more strongly physicalist or biological connotations. The value of a theory is surely a matter of empirical fruitfulness and not a matter of the speculative content of its fundamental concepts.[31]

It is, however, quite legitimate to ask how it is that I can hold onto those materialist motifs that Freudo-Marxism drew on in its theory of drives. Whitebook suspects that a theory of society that no longer takes over intact the Freudian theory of drives necessarily truncates an important normative dimension, namely, that of happiness. At the same time, he also sees an excess of utopianism built into "linguistic idealism." The "concern for happiness" seems necessarily to become secondary to the "passion for justice" in a theory that gets involved with genetic structuralism and directs its interest to general structures of rationality, both in the development of the individual and in social evolution. I shall limit myself here to the moral and legal dimension, since both Whitebook and McCarthy, each in his own way, renew the critique of ethical formalism (and both with reference to the same passage in my essay on Benjamin).

First of all, I have to point out that I have revised my earlier interpretation[32] of the postconventional stage of moral judgment.[33] Even if the approach of a discourse ethics favored by Apel and myself were to be accepted in philosophical discussions, it would only have achieved an adequate description of the *conditions* of principled moral judgment as such. Previously, I was not sufficiently clear about the fact that such a competence for judgment does not *eo ipso* presuppose a flexible ego identity, even if it no longer accepts as given the interpretation of needs (as does Kantian ethics) but rather (as in discourse ethics) opens them to an unconstrained intersubjective process of will formation. The cognitive capacity to justify moral actions and norms has to be supplemented if it is to become effective in the context of ethical life. Only a capacity for judgment (informed by practical reason) makes possible an application of abstract and general norms that is appropriate to particular situations; only motivational resources and structures of inner control makes possible actions that are in accord with moral insight. Without the capacity for judgment and motivation, the psychological conditions for translating morality into ethical life are missing; without the corresponding patterns of socialization and institutions, that is, without "fitting" forms of life to embodied moral principles, the social conditions for their concrete existence are missing. This is the substance of Hegel's critique of Kant's theory of morality, a critique that has always been recognized in the critical theory of society. Autonomy in Kant's sense, with the strict separation of duty and inclination and without the awareness of the ego's communicative access to its own inner nature, also signifies unfreedom; Adorno developed the implications of this in the third part of his *Negative Dialectics*. In psychological terms, this means that inner nature is not transformed into the perspective of reconciliation merely through the capacity of moral judgment (as it is reconstructed in terms of a discourse ethics). Rather, such a perspective is attained only through the structures of an ego-identity making possible "a freedom that limits itself in the intention of reconciling, if not of identifying, worthiness with happiness."[34]

In the theory of society, the relation between morality and ethical life can be found in the contrast between general structures of the lifeworld that are capable of being rationalized, on the one hand, and the plurality of existing lifeworlds in their specific, concrete historical totalities, on the other. Particular forms of life and life-histories form a context that remains in the background and is experienced by us only as a horizon; this context cannot be objectivated *in toto*. Certainly, different lifeworlds may be compared under different abstract points of view; but only a few such aspects are so general that they can be detached from the cultural paradigms of a specific lifeworld. This is true, for instance, of problemsolving capacities that can be measured against the standard of universal validity claims (such as propositional truth and normative rightness) and that can accumulate in the development of the forces of production, in the growth of theoretical knowledge, as well as in progress in the stages of moral judgment. However, happiness, unlike justice or knowledge, is not a concept that relates to only one of these dimensions and to general structures of the lifeworld. It is related to particular constellations of lived practices, value orientations, traditions, and competencies as a whole. Its object is always a historically unique configuration. We do indeed have more or less definite feelings about the success of modes of life and—with less deception—about their failure. But enormous difficulties stand in the way of conceptualizing, as we can do in the case of morality, these *clinical* intuitions about the "good life" in a universally binding way, although this was once the aim of classical ethics. One has to be satisfied with recognizing *necessary* conditions for such a life.

Many of those who have been raised in a Protestant milieu tend toward the presumption that the balance of happiness, overall and in the long run, cannot be drastically altered. But even this goal would not be achieved if every generation did not set *other* goals for themselves and undertake anew utopian efforts to change the balance of happiness. Perhaps it is a remnant of theodicy to assume that every form of life inherently possesses the same chance to find its happiness. Such speculations are surely idealist in the bad sense given the overwhelming experience of individual unhappiness and collective suffering, and in view of social catastrophes that are so terrible because, for all their quasi-naturalness, they do not arise from natural necessity. Over and over again, the necessary conditions for a "good life" are carelessly and arbitrarily violated. It is from this experience that the tradition of thought that unites Marx and Freud draws its inspiration. I am in full agreement with Whitebook in my desire not to give up *this* form of materialism.

In conclusion, I do not want to pass over in silence the fact that McCarthy and Whitebook touch upon a basic philosophical problem that, if I am correct, still awaits an adequate resolution this side of Hegelian logic: How is it possible to weaken the claims of statements about totalities so that they may be joined together with stronger statements about general structures?

Note

1. [Editor's note:] The reference is to the following essays in R. Bernstein, ed., *Habermas and Modernity* (Cambridge, Mass., 1985): R. Rorty, "Habermas and Lyotard on Postmodernity;" M. Jay, "Habermas and Modernism;" T. McCarthy, "Reflections on Rationalization in *The Theory of Communicative Action;*" J. Whitebook, "Reason and Happiness: Some Psychoanalytic Themes in Critical Theory."

2. R. Rorty, *Philosophy and the Mirror of Nature* (Princeton, N.J., 1979), p. 390.

3. R. Bernstein, *Beyond Objectivism and Relativism* (Philadelphia, 1983).

4. H. Schnädelbach, in W. Kuhlmann and D. Böhler, eds., *Kommunikation und Reflexion* (Frankfurt, 1983), p. 361.

5. J. Habermas, "Philosophy as Stand-In and Interpreter," in *Moral Consciousness and Communicative Action*, trans. C. Lenhardt and S. W. Nicholsen (Cambridge, Mass., 1990).

6. J. Habermas, *The Theory of Communicative Action*, vol. 2, trans. T. McCarthy (Boston, 1987), pp. 398ff.

7. I have never used the term "neoconservative" in this connection. I did once, in passing, compare the critique of reason in Foucault and Derrida to the "Young Conservatives" of the Weimar Republic. Usually Hans Freyer, Arnold Gehlen, Martin Heidegger, Ernst Jünger, and Carl Schmitt are numbered among this group. They all take from Nietzsche the radical gesture of a break with modernity and a revolutionary renewal of premodern energies, most often reaching back to archaic times. Like any comparison, it has its weaknesses, but in the German context it does illuminate

intellectual affinities that, notwithstanding the politically contrasting positions, stem from the authority of Nietzsche (see my essay "Modernity versus Postmodernity," *New German Critique* 22 (1981): 3–22).

8. Cf. P. Bürger, *Theory of the Avant Garde* (Minneapolis, 1983). Cf. also his "Institution Kunst," in *Vermittlung, Rezeption, Funktion* (Frankfurt, 1979), and *Kritik der idealistischen Ästhetik* (Frankfurt, 1983).

9. J. Habermas, *The Theory of Communicative Action*, vol. 1, trans. T. McCarthy (Boston, 1984), pp. 157ff.

10. Ibid., pp. 40ff., and the references given there.

11. Bürger, *Kritik der idealistischen Ästhetik*, pp. 104ff.

12. Cf. also P. Bürger, "Das Altern der Moderne," in J. Habermas and L. von Friedeberg, eds., *Adorno Konferenz 1983* (Frankfurt, 1983), pp. 177ff.

13. Habermas, "Modernity versus Postmodernity," pp. 12ff.

14. See A. Wellmer, "Truth, Semblance, Reconciliation," in *The Persistence of Modernity: Essays on Aesthetics, Ethics, and Postmodernism*, trans. D. Midgely (Cambridge, Mass., 1991).

15. Ibid., p. 165.

16. Habermas, *Theory of Communicative Action*, vol. 1, pp. 120ff. and 130ff.; and "Interpretative Social Science and Hermeneuticism," in N. Hann, R. Bellah, P. Rabinow, and W. Sullivan, eds., *Social Science as Moral Inquiry* (Berkeley, 1983), pp. 251–270.

17. J. Habermas, *On the Logic of the Social Sciences*, trans. S. W. Nicholsen and G. A. Stark (Cambridge, Mass., 1988).

18. Habermas, *Theory of Communicative Action*, vol. 1, p. 237.

19. Ibid., p. 238.

20. J. Habermas, "A Reply to My Critics," in J. B. Thompson and D. Held, eds., *Habermas: Critical Debates* (Cambridge, Mass., 1982), pp. 248ff.

21. On this "rather risky model," cf. my *Theory of Communicative Action*, vol. 1, pp. 239ff.

22. Ibid.

23. Cf. my excursus on argumentation theory, ibid., pp. 18–42.

24. "In each of these spheres, the process of differentiation is accompanied by a *countermovement* that always re-incorporates the other two, initially excluded validity aspects under the primacy of the dominant one. In this way, *nonobjectivist approaches* to the human sciences also bring into play the perspectives of moral and aesthetic critique, while not endangering the primacy of the question of truth; only in this way is a critical theory of society possible. The discussion of an ethics of responsibility or

conviction and the more pronounced consideration of hedonistic motives bring the perspectives of the *calculation of consequences* and the *interpretation of needs* into play within universalistic ethics, perspectives that lie within the cognitive and expressive validity domains; in this way, materialistic ideas can also be given their due, without endangering the autonomy of the moral perspective. Finally, post-avant-garde art is characterized by the simultaneous presence of realistic and 'committed' (*engagiert*) tendencies along with the authentic continuation of classical modernity, out of which the independent logic of the aesthetic sphere was distilled. With realistic and 'committed' art, cognitive and moral-practical moments enter once again into art, at the level of the wealth of form set free by the avant-garde" (*Theory of Communicative Action*, vol. 2, pp. 396ff.).

25. Cf. Habermas, "Über Moralität und Sittlichkeit: Was macht eine Lebensform rational?," in *Erläuterungen zur Diskursethik* (Frankfurt, 1991), pp. 31ff.

26. This was, in any case, my intention in the Freud chapter of my *Knowledge and Human Interests*, trans. J. Shapiro (Boston, 1971). I do not find any basis in Freud for the strict separation between a clinically justified theory of neurosis and a metapsychological superstructure that Adolf Grünbaum proposes in "Freud's Theory: The Perspective of a Philosopher of Science," *Proceedings and Addresses of the American Philosophical Association* 57, no. 6 (1983). This separation completely obscures the specific roots of Freudian theory in the experiences of the analytic dialogue. Such an operation may be useful for the argumentative purpose of assimilating Freudian theory to the standard model of unified science, only to reject it then for failing to measure up to its standards. At the same time, it expresses the decision not to consider the hermeneutic character of this science.

27. Cf. J. Habermas, "A Review of Gadamer's *Truth and Method*," in *On the Logic of the Social Sciences*, and "Überlegungen zur Kommunikationspathologie," in *Vorstudien und Ergänzungen zur Theorie des kommunikativen Handelns* (Frankfurt, 1984).

28. Habermas, "Moral Consciousness and Communicative Action," in *Moral Consciousness and Communicative Action*.

29. R. Döbert, J. Habermas, and G. Nunner-Winkler, *Entwicklung des Ichs* (Köln, 1977), pp. 9ff.

30. K. Horn expresses similar reservations in "Geheime kulturalistische Tendenzen der modernen psychoanalytischen Orthodoxie," in *Psychoanalyse als Wissenschaft* (Frankfurt, 1971), pp. 93ff.

31. With respect to the empirical questions, I would like to point out that my reflections on the change in symptoms typical of our times and on the significance of the adolescent crisis are quite similar to those of Whitebook. Cf. *Theory of Communicative Action*, vol. 2, pp. 386ff.

32. Cf. J. Habermas, "Moral Development and Ego Identity," in *Communication and the Evolution of Society*, trans. T. McCarthy (Boston, 1979), pp. 78ff.

33. Cf. Habermas, "A Reply to My Critics." See also the essays in Habermas, *Moral Consciousness and Communicative Action*.

34. Cf. Habermas, "Moral Development and Ego Identity."

Selected Bibliography and Further Reading

This bibliography is meant to lead readers further into the literature related to Habermas's program of formal pragmatics. I have included mainly secondary discussions of Habermas's writings rather than the sources that he cites (these are documented in the notes to the various chapters). The exception is where Habermas mentions a particular writer repeatedly or deals in detail with her or his work. For Habermas's work itself, I have included only those primary texts evidently relevant to formal pragmatics or deemed by him to be correlative. English translations have been cited where available.

Agger, Ben, 1981. "A Critical Theory of Dialogue," *Humanities in Society* 4: 7–30.

Ajzner, Jan, 1994. "Some Problems of Rationality, Understanding, and Universalistic Ethics in the Context of Habermas's Theory of Communicative Action," *Philosophy of the Social Sciences* 24(4): 466–484.

Aladjem, Terry K., 1995. "Of Truth and Disagreement: Habermas, Foucault and Democratic Discourse," *History of European Ideas* 20(4–6): 909–914.

Apel, Karl-Otto, 1967. *Analytic Philosophy of Language and the Geisteswissenschaften* (Dordrecht: Reidel).

Apel, Karl-Otto, ed., 1976a. *Sprachpragmatik und Philosophie* (Frankfurt: Suhrkamp).

Apel, Karl-Otto, 1976b. "Sprechakttheorie und transzendentale Sprachpragmatik—zur Frage ethischer Normen," in Apel, ed., *Sprachpragmatik und Philosophie*, pp. 10–173.

Apel, Karl-Otto, 1980a. *Towards a Transformation of Philosophy*, trans. G. Adey and D. Frisby (London: Routledge and Kegan Paul).

Apel, Karl-Otto, 1980b. "Hermeneutic Philosophy of Understanding as a Heuristic Horizon for Displaying the Problem-Dimension of Analytic Philosophy of Meaning," *Philosophy and Social Criticism* 7: 241–259.

Apel, Karl-Otto, 1980c. "Three Dimensions of Understanding Meaning in Analytic Philosophy: Linguistic Conventions, Inventions, and Reference to Things," *Philosophy and Social Criticism* 7: 115–142.

Selected Bibliography and Further Reading

Apel, Karl-Otto, 1981a. "C. S. Peirce and the Post-Tarskian Problem of an Adequate Explication of the Meaning of Truth," *Transactions of the Charles S. Peirce Society* 18: 3–17.

Apel, Karl-Otto, 1981b. "Intentions, Conventions, and Reference to Things," in H. Parret and J. Bouveresse, eds., *Meaning and Understanding* (Berlin: de Gruyter).

Apel, Karl-Otto, 1987a. "Sprachliche Bedeutung, Wahrheit und normative Gültigkeit," *Archivio di Filosofia* 55 (1987): 51ff.

Apel, Karl-Otto, 1987b. "Fallibilismus, Konsenstheorie der Wahrheit und Letztbegründung," in Forum für Philosophie, ed., *Philosophie und Begründung* (Frankfurt: Suhrkamp), pp. 116–211.

Apel, Karl-Otto, 1992a. "Is Intentionality More Basic than Linguistic Meaning?," in E. Lepore and R. Van Gulick, eds., *John Searle and his Critics* (Oxford: Blackwell), pp. 31–55.

Apel, Karl-Otto, 1992b. "Illokutionäre Bedeutung und normative Gültigkeit: Die transzendentalpragmatische Begründung der uneingeschränkten kommunikativen Verständigung," *Protosoziologie* 2: 2–15.

Apel, Karl-Otto, 1992c. "Normatively Grounding 'Critical Theory,'" in A. Honneth, T. McCarthy, C. Offe, and A. Wellmer, eds., *Philosophical Interventions in the Unfinished Project of Enlightenment* (Cambridge, Mass.: The MIT Press).

Austin, J. L., 1961. "Performative Utterances," in Austin, *Philosophical Papers* (Oxford: Oxford University Press), pp. 233–252.

Austin, J. L., 1962. *How to Do Things with Words* (Oxford: Oxford University Press).

Austin, J. L., 1963. "Performative-Constative," in C. E. Caton, ed., *Philosophy and Ordinary Language* (Urbana, Ill.: University of Illinois Press), pp. 22–33.

Bar-Hillel, Y., 1973. "On Habermas's Hermeneutic Philosophy of Language," *Synthese* 26: 1–12.

Bartels, Martin, 1982. "Sprache und soziales Handeln: eine Auseinandersetzung mit Habermas' Sprachbegriff," *Zeitschrift für Philosophische Forschung* 36: 226–233.

Baurmann, Manfred, 1985. "Understanding as an Aim and Aims of Understanding," in Seebaß and Tuomela, eds., *Social Action.*

Beatty, Joseph, 1979. "Communicative Competence and the Skeptic," *Philosophy and Social Criticism* 6: 267–288.

Belardinelli, Sergio, 1991. "La teoria consensual de la verdad de Jürgen Habermas," *Anuario Filosófico*, pp. 115–123.

Bernstein, Jay, 1992. "De-Divination and the Vindication of Everyday-Life: Reply to Rorty," *Tijdschrift voor Filosofie* 54(4): 668–692.

Bernstein, Richard, 1983. *Beyond Objectivism and Relativism: Science, Hermeneutics, and Practice* (Philadelphia: University of Pennsylvania Press, 1983).

Bernstein, Richard, ed., 1985. *Habermas and Modernity* (Cambridge, Mass.: The MIT Press).

Berten, André, 1989. "L'éthique et la Politique," *Revue Philosophique de Louvain* 87: 74–96.

Bogen, David E., 1989. "Reappraisal of Habermas's *Theory of Communicative Action* in Light of Detailed Investigations of Social Praxis," *Journal for the Theory of Social Behaviour* 19: 47–77.

Bohman, James, 1985. *Language and Social Criticism,* Ph.D. Dissertation, Boston University.

Bohman, James, 1986. "Formal Pragmatics and Social Criticism," *Philosophy and Social Criticism* 11: 331–353.

Bohman, James, 1988. "Emancipation and Rhetoric: The Perlocutions and Illocutions of the Social Critic," *Philosophy and Rhetoric* 21(3): 185–204.

Bohman, James, 1992. "Critique of Ideologies," in M. Dascal, D. Gerhardus, K. Lorenz, and G. Meggle, eds., *Philosophy of Language: An International Handbook of Contemporary Research* (Berlin/New York: de Gruyter).

Bohman, James, 1994. "World Disclosure and Radical Criticism," *Thesis Eleven* 37: 82–97.

Bohman, James, and Terence Kelly, 1996. "Intelligibility, Rationality, and Comparison," *Philosophy and Social Criticism* 22(1): 81–100.

Bühler, Karl, 1934. *Sprachtheorie* (Jena: Fischer).

Canovan, Margaret, 1983. "A Case of Distorted Communication: A Note on Habermas and Arendt," *Political Theory* 11: 105–116.

Chomsky, Noam, 1965. *Aspects of the Theory of Syntax* (Cambridge, Mass.: The MIT Press).

Cobben, P., 1984. "Habermas' *Theorie van het Kommunikatieve Handelen,*" *Tijdschrift voor Filosofie* 46: 216–268.

Comesana, Manuel, 1994. "La Teoria de la Verdad en Habermas," *Dianoia* 40: 245–261.

Cometti, Jean-Pierre, 1992. "Raison, Argumentation et Légitimation: Habermas, Apel et les Apories de la Communication," *Philosophiques* 19(1): 3–24.

Cooke, Maeve, 1993. "Habermas and Consensus," *European Journal of Philosophy* 1(3): 247–267.

Selected Bibliography and Further Reading

Cooke, Maeve, 1994. *Language and Reason: A Study of Habermas's Pragmatics* (Cambridge, Mass.: The MIT Press).

Corredor, Cristina, 1993. "Intentos de formulacíon de una teoria general de actos de habla (J Searle y J Habermas)," *Revista de Filosofía* 6: 119–130.

Cotesta, Vittoria, 1986. "Riferimento e Verita," *AQUINAS* 29: 465–502.

Courtois, Stephane, 1994. "Le faillibilisme de Jürgen Habermas et ses difficultés: un faillibilisme conséquent est-il possible?," *Dialogue: Canadian Philosophical Review* 33(2): 253–282.

Couture, Tony, 1993. "Habermas, Values, and the Rational, Internal Structure of Communication," *Journal of Value Inquiry* 27(3–4): 403–416.

Culler, Jonathan, 1985. "Communicative Competence and Normative Force," *New German Critique* 35: 133ff.

Cushman, D. P., and P. K. Tompkins, 1980. "A Theory of Rhetoric for Contemporary Society," *Philosophy and Rhetoric* 13: 43–67.

Czuma, Hans, 1981. "Rede oder Gewalt," *Conceptus* 15: 102–111.

Dallmayr, Fred, 1987. "Life-World and Communicative Action," in B. Parekh, ed., *Political Discourse* (New Delhi: Sage), pp. 152–178.

Derrida, Jacques, 1977. "Signature Event Context," reprinted in Derrida. *Margins of Philosophy* (Chicago: University of Chicago Press).

Derrida, Jacques, 1977. "Limited Inc abc . . . ." *Glyph* 2: 162–254.

Dews, Peter, 1996. "The Truth of the Subject: Language, Validity and Transcendence in Lacan and Habermas," in P. Dews and S. Critchley, eds., *Deconstructive Subjectivities* (Albany: SUNY Press), pp. 149–168.

Dorschel, Andreas, 1988. "Is There Any Normative Claim Internal to Stating Facts?," *Communication and Cognition* 21: 5–16.

Dorschel, Andreas, 1990. "Handlungstypen und Kriterien: Zu Habermas' *Theorie des kommunikativen Handelns*," *Zeitschrift für Philosophische Forschung* 44(2): 220–252.

Dummett, Michael, 1973. *Frege: Philosophy of Language* (New York: Harper & Row).

Dummett, Michael, 1976. "What Is a Theory of Meaning?," in G. Evans and J. McDowell, eds., *Truth and Meaning* (Oxford: Oxford University Press).

Ferrara, Alessandro, 1987. "A Critique of Habermas's Consensus Theory of Truth," *Philosophy and Social Criticism* 13: 39–67.

Fultner, Barbara, 1995. *Radical Interpretation or Communicative Action*, Ph.D. Dissertation, Northwestern University.

Fultner, Barbara, 1996. "The Redemption of Truth: Idealization, Acceptability and Fallibilism in Habermas' Theory of Meaning," *International Journal of Philosophical Studies* 4(2): 233–251.

Selected Bibliography and Further Reading

Geimann, Kevin Paul, 1990. "Habermas's Early Lifeworld Appropriation: A Critical Assessment," *Man and World* 23(1): 63–83.

Geuss, Raymond, 1981. *The Idea of a Critical Theory* (New York: Cambridge University Press).

Griffioen, Sander, 1991. "The Metaphor of the Covenant in Habermas," *Faith and Philosophy* 8(4): 524–540.

Grondin, Jean, 1989. "Habermas und das Problem der Individualität," *Philosophische Rundschau* 36: 187–205.

Haarscher, Guy, 1986. "Perelman and Habermas," *Law and Philosophy* 5: 331–342.

Habermas, Jürgen, 1971. *Knowledge and Human Interests*, trans. J. Shapiro (Boston: Beacon Press).

Habermas, Jürgen, 1973. "Wahrheitstheorien," reprinted in Habermas, *Vorstudien und Ergänzungen zur Theorie des kommunikativen Handelns.*

Habermas, Jürgen, 1976a. "Some Distinctions in Universal Pragmatics," *Theory and Society* 3: 155–167.

Habermas, Jürgen, 1976b. "Universalpragmatische Hinweise auf das System der Ich-Abgrenzungen," in M. Auwärter, E. Kirsch, and M. Schröter, eds., *Kommunikation, Interaktion, Identität* (Frankfurt: Suhrkamp).

Habermas, Jürgen, 1979. *Communication and the Evolution of Society*, trans. T. McCarthy (Boston: Beacon Press).

Habermas, Jürgen, 1982. "A Reply to my Critics," in J. B. Thompson and D. Held, eds., *Habermas: Critical Debates* (Cambridge, Mass.: The MIT Press), pp. 219–283.

Habermas, Jürgen, 1983. "Interpretative Social Science and Hermeneuticism," in N. Haan, R. Bellah, P. Rabinow, and W. Sullivan, eds., *Social Science as Moral Inquiry* (New York: Columbia University Press).

Habermas, Jürgen, 1984. *Vorstudien und Ergänzungen zur Theorie des kommunikativen Handelns* (Frankfurt: Suhrkamp).

Habermas, Jürgen, 1984/1987. *The Theory of Communicative Action*, 2 vols., trans. T. McCarthy (Boston: Beacon Press).

Habermas, Jürgen, 1985a. "A Reply to Skjei's 'A Comment on Performative, Subject, and Proposition in Habermas's Theory of Communication,'" *Inquiry* 28: 87–122.

Habermas, Jürgen, 1985b. "Remarks on the Concept of Communicative Action," in Seebaß and Tuomela, eds., *Social Action.*

Habermas, Jürgen, 1987. *The Philosophical Discourse of Modernity*, trans. F. Lawrence (Cambridge, Mass.: The MIT Press).

Habermas, Jürgen, 1988. *On the Logic of the Social Sciences,* trans. S. W. Nicholsen and G. A. Stark (Cambridge, Mass.: The MIT Press).

Habermas, Jürgen, 1990. "Philosophy as Stand-In and Interpreter," in *Moral Consciousness and Communicative Action,* trans. C. Lenhardt and S. W. Nicholsen (Cambridge, Mass: The MIT Press).

Habermas, Jürgen, 1992. *Postmetaphysical Thinking,* trans. W. M. Hohengarten (Cambridge, Mass.: The MIT Press).

Habermas, Jürgen, 1993. "Remarks on Discourse Ethics," in Habermas, *Justification and Application,* trans. C. Cronin (Cambridge, Mass.: The MIT Press).

Habermas, Jürgen, 1996. *Between Facts and Norms,* trans. W. Rehg (Cambridge, Mass.: The MIT Press).

Hall, J. A., 1982. "Gellner and Habermas on Epistemology and Politics. Or, Need We Feel Disenchanted?," *Philosophy of the Social Sciences* 12: 384–408.

Healy, Paul, 1987. "Is Habermas's Consensus Theory a Theory of Truth?," *Irish Philosophical Journal* 4: 145–152.

Heath, Joseph, 1995. "Threats, Promises and Communicative Action," *European Journal of Philosophy* 3(3): 225–241.

Hesse, Mary, 1995. "Habermas and the Force of Dialectical Argument," *History of European Ideas* 21(3): 367–378.

Hohn, Hans-Joachim, 1989. "Vernunft—Kommunikation—Diskurs: Zu Anspruch und Grenze der Transzendentalpragmatik als Basistheorie der Philosophie," *Freie Zeitschrift für Philosophie und Theologie* 36: 93–128.

Honneth, Axel, 1979. "Communication and Reconciliation: Habermas's Critique of Adorno," *Telos* 39(1): 45–61.

Husserl, Edmund, 1970. *The Crisis of the European Sciences,* trans. D. Carr (Evanston, Ill.: Northwestern University Press).

Ilting, Karl-Heinz, 1976. "Geltung als Konsens," *Neue Hefte für Philosophie* 10: 20–50.

Ingram, David, 1982. "The Possibility of a Communication Ethic Reconsidered: Habermas, Gadamer, and Bourdieu on Discourse," *Man and World* 15: 149–161.

Ingram, David, 1987. *Habermas and the Dialectic of Reason* (New Haven: Yale University Press).

Johnson, James, 1991. "Habermas on Strategic and Communicative Action," *Political Theory* 19(2): 181–201.

Johnson, James, 1993. "Is Talk Really Cheap? Prompting Conversation between Critical Theory and Rational Choice," *American Political Science Review* 87(1): 74–93.

Selected Bibliography and Further Reading

Kambartel, F., and H. J. Schneider, 1981. "Constructing a Pragmatic Foundation for Semantics," in G. Fløistad, ed., *Contemporary Philosophy: A New Survey*, vol. 1 (The Hague: Nijhoff), pp. 155–178.

Keuth, Herbert, 1979. "Erkenntnis oder Entscheidung: die Konsenstheorien der Wahrheit und der Richtigkeit von Jürgen Habermas," *Zeitschrift für allgemeine Wissenschaftstheorie* 10: 375–393.

Kissling, Christian, 1991. "Habermas et la theologie: Notes pour une discussion entre la theologie et la *Theorie de l'agir communicationnel*," *Freiburger Zeitschrift für Philosophie und Theologie*, pp. 235–244.

Kolb, David, 1992. "Heidegger and Habermas on Criticism and Totality," *Philosophy and Phenomenological Research* 52(3): 683–693.

Kompridis, Nikolas, 1994. "On World Disclosure: Heidegger, Habermas, and Dewey," *Thesis Eleven* 37: 29–45.

Kujundzic, Nebojsa, and William Buschert, 1993. "Staging the Life-World: Habermas and the Recuperation of Austin's Speech Act Theory," *Journal for the Theory of Social Behaviour* 23(1): 105–116.

Lafont, Cristina, 1993. *La Razon como Lenguaje* (Madrid: Visor).

Lafont, Cristina, 1994. "Spannungen im Wahrheitsbegriff," *Deutsche Zeitschrift für Philosophie* 42(6): 1007–1023.

Lara, Maria Pia, 1995. "Albrecht Wellmer: Between Spheres of Validity," *Philosophy and Social Criticism* 21(2): 1–22.

Leist, Anton, 1977. "Was heißt Universalpragmatik?," *Germanistische Linguistik* 5/6.

Leist, Anton, 1989. "Dieseits der 'Transzendentalpragmatik': gibt es sprachpragmatische Argumente für Moral?," *Zeitschrift für Philosophische Forschung* 43: 301–317.

Levin, David Michael, 1994. "Making Sense: The Work of Eugene Gendlin," *Human Studies* 17(3): 343–353.

Machado, C. E. J., 1988. "The Concept of Rationality in Habermas: The 'Linguistic Turn' of the Critical Theory" (in Portuguese), *Trans/Form/Açao*, pp. 31–44.

McCarthy, Thomas, 1978. *The Critical Theory of Jürgen Habermas* (Cambridge, Mass.: The MIT Press).

McCarthy, Thomas, 1979. "Translator's Introduction," in J. Habermas, *Communication and the Evolution of Society* (Boston: Beacon Press).

McCarthy, Thomas, 1980. "Reflections on Rationalization in *The Theory of Communicative Action*," in Bernstein, ed. *Habermas and Modernity*.

McCarthy, Thomas, 1991. "Practical Discourse: On the Relation of Morality to Politics," in *Ideals and Illusions* (Cambridge, Mass.: The MIT Press).

McCumber, John, 1985. "Critical Theory and Poetic Interaction," *Praxis International* 5: 268–282.

McGuire, R., 1977. "Speech Acts, Communicative Competence and the Paradox of Authority," *Philosophy and Rhetoric* 10: 30–45.

Merrill, Sarah A., 1990. "Linguistics as a Borderline Case," in Merrill, ed., *Abeunt Studia in Mores: A Festschrift for Helga Doblin on Philosophies of Education and Personal Learning or Teaching in the Humanities and Moral Sciences* (New York: Lang).

Mertens, T., 1986. "Habermas en Searle: Kritische Beschouwingen bij de *Theorie van het Communicatieve Handelen*," *Tijdschrift voor Filosofie* 48: 66–93.

Misak, Cheryl, 1994. "Pragmatism and the Transcendental Turn in Truth and Ethics," *Transactions of the Charles S. Peirce Society* 30(4): 739–775.

Misgeld, Dieter, 1977. "Discourse and Conversation: The Theory of Communicative Competence and Hermeneutics in the Light of the Debate between Habermas and Gadamer," *Cultural Hermeneutics* 4: 321–344.

Murphy, Peter, 1985. "Meaning, Truth, and Ethical-Value," *Praxis International* 5: 225–246.

Nagl, Ludwig, 1984. "Die Wahrheitsfrage zwischen sprachanalytischer Transformation und historisch-systematischer Dimensionierung," *Philosophische Rundschau* 31: 85–94.

Nielsen, Kai, 1994. "How to Proceed in Philosophy: Remarks after Habermas," *Thesis Eleven* 37: 10–28.

Nordquist, Joan, 1986. *Social Theory: A Bibliographic Series*, no. 1: *Jürgen Habermas: A Bibliography* (Santa Cruz: Reference & Research).

Nordquist, Joan, 1991. *Social Theory: A Bibliographic Series*, no. 22: *Jürgen Habermas II: A Bibliography* (Santa Cruz: Reference & Research).

Nusser, Karl-Heinz, 1985. "Totalität ohne Subjekt," *Zeitschrift für Philosophische Forschung* 39: 590–599.

Oehler, Klaus, 1995. "A Response to Habermas," in K. L. Ketner, ed., *Peirce and Contemporary Thought: Philosophical Inquiries* (New York: Fordham University Press).

Pettit, Philip, 1982. "Habermas on Truth and Justice," in G. H. Parkinson, ed., *Marx and Marxisms* (Cambridge: Cambridge University Press), pp. 207–228.

Pickard, Dean, 1993. "Habermas, A Postmodern Critique," *Auslegung* 19(1): 1–21.

Power, Michael, 1993. "Habermas and Transcendental Arguments: A Reappraisal," *Philosophy of the Social Sciences* 23(1): 26–49.

Rasmussen, David M., 1990. *Reading Habermas* (Oxford: Blackwell).

Redding, Paul, 1989. "Habermas's Theory of Argumentation," *The Journal of Value Inquiry* 23: 15–32.

Roderick, Rick, 1985. "Habermas on Rationality," *Man and World* 18: 203–218.

Roderick, Rick, 1986. *Habermas and the Foundations of Critical Theory* (New York: St. Martin's Press).

Rorty, Richard, 1979. *Philosophy and the Mirror of Nature* (Princeton, N.J.: Princeton University Press).

Rorty, Richard, 1989. *Contingency, Irony, and Solidarity* (Cambridge: University of Cambridge Press).

Rorty, Richard, 1991a. *Philosophical Papers I: Objectivity, Relativism, and Truth* (Cambridge: Cambridge University Press).

Rorty, Richard, 1991b. *Philosophical Papers II: Essays on Heidegger and Others* (Cambridge: Cambridge University Press).

Rorty, Richard, 1994. "Sind Aussagen universelle Geltungsansprüche?," *Deutsche Zeitschrift für Philosophie* 42(6): 975–988.

Rosenberg, J. and C. Travis, eds., 1971. *Readings in the Philosophy of Language* (Englewood Cliffs, N.J.: Prentice Hall).

Saiedi, Nader, 1987. "A Critique of Habermas's Theory of Practical Rationality," *Studies in Soviet Thought* 33: 251–265.

Schatzki, Theodore, 1986. "The Rationalization of Meaning and Understanding: Davidson and Habermas," *Synthese* 69: 51–79.

Scheit, Herbert, 1991. *Wahrheit—Diskurs—Demokratie: Studien zur "Konsensustheorie der Wahrheit"* (Freiburg: Karl Alber).

Schiller, Hans-Ernst, 1990. "Zur sozialphilosophischen Bedeutung des Sprachbegriffs Wilhelm von Humboldts," *Zeitschrift für Philosophische Forschung* 44(2): 253–272.

Schmidt, James, 1979. "Offensive Critical Theory: Reply to Honneth," *Telos* 39(1): 62–70.

Schnädelbach, Herbert, 1977. *Reflexion und Diskurs* (Frankfurt: Suhrkamp).

Schnädelbach, Herbert, 1992. "Thesen über Geltung und Wahrheit," in Schnädelbach, *Zur Rehabilitierung des animal rationale* (Frankfurt: Suhrkamp).

Schneider, Hans J., 1982. "Gibt es eine 'Transzendental-' Universalpragmatik'?," *Zeitschrift für Philosophische Forschung* 36: 208–225.

Schurz, Gerhard, 1980. "Soziale Erwartungen und ideale Sprechsituation: ein formales Modell," *Conceptus* 14: 47–57.

Searle, J. R., 1969. *Speech Acts: An Essay in the Philosophy of Language* (Cambridge: Cambridge University Press).

Searle, J. R., 1971a. "Austin on Locutionary and Illocutionary Acts," in Rosenberg and Travis, eds., *Readings in the Philosophy of Language*, pp. 262–275.

Searle, J. R., 1971b. "What Is a Speech Act?," in Rosenberg and Travis, eds., *Readings in the Philosophy of Language*, pp. 614–628.

Searle, J. R., 1977. "Reiterating the Differences: A Reply to Derrida," *Glyph* 1: 198–208.

Searle, J. R., 1979. *Expression and Meaning: Studies in the Theory of Speech Acts* (Cambridge: Cambridge University Press).

Searle, J. R., 1981. "Intentionality and Method," *Journal of Philosophy* 78: 720–733.

Searle, J. R., 1983. *Intentionality: An Essay in the Philosophy of Mind* (Cambridge: Cambridge University Press).

Searle, J. R., 1984. *Minds, Brains, and Science* (Cambridge, Mass.: Harvard University Press).

Searle, J. R., 1986. "Meaning, Communication, and Representation," in R. E. Grandy and R. Warner, eds., *Philosophical Grounds of Rationality* (Oxford: Oxford University Press).

Searle, J. R., 1989. "How Performatives Work," *Linguistics and Philosophy* 12: 535–558.

Seebaß, G., and R. Tuomela, eds., 1985. *Social Action* (Dordrecht: Reidel).

Skirbekk, Gunnar, 1983. "Pragmatism in Apel and Habermas," in G. Fløistad, ed., *Contemporary Philosophy: A New Survey* (The Hague: Nijhoff), pp. 387–416.

Skjei, Erling, 1985. "A Comment on Performative, Subject, and Proposition in Habermas's Theory of Communication," *Inquiry* 28: 87–104.

Southgate, David, 1995. "Insanity Ascriptions: A Formal Pragmatic Analysis," *Journal for the Theory of Social Behaviour* 25(3): 219–235.

Speranza, Jorge L., 1991. "Un Grice aleman? En torno de las estrategias conversacionales: acercade Habermas acerca de Grice," *Revista Latin de Filosofía* 17(1): 133–148.

Sullivan, William M., 1978. "Communication and the Recovery of Meaning: An Interpretation of Habermas," *International Philosophical Quarterly* 18: 69–86.

Swart, H. A. P., 1979. "Kritiek van Habermas' Consensus-Theorie van de Waarheid," *Algemeen Nederlands Tijdschrift voor Wijsbegeerte* 71: 167–172.

Swindal, James, 1994. "The Problem of Problematization in Discourse Ethics," *Philosophy and Social Criticism* 20(3): 1–18.

Tejera, Victorino, 1996. "Has Habermas Understood Peirce?," *Transactions of the Charles S. Peirce Society* 32(1): 107–125.

Thompson, John B., 1982. "Universal Pragmatics," in Thompson and Held, eds., *Habermas: Critical Debates* (Cambridge, Mass.: The MIT Press), pp. 116–133.

Tietz, Udo, 1994. "Transformation der Sprachanalyse," *Deutsche Zeitschrift für Philosophie* 42(5): 861–881.

Trans, Van-Doan, 1989. "On Human Rationality. Habermas's Theory of Consensus," *Philosophical Review* (Taiwan) 12: 389–430.

Tugendhat, Ernst, 1982. *Traditional and Analytical Philosophy*, trans. P. A. Gorner (Cambridge: Cambridge University Press).

Tugendhat, Ernst, 1985. "J. Habermas on Communicative Action," in Seebaß and Tuomela, eds., *Social Action*.

Tugendhat, Ernst, 1986. *Self-Consciousness and Self-Determination*, trans. P. Stern (Cambridge, Mass.: The MIT Press).

Turski, George, 1979. "Some Considerations on Intersubjectivity and Language," *Gnosis* 1: 29–44.

Umhauer, Gerd, 1983. "Zum normativen Fundament sprachlicher Verständigung in der Konzeption einer 'idealen Sprechsituation,'" *Zeitschrift für Philosophische Forschung* 37: 88–101.

Van Nieuwstadt, J., 1983. "De Relatieve Zelfstandigheid van Taalhandelingen," *Kennis en Methode* 7: 356–367.

Van Zyl, Albert, 1995. "The Dilemma of Grounding in the Modernity-Postmodernity Debate," *South African Journal of Philosophy* 14(4): 168–174.

Visker, Rudi, 1992. "Habermas on Heidegger and Foucault: Meaning and Validity in the Philosophical Discourse of Modernity," *Radical Philosophy* 61: 15–22.

Wagner, Gerhard, and Heinz Zipprian, 1991. "Intersubjectivity and Critical Consciousness: Remarks on Habermas's *Theory of Communicative Action*," *Inquiry* 34(1): 49–62.

Ware, Robert X., 1982. "Habermas's Evolutions," *Canadian Journal of Philosophy* 12: 591–620.

Weber, Max, 1978. *Economy and Society: An Outline of Interpretive Sociology*, ed. G. Roth and C. Wittich, 2 vols. (Berkeley: University of California Press).

Weber, Max, 1981. "Some Categories of Interpretive Understanding," *Sociological Quarterly* 22: 151–180.

Wellmer, Albrecht, 1991. *The Persistence of Modernity: Essays on Aesthetics, Ethics, and Postmodernism*, trans. D. Midgely (Cambridge, Mass.: The MIT Press).

Wellmer, Albrecht, 1992. "What Is a Pragmatic Theory of Meaning?," in A. Honneth, T. McCarthy, C. Offe, and A. Wellmer, eds., *Philosophical Interventions in the Unfinished Project of Enlightenment* (Cambridge, Mass.: The MIT Press).

Wellmer, Albrecht, 1998. *Endgames: Essays and Lectures on the Irreconcilable Nature of Modernity* (Cambridge, Mass.: The MIT Press).

Selected Bibliography and Further Reading

White, Stephen K., 1988. *The Recent Work of Jürgen Habermas: Reason, Justice and Modernity* (Cambridge: Cambridge University Press).

Whitton, Brian J., 1992. "Universal Pragmatics and the Formation of Western Civilization: A Critique of Habermas's Theory of Human Moral Evolution," *History and Theory* 31(3): 299–312.

Wood, Allen, 1985. "Habermas's Defence of Rationalism," *New German Critique* 25: 145ff.

Zimmermann, Rolf, 1984. "Emancipation and Rationality: Foundational Problems in the Theories of Marx and Habermas," *Ratio* 26: 143–166.

Zimmermann, Rolf, 1985. *Utopie—Rationalität—Politik* (Freiburg: Karl Alber).

Index

Index

Index